URBANIZATION
IN LATIN AMERICA:

Approaches and Issues

D0913451

URBANIZATION
IN LATIN AMERICA:
APPROACHES AND ISSUES

EDITED AND WITH A PREFACE BY

JORGE E. HARDOY

ANCHOR BOOKS

ANCHOR PRESS/DOUBLEDAY

GARDEN CITY, NEW YORK

1975

Anchor Books edition: 1975

Library of Congress Cataloging in Publication Data

Main entry under title:
Urbanization in Latin America

Includes bibliographical references.
1. Urbanization—Latin America—Addresses, essays,
lectures. 2. Cities and towns—Latin America—Addresses,
essays, lectures. I. Hardoy, Jorge Enrique.
HT127.5.U72   301.36′3′098
ISBN 0-385-08240-1
Library of Congress Catalog Card Number 73-93594

CONTENTS

IV. URBANIZATION IN SELECTED COUNTRIES AND CITIES

PREFACE*

Every year until the close of the 1970–85 period, a population estimated at 8,766,000 persons will be incorporated into the cities of Latin America. Every year between 1985 and the year 2000, a population estimated at 11 million to 12 million persons will be absorbed into these same cities and into other new cities that may be built. This accelerated urban growth is due to the persistence of a high rate of natural population increase and to migrations from rural areas to the main metropolitan areas and medium-sized cities. These data and these characteristics of Latin American urbanization have been analyzed on numerous occasions.

Latin American urbanization is principally peripheral or coastal, with Mexico and Central America the exceptions to this norm. In South America and the Antilles, urbanization is concentrated in extremely small coastal areas, and the main cities are ports or are located near the principal ports of each country. The main conurbations of each country are coastal: the industrial belt between Buenos Aires and Rosario; the São Paulo–Rio de Janeiro, Santiago–Valparaíso, Lima–Callao, and Caracas–La Guayra complexes; the metropolitan areas of Montevideo, Recife, Salvador, and Porto Alegre in South America; and the Havana metropolitan area in the Antilles. Among the urban clusters in Latin America having more than one million inhabitants, only the metropolitan areas of Mexico and Colombia are located in the interior of the continent.

The origin of the peripheral concentration of urbanization in Latin America dates from the beginning of the six-

* English translation by Felicity M. Trueblood.

teenth century, when the Spanish and Portuguese formulated their objectives in occupying these lands. When the
Spanish arrived, they found two great indigenous political
experiments in America—the Aztec confederation and the
Inca empire—which radiated outward from the interior to
the coast. They constituted the culmination of a process
begun two thousand years before, a process that took
place in complete independence from influences external
to the continent. But the course of the European conquest
and colonization of Latin America was different. Rapid establishment of fortified trading posts and, later, cities, permitted at the same time territorial control and exploitation
of natural and human resources, as well as commercial,
cultural, and administrative links between the new colonies and Lisbon and, through Sevilla and Cádiz, the
Spanish crown. With the exception of Montevideo, all
metropolitan areas that had more than one million inhabitants in 1960 were founded in the sixteenth century.

The passage of time accentuated the peripheral course
of colonization. Independence from the old Spanish and
Portuguese colonies accomplished nothing more than increasing the dependence of the new republics upon European industrial powers and the United States, with the
consequent primacy of the principal colonial centers.
Railroad and highway networks accentuated this historical
tendency. A national model was formed of one or two
centers in close contact with external markets and with the
European and U.S. interests that determined each
country's economic policy, and a periphery made up of a
scarcely evolved interior. Contact of each Latin American
country with the outside world was achieved through the
capital city, and only occasionally through two or three
cities. This situation persists. Argentina's external image is
provided by Buenos Aires, Uruguay's by Montevideo,
Peru's by Lima, Brazil's by Rio de Janeiro and São Paulo,
Mexico's by Mexico City, and thus successively. This

identification of a nation with its principal city is even stronger in less populous and smaller countries in which the capital is possibly the only city and the only market of any magnitude. These single cities and their metropolitan areas are the centers of political and economic power, finance, the most important cultural activities and universities, and, in general, the main trade ports. This concentration of function and power in extremely limited land areas only widens the breach between the developed and underdeveloped regions of each country.

Not only are contemporary Latin American cities larger and more complex than those of ten or thirty years ago, but also their links within their own national space are closer and more varied. The void that characterized each nation's territory during the nineteenth century and, in certain cases, well into the twentieth century, was finally filled with railroad lines and/or highways and/or airlines, and was also partially populated in the face of demographic pressure and the discovery and exploitation of new natural resources of greater external demand. Gradually, national urban systems expanded, and contacts among the cities of these systems increased. Isolation of the cities from each other decreased, as did the isolation of rural areas which, in zones most closely linked to these cities, were affected by the expansion of urban culture. On the other hand, underdevelopment, poverty, and differences in income and opportunities among regions and among various socioeconomic sectors of the population did not decrease. Neither were basic problems of conservation, health, education, housing, stable employment, and salaries solved for a majority of the population.

In spite of the lack of employment, housing, and urban services, in spite of the fact that the physical environment resulting from this accelerated, fragmented, and spontaneous urbanization deteriorates rapidly, and in spite of the fact that urban life does not permit large sectors of the population to enjoy spiritual and material goods, present-day Latin American cities are serving a greater number of inhabitants in improved fashion. These inhabitants find in the cities sources of employment, opportunities for education and recreation, modes of living together, and general progress, which formerly did not exist and which still do not exist in rural areas and small cities. Thus one could say that urbanization has facilitated improved education and sanitary levels, higher levels and better distribution of income, and a more open attitude on the part of growing percentages of the population toward political, cultural, and technological innovations. Possibly, unemployment and underemployment in the main industrial cities of each Latin American country are presently less than or the same as a generation ago. Possibly, proximity to centers of technical and higher education permits at least some children of working-class families to receive more adequate training. But where and when will it be possible to attempt technical solutions to human problems which persist and worsen, problems such as injustice, violence, and the humiliations imposed upon the population by a system which values profit, superfluity, competition, power, and ostentation at the cost of social justice, harmonious co-operative living, and satisfaction of basic necessities?

There is great variation, not only in the present degree of urbanization of each Latin American country, but also in present rates of urbanization and in urban potential. For example, Uruguay is a country in which 81 per cent of the population lives in centers of 2,000 inhabitants or more (about 50 per cent lives in the capital city, Montevideo), and the country has an extremely low rate of demographic growth. Since Uruguay is small in size and underpopulated, natural growth of its population, completely channeled into the cities, does not signify very great pressure quantitatively: barely 46,000 per year during the 1970–85 period. On the other hand, Brazil must absorb about 3,300,000 new inhabitants per year. This is due to the fact that Brazil is not highly urbanized and has an extremely high rate of demographic growth. As a consequence, Brazil's urban population is growing at a rate of 5.67 per cent per year, and in certain metropolitan areas the annual rate approaches 10 per cent. Argentina, Chile, and Cuba are closer to the Uruguayan case, while Ecuador, certain Central American countries, Paraguay, and Bolivia, all of which are still predominantly rural, have an urbanistic potential that in the long run, on a percentage basis, will surpass even that of Brazil, as well as of Mexico, Colombia, and Peru.

Until a few decades ago, the majority of the world's large metropolitan areas grew because they were industrial centers of world, national, or regional importance. But there is ample evidence that the accelerated process of current urbanization is taking place in less-developed economies without simultaneous industrialization. In Latin America, even though there is a correlation by country and, in fact, by region within each country, in urbanization, *per capita* income, energy consumption, and percentage of gross national product produced by the industrial sector, it is also clear that the developed, industrialized, and urbanized countries of Latin America do not maintain correlations of the type estimated to exist in countries with more highly developed economies.

In other words, in Latin America, urbanization has not been accompanied by simultaneous and adequate industrialization, or by better distribution of opportunity, income, and consumption. Nor has it been accompanied by the rates of demographic growth already observed for decades in the developed countries. This precarious situation is becoming more acute, since the tertiary sector, already highly supercharged in relation to the development of each Latin American country, is not in a position to provide the employment necessary to maintain by itself an extremely large urban population.

To create employment and provide housing, urban services, and community facilities for a new urban population which, like Latin America's, increases by more than 8.5 million people per year, requires extremely large investment and operating costs. Yet little is known about this entire process. The situation, as I explained earlier, is substantially different in Brazil and Uruguay, both extreme cases. In general, however, it seems that few Latin American countries are in position, in the short and medium run, to provide housing, urban services, and facilities, to say nothing of employment, to the new urban population if present criteria and values are maintained. Here, once again, the possibilities of Argentina and Bolivia, which in this aspect are extreme cases, are also very different. My own conclusion is that, given the present power structure, there is no solution to the urban problem of Latin America, just as there is no solution to its development. In part this is due to the fact that, for historical reasons that not only have been maintained but that also appear to be increasing, the Latin American countries are organized as primary, export economies. There are too many powerful internal and external interests in almost all Latin American countries for this situation not to continue. The infrastructure networks and the spatial structure within each country, aspects that may be analyzed on any map and with statistical data, confirm this conclusion. In part this is due to the fact that for internal and external reasons it is difficult for national movements with broad popular participation to arise, movements that could shake the peoples of Latin America out of an apathy that is nothing more than a reflection of ancestral exploitation. These same interests have been careful to see that these movements do not take root, or have weakened them. Yet, in Latin America, the search is continuing for new initiatives, new ideas and experiences, permitting conscious affirmation of the collective responsibility of the peoples of Latin America and of the necessity of self-determination and participation.

The existing Latin American urban situation can be dealt with only through a broad, co-ordinated, and revolutionary approach of general scope for each country and particular focus for each city. It involves the definition of policies, elaboration of plans, and co-ordination of programs and investment. It involves the simultaneous action of creating and executing, restating the concepts of property and inheritance of material goods, denouncing an aristocratic society and a power structure that bases perpetuation of political control (*continuismo*) and, as a consequence, exploitation of poverty upon the control of wealth and justice.

There is hardly a municipal administration in Latin America that enjoys the financial resources, political power, technical personnel, and knowledge of existing problems to direct the growth of its particular city in an orderly manner. It is a fact that municipal governments do not have planning organisms of adequate technical competence, or, if they do exist, local planning agencies are unable to pressure similar organisms at the national, regional, and provincial levels. National governments and intermediate decision-making levels—provinces, states, or departments—have delayed in recognizing this situation, and still do not face it with concrete action.

Gradually, the Latin American governments have embraced economic planning as a means of governmental action. Even though it has been far from effective, in certain countries it has been accepted. Nevertheless, social and spatial aspects of development have not enjoyed equal attention, and no Latin American country to date has attempted to incorporate urban policies at the national and regional levels. The private sector in turn has profited from this situation, and its activities have been instrumental in increasing the disorderly and speculative character of current urbanization in the face of the passive attitude of the public sector.

Information and research are required in order to make adequate decisions, and it is safe to say that research into Latin American urban problems is still insufficient. Information gathered by censuses undertaken by different levels of government is fragmentary and highly diverse. A large portion is of little use for serious urban studies. Basic information is also lacking regarding transportation, investment, consumption, labor, the housing and land market, etc. Many advances have been made during the past ten years, but it has still been difficult to elicit broad interest from economists, sociologists, anthropologists, and political scientists, and only a few lawyers and groups of architects and engineers have become involved. Technological research directed at urban problems is nonexistent. More notable advances are achieved in conceptual clarification than in the research that would serve to determine policy. This should not surprise us from a continent that dedicates more money to promoting the sale of frequently unnecessary products and artifacts than to urban studies, or that spends on armaments a sum that could satisfy 50 per cent of the annual housing demand caused by natural population increase.

The precarious nature of the construction industry is significant for an urban population with the previously mentioned characteristics. Even in the most economically and technically advanced countries of Latin America, the construction industry has only recently begun to apply the techniques and systems that have revolutionized other industries. In addition, methods to achieve the rapid and well-co-ordinated construction of cities are not used since other essential preconditions do not exist. Traditional construction systems persist in Latin America. Heavy industrialism has recently been applied to construction, but its action will continue to be shackled if the diffused system of individual credit applying to isolated housing units is not overcome, fragmentation of urban land is not checked, and construction programs in urban services and facilities are not better co-ordinated. All of this contributes to the costly and chaotic panorama of Latin American urban development.

Urbanization of the magnitude and tendencies of Latin America would constitute a threat to any industrialized and economically developed country or region. If it is faced by less-developed countries that for the moment have precarious sources of investment, scarce technical resources, and low technological levels, it assumes crisis characteristics. While it is possible to determine what is wrong, it is more difficult to define an urban strategy of national scope, and much more difficult to transform this strategy into plans and programs for subsequent implementation. To date, the passivity with which Latin American governments have faced the growth of cities, and the unilateral physical approach with which they believed they could solve their problems, have not been entirely overcome. In addition, private enterprise has failed to solve the problems posed by economic development, population growth, and urbanization, areas in which it could collaborate by creating new employment, providing housing and urban services, and maintaining an adequate environment, among other contributions. On the other hand, backed by the prevailing power structure, private enterprise has used the giddy process of urbanization and the growing demand for land, housing, and urban services for speculative ends, distorting prices and creating situations that are extremely difficult or costly to overcome.

The future model of the Latin American city without adequate financing is difficult to predict. Many factors influence a country's spatial structure. Similarly, incorporation of new technologies or the adoption of new (for Latin America) social concepts regarding the right to property or the redistribution of power may also affect a city's internal structure. Thus, predictions are subject to great error and drastic change in each Latin American country's sociopolitical organization. In addition, how can such rapid urbanization be financed without investment resources, which are often diverted to what is considered more dynamic investment?

One way is to reduce the costs of urbanization, without lowering the standards permitting a housing unit and complementary urban services to last at least fifty years. This may in part be achieved by massively financed projects with technology appropriate to each country's stage of development. The latter requires avoiding dispersing credit in an isolated manner, advancing the technology employed in transportation and communications and construction, and developing land in logical sizes and locations. Another way of reducing costs is to recover the added value (produced by urbanization) for the benefit of society and not for speculators or fortunate owners. Still another way is to perfect the technique of building makeshift housing, given that such housing is an inescapable fact at the moment, in order to improve its habitability and facilitate its construction in areas already provided with urban services and community facilities. The three formulas suggested, implemented in the short run, are based upon the premise that there is no adequate solution to urban development without an energetic, continuous, and visionary land acquisition policy that would permit order and deter speculation, and without state control of the factors that have carried Latin American cities to their present state.

As foreshadowed above, state control of land for future urban expansion is a guarantee that the city will be reconditioned at levels still difficult to foresee and will incorporate technologies that in the developing countries are still entirely too costly. It is, in addition, the road to abolishing unjust divisions by socioeconomic level caused by the land and rental market, which has exploited existing regulations and codes. Nevertheless, socialization of urban and suburban land is only a precondition, though perhaps the most important, for a national solution to the problem of needed urban transformation. Yet the latter may not be begun without an economy that serves the entire society.

My concept of a city built for the entire population, which for the moment lacks the required investment resources, is concerned more properly with environmental, social, and economic issues than with architecture. I do not wish to suggest that aesthetics are forgotten. It is simply necessary to adopt less individualistic, less monumental aesthetics, combined with adequate use of the natural landscape. This could be the city in less developed countries for many years. It should not, however, serve as an excuse for the improvised, though partially ostentatious, city of the socioeconomic classes which has caused the current misery of a majority of the population. Above all, it should not be the city of extremes so evident in Latin America today.

The authors of the studies in this collection are essentially researchers who represent different disciplines: Unikel and Urquidi from the Colegio de México, Mexico City; Cardoso and Singer from Centro Brasileiro de Análisis e Planejamento (CEBRAP), São Paulo; Hardoy, Basaldúa, Moreno, Yujnovsky, and Vapñarsky from the Centro de Estudios Urbanos y Regionales (CEUR) of the Instituto Torcuato di Tella, Buenos Aires; Quijano from the Instituto de Estudios Peruanos, Lima; Funes and Lander from the Centro de Estudios Nacionales del Desarrollo (CENDES), Caracas; Matus Romo from the UN Instituto Latinoamericano de Planificación Económica y Social (ILPES), Santiago de Chile; and Morse from Yale University.

I have intentionally sought studies by economists, political scientists, sociologists, lawyers, historians, and physical-planning specialists, in order to present as broad a picture as possible of urbanization in Latin America, in spite of the space limitations imposed by any anthology.

I have divided the collection into four parts. The three historical studies making up the first section include a general spatial analysis of a process begun two thousand or more years ago, a case study, and a systematic sociopolitical and economic analysis of the causes and characteristics of contemporary urbanization.

The three essays forming the second section provide an interpretation of political and demographic forces characterizing the current spatial structure of the Latin American countries, as well as an analysis of policies and mechanisms used to regulate the physical growth of cities.

In the third section, one study posits the importance of thinking in terms of horizontal spatial development as an alternative to the excessive concentration existing at present, while the other two essays elaborate upon the possibilities of using the urbanization process in a positive way to accelerate the economic growth and social development of the Latin American countries.

Three studies of Argentina, Brazil, and Mexico form the final section. Different in their approaches, they provide national or metropolitan analyses of the three most populous nations of Latin America.

It should be noted that the twelve essays in this anthology are unknown or little known by English-speaking readers. The studies by Cardoso, Morse, Singer, and Yujnovsky have not previously been published. Those by Hardoy and Vapñarsky have been expanded, revised, and brought up to date. Only those by Urquidi, Quijano, and Vapñarsky, in its original form, have previously been published in English. Although all the previously published studies included herein are part of the current bibliography of university courses in Latin America dealing with the topics discussed in this volume, only rarely have

I seen them included, either because they were unknown or because of language difficulties, in courses dealing with historical and contemporaneous aspects of Latin American society that are periodically offered by universities in Canada, the United States, and Great Britain. I have intentionally avoided purely technical studies in favor of others with a descriptive emphasis. I have also provided a sampling of ideological positions permitting readers to improve their understanding of the economic and sociopolitical background of Latin American urbanization.

JORGE E. HARDOY

I

THE BACKGROUND
OF LATIN AMERICAN
URBANIZATION

CHAPTER ONE

TWO THOUSAND YEARS
OF LATIN AMERICAN
URBANIZATION*

JORGE E. HARDOY

The principal objective of this essay is to synthesize the urbanization process in Latin America from its origins to the moment when, only a few decades ago, the bases of contemporary urbanization became clearly defined. To achieve this purpose, I have isolated six stages covering approximately 2,000 years of increasing and uninterrupted urban history and progressive territorial expansion. In order to explain the characteristics of the urbanization process, I shall analyze for each stage and in relation to the geographic context the size and population of the principal cities and the functions they fulfilled, with brief reference to their design and internal structure.

First Stage

Pre-Columbian urbanization acquired its most relevant characteristics in certain ecologically favorable areas of Mesoamerica and South America. It was preceded in all

* This is an expanded and updated version of the article of the same name appearing in *La urbanización en América Latina,* eds. Jorge E. Hardoy and Carlos Tobar (Buenos Aires: Editorial del Instituto Torcuato di Tella, 1969), pp. 23–64. English translation by Felicity M. Trueblood.

these areas by a prolonged formative period dating from the third millennium before Christ.¹ The geographic areas directly subject to the politico-administrative, institutional, and commercial influence of pre-Columbian cultures and of leadership groups established in their cities barely comprised, at their height, some 5 per cent of the total territory we know today as Latin America. This would include, at maximum expansion, approximately the territories occupied by the Aztec and Inca cultures at the beginning of the sixteenth century. The rest of the continent was occupied by sedentary though nonurban cultures, nomadic or seminomadic cultures, or simply was not occupied at all. Another important aspect is that the pre-Columbian urbanization process was achieved in total independence from external influences. Its intensity and regional or local characteristics depended upon the greater or lesser ability of indigenous cultures to exploit advantageously the resources of the immediate environment, and upon their inclination to adopt an urban way of life. In addition, there was a certain significant parallel in phases of this process in Mesoamerica and South America, although it has not been proven that the urban architectural forms and building techniques used in Mesoamerica have influenced those in South America or vice versa. Both cultural areas maintained a certain interchange of products and ideas.

The development of agriculture preceded the construction of true cities by at least 2,000 years, and facilitated the growth of population and its clustering in permanent if still small centers. Gradually, these agricultural centers were grouped around religious centers whose prestige, in certain cases, came to radiate considerable impact. The first temples were built during the Middle-Formative period in Mesoamerica, corresponding to the last preceramic or initial period in the Andean area. Their appearance in about 1500 B.C. indicates the consolidation of a religious group with sufficient power to mobilize the human resources necessary for their construction. This model

encompasses San Lorenzo and La Venta, in the southern
zone of the Gulf of Mexico; Cerro de Tepalcate and
Cuicuilco, in the central valley of Mexico; Monte Albán, in
Oaxaca, Mexico; Dzibilchatún, in Yucatan; Kotosh and
Chavín, in the central altiplano (high plateau) of Peru;
Las Haldas, on the central Peruvian coast between the
valleys of the Casma and Culebras rivers; possibly Cerro
Sechín, in the Casma River Valley; and others.

The advent of classical cultures during the first centuries
of the Christian era marked the appearance of true cities
with varied functions and a population and size unknown
until that time. The Classical Period in Mesoamerica (A.D.
300–900) corresponds approximately to the end of the
Early Intermediate Period (A.D. 300–600) and to the
Middle Horizon Period (A.D. 600–1000) in the Andean
area. It was undoubtedly the culminating moment of pre-
Hispanic art. Each of the classical Mesoamerican cultures
enjoyed during their prolonged flowering characteristic art
forms, political and social organization, and varied aspects
of regional production. Equally different were the cities
they built, to such an extent that the cultures may easily
be recognized by the physical characteristics of their
urban centers. In the design of cities (rather than in architectural forms), in the conception of urban space, and in
the feeling and use of streets (rather than the way in
which sculpture and frescos were incorporated into architecture), each of the classical cultures displayed very
different criteria.

Teotihuacán, in the central valley of Mexico, is totally
distinct urbanistically from Tikal and Uaxactún in the
Petén, or from other centers of Maya culture such as Palenque, Piedras Negras, and Yaxchilán in the Usumacinta
Valley. In Monte Albán in Oaxaca, in El Tajín on the
Mexican Gulf Coast, and in Xochicalco on the eastern
slopes of the central valley of Mexico, the influence of
these two main classical cultural areas in Mesoamerica
may be observed to lesser or greater degrees. Distinctions

are explained by differing environmental characteristics, and therefore by differing agricultural techniques, some of which favored population concentration and others dispersion.

The radiating center of the classical cultures must have been the hot and humid coast of the Gulf of Mexico.[2] There the Olmec culture flowered between the end of the second millennium and the middle of the first millennium before Christ. Its principal ceremonial centers were San Lorenzo, La Venta, and Tres Zapotes. La Venta, which was a ceremonial center rather than a city, is perhaps the key example of the monumental urbanistic concept, which would endure in central Mexico until the arrival of the Spanish. Its outskirts do not contain enough housing to justify the existence of a permanent population dedicated to activities we would call urban. Nevertheless, the builders of La Venta perfectly defined their axial concept, culminating in a pyramidal temple with a regular base and a plaza of regular shape, flanked by low and rectangular buildings marking the only access to the pyramid. They used the talus as an architectural element, alternating it with vertical panels on the pyramid's lateral faces. These elements and others of lesser importance were incorporated between six and eight centuries later into the general design and architecture of the ceremonial center of the city of Teotihuacán, but on a scale and with a perfection of conception not to be repeated again in Mesoamerica.

Teotihuacán was the main religious and service center of a dense agricultural population occupying the valley in which it was built as well as neighboring valleys. Thus sustenance was assured for an urban population that at its peak, between A.D. 450 and 650, must have numbered 85,000 inhabitants distributed over an area of some twenty square kilometers. It was the residence of a leadership group whose system of political organization, still not well understood, radiated outward over central Mexico and a large part of Mesoamerica. It was also a transformation center for raw materials that were brought from other regions to be manufactured and traded all over Mesoamerica.

Recent urban studies indicate that the builders of Teotihuacán established two enormous axes in the shape of a cross, serving as the basis for a grid that not only defined residential areas but also permitted easy displacement and drainage of water.[3] The civic-ceremonial center was distinguished by the complex of buildings and plazas bordering the Avenue of the Dead, undoubtedly one of the most brilliant monumental conceptions in urban history. Although conceived for a population of pedestrians, spatially it was a true urban street. The Avenue of the Dead was a perfect example of lineal progression and subtlety of design, its builders overcoming the uneven topography between the cross formed by the two axes and the extreme north of the avenue by means of grouped steps, which partially checked the frontal vision and the visual length of the complex. Surrounding this planned and densely occupied urban core, which included the principal ceremonial buildings like the Pyramids of the Sun and the Moon and the main civic groups and residential districts, were other neighborhoods of inferior housing. This housing was occupied by artisans and possibly by minor members of the administration of this society, hierarchical, heterogeneous, and specialized in a way none of its predecessors had been.

At the crossing of the two axes are reconstructed ruins of the Citadel (Ciudadela), an almost square complex formed by a platform enclosing an enormous sunken patio accessible only from the Avenue of the Dead. The Citadel was another ceremonial complex, possibly consecrated to the worship of Quetzalcóatl. In front of the main access to the Citadel, crossing the Avenue of the Dead, ruins have been found of another enormous complex, which might have been a marketplace.

The image and density of Mayan cities, as well as the environment in which they were built, were completely different. If to define a city we rely upon criteria of permanent settlement, heterogeneity, differentiation of inhabitants by socioeconomic level, its function as a center of urban economy devoted to transformation of raw materials, redistribution of imported products, and dependence upon the primary production of the immediate area, then the Mayan centers must be classified as cities.[4] If cities at one time were centers for specialized nonagricultural tasks, and fulfilled certain typically urban functions such as market and/or cultural and/or religious centers, with an architecture of greater refinement and scale than that of rural groupings, it is possible that Mayan centers could have been defined as cities. Yet they should undoubtedly not be considered as cities if, on the other hand, we focus on their density and plan. Mayan cities had no streets as we conceive them today or as they were conceived by the builders of Teotihuacán. That is to say, in Mayan centers houses were not aligned parallel to streets or organized around patios, but rather were grouped by two, three, or four units and built on platforms, avoiding low areas and zones subject to flooding. Even the housing sectors closest to the central ceremonial complex had an extremely low density, much lower than that of Teotihuacán's true urban districts. Because of their density and plan, Mayan centers more closely resembled Zapotec and Totonec urban centers, like Monte Albán and El Tajín, than Teotihuacán the postclassical urban centers of central Mexico. In the use of topography; in the design of plazas and of sequences of urban space; and in the arrangement of tall pyramids, which served as bases for temples crowned with elegant limestone cresting, the Maya attained combinations filled with premeditated visual perspectives and counterpoint in contrast to the urban design of the classical centuries of Tikal, Piedras Negras, Yaxchilán, Palenque, and other centers in the Petén and the Usumacinta

Valley. The Maya's achievements constitute one of the crowning moments of urban history.

The phases of the urbanization process among Andean cultures occurred with a difference of many centuries as compared to Mesoamerican cultures. The most significant urban examples had neither the scale of Teotihuacán nor the quality and spatial variety of Maya centers, Xochicalco, or Monte Albán. The urban design of indigenous Andean cultures during the Middle Horizon Period, which coincided in time with Mesoamerican classical cultures, was generally less monumental and less elaborated. Their architecture and sculpture, in spite of the use of similar materials and many of the same elements, were coarser and less polished than those of Teotihuacán, the Maya, or Zapotec. In Tiahuanaco, for example, there may not have been a premeditated general design based upon axes cutting perpendicularly, as in Teotihuacán, but its pyramidal masses and regularly shaped complexes are similarly arranged according to secondary axes, and their interrelation demonstrates a premeditated plan. Tiahuanaco was the southern altiplano's most important urban center during the Middle Horizon Period, and possibly one of the most extensive and highly populated centers of the entire Andean area during those centuries. Yet its population could not have been greater than 20,000 inhabitants, and its urbanized land area must have been between 2.4 and 4 square kilometers.

It is possible that the explanation for this resides in the fact that during the entire pre-Columbian period the Andean area had a smaller population than Mesoamerica. In the arid coastal valleys of Peru, the volume of river water limited potentially irrigable land areas and therefore demographic growth. In the sierra, or at heights in excess of 3,000 meters above sea level, the region's ecological characteristics imposed an extensive pastoral economy alternating with intensive cultivation of small valleys, which were frequently extended by man up the slopes of surrounding mountains. The Sierra's agricultural economy forced dispersal of the small communities, while the coast's intensive agriculture favored population concentration. It is logical, then, that beginning with the Middle Horizon Period the largest urban centers were built on the coast.

On the other hand, despite environmental limitations, members of Andean cultures were unsurpassed ceramists, gold- and silversmiths, and weavers during the Middle Horizon Period. The textile arts along the southern coast acquired unique technique, coloring, and originality, and Mochica ceramics on the northern coast developed an unequaled perfection in the representation of the human face and scenes of daily life. Similarly, Nazca ceramics on the southern coast were outstanding for the symbolism and abstraction of their designs. Nevertheless, the Mochicas and Nazcas only built large villages, greater in size and population than those of Formative centuries, but without the total urbanistic conception or the monumental civil and religious architecture and works of urban engineering of contemporaneous Mesoamerican cultures.

The decline of classical Mesoamerican cultures was marked by the almost total abandonment of Teotihuacán in about A.D. 750. Peoples of a lower culture originating in northern Mexico invaded the central valley, causing cultural regression and the loss of the politico-administrative unity achieved during classical centuries. Two centuries later, due to causes still not well established, the ceremonial centers of Petén and the Usumacinta Valley were also abandoned. Xochicalco and El Tajín befell the same fate. The heyday of Monte Albán was also past. By the end of the tenth century, the classical cultures of Mesoamerica and their nuclear centers belonged entirely to the past.

Between the end of the tenth century and the beginning of the thirteenth, Tula was the principal city of central Mexico. It was founded in about A.D. 980 by Quetzalcóatl-Topiltzin as the capital of the Toltec-Chichimec, one of the northern invading groups, and was controlled slightly later by a military-religious faction that renounced the peaceful and monotheistic worship of Quetzalcóatl and imposed Tezcatlipoca, the god preferred by the military. The prestige of Tula and the Toltec, even in their decline, was such that it endured after their destruction and was exploited by the Aztec, who selected from among Toltec descendants the beginnings of the Aztec dynastic line. With the aid of the lords of Texcoco and Tacuba, two city-states consolidated in central Mexico in the fourteenth century, the Aztec lords of Tenochtitlán and Tlatelolco dominated the political, commercial, and cultural panorama of Mesoamerica until the arrival of the Spanish.

In the thirteenth century, a well-integrated system of cities began to be consolidated around the lacustrine basin of Texcoco Lake. The two original Aztec cities, Tenochtitlán and Tlatelolco, were founded on two tiny islets in the southwestern part of the lake in 1325 and 1327, respectively. These two cities, as well as Texcoco (a Chichimec center originating in approximately the same epoch), Azcapotzalco, Tlacopán, Coyoacán, Tenayuca, Culhuacán, Xico, Cuauhtitlán, and others were cities of considerable size and activity for the age. Bearers and canoes overcame the lack of beasts of burden in transporting the merchandise that filled their markets and supplied the needs of their artisans. Arriving continually in the markets of Tenochtitlán and Tlatelolco were green Quetzal plumes and turquoise and yellow feathers from Coayxtlahuaca and Soconochco to be made into symbolic headdresses and shields; deerskins from Tepeacac; ready-made clothing from Xilotepec, Axopoacan, Tlapán, and other provinces; cotton and hempen blankets from Cihuatlan, Cuetlaxtlan, Tepequacuilco, and other provinces; cacao from Ahuatlán and Techtepec; dried chile peppers from Tuchpa and Oxtipán; packages of paper from Huaxtepec and Quauhnahuac; balls of rubber from Tochtepec; amber, seashells, and copal; copper and gold objects; and precious stones from Yealtepec, Tuchpa, and Quiauhteopán for mosaics adorning temples and houses. Everything consumed by the Aztec capital was imported daily by bearers who traveled the highways linking the city and the lake's edge, or was unloaded from canoes. Tenochtitlán and Tlatelolco procured goods from the provinces by means of tribute imposed after successful military campaigns or the threat of military occupation. Their artisans, among them specialists in luxury articles, found sure buyers for their work in the city and among the local merchants who controlled regional trade. Tenochtitlán based a large part of its economic strength, which was unrivaled in Mesoamerica after the mid-fifteenth century, upon commerce and tribute.

The Aztec city grew in a disorderly way during its first century of life. During the reigns of Izcóatl (1427–40) and Moctezuma I (1440–69), Tenochtitlán's urban outlines were almost completely defined, and basic public works were introduced for the population's health and safety. During the reign of Moctezuma II (1502–20), Tenochtitlán attained its maximum extension and population, its greatest political and military strength, and its greatest prestige. Half city and half floating garden (*chinampa*), its profile etched by dozens of temples dominated by the Pyramid dedicated to the worship of Huitzilopochtli and Tlaloc, it rose majestically above the lake and green groves of trees. The setting was imposing: snow-covered peaks, cultivated slopes, and the densely populated fertile valley.

It is not easy to establish the Aztec capital's precise population. Some chroniclers mention 300,000 inhabitants or 60,000 houses.[5] This figure was accepted by various ancient authors and modern researchers, while others believe that the population must have oscillated between 1 million and 500,000 inhabitants.[6] Yet all these are undoubtedly exaggerated figures. Recent research has set the city's area at 12 and possibly 15 square kilometers.[7] The districts of the central part of Tenochtitlán and Tlatelolco, built upon rocky islets, were the only ones with urban characteristics and occupied about 40 per cent of the city's total area; the remainder was made up of *chinampas*, which enlarged year after year, modifying the shape of the city and moving it closer to the lake's shores on the west. Estimating the density of districts built on dry land at 300 inhabitants per hectare and those on *chinampas* at between 90 and 74.3 inhabitants per hectare, we obtain a total population (a short time before the arrival of the Spanish) of from 165,000 to 154,584 inhabitants, depending upon the density accepted for *chinampa* districts.[8]

In Peru, due to the dense population concentrated in irrigated coastal valleys and the political centralization of the Late Intermediate Period (cir. A.D. 1000–1400), urban systems with complementary and well-defined functions arose along the coast's largest valleys. On the northern coast, coinciding with the expansion of the Chimú kingdom, Chan Chan became the capital of a kingdom controlling a series of adjacent valleys. Chan Chan's population has been estimated at 100,000 inhabitants. Its adobe ruins cover an area of 15 square kilometers. The complex lacks a general plan, although in the city's central districts a group of ten or more walled complexes or citadels are formed by identical elements arranged in a similar manner. The functions of these citadels have not been clarified, but their architecture and the interiors of houses, plazas, courts, sunken gardens or *puquios*, arranged according to a planned and rectilinear design, were repeated in other northern coastal cities such as Pacatnamú, Apurle, and Purgatorio.

All Inca political, institutional, and economic life was centralized in Cuzco, where the Inca resided. The Inca expansion occurred during the reign of Pachacuti (1438–71) and was consolidated by his son, Topa Inca Yupanqui (1471–93), and his grandson, Huayna Capac (1493–1527). In less than 80 years, the Inca empire attained a land area of approximately 1.5 million square kilometers and a population estimated at 6 million inhabitants, extending from northern Ecuador to central Chile.[9] As the Inca empire expanded, the ancient capitals and cities of states incorporated into the empire were converted into regional capitals serving the new regime: such was the fate of Quito, Tomebamba, Chan Chan, Cajamarca, Pachacamac, Tumbez, and other administrative and religious centers of coast and sierra. To complement the network of conquered urban centers, the Incas founded other centers of different size and function, like Huanuco and Tumpu in the central sierra, Ollantaytambo in the Urubamba Valley, and Tambo Colorado and Incahuasi on the southern coast. In all centers, the Incas introduced urban and architectural elements already employed in Cuzco: the great central plaza, surrounded by the most important buildings; the links with the Incas' roads; the cereal granaries or *collcas,* as well as the characteristic stone construction with trapezoidal openings, and floor plans of main houses organized around patios. Among the urban centers founded by the Incas, Ollantaytambo, in spite of its small size, is outstanding for its regular plan, almost a perfect grid, with its regularly shaped plaza formed by two of the blocks of housing left unbuilt.

The network of roads built by Incan engineers as the empire expanded facilitated an efficient and rapid communications system and the movement of troops to territories very different in geographic and ecological characteristics. An objective of the Incan administration was incorporation of each region's population and resources into a co-ordinated effort designed to satisfy the basic needs of inhabitants. Granaries, storehouses of tools and equipment, and efficient administrative and engineering techniques served this objective.

Cuzco's symbolic origin in about the year 1200 is confused with the origin of the Inca dynasty. Until the reign of Inca Roca, the dynasty's sixth member, all Incas inhabited the lower part of the city, or Hurin-Cuzco, near the site originally selected for construction of the Temple of the Sun. The tendency to live at higher altitude levels initiated by Inca Roca was further developed by the dynasty's ninth member, Pachacuti, a man of extraordinary vision and energy, who not only consolidated and gave direction to Inca conquests and established the empire's organizational bases, but also defined the plan and physical characteristics of the Inca capital. The city's center was indicated by an enormous trapezoidal plaza of some ten hectares, surrounded by the palaces of Incas succeeding to power and important religious buildings.

The center of Cuzco has not changed location since the time of Pachacuti, although its plaza was subdivided into two during the colonial period. Four roads pointing to the four corners of the empire ran from the plaza, giving a certain order to the streets without forming a regular plan due to the site's topography and the spontaneous nature of the city's growth. Twelve neighborhoods, some of which survive today under other names, surrounded the city's center, extending randomly throughout the valley.

Here, too, it is difficult to estimate the capital's population and area, especially since estimates of the first chroniclers were generally exaggerated. Juan Ruiz de Arce, a witness to the conquest, estimated that the city had 4,000 houses; another chronicler, Father Valverde, confirmed this figure and enlarged it by 20,000 houses in the suburbs. Pedro Sancho mentions 100,000 houses in the valley in which Cuzco is located. For the moment, then, there is no way to know.

The arrival of the Spanish occurred at a moment when the Inca empire was divided by a civil struggle that might possibly have been solved had a victor emerged. Nevertheless, the empire's future must have been uncertain due to its vast extension and complex internal situation. It is possible that the empire's population, as well as that of the

Aztec confederation, was already in decline, the latter decimated by continuous human sacrifice and both by war.

Second Stage

Between 1492 and 1519, the Spanish founded many dozens of forts, villages, and cities on the Caribbean islands, the northern South American coast, and the coasts and interior of Panama. The great majority were temporary settlements established as bases for bartering with the Indians, for exploration, conquest, and exploitation of new territory, and for assuring eventual protection and retreat in case of attack. In addition, due to ignorance of the characteristics of sites chosen, the majority of settlements lacked the necessary conditions for survival, and many were abandoned a few months or years after their founding. Santo Domingo and Santiago de Cuba were the two main settlements founded in those years that still exist in their original locations. Other cities, like Havana and Sancti Spíritus in Cuba, enjoyed importance during the colonial period, especially the former, but were moved to new locations in the same region.

In 1519, Pedrarias founded Panama, and Cortés entered into contact with the most advanced indigenous cultures of Mexico. After this date, the exploration and conquest of America acquired broader geographic dimensions and sparked renewed interest on the part of the Crown and nobility, thereby accelerating the rate of urban settlement in Mexico and Central America.

In late 1492, the shipwreck of one of his vessels forced Columbus to leave several members of his crew in a precariously built fort on the northern coast of the island of Santo Domingo (Hispaniola), which was destroyed months later by the Indians. A year later, on January 2, 1494, Columbus founded La Isabela on the same coast. In

1498, La Isabela was replaced by Santo Domingo, built near the Ozama River on the island's southern coast. In 1502, Santo Domingo was moved to the opposite bank of the Ozama River and built following a regular plan that facilitated its subdivision into lots and its land-use design. Nevertheless, Santo Domingo's plan was not square, and its plaza did not foreshadow the models used decades later by the Spanish in America, even though the church and some of the most representative buildings of the colony's politico-administrative structure were grouped around the plaza. Until the 1520s, Santo Domingo was the unquestioned capital of Spain in America. It was the seat of the first governor and the first archbishop, as well as the supply port for expeditions leaving for the conquest of Puerto Rico, Cuba, and other smaller islands, and Tierra Firme. In Santo Domingo, for the first time in America, certain institutions and practices were attempted, such as the *audiencia*, the *cabildo*, and the viceregal inspection tour (*visita*), which fulfilled basic roles in colonial administration.

During those years, various settlements were also founded in the interior of the island. The first, ordered by Columbus, were forts; those founded at Ovando's initiative aspired to be towns. The majority of towns and all of the forts were abandoned or moved within a few years.

About 1519, urban life in America was precarious. Almost all the Spanish lived in isolated and precarious cities and towns. The pompous title of city was a legal figment, not a physical reality. The coats of arms given to certain Hispaniola cities had no significance other than that of a royal gift, easily bestowed. Like the court's attempt to establish Diego Columbus in Santo Domingo, it was nothing more than a dream out of all proportion to reality. In about 1510 and during the succeeding decade, the economic base did not exist in the Caribbean islands to sustain adequately a white urban population not directly involved in production. Gold was scarce; the sugar cane introduced by Columbus on his second voyage, some subsistence agriculture, and cattle were the only sources of wealth. The daily sustenance of the Spanish and the enrichment of a few depended upon the availability of indigenous labor. The latter, ill-treated and malnourished, soon began to disappear. The Crown ordered the indigenous population to be grouped in villages for the avowed purpose of facilitating their evangelization, but in reality for permitting their control and exploitation. We should not confuse the vision and generosity of certain laws of those first decades with the possibilities and the true interest of royal representatives, conquerors, and new landed proprietors in applying them. The history of America should be analyzed by taking into account the double standard that existed between the apparent and, at times, real intention of protecting the indigenous population, and reality.

The cities, towns, and forts founded between 1492 and 1519 were located on the basis of the natural advantages of a particular site. The proximity of indigenous villages was generally taken into account, due to the interest of the first conquerors in bartering their merchandise for gold and pearls. Eventually, certain settlements were founded next to indigenous villages conceived of as friendly, since the Spanish, little given to agricultural labor and the washing of gold, needed indigenous labor for building, sowing, and other tasks. Santa María la Antigua del Darién, and almost all the first settlements of Cortés in Mexico, were built near or actually on indigenous cities and villages. Nueva Sevilla, Oristán, and Melilla in Jamaica; Caparra in Puerto Rico; and San Sebastián de Uraba in Colombia were, on the other hand, established to promote interchange and/or to assure the conquest of territory in a precarious location, and their inhabitants were sometimes forced to abandon them a few months after they were built. The indigenous cultures of the Caribbean and of the coast of Tierra Firme possessed only an incipient agriculture that had not permitted their advance to an urban stage. In addition, they lacked an economy and a political organization that could have been exploited by the Spanish to consolidate their permanent settlements. Thus, town building for the Spanish was difficult.

In the chain of frustrations ending the lives and fortunes of some of the most noble and ignoble of the *conquistadores* and *adelantados,* the conquest of Mexico signified the renewed hope of power and riches. The undertaking of Cortés and his men justified for many of the survivors the efforts and dangers they had faced. For those not participating directly in the conquest and in the distribution of riches, there was the possibility of an *encomienda* (landed estate) and the position this implied. For certain younger sons in Spain, posts were reserved in the new administrative, judicial, ecclesiastical, or military hierarchies. Simultaneously, millions of submissive Indians were distributed among members of the new land-owning class and subjected to evangelizing by religious orders.

Santo Domingo lost importance once the Aztec confederation had been conquered, the conquest of the Inca empire begun, and their material and human riches distributed among recent arrivals, the Crown, and the Church. The capital of America became the new city of Mexico. Veracruz and Panama were the ports of contact with Spain, its courts and merchants.

The strategies followed by Cortés and Pizarro had many points in common. Each tried to replace one culture with another without dismembering a taxable population that could satisfy the conquerors' material wants. The results obtained were rapid and went far beyond previous attempts. Thus, a Spanish city replaced an indigenous one, a Christian temple or a conqueror's palace replaced an Indian temple or palace.

The years between 1521, the date of the capture of Tenochtitlán and the beginning of its reconstruction, and the mid-1530s are essential to an understanding of the subsequent urbanization process. In those fifteen short

years, the Spanish founded numerous cities. Two criteria
were dominant in their location. The existence of indigenous cities on the same site or very nearby determined the
location of Mexico City, Santiago de los Caballeros de
Guatemala, Oaxaca, Cholula, Tlaxcala, Quetzaltenango,
and others in what would become the Viceroyalty of New
Spain, and of Cuzco, Cuenca, Cajamarca, Quito, and
Piura in what was to be the Viceroyalty of Peru. The second criterion was the existence of dense concentrations of
indigenous rural population. On this basis, Puebla, Guadalajara, Tepic, Pátzcuaro, Lima, Trujillo, Arequipa, and
many others were founded. Almost all of these sites were
located in the interior; in none did mineral resources determine location, for the cities were essentially centers of
conquest and colonization. By means of such ports as
Veracruz, Nombre de Dios, Piura, Panama, and Callao,
contacts with Spain were maintained. Cartagena was, at
the end of this stage, a humble hamlet without a hinterland to back its potentially excellent port location.

In 1531, Puebla was founded, and in 1535, Lima and
Trujillo. The blocks of Puebla's grid were rectangular;
those of Lima and Trujillo were square. In Puebla, the ca-
thedral's nave was parallel to the plaza, and its façade did
not face it; in Lima and Trujillo, naves were perpen-
dicular to the respective plazas, and façades became basic
architectonic elements of the whole. In Lima, the governor's house and the Cabildo were located on opposite sides
of the plaza. The grids were perfect. Facing the main
façades of churches were small squares provided for in
advance; entrances were planned around the principal
plaza. The plaza was thus converted into a checkerboard,
identical in its form and proportions to the others but intentionally left unbuilt. These were the characteristics of
the classic model of the Hispano-American colonial city,
repeated in all regions of America, and followed in the
construction of urban centers with different functions and
distinct locations after the second founding of Santiago de

los Caballeros de Guatemala in 1527. On the other hand, in Mexico and Cuzco, the plan and architecture of indigenous cities were incorporated into the general urban scheme of the Spanish city and the location of its plazas and principal buildings.

During these first 4½ decades of the century, the Spanish founded or witnessed the spontaneous growth of various ports, mining towns, and centers of conquest in the interior of the continent, which, on each new voyage of exploration, became formally incorporated into the Spanish Crown. In many of these cities and towns, especially in ports and mining centers, spontaneous growth was reflected in an irregular or apparently formless plan, as in Acapulco, Cartagena, and Veracruz. At some moment in their evolution, certain regulatory measures were introduced into some of these centers, especially the most important, to bring order to their physical growth. They never adjusted totally to the physical characteristics of the cities founded according to the classic model. The topography of sites selected to serve as ports for international or interregional trade made a checkerboard solution difficult. In addition, the interests of the first Spanish owners undoubtedly influenced the design of solutions directly affecting them.

At the end of this stage, the great majority of Spanish settlements were little more than camps, with flimsy houses dispersed over ample lots distributed gratis to the Spanish who witnessed the founding of the city or town, and to settlers arriving in succeeding years. Only those cities founded on Indian ones presented an urban image and possessed a considerable population, although still smaller than the population during the years of the Inca empire and the Aztec confederation. Those were the heroic decades of the colony, those of discoverers and conquerors who left Cádiz or Sevilla or San Lucar, or Santo Domingo, Santiago de Cuba, or Panama, with instructions and contracts they did not always fulfill, or simply without instructions. The kings of Spain, awed by the adventure of distant and unknown America, had no option but to trust their representatives and to insist upon the mission that the Crown and the Church expected of them. It was a stage of trial and error that established a system of living whose institutions, social structure, regional economies, and urban forms would endure more than three centuries, until the wars of independence broke the American territories' political dependence upon Spain.

Third Stage

The Spanish conquest of territories occupied by pre-Hispanic urban cultures and the establishment of colonial institutions caused a sharp decrease in indigenous population. Even though the decline was general, in no other region did it assume such dramatic proportions as in central Mexico, in which a decrease of from 25,200,000 to 1,075,000 Indians has been estimated from the conquest to 1605. In Ecuador, Peru, Chile, and Bolivia the losses were also numerous. Various factors may explain this decline; new illnesses; wars; implantation of the *encomienda* system and consequent social disorganization; the effort demanded by new architectural works initiated by the Crown, religious orders, and private interests; obligatory tribute in agricultural products; and the introduction of European cattle ranchers whose farming and breeding practices gradually provoked ecological disequilibrium and consequent dietary change and hunger in the Indian population.

When the conquest occurred, a population estimated at not less than 30 million and probably more than 35 to 40 million lived in the Spanish-speaking American territories of today. The drastic decline in Indian population was not even remotely compensated for by Spanish immigration or importation of African slaves authorized as a substitute for autochthonous labor. During the three centuries of the colonial period, the total population of territories subject to the Spanish Crown was always lower than the estimated Indian population at the beginning of the sixteenth century.

It is very difficult to find valid estimates of percentages of urban population during the pre-Hispanic period. Yet given the agricultural economy characteristic of indigenous cultures, it is obvious that the great majority of the population was rural, concentrated in self-sufficient towns and rural villages as taxpayers for power groups living in the capitals of states and regional centers. Nevertheless, it is interesting to note that in spite of the decline in the predominantly rural indigenous population after the conquest, urban population grew in slow but sustained fashion during the sixteenth, seventeenth, and eighteenth centuries, especially in the main administrative centers, ports, and mining centers. Despite the lack of statistics on the importance of indigenous groups within urban populations during the colonial period, my impression is that the conquest and the nature of the Spanish way of life caused concentration of the white population in certain cities of each region. The Indian population serving this white population, as well as the majority of free artisans, tended to locate near the urban markets that could use them. Withal, the immense majority of the indigenous population maintained rural ways of life during the colonial period.

Known censuses of urban population in the sixteenth and early seventeenth centuries are scarce and do not permit valid comparisons. If we take as a measure of urban population during those decades the number of residents of each city, continuous general growth may also be noted in every *audiencia*. Between 1580 and 1630, for example, the number of residents grew from 23,023 in 191 centers having population data, to 77,623 in 165 cities with data, for an index of relative growth of 2.88 for all Spanish

America, excluding Florida.[10] The index of relative growth for the Viceroyalty of New Spain was 3.33, and 2.37 for the Viceroyalty of Peru. Disaggregating the index of relative growth according to the ten *audiencias* existing in those decades, five had higher rates than the total; those of Quito (7.25), Mexico (4.77), and Bogotá (3.67) were the highest. In the *audiencia* of Guadalajara (2.81), the index was almost equal to the total for Spanish America. The indices for the *audiencias* of Guatemala (0.40) and Panama (0.32) denote extremely low growth. The *audiencia* of Chile lost urban population during those fifty years.

The number of citizens constituted a relatively low proportion of the total population of a city, as did the white population of any Spanish city in which, according to size, functions, and geographic location, indigenous, black, mestizo, or mulatto groups were dominant. Nevertheless, the growth of the population of principal cities during the entire colonial period may be confirmed by means of analysis of certain censuses and estimates. In 1599, Lima had 14,262 inhabitants; in 1614, 25,434; in 1700, 37,234; in 1755, 54,000 (est.); and in 1812, 63,900 (est.). Data for Mexico City are not so precise. According to Vargas Machuca, in 1591 some 50,000 settlers lived in Mexico City; it took two centuries to double this number to 112,926, as indicated in the 1790 census ordered by Viceroy Revillagigedo. In 1657, Santiago de Chile had 4,986 inhabitants, whose numbers rose to some 40,000 just after independence, about 1820. In 1609, Buenos Aires was estimated to have 1,060 inhabitants; 4,738 in 1738; 24,205 in 1778 (Vertiz census); and 42,252 in August 1810. Thus, in spite of the general decline in population until the mid-seventeenth century and its slow recovery after that time, population growth in the main administrative centers and ports continued without pause.

Even a city of extremely slow growth, such as San Juan de Puerto Rico, grew from approximately 1,000 inhabitants in 1571 to 1,791 inhabitants in 1673. Population growth in Cartagena, Havana, Veracruz, and Callao, the main trading ports with Spain, was much more rapid, with the exception of Portobelo, due to its unfavorable climate. On the other hand, the population of mining centers sustained strong oscillations, with rapid peaks and drastic declines, reflecting the imbalance between the technical extraction of minerals and exhaustion of the richest veins. Cerro de Potosí's growth, for example, was possibly the most accelerated in all America, reaching 140,000 inhabitants by around 1630. However, some 85 years after the beginning of mining operations there, at the beginning of the eighteenth century, its population had declined to some 30,000 persons. The period of rapid growth was also the stage of administrative and economic consolidation of the colony. Shortly after its beginning in the late sixteenth century, the viceroyalties of New Spain and Peru were created, suggesting an administrative subdivision of territory that was to last until the beginning of the eighteenth century. With the organization of the *audiencias*, the number of viceroyalties rose to ten, with jurisdiction over governance and the administration of justice. This administrative organization also defined the possibilities and roles of the viceregal capitals and *audiencia* seats.

Between approximately 1540 and 1600, the spatial structure of the Spanish colonies in America was established in practically definitive form. This structure survived essentially without variation, except for changes in the order of regional importance of urban centers, extension of certain interior frontiers, and growth of certain new centers, until well into the nineteenth century. This spatial structure constitutes the basis of the present-day scheme of continental urbanization. At the end of this stage, the Spanish had swept over the most propitious American areas, and their empire had almost achieved its definitive limits. Similarly, the principal cities had been founded, confirming occupation of those territories and establishing the maritime and land routes that would unite the colonies among themselves and with Spain. As we shall see in another section of this essay, the Portuguese underwent a similar stage in Brazil between 1540 and 1600.

Santiago de Chile (1541), La Serena (1544), Concepción (1550), and Mendoza (1561) in the *audiencia* of Chile; Asunción (1537), Tucumán (1565), Santa Fe (1573), Córdoba (1573), Buenos Aires (1536 and 1580), Corrientes (1588), Potosí (1547), Chuquisaca (1538), La Paz (1548), Cochabamba (1574), and Santa Cruz de la Sierra (1560) in the *audiencia* of Sucre; Huancavelica (1572) in the *audiencia* of Lima; Cuenca (1557) in the *audiencia* of Quito; Bogotá (1538), Calí (1536), and Popayán (1536) in the *audiencia* of Bogotá; Caracas (1567), Valencia (1556), Barquisimeto (1563), Maracaibo (1524 and 1571), and Mérida (1558) in the province of Venezuela; Portobelo (1597) in the *audiencia* of Panama; Campeche (1540), Mérida (1541), San Luis Potosí (around 1550), and Durango (around 1560) in the *audiencia* of Mexico, and many other cities were founded or established during those sixty or seventy years. Geography set limits to Spanish penetration of the interior during the colonial period, and these limits were only partially overcome in the nineteenth and twentieth centuries.

Spain imposed a regime that in practice permitted the colonies to trade only with the Iberian peninsula, granting preferential treatment to peninsular industries over those located in the colonies. Certain American industries achieved considerable volume and employed numerous workers, such as the silk industry in the Viceroyalty of New Spain, especially in the cities of Mexico and Puebla; the tobacco industry in Mexico and Querétaro; ceramics and glass in Puebla; the weaving mills in certain Peruvian and Ecuadoran cities; and the shipyards in Havana, Panama, Guayaquil, and other ports. Nevertheless, only rarely did industrial products from one region enter the markets of other regions. The progress achieved regionally by certain cities over others was due to their pre-eminence as administrative centers of the Crown and Church and to important differences in the commercial areas of influence of some cities with respect to others.

Between 1540 and 1600, Spanish exploitation of the most important mineral resources began, and the principal ports were definitively established. In many cases, the mining industry gave rise to the establishment of some of the colony's most important cities in terms of numbers of inhabitants. In addition, a mining area almost always required development of a complementary area with improved conditions for agricultural and livestock production for its provision and supply. The mining district of Zacatecas, which included the silver mining camps of Fresnillo, Sombrerete, San Martín, and Santa Bárbara, the district of Parral, and the mining region of San Luis, were the most important in New Spain. Yet no other mining center in America equaled Potosí in fame and opulence until its decline during the second half of the seventeenth century.

During those decades the system of merchant fleets transporting passengers and cargo between Spain and America was definitively established by law. Measures adopted guaranteed the continental importance of the ports of Cartagena and Havana, complementing Portobelo, Panama, Veracruz, and Callao. These ports were duly protected by systems of ramparts and walls designed by the most distinguished engineers in the service of the Crown.

During this same period, the first universities of America were founded on the model of the University of Salamanca. Some were established by royal initiative and others by religious orders, but all had a theological orientation. The universities of Mexico and Lima were created in 1551; the latter, however, did not begin its activities until twenty years later. In 1538 and 1558, the universities of Santo Tomás de Aquino and Santiago de La Paz were authorized, both in Santo Domingo; in 1563, that of Bogotá; and in 1586, that of Quito, which actually began to function in 1603. Between 1613 and 1624, the Jesuits founded four universities, among which was San Francisco Javier in Chuquisaca. At lower levels there were primary and secondary schools (*colegios*). Education was essentially urban, and the Indian population concentrated in rural areas and towns had almost no access to schools.

Almost all cities formally founded after the 1530s followed the classic model—that is, the model used in Santiago de los Caballeros de Guatemala, Puebla, and Lima, among others. Within the limited body of sixteenth-century urban cartography, various basic maps exist, such as those of Mendoza (1561), San Juan (1562), Caracas (1573), Buenos Aires (1538), and others included in the *Relaciones Geográficas* ordered by Philip II in the 1570s. If these maps are compared with others drawn earlier or later but representing cities founded before 1530 (such as the one of Panama drawn by Cristóbal de Roda in 1609, or those of sectors of Havana and Cartagena at the end of the sixteenth century, or of Santo Domingo in different epochs), it may be clearly appreciated how, after various decades of attempts, a city model was gradually refined and solidified that was soon to be constantly repeated once technical improvisation and the urgency of the conquest's first decades were overcome.

In 1573, Philip II signed in the Bosque de Segovia the famous *Discovery and Settlement Ordinances* (*Ordenanzas de Descubrimento y Población*). Of the 148 articles, 44 were directly related to regulation of new population centers, site selection, the form and elements of cities, distribution of lots, etc.—that is, directly related to problems we may define as urban. At least 20 of the articles were based upon the text of advance instructions (*Instrucciones*) given by the kings of Spain to the discoverers and conquerors and their representatives in the Indies. The orders given to Nicolás de Ovando in 1501, to Pedrarias

Dávila in 1513, and to Cortés in 1523 are basic. In 1681, when, after a lengthy process, the *Recopilación de leyes de los Reinos de las Indias* was published for the first time, the text and laws of Book IV concerning the settlement of cities were based upon the ordinances of 1573.[11]

An analysis of these instructions, contracts (*capitulaciones*), and royal cedulas issued prior to the mid-1520s, when compared with existing cartography and the descriptions of cities included in written works by the first discoverers, conquerors, and chroniclers, permits certain conclusions:

1. The Spanish did not bring to America a well-defined urban model, but rather a certain appreciation for the practical advantages of a regular, though not necessarily perfectly square, urban plan.

2. Locational factors for a new city, which constituted an important part of the royal instructions to Pedrarias Dávila, were so obvious that they did not require regulation. Indeed, they had already been suggested by Christopher Columbus in his diary of his first voyage, and by Dr. Chanca in 1493, on the occasion of Columbus's second voyage in which he participated, in the absence of prior royal instruction.

3. Royal instructions did not take into account the location of indigenous cities on the continent, which as I have already indicated was extremely important in the location of many colonial cities and in the design of some of them.

4. The Spanish did not even adopt a regular urban plan for the first cities founded on the Caribbean islands and Tierra Firme.

5. The first regular urban plan was adopted without royal instruction in the second founding of Santo Domingo (1504). Henceforth, Santo Domingo became a visible model, repeated and perfected in successive cities such as Panama la Vieja (old Panama City), among others, until its possibly definitive characteristics were achieved in the

second founding of Santiago de los Caballeros de Guatemala (1527) or perhaps in certain lesser cities.

6. Legislation only formalized a situation already perfectly defined in practice. In other words, royal instructions and contracts did not determine the policy followed in founding cities and creating urban forms. Each founder, until tacit adoption of the classic model in the mid-1520s, based his work upon his own personal knowledge, or that of his companions' previous experience in the Iberian peninsula or the Indies—in advance, therefore, of royal instruction.

Not all Spanish settlements founded in America adjusted to the classic model once it was adopted. Mining camps and centers rarely did so, given the topography of their sites and their spontaneous growth. Frequently, ports served as landing sites before becoming cities. Their slow evolution prior to the consolidation of the fleet system and their subsequent insurance of a secure economic base for development, and the characteristics of sites selected, were also reflected in irregular physical growth such as occurred in Valparaíso, Acapulco, and La Guaira, or in plans partially regularized long after the original founding, as in Cartagena. Even certain administrative and service centers founded in the interior after 1530 lacked either a grid or regular plan at the time of founding. Asunción, for example, was remodeled in accordance with a regular urban plan only at the beginning of the nineteenth century.

Fourth Stage

At the beginning of the seventeenth century, relations between Spain and its colonies and among the colonies themselves had conformed to a system that did not permit major innovation. The impetus of the conquest gave way to the rigidity and sluggishness of an opaque colonial administration. Spanish centralism reached such a degree that permission was required from the central administration even to move a small settlement, permission that could be delayed for three years or more.

Beginning with the early decades of the seventeenth century, the population of the Spanish colonies in America grew slowly. At the end of the colonial period, the population of certain regions was double or even triple that of 1620 or 1630, but it was still far from population figures before the conquest. If we rely upon the limited census figures for the remainder of the seventeenth century and the first half of the eighteenth, it would appear that urban population continued to grow more rapidly than total population. In addition, the tendency toward population concentration in the principal administrative cities, in ports of continental importance, and in the most productive mining centers was maintained. Thus, the continental importance of Mexico City, Lima, and Bahia, soon to be supplanted by Rio de Janeiro, was confirmed. Beginning with the eighteenth century, the regional gravitation toward Havana, Bogotá, Cartagena, Buenos Aires, Santiago de Chile, and Recife was equally confirmed. Within interior territorial limits, which had almost been defined by the close of the sixteenth century, the Spanish founded a number of new cities for the purposes of colonization, exploitation of mineral resources, protection of their borders against attack by rival European powers, and control of territories threatened by rebel Indian groups, and as garrisons or new ports. Although I have not studied this topic in detail, I believe that the most significant accomplishments with respect to spatial structure between 1600 and 1800 were:

1. the founding of Montevideo (1726) and Medellín (1675), the capture of the Sacramento colony founded in 1680 by the Portuguese, and Panama City's move after it was sacked and burned in 1681;

2. the well-known decline of Potosí after about 1640, at which time it was the most populous city of America, and the rapid growth of Guanajuato and Taxco and to a lesser degree Pasco and Huancavelica; and

3. the scientific discovery of the South American continent.

There are many descriptions of the characteristics of the principal Hispano-American cities during those two centuries and of their monotonous life, barely interrupted seasonally by the arrival of Spanish fleets at nearby ports with products, news, and travelers. The arrival of a new viceroy was a great event, celebrated with bulls, masquerades, parades, and by adorning approaches to the city, plaza, and central streets. The birth notice of a member of the royal family was an occasion of great fiestas (such as those celebrated in Potosí, which lasted two weeks), "during which time all work ceased in the city, in the mines, and in adjacent villages, and among all the people, high and low, Spanish and foreign, Indians or blacks, the only concern was to do something extraordinary for the solemnization of the fiestas."[12] Announcement of an execution or an *auto-da-fé* attracted the city's population to the main plaza. Comedies performed in a theater or some other specified place, meetings of poets, horse races, and promenades to gardens on the outskirts of the city constituted other forms of diversion especially favored by the cities' moneyed classes. This was the situation in Mexico City and Lima, and in the best of cases in Havana, Puebla, and Bogotá. All were cities with one-story houses aligned along central streets paved with dusty stone, which served as thoroughfares for coaches, numerous clerics, and hundreds of artisans and laborers.

At times the people of Cartagena, Havana, Portobelo, Veracruz, Panama, Santo Domingo, or San Juan de Puerto Rico, as well as Callao, Valparaíso, or La Serena, resorted to arms at the announcement of an enemy fleet or an unknown sailing ship. In that world of permanent conflict and broken alliances, of pacts, challenges, and counteralliances, more than once a Spanish port in America was captured and burned by pirates or by English, French, or Dutch fleets, only to be recaptured by the Spanish within a short time.

Sanitation was abysmal even in the principal cities. Constant pestilence and plague, together with general technological backwardness and limited production, were the reasons for the slow demographic and economic development of the majority of the colonies. Fifty years in the life of a city, not necessarily one of the smaller ones, could be a catalogue of misfortunes. In 1641, an earthquake in Caracas killed between 300 and 500 persons; in 1658, pestilence followed; in 1662, mice and locusts destroyed crops; in 1667, smallpox followed; and in 1687, a new smallpox epidemic spread to the principal cities of Venezuela.[13] It is therefore not surprising that in 1804, "the city of Caracas possesse[d] no public buildings other than those dedicated to religion. The captaincy-general, the royal *audiencia,* the Intendancy, and all courts of justice occupied rented houses. The Army hospital [was] located in a private house. The accounting office or treasury [was] the only building belonging to the King and its construction [was] far from mirroring the majesty of its owner."[14]

Provision of potable water was uncertain in the majority of cities, whose inhabitants were supplied with cisterns and wells. In Buenos Aires, until well into the nineteenth century, water carriers furnished the population with the grayish water of the Río de la Plata. On the other hand, an aqueduct was built in Mexico City at the beginning of the seventeenth century, and another was completed in 1779. Both had branches conducting water to public fountains distributed throughout the city.

We might ask at this point, what is it that still attracts us about a colonial city, some of whose main buildings and

general atmosphere are preserved moderately intact?
What is the attraction of Pátzcuaro, Antigua, Alamos,
Potosí, Cajamarca, Ayachucho, Popayán, or Cuzco, of certain neighborhoods of Guanajuato, of La Paz or Sucre, of
the old cities of Cartagena or Quito? Their first attraction
is their visual unity, without discord, within a simple and
logical spatial sequence; then, the pleasure of traveling between wide tapestries of walls, with their materials barely
whitewashed, and the spontaneity and logical location of
balconies and windows, following a functional criterion
and unpretentious in external composition; in certain
cases, the colors: reds on whites, blue curtains outlined by
the white frames of windows, reds on yellows, rose-col-
ored panels above wine-red squares. Seen from the outside,
the colonial city was immediately understood. Everything was revealed at first glance: the location of the ca-
thedral and the Plaza de Armas, parish churches, access
streets, the fort when it existed. The remainder consisted
of houses, tiled or flat-roofed. Near the center were the
homes of the moneyed classes, grouped around two or
three patios entered from the street through an elaborate
doorway; the houses farthest from the center were very
simple, almost country houses. The plaza was left naked,
lightly decorated with a fountain, ready for the many
daily and occasional uses to which it was put.

Visually, the central streets were not greatly differentiated. Urban complexes of significant architectural value
did not exist in colonial cities, except for those formed
around the Plaza de Armas in Mexico City or certain
public gardens, such as the Alameda of Lima or Mexico
City. The colonial period did not leave transcendental
works of urban design. This may be due to the fact that
there was no court, no princes or prelates interested in
such works. Perhaps the explanation resides in the scarcity
of available resources and in the predominantly mercantile
spirit of leadership groups. The reality is that during the
colonial period there does not appear to have been great

interest in embellishing the cities, which for the most part were only simple villages, precariously built and served.

In about 1800, only Mexico City and Salvador (Bahia) had more than 100,000 inhabitants. Havana had some thousands of inhabitants less, and the growth of Rio de Janeiro, as a consequence of the transfer of the Portuguese court, still had not begun. Lima had less than 60,000 inhabitants, and Buenos Aires and Santiago, less than 50,000.

Fifty years later, when the total population of Latin America reached about 30 million inhabitants, only four cities—Rio de Janeiro, Salvador (Bahia), Mexico City, and Havana—had more than 100,000 inhabitants; Lima, Buenos Aires, and Santiago had between 80,000 and 90,000 inhabitants; Recife between 70,000 and 80,000; and Caracas and Montevideo between 50,000 and 60,000. These were the ten most populous cities in Latin America in the mid-nineteenth century.

The spatial structure of the continent and of each country was maintained without modification during the first fifty or sixty years of the nineteenth century. In certain countries, changes began only after the beginning of the twentieth century. During the nineteenth century, lines of maritime and land transportation were maintained, reflecting reduced foreign and interregional trade. The continent was an immense void, with an average population density of barely 1.5 inhabitants, with El Salvador, Guatemala, and Mexico, countries with large Indian populations, the most densely populated.

The cities of 1850 presented few differences from those of the late colonial period. They were not much larger either in population or in size. Their demographic growth depended upon natural increase, since migrations from Europe scarcely existed; and natural increase, in spite of high birth rates, was reduced by equally high death rates. The civil conflicts characterizing the political history of the majority of Latin American countries from 1810 to

1850 discouraged industrial investment and caused population displacement. Under these circumstances, rates of urbanization were necessarily slow.

The Brazilian City

The urbanization process that took place in Brazil between the sixteenth and eighteenth centuries was independent of that described for the Spanish colonies of America, with independent stages of growth. It was totally different in terms of urban form, internal structure, and architecture.

Portugal's decades of greatest power and prestige coincided with the reigns of Afonso V (1438–81), João II (1481–95), and Manoel I (1495–1521). The voyages of exploration, commerce, and conquest during those years were not achieved by chance, but rather by an undertaking meticulously drafted and supported by members of the royal family. Some of the best navigators and mathematicians of the age participated, among them Duarte Pacheco Pereira, João de Castro, Pedro Nuñez, Gil Eannes, Antão Gonçalvez, Nuño Traistão, Fernando Po, Diego Cão, Bartolomé Diaz, and Vasco da Gama. Collaborating with them were botanists like García de Orta and Chistoval Acosta, and other specialists. A total revolution in the design of warships paralleled these developments. The caravel, with its three masts, lateen sail, trim lines, and medium tonnage, was converted into the preferred vessel for the great maritime explorations of the fifteenth and sixteenth centuries.

The center of all these activities was Lisbon. At the close of the fifteenth century, the capital of Portugal had some 80,000 inhabitants, most of them concentrated in some 100 hectares surrounded by walls and distributed according to a medieval plan of tortuous streets and sudden drops, of churches and castles built on the heights of hills. In Lisbon, as in other Portuguese cities of those centuries, planned plazas did not exist, and regulatory designs were not attempted.

In 1500, Cabral arrived on the northeastern coast of Brazil and took possession of those territories in the name of the King of Portugal. After sending home a rather lukewarm report, he continued his voyage toward his destination, India. Between Cabral's voyage and 1530, approximately, Portugal sent various expeditions to Brazil with unsatisfactory practical results. Gold, silver, or spices were not found, and advanced cultures with which to trade did not exist in the area. Neither was there a dense, sedentary, indigenous population that could be dominated and used in agricultural and construction work, as the Spanish found for their colonies. Only exploitation of fine woods and dyes caused a certain interest, resulting in establishment of the first trading posts.

Spanish advances in the Río de la Plata and French commercial claims on the Brazilian coast induced the Portuguese Crown to send an expedition to populate and colonize the new territory. The expedition was commanded by Martín Afonso de Souza and culminated in the founding of São Vicente, a few kilometers from Santos, in 1532.

In spite of its great interest in the new colonies of the Indies and Southeast Asia and in trade along the West African coast, and in spite of the kingdom's limited population and lack of capital, Portugal attempted in Brazil the *encomienda* system that it had successfully tried in the colonization of the Azores and Madeira. This consisted of giving enormous extensions of land—up to 50 leagues in width from north to south, with an unlimited depth—to noblemen and men with economic resources who, as a consequence of the privileges they obtained, were converted into true feudal lords of the new territories.

The fifteen captaincies (*capitanias*) into which early colonial Brazil was divided developed as independent states without major links among themselves. The beneficiaries or grantees did not always establish themselves in Brazil, and the economic results obtained were rarely encouraging. Prior to 1540, the grantees founded a series of ports for the purpose of assuring trade with Portugal: Olinda (1537), Pôrto Seguro (1535), Espíritu Santo and Igaraçu (1536), Santa Cruz Cabrália (1536), Ilheus (1536), and an expanded São Vicente. In 1548, when the captaincy system was replaced by a captaincy-general, wood, dyes, cotton, and Indian slaves were sent regularly to Portugal through a series of ports and landing sites. This initial settlement scheme constituted the basis of Brazilian spatial structure during the colonial period.

Olinda's plan to some degree reflects a Portuguese city of the age. Its medieval plan, determined by the topography of a location selected for reasons of defense, in spite of being somewhat far from the natural landing site, lacks straight streets and regularly shaped plazas or blocks. Olinda was the only *"vila"* (town) of some importance. São Vicente and Pôrto Seguro, the first Portuguese city founded on the Bahia de Todos los Santos, were trading posts.

When the captaincy-general was created, Tomé de Souza was named to fill the office. Among his duties was the founding of a city. In 1549, Bahia was duly founded, and served as the capital of Brazil until the end of the eighteenth century. In 1565, Rio de Janeiro was founded, and twenty years later, Paraíba.

Bahia grew in importance, prompted by its administrative functions and by development of the sugar industry in the Brazilian Northeast. By 1600, with a population of approximately 8,000 inhabitants, Bahia was the most populous and prosperous city of Brazil. Only two other cities and fourteen *"vilas"* had been founded during the first hundred years. All, with the exception of São Paulo, were coastal settlements.

Bahia's internal plan and line of peripheral fortifications were determined by the site chosen: a triangularly shaped platform 25 meters above sea level, limited by ravines at either end. Its plan was basically formed by four longitudinal and three transversal streets. The Rua Direita was the principal axis and united the two gates to the city. The other streets were also rectilinear, ending at the city walls. Bahia's ordinate plan was adjusted, therefore, to topographical characteristics of a site selected for defensive and strategic reasons—a radical change from Olinda, Vila Velha, and other first settlements. It is possible that Tomé de Souza or Luis Diaz, the architect taking part in the expedition, had received instructions from the King of Portugal regarding the way to design a city. The Crown was accustomed to sending architects to its eastern dominions, and the mission of Diaz to Brazil is significant.

São Paulo's plan (1558) presents certain characteristics imposed by a site small in size and selected, as in Olinda, Bahia, and other early settlements, for reasons of defense. São Paulo was the first town of any importance to be established in the interior, even though it was only a few kilometers from the coast. Olinda, Bahia, and São Paulo were the points of departure for exploration and colonization of the interior, in which the Jesuits played a predominant role, opening the way for colonists.

Olinda and Bahia prospered as a result of the development of the sugar industry. The growing difficulties experienced by Portugal during the sixteenth century in the administration and control of her faraway Asian possessions, due to distance, costs, and continual loss of men and ships, weighed heavily in the decision to give more attention to Brazil. Portuguese financiers became interested in the new territories and invested in the exploitation of sugar and the construction of sugar mills, to such an extent that by 1570 there were already 60 actively producing sugar mills in Brazil.

Since Olinda had no port, the region's sugar was shipped from a site located 5 kilometers to the south, where warehouses, housing, and installations were built.

This was the beginning of Recife, its port protected from the sea by a long and narrow reef. Recife-Olinda was a binuclear conglomerate defended by a series of forts at 500-meter intervals. Recife grew toward Olinda and might have physically united with it eventually, except for the Dutch invasion of 1630, which forced its growth to turn in a different direction.

São Paulo's influence was decisive in development of the Brazilian interior, and in formation of the settlement scheme of the center and North. São Paulo became the area's administrative center, the point of interchange between Portugal and the interior, and the point at which the region's agricultural production, salt from the coast, and tools, arms, and gunpowder brought from metropolitan Portugal all converged. In spite of São Paulo's excellent location, the sugar economy of the Brazilian Northeast was too all-encompassing and important, and during the colonial period the city achieved the status only of a small frontier city. Sugar was Brazil's main export until the beginning of the eighteenth century. Cotton, hides, Indian slaves, and fine woods followed in order of importance. Very little may be added with respect to the founding of urban settlements in Brazil during the rest of the sixteenth century. At the end of that century, the total urban population had reached some 60,000 persons, half of whom were white. The interior of Brazil was an almost unknown territory. In 1567, Rio de Janeiro was definitively established at one end of a bay where there had previously been other settlements and trading posts. Its plan was not a grid, although cartography reveals a slow regularization of its urban design.

Gradually, England, France, Holland, and the Scandinavian countries began to compete commercially with Spain and Portugal in America. Commercial companies with great civil and military powers were created in those countries for this purpose. The West India Company was established in Holland in 1621 to trade with America. At the beginning of the seventeenth century, Holland was the principal commercial power in Europe, and its merchant fleet was the most complete and the best-equipped. The Dutch maritime technology of the sixteenth and seventeenth centuries was also the most advanced in Europe.

Between 1624 and 1654, with brief interludes, the Dutch controlled the Brazilian Northeast militarily. Their invasion had been carefully planned. The Dutch captured Bahia and its immediate vicinity, which they eventually controlled for a short period; but their influence was very much stronger somewhat to the north, where in 1631 they decided to build an entire city, which they called Mauricia, at the village of Recife, Olinda's port.

In urban matters, the Dutch had completely different experiences and ideas from the Portuguese. Dutch cities were compact and regular for practical reasons derived from the need to drain expensively filled-in land by means of canals, which in turn were used for transportation. Location, rather than topography, was of major importance to the Dutch.

This new concept was reflected in 1637, during the government of Mauricio de Nassau, when the building of Mauricia was begun. The site selected was swampy and therefore lacked adequate sanitary conditions. But it had in its favor, in addition to defense advantages, improved links with Olinda's port and good communication with the interior. Neither was the site appropriate for building. The builders were forced to dig canals and employ dikes and pilings, following the ancient Dutch tradition. This they executed with the same organization and military precision characterizing the construction of Batavia, founded in 1619 on the island of Java to achieve similar ends, and of other cities both in Holland and in its colonies.

Mauricia's original plan was rectilinear, cut in two by a 30-meter-wide canal, with the main plaza in the center of the city. Its architecture was also imported, and a few two- and three-story brick houses may still be seen, with inclined roofs and narrow, colored façades. As opposed to the cities founded for the purpose of colonizing the interior, Mauricia was a gigantic trading post inhabited by a population that had no interest in establishing roots in Brazilian soil. Yet, the city had a zoo, an observatory, a botanical garden with hundreds of imported plants, and a palace for Mauricio de Nassau, which in size and magnificence was unrivaled in Brazil in that era.

At the end of the Dutch period, Mauricia-Recife had 2,000 houses and 10,000 inhabitants. In population and commerce, it was Brazil's most important city. Nevertheless, the gradual decline in the European sugar market caused growing economic instability in Recife, Bahia, and the cities of the Brazilian Northeast. To a certain extent, the end of the Dutch period also signaled the beginning of the end of the sugar cycle in the Northeast. At the start of the second half of the seventeenth century, Brazil was not a colony but rather a series of colonies so unrelated among themselves and so cut off from Lisbon that, for example, the governor of Bahia had no effective control over São Paulo.

In 1695, the Paulistas discovered gold in the present-day state of Minas Gerais, and although they were forced to abandon the territory, the discovery was sufficient to revitalize the languishing Portuguese economy and elicit greater attention from the Crown. Gold and diamonds found in the mountains near the central coast attracted many people. They came from Portugal and the central coast, and from the northeastern colonies whose economies had faded because of the inability of producers to sell their sugar on the world market at a price competitive with that of the Dutch, English, and French in their new Antillean colonies. This situation was reflected in the decline in population of cities of the Brazilian Northeast, as well as of the villages founded by the Jesuits along the São Francisco, the Amazon, and principal interior rivers.

Beginning around 1700, phenomenal urbanization occurred in Minas Gerais. The mining cities of the eighteenth century synthesized in the short span of 100 years the impact, peak, richness, and decline of the Brazilian mining economy. Vila Rica (or Ouro Preto) was the most notable example, and the most prosperous of all eighteenth-century mining communities. Built in an area that did not produce food and was difficult of access, its inhabitants had the luxury of importing what they needed and desired. This was also possible for inhabitants of other mining centers in the region, since between 1690 and 1770 half of the world's gold was produced in Brazil.

Vila Rica was built, beginning in 1711, on hilly terrain which, coupled with the rapidity of its growth and lack of prior planning, caused haphazard physical development. Its greatest prosperity occurred some thirty years after its founding. Travelers visiting the city in the early nineteenth century all attributed its decline to a decrease in mining profits over those of the previous century, and the exodus of mining producers to the seaports, where many became merchants. In that same early nineteenth-century period, the baroque churches and chapels designed by Aleijandinho and other masters of the age were still intact. Vila Rica was and is still a city of low houses, whitewashed walls, and tiled roofs, aligned along narrow and serpentine streets paved with giant blue rock, with sharp drops and indirect perspectives, and richness in variety of urban detail, all of which made the city a unique example of the American colonial period.

On the other hand, Mariana, which arose spontaneously about 1710 in flatter country a short distance from Vila Rica, attracts attention for the regular plan partially incorporated into its urban design around 1740. Mariana, like Vila del Príncipe, Tejuco, and other cities and *"vilas"* that arose from the prosperity derived from mineral exploitation, also declined at the same time as Vila Rica.

About the mid-eighteenth century, Rio de Janeiro was already the most powerful city in Brazil, in spite of the exodus of thousands of its inhabitants and much of the population of neighboring agricultural areas to mining centers in the interior. Until that time, Rio had grown without architectural or urban pretensions in its location near the coast. Indirectly, then, the mining climax prompted Rio de Janeiro's development, thanks to the role of its port in exporting ore cargoes to Portugal, and in importing merchandise destined for the interior. In Rio de Janeiro, as in other coastal cities, certain regulatory measures were introduced beginning in the eighteenth century in response to the demands of urban growth and traffic.

In 1762, for political and economic reasons, Rio de Janeiro was designated as the capital of Brazil. One reason was that the Portuguese expansion toward the south and southeast had encountered great resistance from the Spanish established in Buenos Aires, Montevideo, and Paraguay, and Rio de Janeiro was better located geographically than Bahia in relation to the scene of these new events. Another was that gold and diamonds had replaced sugar as the main source of the colony's income, and Rio de Janeiro had become the center of interchange with Portugal.

During the entire nineteenth century, Rio de Janeiro was the unquestioned political, economic, and cultural center of Brazil. This role was confirmed in 1807, when the Portuguese royal family, in the face of Napoleon's invasion, decided to abandon Lisbon and install themselves in Rio de Janeiro. In 1882, a year after the Court's return to Portugal, it was thus only logical that Rio de Janeiro become the capital of an independent Brazil.

Fifth Stage

The urban history of the second half of the nineteenth century and the early decades of the twentieth is virtually unknown, in spite of the extremely rich material left to us by innumerable travelers, scientists, and men of state; chronicles and articles published by newspapers and periodicals; and certain valuable specialized studies undertaken in those decades. In addition, after the second half of the nineteenth century, national and municipal population censuses began to be systematically undertaken and sectoral statistics gathered. Certain conclusions may be drawn regarding this period, during which the bases of contemporary urbanization developed, as much in the configuration of national space as in the internal structure of cities.

Independence caused few changes in the spatial structure established during the colonial period and in the respective hierarchies of urban centers. I cannot think of a single city founded between 1800 and 1860 that later acquired national importance in any of the former Spanish or Portuguese colonies. Its armies expelled from almost all of America, the Spanish Crown retained control of only Cuba and Puerto Rico until 1898. Spain's commercial influence declined rapidly and was replaced by English, French, U.S., and, to a lesser degree, other European influences.

The traveler who, for commercial reasons or in the simple interests of tourism, visited the former Spanish or Portuguese colonies during the first half of the nineteenth century was faced with inconveniences of all kinds and unexpected dangers. The journey between Buenos Aires and Mendoza, an almost obligatory route for travelers who wanted to reach Chile from Europe or the United States, was over an immense uninhabited plain. It took one long month to make a rapid journey between the capitals of Argentina and Chile. Mendoza was the only city that offered a few comforts to the traveler in this area. Even well into the nineteenth century, the journey to Alto Peru from the Río de la Plata or from Lima, or the descent from Bogotá to the sea, were adventures attempted only in cases of extreme necessity. In almost all the new republics, a prolonged period of civil struggle and anarchy followed independence. As a result, internal organization was slow, as was formation of a national bureaucracy, and positive measures to activate the economy were scarce. Civil wars, regional political bossism (*caudillismo*), and confrontations between groups residing in the new capitals and cities in the interior formed a general picture that endured until almost the end of the nineteenth century. In that situation of extreme isolation and the struggle of regional interests, it is understandable that regional economies maintained a great deal of the self-sufficiency and many social characteristics of the colonial period. Around 1850, the approximate beginning of the fifth stage of the urbanization process in Latin America, its total population was some 30,000,000 inhabitants. Brazil had some 8,000,000; Mexico, some 7,600,000; Peru, 1,888,000; Colombia, 1,490,000; and Cuba, 1,186,000. Only 4.1 per cent of the population of Latin America, or about 1,230,000 persons, lived in Argentina and Uruguay, the two countries that in succeeding decades would experience the area's highest rates of demographic growth.

By 1900, the total population of Latin America had reached something more than 60,000,000 inhabitants. Of this figure, 17,318,556 persons lived in Brazil. The area's average density had doubled since 1850. Uruguay's population grew almost 700 per cent in those 50 years; that of Argentina, 430 per cent; that of Chile and Peru, 240 per cent; and that of Brazil, 215 per cent, but with a marked tendency toward concentration in the states of São Paulo, Rio de Janeiro, Paraná, and Rio Grande do Sul. The growth rates for capital cities, which in the majority of cases were the principal ports, were more rapid than national rates. In 1900, Buenos Aires had a population estimated at 867,000 inhabitants; Rio de Janeiro had 691,000 inhabitants; Mexico City, 541,000; Montevideo, 309,000; Santiago, some 287,000; São Paulo, 239,000; Havana, 236,000; Salvador (Bahia), 208,000; Lima, some

130,000; and Recife, 113,000.[15] They were the ten most populous cities of Latin America. With the exception of Mexico City, the others formed part of the previously noted city-port complex, reflecting the commercial policy followed by national government and the increasingly strong links between national agro-export interests and foreign interests.

Meat and cereals, wool and hides, coffee and cacao, fruit, tannin, minerals, and other raw materials were exported to Europe. Textiles, coal, tools, iron and steel, machinery, railroad materials, canned foodstuffs, and drinks were imported. This growing interchange was concentrated through one or two ports in each country. Foreign capital, interested in assuring continuous flow of foodstuffs needed for the population and raw materials for its factories, as well as in expanding markets for its manufactured products, was channeled into the creation of banks and insurance companies, construction, and the exploitation of ports, railroads, urban services, and communications services. British capital cemented its control of the economy of these countries with its shipping lines and intervention in the development of the refrigerating industry, which, after the 1890s, began to displace the primitive drying industry, in the development of grain mills, and other attempts at transformation of primary production. These were decades of limited political participation, governed by foreign and national interests that rejected any state intervention.

The railroad dazzled leaders of these new countries. Even though the first railroads were built in many cases at the initiative of national capital, the companies soon became totally British, or, to a lesser degree, French. In exchange for construction of the railroads, the companies received enormous tracts of uncultivated lands bordering the railroad tracks, excessively large urban tracts for marshaling yards and other uses, exemption from taxes, dispensation from tariffs, special privileges for their personnel, assured profits, and other advantages. Liberal governments (composed of Brazilian growers, cattle ranchers in Argentina and Uruguay, miners in Mexico, sugar planters in Cuba) were associated with foreign capitalists, who managed their companies in total freedom. In this way, between 1880 and 1920, the railroad networks of Argentina, Uruguay, Mexico, Chile, Cuba, Brazil, and Peru were formed with fan-shaped lines centralized in the only ports having export-import facilities, thus reinforcing the primacy of one or two urban centers in each of these countries. The policy was to attract foreign capital at any cost; no privilege or concession appeared too extreme.

National policies remained controlled by agro-export interests located in the capital cities. Major technological innovations, drainage, running water, technical schools, and universities, telephones and telegraph, trolleys, and even suburban trains were concentrated in those cities. When World War I isolated the Latin American countries from their habitual providers of consumer and half-finished goods and equipment, certain governments—those of Argentina, Uruguay, and Brazil, for example—encouraged the manufacture of such goods, initiating the first phase of industrialization. Without the indispensable base for such industrialization, it was soon displaced once the European conflict ended, and the industrial powers resumed their control over Latin American markets.

A second aspect contributed to modifying the colonial urbanization scheme that existed until 1860 or 1870: immigration. Immigrants from impoverished provinces of Italy and Spain, Jewish agriculturalists of Russian and Polish origin, Swiss and German farmers, skilled and semi-skilled workers from Catalonia and northern Italy, and Syrians destined for petty urban commerce decided to abandon their countries of origin. They were impelled by socioeconomic conditions unchanged over centuries, or by political or racial situations, to seek their fortunes in the "new" countries of America. Trained contingents for foreign offices and firms controlled by their fellow countrymen also emigrated from England and France.

Between 1870 and 1914, Argentina, Uruguay, southern Brazil, and Cuba absorbed the immense majority of immigrants. Immigration was renewed after 1919, and enjoyed a new peak period until the world crisis in 1930 confirmed the weakness of Latin American economies in producing the most essential consumer goods and their complete dependence upon the markets of the industrial powers.

English, Italian, French, and Spanish shipping companies encouraged immigration to America, immigration whose impact upon the demographic growth of the Argentine and Uruguayan coasts, southern Brazil, and certain areas of Cuba and Chile was enormous. The expected destinations of these masses of immigrants were the fertile and uncultivated Argentine *pampas;* the coffee plantations of Brazil, where they were to replace freed slave labor; and the sugar plantations of Cuba. They were also employed as laborers in the construction of railroads and urban sanitary works, or in the construction industry itself. Those who actually achieved their dreams of becoming rural property owners were relatively small in number, since the best and most accessible lands had already been cornered by the large land-owning groups (*latifundistas*). The colonization policy of Latin American governments was in the best of cases absolutely incoherent. Enormous fortunes were made in only a few years through the rise in the price of land as a result of the opening of the railroads and the demand for agricultural products. The actual destination of the majority of immigrants, therefore, was the city. Immigrants comprised a high percentage of the populations of Buenos Aires, Rosario, Santa Fe, La Plata, Montevideo, São Paulo, Santos, Rio de Janeiro, Pôrto Alegre, and Havana, and in some cities as much as 50 per cent. In many cases, they controlled petty commerce and the construction industry, and promoted numerous small industries and workshops. Immigrant activity in the creation of institutions and development of labor-union and grass-roots political movements was enormous. As a consequence of foreign investment and European immigration, profound changes occurred in the spatial structure of the countries most affected by these factors between 1870 and World War I. Even though the basic urban centers of these national structures maintained their pre-eminence, the building of railroads and the opening up of new lands, the exploitation of coal and mineral resources, and the administrative needs of new political subdivisions motivated the construction of thousands of new cities and towns. Since the sixteenth century, never had so many new urban settlements been founded in Latin America. Some were built at the initiative of national governments, others by provincial or state governments, and many through the private initiative of colonizing groups, railroads, speculative enterprises, or mining consortia. Belo Horizonte and La Plata were the two most characteristic examples of French-influenced urban design introduced into America during those decades, an influence that also affected the opening and design of new avenues, the placement of monuments, the design of parks, and architecture. The majority of new cities founded, however, were simple service centers and transportation hubs for shipment of agricultural products to the ports. Very few of the cities that were begun between 1870 and 1920 achieved the population and importance of urban centers forming the old network inherited from the colonial period.

Sixth Stage

When the 1930 crisis occurred, Argentina, Uruguay, Chile, and Cuba figured among the world's most urbanized countries. An important percentage of their national population was already concentrated in their capital cities. Buenos Aires was inhabited by more than 25 per cent of the country's population around 1930, and Havana by 16.5 per cent in 1931. This was in contrast to the lower primacy of capitals of less-urbanized countries, such as Caracas, where only 4.5 per cent of the Venezuelan population lived in 1926, and Rio de Janeiro, with 3.8 per cent of the Brazilian population in 1920. The annual growth rates of the principal metropolitan areas of the most urbanized countries were higher than the annual growth rates of national population. That of São Paulo was one of the highest in the world. That of Mexico City, between 1930 and 1940, was higher than 3.5 per cent. The physical expansion of main cities occurred in parallel fashion. Buenos Aires was the only agglomeration approaching 3,000,000 inhabitants in 1930. Rio de Janeiro was close to 1,500,000, while Mexico City's population was 1,229,576 persons, and São Paulo had not yet reached 1,000,000 inhabitants. Santiago de Chile had 712,533 persons in 1930; Havana, 655,823 in 1931. They were the six agglomerations with more than 500,000 inhabitants around 1930. In toto, in the Latin America of 1930, there were twenty-eight cities of more than 100,000 inhabitants; seven in Brazil, six in Argentina, four in Mexico, three in Colombia, two each in Chile and Ecuador, and only one each in Bolivia, Cuba, Peru, and Venezuela. There were none in Haiti, the Dominican Republic, or the majority of Central American countries, still only slightly urbanized.

The spatial structure of certain countries began to reflect the formation of four conurbations, two on the central-southern coast of Brazil, another along the southern border of the La Plata and Paraná rivers, and the fourth in central Mexico. In almost all countries, the historical tendency to peripheral occupation of lands near the coasts continued to be accentuated. For historical and productive reasons, urbanization in Colombia and Mexico was concentrated in the highlands. Urbanization confirmed the politico-administrative structure formed during the nineteenth century, and reflected the growing economic dependence of less industrialized countries upon industrialized nations.

After 1930, the population of almost all Latin America began to grow at ever-increasing rates. It decreased in Argentina and Uruguay, perhaps because of the effects of the urbanization already achieved, but undoubtedly also because of the decrease in European immigration, the most dynamic factor in the demographic formation of those two countries from the mid-nineteenth century. In Mexico, the annual growth rate of national population jumped from 2.6 per cent in the 1940s to 3.0 per cent in the following decade; in Venezuela, from 3.0 to 3.9 per cent in the same time period; in Brazil, from 2.3 to 3.0 per cent; and in Chile, from 1.4 to 2.5 per cent.

Spatially, urbanization was extremely uneven and had almost no effect upon countries and regions afflicted with monoculture, great landowners (*latifundistas*), poor transportation, primitive technology, and low socioeconomic levels. The Brazilian Northeast, the Argentine Northwest, the Andean area, southwestern Venezuela, Haiti, and Central America, for example, geographic areas combining all or some of these characteristics, were not highly urbanized and continue to be the least-urbanized regions of the continent.

After 1930, few new urban centers were founded or arose spontaneously. Population tended to concentrate in the large agglomerations, increasing their size, while within them the decentralization population to the suburbs was begun or consolidated. This was not, as in the most industrialized and developed countries, a consequence of the automobile or the building of urban rapid-transit services or suburban railroads. Until 1968, Buenos Aires was the only Latin American city with a subway network, and it is the only agglomeration in Latin America in which suburban trains are important in the transportation of its population. The automobile undoubtedly influenced the formation of upper- and middle-class residential districts, just as the truck facilitated the decentralization of industry, but the mass of population lacks automobiles and depends upon unreliable bus systems for transportation.

The 1930 crisis forced increasing numbers of the rural population to seek employment in urban centers, especially in those undergoing industrial expansion. Lacking resources and adequate training, affected by the frequent structural crises of national and regional economies, these rural migrants swelled a floating population of unemployed and underemployed. They built *villas miserias,* or *favelas* or *callampas* (shacks and shantytowns) wherever they encountered vacant land, preferably near transportation lines and concentrations of employment. At first their locations were central; gradually, they spread to suburban municipalities by following new industrial locations, or, for lack of land, built *villas miserias* on the periphery of the large agglomeration.

One could say that the physical metropolitanization of recent decades is incomplete; yet this is not the case. It reflects, in the growing physical marginality of ever-increasing sectors of new urban population, general socioeconomic marginality and the increasing deficit in employment, housing, and urban services characterizing modern and contemporary urbanization in Latin America.

In a brief essay it is impossible to point out all the salient aspects of the contemporary urbanization process. This stage is the best known, and its existing bibliography is full and varied. On the other hand, this stage is undergoing geographic and demographic expansion, and its characteristics are still far removed from complete definition. They reflect, however, the historical spatial tendencies noted in the analysis of preceding stages, and the social contradictions of countries rich in resources, which nevertheless have not been able to break their ties to the industrial powers of the capitalist world.

NOTES

1. At the beginning of the sixteenth century, the boundaries of Mesoamerica were approximately the following: on the north, a line formed by the Pánuco River and the Lerma and Sinaloa rivers; on the south, the Motagua River, in Nicaragua; on the west, the Pacific Ocean; and on the east, the Gulf of Mexico and the Caribbean.

2. This thesis was proposed by Miguel Covarrubias in *Indian Art of Mexico and Central America* (New York: Knopf, 1957), and reformulated by Michael Coe in various works, especially, "The Olmec Style and Its Distribution," *Handbook of Middle American Indians,* Vol. III (Austin: University of Texas Press, 1965).

3. Concerning Teotihuacán see René Millon, "Teotihuacán," *Scientific American* CCXVI (6) (1967):38–48.

4. See the Preface to Jorge E. Hardoy, *Pre-Columbian Cities* (New York: Walker & Company, 1972), for a selection of criteria defining a city during the pre-Columbian period.

5. Among other ancient authors who corroborate this estimate are Pedro Mártir, López de Gomara, and Antonio de Herrera. This figure was accepted by Prescott and Vaillant.

6. Torquemada, in his *Monarquía Indiana,* estimated it at 120,000 houses occupied by from three to ten persons each. Soustelle calculated it at 180,000 houses and a total number of inhabitants that oscillated between 1 million and 500,000.

7. See Edward Callnek, "Urbanization at Tenochtitlán" and "Subsistence Agriculture and the Urban Development of Tenochtitlán," papers presented at the 1968 and 1969 annual meetings, respectively, of the American Anthropological Association.

8. See Chapter Ten of Hardoy, op. cit.

9. Rowe estimated the population of the Inca empire at 6,000,000, Bandin at 11,000,000 or 12,000,000, and Tello at at least 10,000,000. The lowest estimate is that of Steward: 3,500,000. A good summary is that provided by Henry F. Dobyns, "Estimating Aboriginal American Population: An Appraisal of Techniques with a New Hemispheric Estimate," *Current Anthropology* VII (4) (1966):395–416.

10. Jorge E. Hardoy and Carmen Aranovich, "Urbanización en América Hispánica entre 1580 y 1630," *Boletín del Centro de Investigaciones Históricas y Estéticas* (Universidad Central de Venezuela, Caracas) 11 (May 1969):22, Table 2. To find

the relative index of growth, the absolute index formula was applied to the ratio (or quotient) of the number of resources and the number of cities with population data.

11. Jorge E. Hardoy, "El modelo clásico de la ciudad colonial hispanoamericana." (Buenos Aires: Editorial del Instituto Torcuato di Tella, 1968), paper presented at XXXVIII International Congress of Americanists, Stuttgart, 1968.

12. Acarette du Biscay, *Relación de un viaje al Río de la Plata y de allí por tierra al Perú* (Buenos Aires: 1943).

13. Federico Brito Figueroa, *La estructura social y demográfica de Venezuela colonial* (Caracas: 1961).

14. F. de Pons, *A Voyage to the Eastern Part of Tierra Firme* (New York: 1806), p. 68.

15. Figures extracted from various official censuses and travelers' estimates or interpolations by the author.

CHAPTER TWO

A FRAMEWORK FOR
LATIN AMERICAN
URBAN HISTORY

RICHARD M. MORSE

The Preindustrial-Industrial Dichotomy

Much of the contemporary interest in the urban history of Third World countries attaches to the role of cities as agents or arenas for the transition to industrial societies. Usually, this evolution involves transactions and accommodations between a non-Western civilization and certain ideological and organizational imperatives of Western origin. The Latin American case is different, for here European conquest terminated or violently redirected the development of Amerindian societies. The new societies of the sixteenth century were at once "colonial" and Western. The drama occurring in contemporary Latin America is therefore an encounter between two fragments, or successive moments, of Western experience. Oddly enough, this encounter is yielding an outcome less conclusively "modern" than that produced by the impingement of Western capitalism and technology on the alien cultural and feudal institutions of Japan.

Until recently, the "development" mania has focused the analysis of Third World urban societies on the supersession of archaic or traditional features as they enter the era of the industrializing, mass-based polity. More cursory attention is paid to the preservation and reworking of preindustrial features. Typical of this propensity is Gideon Sjoberg's influential, or at least widely read, *The Preindustrial City* (1960), which divides the world's cities into two primary categories, preindustrial and industrial. Though claiming, unconvincingly, to avoid determinism, Sjoberg isolates industrial technology as a key variable that conditions social structure, allocation of political power, criteria for social mobility, division of labor, standardization of means of exchange, and man's relation to nature. By his reckoning all the world's cities before the nineteenth century, as well as contemporary cities in parts of Asia, Africa, southern Europe, and Latin America, run to a common preindustrial type. Pre-Columbian Chichén Itzá, seventeenth-century Paris, and a contemporary Yoruba "mud town" turn out similarly in respect to social structure and economic institutions. He offers little ground for differentiating Tenochtitlán from the Spanish city of Mexico City, which succeeded it. Similarly, his criteria discourage inclusion of two cities of Colombia, industrial Medellín and preindustrial Popayán, in a common Latin American urban family. Wheatley (1963) elegantly exposes Sjoberg's conceptual and factual infelicities. Here it suffices to point out that Sjoberg's dual taxonomy stems from two sets of Parsonian pattern variables—the particularistic-ascriptive and the universal-achievement—with no acknowledgment that from these variables Parsons constructs not two but four ideal types of social structure (Sjoberg 1960:332, 339).

The trouble with Sjoberg's dichotomy is not oversimplification but improper dichotomization. Industrial or technological determinism is no less defensible than other varieties. But if cities are conceived as societies embedded in larger societies rather than as artifacts, and if our concern is with sociological and institutional change, then we cannot chart the wider impact of industrialism without tracing it through men's minds. At this point preindustrial culture and beliefs assume critical importance. Or, if one suspends the cultural variable, one must be prepared, as was Durkheim, to allow for a range of institutional outcomes to division of labor in industrializing societies. Geertz makes precisely the point at issue in his comparative study of two culturally distinct Indonesian towns, a market town and a court town. From a narrowly economic outlook, development might, he concludes, be seen as a uniform process of economic rationalization. Sociologically, however, this uniformity does not extend to changes in religious orientation, class structure, or family organization; "a modern economic system may be compatible with a wider range of non-economic cultural patterns and social structures than has often been thought" (Geertz 1963:144–45).

A century ago Karl Marx analyzed the social effects of machinery in terms more clinical then Sjoberg's deceptive sociologism, despite Marx's propensity to mythicize the machine as a "monster whose body fills whole factories, and whose demon power . . . breaks out into the fast and furious whirl of his countless working organs." Because it sustains relentless focus on the nexus of machine-induced change, Marx's chapter "Machinery and Modern Industry" in *Capital* yields a series of culture-free propositions about industrialization (alienation of workers from their product and from their own selves; reification of personal relations into "objective" ones; socialization of means of production but not of exchange and appropriation) that are pertinent, with reformulations, to any historical context.

Sjoberg, in contrast, itemizes sociological changes that seem to have occurred in the West during the past century and a half and attributes them to industrialization. He never locates us at the site of the machine to demonstrate, as does Marx, what inevitable changes machines by their nature *dictate* to a community—in the way, as we shall see, that Fustel identifies the sociological imperatives of a universal religion, or Pirenne those of a commercial revolution.[1] Instead of showing "what industrialization does," Sjoberg offers a melioristic version of "what has happened in the West since industrialization." By loosely attributing a Protestant work ethic to industrial urban societies (1960:186), and thus mixing religion-derived and technology-derived phenomena, he makes it impossible to apply his paradigm of the industrial city to societies outside this religious tradition.

The extensive research now being invested in Latin American urban change is seldom conducted with clear or consistent reference to the historical context—partly because researchers so often are, or purport to be, "activists," partly because so many contexts can be identified: regional, national, Hispanic vs. Luso American, and so forth. This essay takes Latin (or more precisely Ibero) America as a single culture area for purposes of examining the process of urban development and its antecedents. Despite the considerable heterogeneity of the area, one can reasonably entertain the contentions of Tricart (1965) that Latin American cities comprise a "family" and of Holzner (1967) that Latin America constitutes one of twelve world regions for the urban geographer.

It will not serve our purpose merely to describe Iberian urban institutions on the eve of conquest, then trace their transplantation and modification overseas. We must locate them within a larger polity and economy. We must also look beyond institutions to an "idea of the city" associated with central beliefs. Moreover, if Iberian cities prove to be a special case, their idiosyncrasies require elucidation within the panorama of European urban development. So ambitious an assignment requires that we first revert to the Mediterranean matrix of antiquity.

Two Dichotomies: Tribal-Secular and Local-Universal

From a global perspective, as we have seen, Sjoberg signalizes the Industrial Revolution of northwestern Europe as the pre-eminent watershed for urban develop-

ment. Fustel de Coulanges, restricting his horizons to
Europe and the ancient Mediterranean, took the third to
fourth centuries A.D. as the critical juncture, a time when
distinctions between Roman citizens and subject peoples
were effaced, causing the decay of the Roman municipal
system, and when the "victory of Christianity marks the
end of ancient society" (1956:389). These two turning
points are each a threshold of disintegration. Sjoberg's industrialism erodes urban-rural boundaries, spewing technological change and the standardized educational system required by industrial societies into remote rural
corners. Fustel saw the universalism of the late Roman
Empire and early Christianity as similarly annihilative for
ancient cities. Whether the municipal community were
taken to be expanded into world empire or perceived
as a shadowy antechamber to the City of God, no man
could pay ultimate allegiance to both the polis and a universal order. Slowly the municipal system perished.
"There came a time when the city was a mere framework that contained nothing, where the local laws applied to hardly a person, where the municipal judges
no longer had anything to adjudicate upon" (1956:386–
87).[2]

Fustel's historical nexus lies deeper than Sjoberg's. For
while industrialism induced sweeping social, economic,
and institutional changes and engendered a new range of
attitude and sensibility, it left the substrate of belief relatively undisturbed. The past two centuries have witnessed
no reorientation of consciousness so deep-cutting as those
that Fustel treats in the realms of politics (universal empire), philosophy (Stoicism), and religion (Christianity).
Indeed, it is commonplace to deplore the archaism of the
systems or fragments of belief available to modern man
as he confronts the massive dislocations that industrialism continues to spawn. Even with Marx's mythopoetic
assistance, the machine, understandably, has failed to

renovate the moral and spiritual realms so sweepingly as
did the incarnation of God's Son.

Fustel explained the origin of the ancient city not as
technological response to economic challenge but as an
aggregation of autonomous religious groups. He perceived
no quantum jump between "village" and "city." For him
an early city was segmentally constructed, a tribe writ
large. It did not take shape gradually but appeared in a
moment of time as an alliance of tribes, they in turn composed of phratries or curiae and their constituent families.
A youth born in the city was successively initiated into
these groups, his rise from worship to worship recapit-
ulating the historic course of human association. The city
could not impose a legal order on the family or intrude on
its domestic religion and the paternal authority of its head.
Thus the ancient city was not legally innovative, as Max
Weber saw the medieval city to have been.

In forming a city the founders each threw a clod of
earth from their former dwelling places into a trench
(*mundus*) to enclose the souls of their ancestors. At this
site an altar was erected and the holy fire of the city lit.
Thus family, tribe, and city each perpetuated an ancestral
cult, tending fires that symbolized the sacred flame of the
human soul. Another complementary religion found its
gods in physical rather than human nature (the Hellenic
Olympus, the Roman Capitol); it acknowledged the won-
der of the external world and deified its surging forces.
This religion of the gods of nature was more comprehen-
sive than that of ancestors, heroes, and manes. While
worship of the dead was fixed and particularistic, worship
of nature, of the Olympian gods, was expansive, progressive, open to all men, mutable in its legends and dogmas
as its circle of authority widened. Gradually the god of nature moved from his modest *cella* near the domestic hearth
to claim sacrifices in his own sanctuary or temple. Once
his statue became invested with divinity, the holy fire at
the temple door was no longer a god but a mere in-

strument for sacrifice. "When we see these temples rise and open their doors to the multitude of worshippers, we may be assured that human associations have become enlarged" (1956:126). The transformation from tribal to secular city has occurred, and the stage is set for the city of empire.[3]

Needless to say, Fustel's century-old scholarship must be accepted with caution. Ehrenberg (1964:245), whose account of the early polis usefully supplements Fustel, calls the latter's work "in substance and method fanciful, but a great concept, showing a deep realization of the importance of religion and of kinship groups for the state." Zimmern (1961:82) calls the first half of *The Ancient City* "the best general account, not of the City State in itself but of the lesser loyalties out of which it grew," then lists qualifications: Fustel's Gallic tidiness and *esprit de système*, his neglect of the realm of criminal law, his jaundiced opinion that men in ancient cities neither enjoyed liberty nor had "even the idea of it." Important to our discussion is the charge that Fustel, faithful to the notion of a parent Aryan civilization, dealt simultaneously with Greece and Rome, reaching conclusions that may "fall between two stools and fit neither." There are of course studies, such as W. W. Fowler's history of the city-state or Max Weber's comparison of ancient and medieval cities, that show the "ancient city" to be a manageable subject. Here, in any case, our concern is with Fustel's conceptualization, not his historiography.

We may now proceed to consider in what respects the example of ancient Mediterranean cities elucidates the urban history of Latin America. In part we shall be examining historical analogies, for, as Hinojosa, Sánchez Albornoz, and others have long since proven, there was no institutional continuity between Roman and medieval towns of the Iberian peninsula. At the same time Spain and Portugal on the eve of overseas expansion shared intellectual legacies from the ancient world—juridical,

philosophical, religious—so that the question of analogy
vs. continuity is on some points moot. The following discussion first examines tensions in these two historical
settings between the local and the universal (city and
empire) and between the mundane and the otherworldly
(city of man and City of God). The polis and the Roman
legionary town are then adduced as prototypes for certain features of Latin American urban society.

The conquests of Alexander in the late fourth century
B.C. set an important precedent for the transformation of
Rome from republic to empire and, concomitantly, the
idea of "Rome" from polis to universal City of Justice. The
conceptual challenge was how to translate the political
ideal of the small city-state, that its citizens are both ruled
and rulers, into a political philosophy for empire. The
Stoic answer, which heavily influenced the Romans,
stressed duty and discipline under a universal, natural law
that had a wise ruler as spokesman. Such a theory implied
the Hellenistic monarchical ideal that was espoused by
Caesar and Antony and caused their downfall. It was left
for Cicero to formulate and for Augustus to apply a
compromise between republican institutions and princely
authority, *Respublica restituta* and *auctoritas principis*. Although the orthodox city-state tradition of direct exercise
of citizenship fitted the imperial context awkwardly, Cicero must largely be credited with preserving for later
ages the Greek idea that government is for the commonwealth and that the commonwealth is the source of sovereignty (Ehrenberg 1964:135–240; Hammond 1951).

In the religious sphere the ecumenical Hellenistic-
Roman conviction that the City of Mankind is the whole
earth, that it overrides hermetic compartments of city-
state, race, and class, drew emotional force from those
Eastern cults that professed that all men are spiritual
brothers and, as Philo of Alexandria wrote, that the true
citizen is found among "those who have never been upon
the burgess roles, or [who] have been condemned to

disfranchisement or banishment." Philo dreamed of a single monarch who would rule mankind as a philosopher, a mild shepherd, an alert helmsman. From such sources came monotheistic ideas and messianic hints (as in Vergil's *Fourth Eclogue*) long before the triumph of Christianity. Thus the two cities came to be distinguished not only as geographical and statutory (Cicero) or national and worldwide (Philo) but also as transitory and eternal (Seneca). Eventually, the tyranny of imperial Rome, its depredations against the municipalities, and the collapse of civic spirit opened paths for Christianity and vitalized the transcendental version of the two cities. The Great City was no longer a universal earthly city under one law and faith but a City of the Soul, which approached realization precisely as its links with the misfortune-plagued city of man were severed. In envisioning the City of God, St. Augustine perceived that the destinies of Christendom and empire were disjoined, that earthly society was but a shadow of the heavenly, and that Rome, city of this world, was only Babylon, while Jerusalem symbolized the City of the Beyond (Mazzolani 1970).

The preoccupation with city and empire remained lively throughout the Middle Ages, then took a new lease as the Iberian conquest of America recapitulated the historical moment when the city-idea had been universalized more than a millennium earlier in its Roman and Christian versions. New World images of the ideal city fall within Phelan's classification (1970) of the three main currents of Spanish politico-ecclesiastical theory in the sixteenth and seventeenth centuries: the humanist, Renaissance outlook, which stressed Spain's civilizing mission; the messianic, mystical interpretation of the conquest, inspired by Old Testament prophecies; and the thought of the Dominicans flowing from Aristotelian, Roman, and canon law sources, which looked to a world community of nations grounded on Roman *jus gentium*.

The ideal community of the humanists was conceived

as actually reproducible in the world, the most notable exemplar being the mission towns erected by Vasco de Quiroga in Michoacán on the model of Thomas More's "utopia" (a word meaning, ironically, "nowhere").

The edenic or chiliastic city-image had two principal versions. One featured various pre-existing cities: a plunderable city of gold, the seven cities of Cíbola, the cities of the seven legendary Portuguese bishops who fled the Saracens, or else a terrestrial paradise, possibly inaccessible to mortals, such as Columbus surmised to exist at the Orinoco headwaters. (Gandía 1929). The Portuguese in Brazil shared these edenic visions, although they were less given than the Spaniards to witnessing miraculous interventions, and their chroniclers purveyed fabulous legends with a sense of "plausible attenuation" (Holanda 1969).

There was also a prospective rather than an extant paradise, of the sort Phelan studies in the writings of Gerónimo de Mendieta (1525–1604), foremost of the Franciscan New World millennialists. Mendieta felt that the friars, protected by paternal kings and viceroys, were to lead the Indians to a City of God wherein the poverty and piety of the pre-Constantinian Church would be reborn in anticipation of the Apocalypse. Though situated on earth, Mendieta's City was not a this-worldly utopia like Quiroga's but an other-worldly Celestial City heralding reconsecration to apostolic humility. This chiliastic vision had its Luso Brazilian parallel in the *História do futuro* and other eschatological writings of the seventeenth-century Jesuit orator, missionary, and statesman Antônio Vieira (Cantel 1960).

For a modern audience Larrea (1943) re-creates the millennial theme in poetico-mystical rather than theological terms, describing the course of the universal city from its Judeo-Christian genesis to its apotheosis in the New World. Three historic cities occupy successive points of the trajectory: Jerusalem to the east, mistress of the past, built on the tomb of Christ; Rome in the center, mistress of the present, built on the tomb of Peter; and Santiago at the western rim of Europe (Finis-terre), built on the tomb of James, its name, Compostela or *campo de la estrella,* portending a luminous future. As the battleground for the Europocentric and the universal, Spain released Cristoforo Colombo (a name meaning "bearer of Christ's spirit") to discover the New World. Inexorably the dialectic reaches its term, faithful to the message that Roma, meaning "force," spells Amor when reversed and that the river Ebro, flowing past Zaragoza (city of Caesars), becomes in inversion the universal Orbe.

Policies of colonial government were centrally informed by neither utopianism nor millennialism but by a pragmatic moral philosophy with a strong Thomist accent that could purport to reconcile Christian principles of justice with the harsh realities of conquest and exploitation and with the diversity and intractability of the immense New World empires. In this as in the millennialist tradition, the city idea preserves its ancient local and universal connotations. The *Política indiana* (1648) of the jurisconsult Solórzano (1736–39: *lib.* II, *chaps.* vi, xxiv) offers some representative statements. Citing Greek and Roman authors, Church Fathers, and Scholastic sources, he asserted the "republics" of Spaniards and Indians to form a single mystical body whose members were to be designated rulers and followers according to their capacity and assigned to trades and professions in agriculture, commerce, mechanical arts, liberal vocations, and the magistracy. St. Thomas Aquinas is given as authority for the ideal that "a City will be perfect and well ruled when the Citizens are disposed to assist one another and each one complies punctually and conscientiously with his duty."

Moral principles for the *Ciudad perfecta* were reinforced by ecological ones. Solórzano perceived the city to have the civilizing function of "reducing" wild, nomadic groups who lacked laws and kings to community life for defense and mutual aid. Just as the Romans once assembled wandering peoples in industrious farm communities controlled by larger mother cities (*metrocomias*), so the Spaniards were right to gather the Indians in *reducciones* or *agregaciones,* establishing their leaders in the larger *cabeceras* of each province. This policy flowed from a grand notion that the whole world forms "a great City where all men live, divided into lesser ones composed of different nations." Solórzano makes explicit the ambivalent meaning of "republic" in Spanish political doctrine. The task of government was to cultivate the prosperity of towns of Spaniards and urbanized groups of Indians linking them to larger juridical, administrative, and ecclesiastical structures. "The State is eminently civilizing, in the original meaning of the word. The founding of urban 'republics' of Spaniards and natives assures the general order of the Republic in the sense of 'state'" (Góngora 1951:234).

Affinities between the Iberian and the ancient Mediterranean concept of the city have two implications for understanding the character of urban development in the Spanish Indies and Brazil. First, the Ibero-Catholic-Mediterranean ideal city, in its edenic and juridical versions, was an exemplar or paradigm that transcended mortal strivings and passions. It occupied a higher plane of reality. The two orders might in principle converge—once an Indian tribe was settled in a benign mission, or once the conquistador or bandeirante stumbled on the Shining City, or once the Apocalypse arrived—but for practical day-to-day purposes the higher reality could only imperfectly penetrate the lower. The pragmatic arrangements and hierarchies of society could not replicate the ideal and required constant legitimation by strenuous exercises in casuistry.

The significance of this tradition is accented when one contrasts it with the "covenanted community" of the New England Puritans (Smith 1966:3–16). The "covenant" implied a "bond of marriage" between God and the com-

munity. As long as the covenanters observed the Articles
and refused "to embrace this present world and prosecute
our carnal intentions," then the God of Israel was among
them and their settlement was "as a city upon a hill."
While its members remained sinless, the community was
an embodiment, not an imperfect replica, of the divine
order. Moreover, its emigrants could reproduce new con-
gregations that would each stand "in the same relation to
God as did its parent community. There was no suggestion
of subordination." The psychological pressures required
to maintain this communal self-purification were not
generalized in Ibero American societies, where the "perfected" communities of disciplined religious elites—however ecumenical their pretensions—served in fact only
paradigmatic functions.

A second implication of the discussion relates to the notion of universal city-empire. Iberian subjects in America
shared an allegiance to a far-flung religio-political community not of their own making. Because this community was
weakly articulated, particularly in the formative period, its
eventual disposition of parts and inner linkages were not
clearly prescribed. In the case specifically of cities, it is
sometimes asserted that the repetitive grid layout and
spacious plaza of Spanish America was both symbol and
vehicle for an imperial master plan. In fact, however, this
bold geometrism flowed from local, pragmatic experiments, which crystallized only gradually into a legislative
archetype. "In other words, the legislation confirmed and
legalized a process that had been anticipated in practice"
(Hardoy 1968:40). Urban institutions, like urban form,
were in this dialectic relationship to the theory of empire.
In sixteenth-century Latin America, town and mission
founding was the primary act that asserted sovereignty,
settled colonists, appropriated land, and enforced economic demands on Amerind communities. These municipal functions frequently originated beyond reach of effective imperial control, developed within an armature of

local interests, and stubbornly resisted royal encroachment. The colonial Latin American town is therefore sometimes more appropriately conceived as a semiautonomous, agrourban polis than as an outpost of empire.

We distinguish, then, two types of affinity between ancient and Ibero American cities. Affinity of descent allows us to trace the late-medieval Scholastic, juridical, and chiliastic versions of the universal or transcendental city back to Ciceronian and Augustinian sources. Affinity of analogy allows us to perceive that American colonization recapitulated an early stage of the long historical process from which it had issued. New World urban societies produced historical echoes not only of the tension between the local and the universal (Aristotelian and Ciceronian) political orders but also of tensions along the tribal-secular gradient that Fustel defined for the ancient polis.

In applying the tribal-secular continuum to Latin America, it might seem logical to trace how the clannish, patriarchal colonial town evolved into the primate bureaucratic-commercial city, with its plebs and populist politics. To capture the full force of the distinction, however, one must roll back the historical horizon to include pre-Columbian cities. The Inca empire fits the case well. Not infrequently, the Incas are described as stern and noble "Romans" who calculatingly constructed a large empire centered on Cuzco, knit by highways, supplied by technologically advanced agriculture, and defended by strategically placed forts. In socialist interpretations particularly, the Spanish period is seen as a reversion to a more primitive, predatory economy that destroyed the transportation network and the urban-rural ecology of the Inca empire. Such a view, responsive to Western "developmental" criteria, misses the texture and historical logic of Incaic institutions. As Zuidema (1962) demonstrates, it is misleading to describe Cuzco as an "imperial" capital that projected a "rational" order on its hinterland, given the fact that the city's complex religio-social system seems related to the village organization of the contemporary Borôro and Gê tribes of eastern Brazil. The structure of empire emanating from Cuzco was not a "Roman" design but an extrapolation from urban (one wishes to say "preurban") social organization "based on kinship and on the application of kinship principles." The cells of this organization were endogamous groups, their territories, and the holy sites (*huacas*) identified with their forebears. Thus the famous decempartition, which characterized the Incas' administration and the temporal ordering of their dynasties, emanated from kinship structures. The place of any person in the hierarchic social order was fixed by a threefold relationship with present and abandoned marriage groups and with the rest of society.[4] Comparing Incaic Cuzco with Spanish colonial Lima, then, yields a quantum jump along Fustel's evolutionary tribal-secular gradient. Occasionally the two forms may have coexisted under Spanish rule but, as Gibson (1964:368–402) shows for the Indian *parcialidades* and *barrios* of Mexico City, with Indian organization subordinate to the design and purposes of Spanish control.

Once we narrow our focus to the ancient secular city, or polis, and the colonial Latin American town, we find that tribalism or kinship is no longer the organizing principle for urban life. The city is now constituted as a *public* order, but a public order in chronic conflict with the private one of patriarchal familialism. The urban histories of the ancient Mediterranean and colonial Latin America are grounded in persistent tensions between universalism and particularism, legalism and personalism, populism and elitism, public equity and clientage. Treatments of these themes for Latin America—such as the classic study of patrician domination in Buenos Aires (García 1955), accounts of plebeian revolts (Sigüenza 1929; Guthrie 1945), or analyses of the interplay of the public and private orders (Duarte 1966; Faoro 1958)—recall the matrix situation confronted by Thucydides, Plato, and Aristotle, and imaginatively rendered in *Antigone* and the *Oresteia*. Indeed, echoes persist even in modern industrial Latin America, where elite clientist structures and intermittent, weakly articulated populist protest—the interaction of patriciate and demos—weigh more heavily than do "class ideologies" or "interest groups" in defining the social order.

Just as the age-old categories of Aristotle's *Politics* illuminate *internal processes* of the Latin American urban polity, so the example of the Roman legionary outpost helps one characterize the *external relations,* political and ecological, of Latin American towns. The location of the Roman *colonia* (related to *colere,* to cultivate) or New World town was dictated more by political, strategic, and agricultural than by commercial or industrial considerations. The administrative unit was the *civitas* or municipality, centering on a grid plan surrounded by lands that were allotted to first comers or else held aside as an *ager publicus* or *ejido.* The Roman civitas was an old tribal unit comprising a tribe and its territory. Its chief town was the administrative center, organized on the standard Roman model and controlling subtribes or client tribes, each with its *pagus* (territorial unit) and *vicus* (settlement) (Lot 1931:115–18). "Gaul was . . . too large, its tribes too backward and scattered, to be welded into the Italian type of a network of municipalities. A tribal territory was like a French department, or often larger" (Brogan 1953:66–67). In the New World, similarly, municipal jurisdictions might extend scores, even hundreds of miles, and in an area like central Mexico they fastened on Amerindian tribal systems (Gibson 1964:32–57). Roman colonists were soldier-farmers, and their towns had a camplike appearance; in Spanish America, foot soldiers and horse soldiers received land grants called *peonías* and *caballerías.*

If both situations yield the example of the rectilinear

town functioning as metropolitan outpost and as colonizing agent, so do they exhibit functionally comparable agrarian institutions. The latifundium, controlled by a single proprietor originally from an urban background, becomes the agency that organizes rural workers for production. In both cases the workers are typically of an alien culture and, whatever the dictates of the metropolis may be, it is largely the latifundium that determines the workers' relation to the soil and the kind of justice they may expect to receive. Proprietors have mixed rural-urban allegiances. When the social or economic promise of the hinterland is great, or when town life becomes penurious and oppressive, they are drawn to reside in the country. This deprives the town of leadership and, to the extent that the rural domain becomes self-sufficient, of economic vitality as well.

In exploring such historical analogies one cannot of course neglect fresh economic and psychic ingredients in the ethos of New World city-building. Ancient Greek political (or "polis") ideals of paideia, areté, and sophrosyné—emphasizing the wholeness and balance of personal development, the organic identity of man and community, the polis as ultimate embodiment of justice and spiritual life—would not reappear in Latin American communities where dominance and subjection, prestige and humiliation, beatitude and sin, salvation and damnation were determined by a politico-moral order far transcending the bounds of the polis. And while imperial Rome, which failed to effectuate Greek polis ideals, may seem to offer fuller comparisons with the post-medieval empires, here again one cannot overlook important differences of sensibility. In characterizing the politico-urban imagery of the Romans, Mazzolani (1970:183) highlights two contending impulses: the literary ideal of universal egalitarianism under the aegis of a beneficent Olympian monarchy, and the theme of brute force, violence, and oppression which, in the visual arts, coexists with the paternal egalitarian theme. In the Iberian case one might venture that the theme of paternalism is imbued with hierarchical and compassionate rather than egalitarian motifs and that its richest statement is in ecclesiastical imagery, literary, visual, architectural, and liturgical. The theme of domination found abundant expression, largely literary or expository, on a spectrum from legalism to militancy but without Roman overtones of militarism.

The comparative discussion of ancient and Latin American cities is problematical because on certain points one cannot assert unequivocally whether direct historical continuity is involved, whether the issue is strictly one of historical analogy, or whether perhaps one is dealing with a case of loose historical replication within the Mediterranean culture area. To give firmer shape and anchorage to the impressions suggested above, we must now consider the development of municipal institutions in western Europe during the centuries preceding the discovery of America. In so doing we abandon the tactic of selective crosstemporal analogy and undertake to reconstruct two patterns of urban development that unfolded simultaneously north and south of the Pyrenees.

The Patrimonial-Commercial Dichotomy

From various quarters exception is taken to the thesis that the northwestern European town of the late Middle Ages was historically unique in that (1) its charter, laws, and institutions were shaped by and oriented to commercial interests and (2) it enjoyed corporate autonomy. Sjoberg (1960:113) holds that bourgeois ascendancy was brief, limited to a few cities, and soon eclipsed by the nobles' reassertion of control. Cahen (1958–59), who accepts the importance of the bourgeois commune of the West, describes both "bourgeois" and popular, egalitarian uprisings in Near Eastern Islamic cities after the ninth century; the bureaucratic state, however, prevented their attaining organizational autonomy. The Islamic bourgeoisie, which anticipated Western economic attitudes and reached its ascendancy in about 1000, "never became an organized body and, as a class, never obtained political power, although many of its members occupied positions as high and highest executives of the state" (Goitein 1957:584). Weber (1958:95–96), who has been charged with overstressing the uniqueness of the Western city, supposed that the legally autonomous commune may have arisen in at least rudimentary form in Mesopotamia, Phoenicia, Palestine, and perhaps maritime cities of other areas. The point of uniqueness is less important to our concern than the point of commercial determinism and municipal "citizenship." For if the "urban revolution" of western Europe preceded the colonization of Latin America by four centuries, one wishes to know what effects the former may have had on urban patterns of the latter.

The discussion starts logically with Pirenne's distinction between ancient and medieval cities. In antiquity, he observed, the city with its temples and magistrates was the center of the whole life of those who had built it. Peasant and urban dweller equally claimed the title "citizen," and the *jus civitatis* applied to all free men within or without the city walls. The medieval city, on the other hand, was legally distinct from the surrounding country. Countryman and townsman shared neither common interests nor common status nor a common magistracy. The city was an island of legal immunity (1939:I, 167). In Pirenne's tentative definition: "The medieval city is a community in the shelter of a fortified sanctum living by commerce and industry, and enjoying an exceptional law, administration, and jurisdiction which make it a privileged body (1939:II, 119). No one belongs to the city who does not reside there. "In short, the citizen exists for the city and not, as in antiquity, the city for the citizen (1939:I, 104). Hence the ingenious suggestion that whereas in Latin the word *civitas* is derived from *civis*, in modern languages the words *bourgeois*, *bürger*, *citizen*, and *cittadino* derive from *bourg*, *burg*, *city*, and *città*. Medieval Latin even closes the circle by deriving *civitatensis* from *civitas*.

Though his more popular writings may suggest that Pirenne overgeneralized his "model," he was explicit as to its complexity. Urban evolution, he observed, was affected by the character of the towns' struggle, if any, against princes, by the nature of their commerce, by the degree to which institutions of surrounding territories were compatible with their needs. Usually a compromise was reached between princely rights and municipal law developed from intimate dialectic between feudal and communal organization. Ecclesiastical princes, on the other hand, had urban residences, quarreled more constantly with burghers, and attempted to impose their ideals of political and social organization. Thus in episcopal towns burghers were more given to "revolutionary" conjurations resulting in powerful communes that stood free of pre-existing public power. Pirenne also distinguishes between cities that developed communal organization internally and the *villes neuves* which, after the twelfth century, might receive a full-blown charter from a prince or lord (1939:I, 87–90, 103–4, 174–77; II, 115–19).

Some institutional differences are classifiable geographically. Paris and the English towns could not effectively challenge royal authority. Flemish towns grew with such speed and power that they accepted a municipal autonomy less complete than that often achieved in France or Germany. Cities of the Low Countries Pirenne subdivided by their constitutions into family groups of the Flanders, Liège, Brabant, and Holland types, highlighting the "Flemish"-"Liège" contrast. In Flanders the commercial and manufacturing impetus was strong. Neither Church nor nobles could offer serious resistance to the burgher communities, and from the eleventh century on, the causes of prince and town were joined. Municipal institutions, commercial privileges, abolition of trial by combat, restrictions on ecclesiastical jurisdiction, and limitation of military service were all gradually sanctioned by the courts. Liège, on the other hand, was an episcopal city with limited trading interests, its soil largely occupied by chapters and abbeys. As the commune developed it failed to displace the lord's tribunal. Dual jurisdiction persisted, with that of the *jurés*, or sworn members of the council, limited to municipal regulation and policing. The Church's financial needs, however, gave rise to a class of financiers and money lenders who eventually played something of the role that the great merchants played in Flemish cities (1939:I, 177–93, 209–11). This contrast illustrates two complementary urban developments in medieval Europe: the appropriation of political power by burghers to create a new institutional and legal regime, and the less distinctively European formation of bureaucratic and intellectual cadres that were to organize and manage the new nation-states and national economies (Hoselitz 1960:165–70; Pizzorno 1962:107).

The critical significance that scholars like Pirenne, Weber (1958), and Petit-Dutaillis (1947) ascribe to the commune or conjuration of northwestern Europe hinges neither on the burgher class being of exclusively commercial origin nor on the widespread triumph of explicitly communal organization. Pizzorno groups historians into those who insist on the merchant origins of the new urban leaders (Pirenne, Bloch), those who see them as an offshoot of the dominant feudal class (Sombart), and those who see them of mixed origins (Sapori, Lestocquoy). None of these positions is incompatible with the view that a new type of city appeared, dominated by the mercantile function and by a class whose power was rooted in that function. The historians' differences do, however, suggest that the larger the role of landed nobility in organizing the commune, the stronger the ties between the city and its surrounding territory. Where the nobility was excluded, the city's regional influence was weaker and its conflicts with the central power were stronger.

Because it answers this second case, the originality of the Western city is more evident, in the sense that it exhibits more clearly the first signs of cumulative economic development. In the case of the Italian and south European cities economic development will halt at a given moment. Opposition, not assimilation, engendered development [Pizzorno 1962:105].

Botero (1956:259–60) observed in 1588 that Italian cities were "more glorious and more populous" than French ones because "the gentlemen in Italy do dwell in cities, and in France in their castles." Pizzorno suggests that the contrast between conspicuous consumption in Italian cities, which Botero praised for its demonstration effect, and the northern burghers' model of thrift is traceable to different relations between urban and rural elites. "In the north, burgher law often worriedly prohibited rural knights and magnates from living in town. In Italy, town law frequently obliged them to live there" (Mundy 1958:45).

Apart from the issue of classifying the origins of burghers there is that of determining the "true" commune. More than a century ago Augustin Thierry divided late-medieval France into three zones: the northern zone of the communes, the middle zone of the *villes franches,* and the southern zone of the *consulats.* For central France Boulet-Sautel (1954) accepts the outline but not the implications of this classification. She recognizes that here the communal movement was limited and did not take "revolutionary" form. The *ville franche* was more frequent and differed from the conjuration because it originated not in the revolt of a single class against feudal power but in the appeal for privileges or freedoms made to a lord by a whole *communitas* of burghers, clerics, soldiery, and even rural serfs. What is significant is that in its triumph over the commune, the *ville franche* "progressively takes over its institutional substance." The competence of the delegates of the communitas expands until they become in effect its representatives. "At that moment it is quite difficult to analyze the distinction between the *ville franche* and the commune stripped of its conjuration." Finally, in the more centralized nation of the fourteenth century, the two types tend to fuse into a third, the *bonne ville*, which consolidates their gains in administrative autonomy under the aegis of the crown.

The late-medieval town of northwestern Europe did not indefinitely supply economic energy and innovation. For one thing, the leaders of the third estate became a closed patriciate. For another, economic institutions oriented to isolated, guild-based, monopolistic cities were no longer viable in face of agricultural enclosure; interurban financial operations; the factory system, with its decentralized energy sources; and the growth of the mercantilist nation-state. "[The] cities which had struggled to affirm a progressive economic system now constitute a knot of interests in conflict with the new type of development" (Pizzorno 1962:109–13). Erosion of the city's autonomy and of its distinctive societal form, however, signified the universalizing, not the evaporation, of the medieval municipal ethos. In the summary of Romero (1967:448):

. . . the great bourgeoisie progressively cast off its urban ties and began to unite as a class having continuity and homogeneity within supraurban territorial units: kingdoms or fiefs. And where the great bourgeoisie did not have that possibility it tried to expand its limits by creating around cities a radius of influence, economic at first but very soon political as well, as in the case of the great bourgeoisie of the Italian or German cities.

With this urban communities as such began to weaken,
but the great bourgeoisie, especially its most powerful
sectors, did not therefore weaken. On the contrary it
gained in independence and above all acquired growing
influence with the territorial powers.

"Burgher law," wrote Weber (1958:112), "is a half-way
house between the old feudal law and the law of territorial units." Elsewhere, in discussing legal sources of the
European nation-state, he developed the point as follows
(1967:275):

[In] the reception of substantive Roman law the "most
modern," i.e., the bourgeois groups, were not interested
at all; their needs were served much better by the institutions of the medieval law merchant and the real estate
of the cities. It was only the general formal qualities of
Roman law which, with the inevitable growth of the
character of the practice of law as a profession, brought
it to supremacy. . . .

Whether or not the western and central European pattern of urban development held for the Iberian peninsula
has important implications for the subsequent urbanization of America, and indeed for the whole legal and institutional inheritance of the Spanish and Portuguese New
World empires. The northern part of the peninsula did receive strong trans-Pyrenean influences when, in the
eleventh century, pilgrims, mostly from France but also
from Italy, Germany, Flanders, and England, began flock-
ing to Santiago de Compostela along the westward route
through Jaca, Pamplona, or San Sebastián, then to Burgos,
Sahagún, León, Astorga, Ponferrada, and Puertomarín
(Vázquez-Lacarra-Uría 1938–49). Importing new ideas,
customs, and skills, many travelers settled permanently in
towns and small settlements or next to monasteries, where
they created walled suburbs (*arrabales*), established

markets, and plied artisans' trades. In Navarre and Aragon the kings founded towns for the newcomers' exclusive residence. (Defourneaux 1949). The generic name for the settlers was *francos,* a term implying both trans-Pyrenean origin (though not all were foreigners) and free juridical status. Francos who lived in cities directly under public power enjoyed statutory privileges of *burgueses,* a royal grant of *franquitas* guaranteeing immunity from services to lords and from commercial imposts. In towns subject to lords or abbots, however, restrictions on trade or manufacture might provoke an "oath of mutual aid and defense" analogous to the commune or conjuration of the French, Flemish, or Rhenish lands. The first wave of outbreaks, which occurred in Sahagún, Lugo, Carrión, Burgos, and Palencia from 1087 to 1184, crested with the commune of Santiago de Compostela (1116–17). Here the *burguesía* united with many of the clergy in a "revolutionary" *hermandad jurada,* which seized authority from the bishop and ruled the city for a year (Vázquez 1945). Yet even this movement, technically a "commune" in the French sense, was directed more toward seizing city government than toward changing its form. The bishop was perceived not as a feudal lord but as the leading entrepreneur in the most prosperous city of Christian Spain, a position for which he was greatly envied.[5] The conjuration unsuccessfully sought the patronage of Queen Urraca and was eventually defeated by the forces of herself, her son Alfonso, and the bishop. In later years the struggle broke out again repeatedly, but although the burgueses acquired internal autonomy in the late twelfth century, their jurisdiction was never enlarged to include the surrounding *alfoz* (Soares 1951:504). The small urban perimeters to which bourgeois power was limited in northern Spain recall the northern European situation rather than that of Italy and southern France.

The Iberian municipal traditions that would orient New World settlement patterns were those forged in the reconquest, not those that filtered over the Pyrenees. Juan Larrea rightly found the significance of Santiago for Spanish overseas expansion to be symbolized in its saintly tomb, not its commune. The reconquest of central Spain occurred in four phases (Valdeavellano 1968:239–42). First came the resettlement of the largely deserted Duero Valley in the ninth and tenth centuries, reaching advance points like Salamanca and Sepúlveda. This was carried out by monasteries and private persons, though often at the initiative and under supervision of the Crown. Colonization by Galicians, Asturians, Basques, and Mozarabs from the South was accomplished by *presura,* which gave control of land in recognition of "squatters' rights," prescription, or effective cultivation (Concha 1946). The resultant agrarian regime was one of small holdings nucleated by villages (*villae*) or monasteries and the forts (*castra*) that protected them. Save for modest development of local handicrafts and weekly markets—and the more intense economic activity of León and Barcelona—the early settlement centers were dominated by military, clerical, and agricultural pursuits.

The second phase of reconquest witnessed the *repoblación concejil* of lands between the Duero and the Tagus during the eleventh century. Here colonization was entrusted to the *concejos* of the former Moorish realm, where Mozarab and Moslem communities provided a certain ecological continuity. Concejos of Avila, Segovia, Madrid, or Toledo were assigned a large territory (*alfoz*), with lands allocable to clusters of free settlers under stipulated conditions and privileges. In the third phase the defense of lands newly conquered between the Tagus and the Guadiana was entrusted to the military orders in the twelfth century, while the last phase saw the frontier pushed south to the Guadalquivir under the combined auspices of Orders, concejos, and nobles.

As early as the phase of *repoblación concejil,* the trade and manufactures of the Leonese and Castilian towns quickened in contact with centers subsequently wrested from Islam; yet the dominant accents of urban life continued to be military, ecclesiastical, agricultural, and pastoral. The new markets were often in rural villages, and even in urban settings the "peace of the market" did not give rise to a distinctive "urban peace" (*pax civitatis*).

> Socially and economically, our medieval cities must have differed considerably from those of Germany or Italy. From what can be told from its common features, the city with us never loses a certain rural character. Often its economy does not seem to be a fully developed urban economy [Valdeavellano 1931:397].

The term *burgués* rarely penetrated south of the pilgrimage route; more usual designations were *civis, cibdadano, vecino,* or *omo bueno.* Castile's thirteenth-century laws, the *Siete Partidas,* identified the estates of society as defenders, preachers, and farmers, omitting mention of burgueses. "Local government of the cities of Castile was in the hands of knights or hidalgos, farmers, landowners, lawyers (*letrados*), but rarely the great merchants, owing of course to their small number rather than to systematic elimination" (Carande 1965:154). The Crown's reliance on private persons and would-be small proprietors for the work of resettlement had created a large class of *caballeros de las villas,* or *caballeros villanos,* who enjoyed relative juridical freedom by dispensation rather than by communal action taken for economic interest. Therefore "residence in an urban center and acquiring the condition of a city 'burgués' were not the only circumstances which determined at least partial liberation from links of subjection to the lordly potentates" (Valdeavellano 1960:55–56).

Leonese and Castilian towns in particular enjoyed considerable internal autonomy in medieval Spain. But municipal governments were embedded in the political and

administrative structure of the state, and organizationally
an "urban" center might differ little from a rural one. Municipal organization was sanctioned by charters, or *fueros*,
which were contractual in Castile but acquired the character of conceded privilege or legal statute as the conquest
advanced south into Andalusia during the Roman-law revival under a more centralized monarchy. In central
Spain, "unlike elsewhere in Europe, there was no communal movement with convulsions and struggles to establish
urban institutions" (Font 1954:271). The thirteenth and
fourteenth centuries witnessed urban revolts in Castile and
Leon. They were not bourgeois or artisans' movements,
however, but actions by *caballeros* to suppress the popular
agrourban classes (loosely, the *ciudadanos, labradores,* or
pueblo), as in Avila, Toro, and Zamora, or else uprisings
of the *pueblo* (who might even proclaim a *comuna*)
against the *caballeros*, as occurred later in Córdoba, Segovia, Ubeda, and Seville (Carlé 1965). The East, where the
large Mediterranean ports of Barcelona and Valencia en-
gaged heavily in commerce and manufacture, had municipal communes akin to the conjuration and *consulat*
of France and Italy. Yet here larger cities were in the
royal domain and even more heavily dependent on the
sovereign than were those to the west (Font 1945). When
in the fourteenth century the Crown further centralized
its power by appointing *corregidores* as chief municipal
magistrates, by suppressing open town assemblies, and by
confirming life terms for town councilors, such measures
were applied more vigorously in Castile than in the East
precisely because, it would seem, the King already enjoyed considerable interventionary power there. To compare the French and Spanish cases, one might say that
the latter offers counterparts to the *ville franche* and *ville
bonne* but is uninfluenced, except in the North, by the
example of the "revolutionary" conjuration.

The urban history of Portugal, it is usually assumed or

implied, differed from Spain's because here the reconquest played a less commanding role, and urban life sprang up along the coast in response to maritime possibilities for fishing and commerce. Portuguese municipal institutions, however, evolved under patrimonial auspices similar to the Spanish (Sampaio 1923:I, 163–66; Soares 1941–43; Sánchez-Albornoz 1943:129), and coastal settlements appeared only in the late twelfth century. An observer who cruised the northern coast in 1147 reported scarcely a single urban cluster (Sampaio 1923:I, 307; also insert maps in Merêa-Girão 1943 and Marques 1965). In its early period the Portuguese realm was "a federation of fiefs (*senhorios*) and cities presided over by the King and symbolized in the Crown; with the military power at his disposal he mediated among the parts and prevented dissolution, thus preserving the state" (Vasconcellos 1916:288). As in Leon and Castile, fairs and markets had little influence on the origins or institutions of Portuguese towns (Rau 1943).

For Portugal as for Spain, the contrasting example of the pilgrimage city clarifies the central institutional development. Sousa Soares (1943) distinguishes the cities of Galicia and northern Portugal—specifically Santiago, Guimarães, and Pôrto—as ones in which a merchant-artisan group created an independent municipal regime (*burgo*) alongside the institutions that controlled the larger agrourban territory. The case of Coimbra, whose charter or *foral* of 1179 seems to have supplied the model for Lisbon and Santarém (Soares 1960), is quite different. Here Cortesão (1964:94–100) was apparently mistaken in interpreting the twelfth-century revolt against Count Dom Henrique as that of a nascent bourgeoisie. The city was not a commercial and manufacturing center, and the *optimates populi* were not, as in Santiago, well-to-do, frequently immigrant merchants but landed, knightly proprietors long rooted in the city who protested the appointment of foreign magis-

trates. The movement aimed to maintain traditional privileges, not to reform administration. The foral that was
won accentuated the aristocratic cast of Coimbra society
and preserved the agrourban character of municipal jurisdiction. It established that the *iudex* should be a native
of Coimbra but otherwise perpetuated the city's position
in the administrative structure of the state (Merêa 1941;
Soares 1951). In the case of Lisbon, on the sea route between Italy and Flanders, pressures generated by its growing commerce and small manufactures led in 1383–85 to
the replacement of the 1179 foral with a statute that conceded certain privileges to the commoners (*povo meudo*
or *povo comum*), notably creation of a body of twenty-
four working men from twelve trades to participate in
municipal deliberations. Previously, however, the trades
had not had corporate structure, and the new privileges
did not merge the workers with the leaders of the city
council (Caetano 1953).

Lest one be tempted to attribute patrimonial features of
Iberian cities to Islamic influence, we should revert here to
the Islamic-western European distinction. In neither case
was there institutional continuity from ancient cities. In
the eastern Mediterranean, however, the Arabs did inherit
the centralized state bureaucracies and the active urban
and industrial life of late antiquity. Absent was the strong
tradition of corporate life, feudal and ecclesiastical, that
sprouted in Christian Europe and gave form and coher-
ence to the communal movements of the twelfth century.
In Islam urban tumults broke out against governors, as in
Syria and Mesopotamia in the eighth to tenth centuries,
but did not culminate in communal, corporate organizations. During interims when central rule had collapsed,
as in Spain or North Africa, local notables might take over
city governments, only to surrender them when territorial
rulers regained power (Stern 1970). Christian Spain and
Portugal shared the corporate tradition of western Europe,

but the reconquest shifted the phasing of its development vis-à-vis central power. The frequent Arabic derivation of Spanish and Portuguese terms for municipal officers dates from the heavy exodus of Mozarabs to Leon during the conquests of the late eleventh and twelfth centuries. Their adoption paid linguistic homage to the brilliant urban civilization of Toledo, Córdoba, and Seville, but did not signify structural change in an already established municipal order (Sánchez-Albornoz 1943:126–29, 142–45).

The fact that municipal power in the Iberian countries was further centralized and bureaucratized on the eve of overseas expansion made it inevitable that the new American towns would be conceived as territorial and jurisdictional units embedded in a patrimonial state structure. Much ink has been spilled in assessing what factors militated against municipal "democracy" in the New World, in identifying periods or regions when "democracy" was most nearly achieved, and in comparing the "democratic" potential of Spanish American *cabildos* and Brazilian *câmaras*. In such discussions the term "democracy" not only shifts meanings (representative government, populist government, municipal autonomy, social justice) but also gives a moralistic bias to an analysis that should take its cues from institutional structure. The degree to which town councils in the Americas were granted, or managed to assert, self-government is a less interesting question than such others as: By what rationale were municipalities inserted into the state structure? What accommodations were made for original settlers and their descendants? On what occasions and by what procedures might communal will be registered? What form did town government take when functioning beyond effective reach of the imperial structure that was conceived to provide its armature?

The Spanish policy of clustering New World settlers in towns to impede rural dispersion shows the whole system of justice, administration, defense, and Church to have rested on an urban base (Góngora 1951:69–90). The Spanish state and that of the Indies were conceived as organic entities arising from natural, not merely economic or utilitarian—nor, for that matter, religious—communities. As the jurist Francisco de Vitoria expressed it, "the source and origin of cities and republics is not an invention of man, nor can it be counted among artificial things, but it arises from nature." The corollary to the organic principle was the irrefragability of political power and of the community's need to exist within the framework of the state that exercised it. Such power is not the arbitrary creation of the multitude but is legitimized by natural law and irrevocable even by universal consensus.

After the early towns on Española had fought to preserve their liberties against Diego Columbus and to place themselves under the Crown, free of seigneurial jurisdiction, the Emperor decreed that the islands and mainland were the patrimony (*realengo*) of Castile and inseparable from its Crown. It was in the spirit—or on the pretext—of this traditional principle that Hernán Cortés, at the start of the Mexican conquest, disavowed the authority of Velázquez, his superior in Cuba, then resigned his command in favor of a duly constituted town council; as its justiciary he was then in direct vassalic relation to the Crown. A decade later the tables were turned when Cortés had himself acquired a vast marquisate in central Mexico. On the same medieval principle of municipal resistance to the *señorío*, Mexico City challenged his attempt to encroach on its public lands and pasture. By and large, however, señoríos were sparingly granted and firmly controlled by the Crown and did not encompass large towns.

Castilian town government had two branches: *justicia* officered by magistrates (*alcaldes*), and *regimiento* officered by councilors (*regidores*). In the fourteenth century the Crown terminated the age of municipal liberty by starting to convert these offices into prebends (*regalías*).

Alcaldes were substituted by corregidores, and local election of regidores gave way to Crown appointment. In America the Crown in principle controlled the regimientos but made concessions to the discoverers and conquistadors with respect to justicia. From this, different outcomes might arise. In Española the settlers asserted their freedoms against Columbus' son, while in Mexico Cortés succeeded in exercising his privileges and curbing municipal powers. In South America diverse formulas reflected diverse reconciliations of the interests of Crown, conqueror, and leading settlers (*vecinos*).

> The liberty of the Cabildo in the Indies, then, flows directly from a privilege of the king, who leaves the regalía essentially intact but who confers a right of election, considered a source of honor for the city and of power for its most important vecinos. The fact of new lands forces the monarchy to renounce application of the system already implanted in Castile. The regalist idea permits bureaucratization of part of the Cabildo . . . and on the other hand concession of regimientos in perpetuity, whether by the king or by the discoverers and conquerors by virtue of *capitulaciones* or special privileges. But these perpetual regimientos are bestowed on vecinos simply as grants; no fiscal advantage is yet taken of the regalía, as will happen later [Góngora 1951:77–78].

Like the Spanish American vecinos, the bourgeoisie of northwestern Europe was acquiring rural property from urban bases in the sixteenth and seventeenth centuries. But here it marked a departure from tradition, prompted by new needs for patrician status or protection against inflation. In Spanish America the vecinos' land hunger had precedents reaching back to the agrarian origins of Castilian municipal organization (Roupnel 1955:211; Góngora 1951:180; Friede 1966:18–21).

The colonial Brazilian municipality functioned more freely at the margin of the state than did the Spanish American, but, formally speaking, the former was even less innovative with respect to the metropolitan prototype. Because the Portuguese Crown lacked resources for discovery and conquest, overseas territories were infeudated to the opulent Order of Christ, and in the case of Brazil subinfeudated, as it were, to proprietors or *donatários*. The latter were empowered to establish municipal centers to nucleate colonization, but because these were contained in *senhorios*, such centers could be no more than *vilas*. Subsequent ecclesiastical organization of the colony forced an accommodation to the fact that bishops, as first-ranking nobles and titular princes, could not be ensconced in vilas that were subject to a proprietor but required "cities" (*cidades*) that stood on alodial land. In creating bishoprics the King, as grand master of the Order of Christ, emancipated the land to be used for the order's central purpose, service of the faith; then, as sovereign, he elevated the designated vila to the status of cidade. (Vasconcellos 1916).

By the end of the colonial period neither had the Crown ever issued an order specifically concerned with municipal administration in Brazil, nor had any distinctive mutation appeared in the colony itself. The only marks of special recognition accorded Brazilian cities were the award to half a dozen câmaras of the privileges of the municipality of Pôrto and an occasional concession reserving a câmara's offices for the native-born or allowing it to appoint interim governors. Otherwise municipal life was governed by codes promulgated for the whole Portuguese realm. The earliest, the *Ordenações Afonsinas* (1446), standardized existing law and usage to bring town government more fully under royal control. Câmaras were regulated by Titles 26 to 29 of the *Ordenações;* they narrowed the definition of *homens bons* who might participate in town government and subjected the election of officials to confirmation by the King or his representative and publication of municipal acts to confirmation by Crown magistrates. The *Ordenações Manuelinas* (1521) reproduced the Afonsine municipal provisions, while the *Ordenações Filipinas* (1603) accentuated the purely administrative function of municipalities (Mourão 1916).

The view of cities within a vertical politico-legal order invites consideration of their horizontal or intermunicipal relationships. For this purpose one may take the *hanse* as the archetypal interurban system of northern Europe and the *hermandad* as that of Iberian Europe. The German Hansa, whose hegemony dates from the late fourteenth century, arose from co-operation among several urban leagues; these in turn had been preceded by the twelfth-century Gotland community of German merchants from Lübeck and the Westphalian and Saxon towns. A merchants' association, that is, was antecedent to the community of towns. The Hansa was a loose commercial confederation with no corporate structure, regular administrative organization, independent judiciary, permanent tax base, fleet, or army. Member towns acquiesced in the leadership of Lübeck, but its authority rested on their moral support; they could exercise coercion only by excluding a town from trade privileges. Nearly all the towns were subject to a lay or ecclesiastical prince, and the principal interest of the Hansa was to maintain a stable commercial regime for a far-flung society of merchants and to avoid the economic sacrifice and threat of piracy that resulted from wars among nations and principalities. Although many towns were located within the Holy Roman Empire, the Hansa developed independently of it while the emperors sought to recoup power in southern Germany after the mid-thirteenth century. An important reason for the Hansa's decline in the fifteenth century was the intensified conflict between towns and princes. In the Germanies no strong national government emerged, vis-à-vis centralized France and England, to consolidate and extend the "rational" commercial regime of the interurban league (Rörig 1967; Dollinger 1970).

Once again northern Spain seems to offer an analogy to developments in northern Europe. In this case it was the Hermandad de la Marina de Castilla, a mercantile, coastal league of Castilian, Basque, and Guipuzcoan towns founded in 1296 having trade links with Flanders, the Atlantic coast of France, and the Hansa, and sometimes acting independently of royal authority. In contrast to the Hansa, however, the Hermandad de la Marina disposed of troops, sixty in each town, and received protection from the kings, who might influence its external policies (Fernández 1894:219–48, 391–96).

The other types of Spanish hermandad, oriented to domestic interests, developed in even closer symbiosis with royal power (Puyol 1913; Suárez 1951). The early thirteenth-century precedent was a series of bilateral agreements between towns, which stipulated guarantees for merchants and measures for protection of cattle. Formation of the Hermandades Generales of 1282, however, responded to the appeal for municipal support of Don Sancho, pretender to the Castilian throne. Once in power he suppressed them in 1284, but on his death (1295) they reappeared spontaneously as a defense against anarchy. By now they had fixed headquarters, a common seal, authority for specified police actions, and coercive power over members. They had become supermunicipal bodies with an identity distinct from their composite membership, effective insurance against anarchy, against royal usurpation, or against depredations by the members. The *hermandad*, representing the interests of the municipal estate (*estamento ciudadano*), was a state within a state and not, as was the hanse, a commercial system at the margin of the states. In 1325 the era of the Hermandades

Generales ended when Alfonso XI established a strong government and turned for collaboration to the Cortes rather than the less manageable hermandades. Under a stable order, however, the hermandades, loyal to the Crown, had lost their *raison d'être* and were peaceably dissolved by the Cortes of Valladolid. Frequent Cortes meetings now afforded municipalities a dependable channel for airing grievances before the King.

Another type of hermandad was the Hermandad Vieja de Toledo, established around 1300 as an association not of towns but of vecinos in several towns. Primarily designed to protect economic activities against banditry, it enjoyed the favor of the kings, who occasionally recruited soldiers from its rural constabulary. When at later times the Crown revived the institution, the Hermandad Vieja, not the General, was the model. The eventual Santa Hermandad, organized by Fernando and Isabel in 1476, was clearly an agent of central power collecting taxes, performing judicial and police functions, and supplying troops; in 1498 it was reduced to little more than a rural militia. The frustrated attempt of the *comuneros* movement under Carlos I to reassert the vigor and prerogatives of the *estamento ciudadano* revived only ephemerally the memory of the ancient hermandades.

One might say that the Spanish American sequel to the earlier hermandad was the procuratorial junta or *ayuntamiento general*. Such assemblies, some convoked by royal officials, some by the towns themselves, were the only regional representative bodies in the Indies. The Crown never authorized a Cortes for its American viceroyalties because, although hungry for the revenues such a body would have delivered, it was apprehensive about the inevitable demands of a Cortes for redress of grievances (Lohmann 1947; Borah 1956).[6]

The assembly of procurators at Santo Domingo in 1518 was convoked under authorization of the Jeronymite *comisarios* and the *justicia mayor*, Alonso de Zuazo. Giménez (1954) felt that it was inspired by the contemporary *comuneros* movement in Castile and anticipated the assumption of municipal liberties by Hernán Cortés in Mexico the following year. The petitions were formulated not jointly but independently by each town, and despite the clannish factionalism of the *colombistas* (partisans of Diego Columbus) and the "bureaucrats" (partisans of royal authority), there was agreement on such issues as tax exemption and harsher servitude for Indians. Delegates to the assemblies held in Cuba from 1515 to 1550 came to be elected by vecinos rather than appointed by town councils. The meetings therefore had a "popular" character and gave "legitimate representation to the whole population of the island"; their petitions to the King might be unrelated to the decisions of individual councils. The Cuban assemblies were officially declared illegal in 1574, long after the island's depopulation and decadence had ended them. Procuratorial functions were then split between a newly defined procurator, who served as municipal inspector and could not meet with colleagues from other towns, and the municipal attorney, who might be empowered as a petitioner before the Crown (Guerra 1921–25:I, 307; II, 134–35).

On the mainland juntas were held in New Spain (1521, 1525, 1560), Peru (1544–62), New Granada (1564), Chile, and elsewhere (Bayle 1952:238–44). The New Spain junta of 1525 was authorized by Crown officials, who attended the sessions but were at one point requested to withdraw, leaving the procurators to discuss and vote in privacy. The 1560 junta included procurators of certain groups (conquerors, settlers, merchants) as well as of towns. The cabildo of Mexico City convoked the meetings, and if the agenda was not of urgent general interest, the cabildo might formulate petitions in behalf of all towns as "representative of the whole realm for being its head"

(Miranda 1952:127–41). Meza (1958:37–47) stresses that in the Chilean case the right of representation through town councils was a concession from the Crown; royal will and vassals' welfare were blended in a unitary system of power. "The superurban unity constituted for purposes of royal administration was . . . a collection of cities, and according to this idea the total representation of the vassals of the realm equaled the sum of the urban representations." The weaker, sometimes desolated towns sent procurators to Santiago as the "head of government" (*cabeza de gobernación*), although without renouncing their right to individual petition. The Santiago cabildo represented them before the King or his agents and, in the King's name, even administered the oath of office to Crown-appointed governors.

In Brazil authority to convoke assemblies was reserved to governors, and they were originally attended by leading Crown and ecclesiastical officials. The câmaras usurped this power, however, and organized juntas to allocate taxes among towns, to assume interim power in a governor's absence, and even to establish leagues or alliances (Zenha 1948:108, 111, 128).

While Iberian and later Ibero American cities, then, were embedded in a framework of empire, those of northwestern Europe had provided an arena for legal innovation that hastened the transition from feudalism to "the law of territorial units." It has long been recognized that the reconquest gave a distinctive cast to the institutions and social fabric of Spain and Portugal and hence to their overseas colonies. The preceding pages attempt to specify the implications for urban history. Although the relation of municipalities to central power has been stressed, the important issues are not narrowly politico-administrative but such larger ones as the structure of political and social action, the relation of parts to wholes in social systems, sources of authority and of its legitimation, and the premises for moral sanction. Once our concern extends to these matters, we perceive that medieval Iberian history is the necessary prolegomenon not simply to studying American cities as administered under the *Leyes de Indias* and *Ordenações Filipinas* but also to understanding modern urban development under the quite different constitutional and administrative systems of the independent republics.

The Ibero-Thomist Synthesis

This essay has explored three points of departure toward a framework for Latin American urban history. First was the distinction between preindustrial and industrial cities. Although much of the current interest in Latin American cities reflects concern with problems of transition to industrialism, we found that the preindustrial-industrial dichotomy yields inadequate primary categories for regional historical analysis and that Sjoberg's contrasting ideal types frequently mislead or equivocate. If we accept that industrialism reworks rather than obliterates pre-existing urban life and institutions, we must particularize that life and those institutions for the urban family of our concern.

Two other lines of inquiry illuminated less fitfully the historical trajectory of Latin American cities. One was a comparative analysis of ancient cities, focused on (1) the transition from tribal city to polis and (2) the tensions between polis and universal city, and between city of man and City of God. The other was a comparative review of medieval town origins in the Iberian peninsula and in the rest of western Europe. It now remains to blend a sensitivity to distant cultural echoes with the perception of institutional continuities. The key is the social and political thought of St. Thomas Aquinas and its commanding influence in the Iberian countries till the seventeenth century.

Thomist ideas, of course, drew generously on ancient traditions: patristic theology, especially Augustinianism, tinctured by neo-Platonic idealism and Roman stoicism; Roman law, revived at Bologna in the late eleventh century; and the new Aristotelianism. Aristotle's logic and science reappeared in the West before his ethics and political thought. The *Politics* was not translated into Latin until about 1260, when Thomas was thirty-five, and its influence increasingly marked his writings thereafter. The practical side of the *Politics* had been rendered obsolete during its own author's lifetime by the conquests of Philip of Macedon and Aristotle's own pupil, Alexander, which heralded the expansion of polis to imperium. Yet precisely in the age of St. Thomas, a millennium and a half later, the Italian republics and embryonic nations of Europe were challenging the imperium. "The compact City-States and centralized Nation-States fulfilled the conditions of the perfect political community described in the *Politics*, and their completeness was capped when their rulers claimed the attributes of the *Princeps* of Roman law" (Gilby 1958:91).

In his political thought the task of St. Thomas was to reconcile convictions about civic life with those concerning personal salvation, to unite Aristotle and St. Augustine.

> With one voice he echoes the Augustinian teaching that the human person is made to the image of God, related immediately to an exemplar outside the order of the universe, and invited to a salvation found outside its collective benefit. With another voice he echoes the Aristotelian teaching that virtue is essentially social, that every act is a political act, and that a man fulfills himself in the service of the community [Gilby 1953:203].

St. Thomas saw the arrangements of the political community, the Christian City, as largely contrived by art (*indus-*

tria) but its principles as grounded in human nature. And although the positive law he took for study was the Mosaic Dispensation—lacking legal sources for Greco-Roman antiquity—it was the Aristotelian polis, suffused with Christian virtues, that supplied his paradigm (Gilby 1953:324). In the specific case of urban form, St. Thomas' *De Regimine Principum*, with its Aristotelian precepts, directly influenced the medieval Spanish treatises of Francesc Eiximenic and Bishop Rodrigo Sánchez de Arévalo, and through them the Spanish colonizing ordinances for the Indies (Torres 1954:89–92; Guarda 1965). The case requires us, however, to go beyond tracing influences and to explain *why* the Thomist concept of the polity found so congenial a reception south of the Pyrenees.

It is interesting, though not portentously so, that St. Dominic, founder of St. Thomas' order, was himself from Castile, and a Castile still distinguished by local *fueros* and free municipalities, not its Inquisition and centralized court (Vicaire 1957:I, 365–76). The crux of the explanation, however, lies in St. Thomas' own writing. It has to do with his disregard for feudal institutions and with the urban character of his polity. Northwestern Europe of the thirteenth century was still very much an agrarian society in the hold of feudal traditions and institutions, merely punctuated by flash points of mercantile, legal, and political change. Yet the Catholic theory to which St. Thomas so centrally contributed was "comparatively independent of feudal tenure and the feudal system" (Troeltsch 1960:I, 314). It retained certain features of the feudal persuasion, such as the superiority of custom to governmental decree, the responsibility of lords for their actions within a system of concessions and services, chivalric honor, and Christian compassion (Gilby 1953:12); but its political sociology was framed for an urban setting—a prebourgeois setting, however, in which profit motive and "individualism" were subordinated to public service and social unity, or corporateness. Though Catholic thought acquired a rural accent centuries later, in the age of nineteenth-century Romanticism and Restoration,

. . . it is solely the city that St. Thomas takes into account. In his view man is naturally a town-dweller, and he regards rural life only as the result of misfortune or of want; the town of which he thinks is itself strongly agrarian, and supports its own life by a system of ordered exchange of goods with the surrounding country which is under its rule [Troeltsch 1960:I, 318].

Why the ethic of St. Thomas features the city ideal so prominently admits of speculation. Gilby (1953:102; 1958:55–72) emphasizes St. Thomas' personal circumstances: that his close relations were officers of state, not landed lords; that his order, the Dominican, was drawn to the strenuous, disputatious life of towns, markets, and universities. Troeltsch discounted such biographical factors; nor did he find St. Thomas wholly faithful to Aristotle's city-state ideal, for, unlike his mentor, St. Thomas preferred independent urban labor to "miserable" agriculture. Instead, Troeltsch (1960:I, 318) felt that Catholic thought fastened on the contemporary European town for evangelical purposes; properly interpreted, the town could be perceived as the natural vehicle for Christian ideals "with its principles of peace, with its basis of free labour and corporate labour-groups, with its stronger intellectual interests, and its care and protection through its administration for everyone."

However one accounts for the cast of St. Thomas' social thought, Iberian hospitality to the ideal of the urban-based polity reflected practical requirements of the political and institutional order; for here, as Sánchez Albornoz and others have established, feudalism could not come to full flower during the reconquest. Settlement was nucleated around agrourban centers, not manorial units of production. Townsmen and rural workers were relatively unencumbered by servile obligations, yet the urban patriciate was lordly, not mercantile. Finally, society was suffused with memories of its evangelical past. The fact that the Thomist scheme was eminently appropriate to such a setting partly explains its long career in the Iberian peninsula, where it received its most detailed and discerning application to the great issues of the times, including governance of the American colonies. In the process, Thomism helped revitalize in Iberian minds certain outlooks of Mediterranean antiquity, a world with which continuity had worn thin over the centuries but never completely snapped.

NOTES

1. Symptomatic of Sjoberg's laxness is his failure to acknowledge that one account of urban development (Patrick Geddes, Lewis Mumford) places a technological watershed, the transition from paleotechnics to neotechnics, squarely in the middle of the industrial age.

2. Fustel (1956:387) ascribed key significance to a fiscal measure issued, he thought, by Caracalla at a date unknown to him: "We meet in history with few more important decrees than this." The ordinance, later identified as the *constitutio Antoniniana* of A.D. 212, was in fact Caracalla's. From discovered fragments it is difficult to determine whether it extended Roman citizenship to free village peasant and rural populations of city territories. Whatever its scope, the intent of the measure was to enlarge the tax base and to flatter outcasts with the grant of citizenship. In this the Emperor's aim was not so much to raise the lower classes (although he notoriously cultivated humble soldiers and the support of the masses) as it was to undermine the self-confidence of the imperial and municipal aristocracy. In a sense, then, Caracalla's grant helped no one and lacked real social or political importance; but symbolically it marked the demise of the state founded on the *Senatus Populusque Romanus* and the advent of an era when Roman citizenship was a mere name, bereft of political or social value, sig-

nifying only that the bearer of the title inhabited one of the cities of the empire (Jones 1954:143; Rostovtzeff 1957:I, 418; Mazzolani 1970:192–93).

3. To the kin-based and Olympian religions Ehrenberg (1964:19) adds the chthonic.

4. Zuidema's analysis reverses the interpretation of Lévi-Strauss, who viewed Brazilian village cultures as pauperized, or "pseudoarchaic," because they retain self-contradictory features from earlier, more complex societies. Zuidema discerns and provides a logic for similar "contradictions" in Incan social organization and suggests that they may derive from more "primitive" situations.

5. Pastor (1965) contrasts the Compostela movement with that against the abbacy of Sahagún from 1110–17.

6. Authorities disagree on the Spanish precedent for the juntas. Guerra y Sánchez felt that the hermandad was the prototype, while Giménez and Miranda thought it to be the Cortes. The fact that the state in the Indies was more markedly patrimonial than estate-based (*estamental*) changes the context and makes a conclusive answer difficult (Konetzke 1951).

REFERENCES

Bayle, Constantino. *Los cabildos seculares en la América Española.* Madrid: Sapientia, 1952.

Borah, Woodrow. "Representative Institutions in the Spanish Empire: The New World," *The Americas* 12 (3) (1956): 246–57.

Botero, Giovanni. *The Reason of State and the Greatness of Cities.* New Haven, Conn.: Yale University Press, 1956.

Boulet-Sautel, Marguerite. 1954. "L'émancipation urbaine dans les villes du centre de la France," *Société Jean Bodin.* La ville. Première partie: Institutions administratives et judiciaries. Brussels: Librarie Encyclopédique, 1954, pp. 371–406.

Brogan, Olwen. *Roman Gaul.* London: G. Bell, 1953.

Caetano, Marcelo. "O concelho de Lisboa na crise de 1383–1385," *Academia Portuguesa da História, Anais,* 2ª série 4 (1953): 175–247.

Cahen, Claude. "Mouvements populaires et autonomisme urbain dans l'Asie musulmane du Moyen Age," *Arabica, Revue d'Etudes Arabes* 5 (3) (1958–59): 225–50; 6 (1): 25–56; 6 (3): 233–65.

102   *Urbanization in Latin America*

Cantel, Raymond. *Prophétisme et messianisme dans l'oeuvre d'Antonio Vieira.* Paris: Ediciones Hispano-americanas, 1960.

Carande, Ramón. *Carlos V y sus banqueros.* Vol. I, *La vida económica en Castilla* (1516–56), 2d ed. Madrid: Sociedad de Estudios y Publicaciones, 1965.

Carlé, María del Carmen. "Tensiones y revueltas urbanas en León y Castilla (siglos XIII–XIV)," Universidad del Litoral, Instituto de Investigaciones Históricas, *Anuario* 8 (1965): 325–56.

Concha, Ignacio de la. *La "presura," la ocupación de tierras en los primeros siglos de la reconquista.* Madrid: Instituto Nacional de Estudios Jurídicos, 1946.

Cortesão, Jaime. "Os factores democráticos na formação de Portugal," *Obras completas,* Vol. I. Lisbon: Portugália, 1964.

Defourneaux, Marcelin. *Les français en Espagne aux XI et XII siècles.* Paris: Presses Universitaires de France, 1949.

Dollinger, Philippe. *The German Hansa.* Stanford, Calif.: Stanford University Press, 1970.

Duarte, Nestor. *A ordem privada e a organização política nacional,* 2d ed. São Paulo: Nacional, 1966.

Ehrenberg, Victor. *The Greek State.* New York: W. W. Norton, 1964.

Faoro, Raymundo. *Os donos do poder, formação do patronato político brasileiro.* Pôrto Alegre: Globo, 1958.

Fernández Duro, Cesareo. *La Marina de Castilla desde su origen y pugna con la de Inglaterra hasta la refundición en la Armada Española.* Madrid: El Progreso Editorial, 1894.

Font y Rius, José-M. "Orígenes del régimen municipal de Cataluña," *Anuario de Historia del Derecho Español* 16 (1945): 389–529.

———. "Les villes dans l'Espagne du Moyen Age," *Société Jean Bodin.* La ville. Première partie: Institutions administratives et judiciaires. Brussels: Librairie Encyclopédique, 1954, pp. 263–95.

Friede, Juan. "Los estamentos sociales en España y su contribución a la emigración a América," *Revista de Indias* 26 (103–4) (1966): 13–30.

Fustel de Coulanges, Numa Denis. *The Ancient City.* Garden City, N.Y.: Doubleday, 1956.

Gandía, Enrique de. *Historia crítica de los mitos de la conquista americana.* Madrid: Sociedad General Española de Librería, 1929.

García, Juan Agustín. "La ciudad indiana," *Obras completas.* Buenos Aires: Antonio Zamora. I (1955): 283–475.

Geertz, Clifford. *Peddlers and Princes, Social Change and Economic Modernization in Two Indonesian Towns.* Chicago: University of Chicago Press, 1963.

Gibson, Charles, *The Aztecs under Spanish Rule: a History of the Indians of the Valley of Mexico, 1519–1810.* Stanford, Calif.: Stanford University Press, 1964.

Gilby, Thomas. *Between Community and Society: A Philosophy and Theology of the State.* London: Longmans Green, 1953.

———. *Principality and Polity: Aquinas and the Rise of State Theory in the West.* London: Longmans Green, 1958.

Giménez Fernández, Manuel. "Las Cortes de la Española en 1518," Universidad Hispalense, *Anales* 15 (1954): 47–154.

Goitein, S. D. "The Rise of the Near-Eastern Bourgeoisie in Early Islamic Times," *Cahiers d'Histoire Mondiale* 3 (1957): 583–604.

Góngora, Mario. *El estado en el derecho indiano, época de fundación 1492–1570.* Santiago: Universidad de Chile, 1951.

Guarda, Gabriel. *Santo Tomás de Aquino y las fuentes del urbanismo indiano.* Santiago: Academia Chilena de Historia, 1965.

Guerra y Sánchez, Ramiro. *Historia de Cuba,* 2 vols. Havana: El Siglo XX, 1921–25.

Guthrie, Chester Lyle. "Riots in Seventeenth-century Mexico City: A Study of Social and Economic Conditions," *Greater America: Essays in Honor of Herbert Eugene Bolton.* Berkeley, Calif.: University of California Press, 1945, pp. 243–58.

Hammond, Mason. *City-State and World State in Greek and Roman Political Theory Until Augustus.* Cambridge, Mass.: Harvard University Press, 1951.

Hardoy, Jorge E. *El modelo clásico de la ciudad colonial hispanoamericana.* Buenos Aires: Instituto Di Tella, 1968.

Holanda, Sérgio Buarque de. *Visão do Paraíso, os motivos edênicos no descobrimento e colonização do Brasil,* 2d ed. São Paulo: Nacional, 1969.

Holzner, Lutz. "World Regions in Urban Geography," *Association of American Geographers, Annals* 57 (4) (1967): 704–12.

Hoselitz, Bert F. *Sociological Aspects of Economic Growth.* New York: The Free Press, 1960.

Jones, A. H. M. "The Cities of the Roman Empire," *Société Jean Bodin.* La ville. Première partie: Institutions administratives et judiciaires. Brussels: Librairie Encyclopédique, 1954, pp. 135–73.

Konetzke, Richard. "La formación de la nobleza en Indias," *Estudios Americanos* 3 (10) (1951): 329–57.

Larrea, Juan. *Rendición de espíritu (introducción a un mundo nuevo)*, 2 vols. Mexico: Cuadernos Americanos, 1943.

Lohmann Villena, Guillermo. "Las Cortes en Indias," *Anuario de Historia del Derecho Español* 18 (1947): 655–62.

Lot, Ferdinand. *The End of the Ancient World and the Beginnings of the Middle Ages*. New York: Alfred A. Knopf, 1931.

Marques, A. H. Oliveira. "A população portuguesa nos fins do século XIII," *Ensaios de história medieval*. Lisbon: Portugália, 1965, pp. 69–123.

Marx, Karl. *Capital: A Critique of Political Economy*. New York: Modern Library, n.d.

Mazzolani, Lidia Storni. *The Idea of the City in Roman Thought from Walled City to Spiritual Commonwealth*. Bloomington, Ind.: Indiana University Press, 1970.

Merêa, Paulo. "Sôbre as origens do Concelho de Coimbra (estudo históricojurídico)," *Revista Portueguesa de História* 1 (1941): 49–69.

———. and Girão, Amorim. "Territórios portugueses no século XI," *Revista Portueguesa de História* 2 (1943): 255–63.

Meza Villalobos, Néstor. *La conciencia política chilena durante la monarquía*. Santiago: Universidad de Chile, 1958.

Miranda, José. *Las ideas y las instituciones políticas mexicanas: primera parte 1521–1820*. Mexico: Instituto de Derecho Comparado, 1952.

Mourão, João Martins de Carvalho. "Os municípios, sua importancia política no Brasil-colonial e no Brasil-reino," *Revista do Instituto Histórico e Geográphico Brasileiro, tomo especial consagrado ao Primeiro Congresso de História Nacional* (7–16 de setembro de 1914) 3 (1916): 299–318.

Mundy, John H. "Medieval Urbanism," *The Medieval Town*, eds. John H. Mundy and Peter Reisenberg. Princeton: Van Nostrand, 1958, pp. 7–94.

Pastor de Togneri, Reyna. "Las primeras rebeliones burguesas en Castilla y León (siglo XII)," *Estudios de Historia Social* 1 (1965): 29–106.

Petit-Dutaillis, Charles Edmond. *Les communes françaises: caractère et évolution des origines au XVIIIe siècle*. Paris: A. Michel, 1947.

Phelan, John L. *The Millennial Kingdom of the Franciscans in the New World*, rev. ed. Berkeley, Calif.: University of California Press, 1970.

Pirenne, Henri. *Les villes et les institutions urbaines*, 6th ed., 2 vols. Paris: Librairie Félix Alcan, 1939.

Pizzorno, Alessandro. "Développement économique et urbanisation," *Fifth World Congress of Sociology, Transactions*. Louvain: International Sociological Association II (1962): 91–123.

Puyol y Alonso, Julio. *Las hermandades de Castilla y León*. Madrid: Minuesa de los Ríos, 1913.

Rau, Virgínia. *Subsídios para o estudo das feiras medievais portuguesas*. Lisbon: Bertrand, 1943.

Romero, José Luis. *La revolución burguesa en el mundo feudal*. Buenos Aires: Sudamericana, 1967.

Rörig, Fritz. *The Medieval Town*. London: B. T. Batsford, 1967.

Rostovtzeff, M. *The Social and Economic History of the Roman Empire*, 2d ed., 2 vols. Oxford: Clarendon Press, 1957.

Roupnel, Gaston. *La ville et la campagne au XVIIe siécle, étude sur les populations du pays dijonnais*. Paris: Armand Colin, 1955.

Sampaio, Alberto. *Estudos históricos e econômicos*, 2 vols. Pôrto: Chardron, 1923.

Sánchez-Albornoz y Menduiña, Claudio. *Ruina y extinción del municipio romano en España e instituciones que le reemplazan*. Buenos Aires: Facultad de Filosofía y Letras, 1943.

Sigüenza y Góngora, Carlos de. "Letter of Don Carlos de Sigüenza y Góngora to Admiral Pez Recounting the Incidents of the Corn Riot in Mexico City, June 8, 1692," *Don Carlos Sigüenza y Góngora, a Mexican Savant of the Seventeenth Century*, ed. Irving A. Leonard. Berkeley, Calif.: University of California Press, 1929, pp. 210–77.

Sjoberg, Gideon. *The Preindustrial City Past and Present*. Glencoe, Ill.: The Free Press, 1960.

Smith, Page. *As a City Upon a Hill, the Town in American History*. New York: Alfred A. Knopf, 1966.

Soares, Torquato de Sousa. 1941–43. "Notas para o estudo das instituições municipais da reconquista," *Revista Portuguesa de História* 1 (1941–43): 71–92 and 2:265–91.

———. "Les bourgs dans le nord est de la Péninsule Iberique," *Bulletin des Etudes Portuguaises et de l'Institut Français au Portugal*, nouvelle série 9, fasc. 2 (1943): 5–15.

————. "Dois casos de constituição urbana: Santiago de Compostela e Coimbra," *Revista Portuguesa de História* 5 (2) (1951): 499–513.

————. "O foral concedido a Coimbra, Santarém e Lisboa em 1179," *Academia Portuguesa da História, Anais*, 2ª série 10 (1960): 173–88.

Solórzano, Juan de. *Política indiana*, 2 vols. Madrid, 1736–39.

Stern, S. M. "The Constitution of the Islamic City," *The Islamic City: A Colloquium*, eds. A. H. Hourani and S. M. Stern. Oxford: Bruno Cassirer, 1970, pp. 25–50.

Suárez Fernández, Luis. "Evolución histórica de las hermandades castellanas," *Cuadernos de Historia de España* 16 (1951): 5–78.

Torres Balbás, Leopoldo et al. *Resumen histórico del urbanismo en España*. Madrid: Instituto de Administración Local, 1954.

Tricart, Jean. "Quelques caractéristiques générales des villes latinoaméricaines," *Civilisations* 15 (1) (1965): 15–30.

Troeltsch, Ernst. *The Social Teachings of the Christian Churches*, 2 vols. New York: Harper, 1960.

Valdeavellano, Luis G. de. "El mercado, apuntes para su estudio en Léon y Castilla durante la Edad Media," *Anuario de Historia del Derecho Español* 8 (1931): 201–405.

————. *Sobre los burgos y los burgueses de la España medieval.* Madrid: Real Academia de la Historia, 1960.

————. *Curso de historia de las instituciones españoles.* Madrid, Revista de Occidente, 1968.

Vasconcellos, Diogo de. "Linhas geraes da administração colonial," *Revista do Instituto Histórico e Geográphico Brasileiro, tomo especial consagrado ao Primeiro Congresso de História Nacional* (7–16 de setembro de 1914) 3 (1916): 281–98.

Vázquez de Parga, Luis. "La revolución comunal de Compostela en los años 1116 y 1117," *Anuario de Historia del Derecho Español* 16 (1945): 685–98.

————; Lacarra, José María; and Riu, Juan Uría. *Las peregrinaciones a Santiago de Compostela*, 3 vols. Madrid: Consejo Superior de Investigaciones Científicas.

Vicaire, M.-H. *Histoire de Saint Dominique*, 2 vols. Paris: Les Editions du Cerf, 1957.

Weber, Max. *The City*. Glencoe, Ill.: The Free Press, 1958.

————. *On Law in Economy and Society*. New York: Simon and Schuster, 1967.

Wheatley, Paul. " 'What the Greatness of a City Is Said to Be,'

Reflections on Sjoberg's 'Preindustrial City,'" *Pacific View-point 4* (2) (1963): 163–88.

Zenha, Edmundo. *O município no Brasil* (1532–1700). São Paulo: IPÊ, 1948.

Zimmern, Alfred. *The Greek Commonwealth, Politics and Eco-nomics in Fifth-Century Athens*, 5th ed. New York: Ox-ford University Press, 1961.

Zuidema, Reiner Tom. *The Ceque System of Cuzco: The Social Organization of the Capital of the Inca*. Leiden: University of Leiden, 1962.

CHAPTER THREE

THE URBANIZATION OF
LATIN AMERICAN SOCIETY*

ANÍBAL QUIJANO

The development of social research in Latin America is increasingly hampered by the inability of the scientific techniques in use to capture the essence of the social situation and its historical background in Latin America, not only because they were generally elaborated in and for different societies and historical contexts, but also—and chiefly—because their basic assumptions are inappropriate. They are intended to deal with a set of problems which are no longer fully relevant, and the question at issue is the historical significance and scientific effectiveness of a system of investigating the social situation.

In these circumstances, the present situation and the development of research are creating a new set of problems. These problems are as yet vague and ill-defined, and if they are to be clearly seen, the isolated attempts to formulate them must be co-ordinated and integrated. These attempts should not consist solely or mainly in revising specific research concepts and techniques, although that may also be necessary. The basic task is to develop a

* Originally published as "La urbanización de la sociedad en Latinoamérica," *Revista Mexicana de Sociología* XXIX (4) (Oct.–Dec. 1967):669–703. The unsigned English version appears as "The Urbanization of Society in Latin America," *Economic Bulletin for Latin America* (UN/ECLA) XIII (2) (Nov. 1968):76–93.

way of looking at the situation which is capable of prompting questions and systems of questions that will effectively capture its shifting and complex nature.

This problem is particularly acute in research on the process of change in society. The specific questions elicited by the approaches generally adopted, which are essentially analytical in nature and lay most emphasis on stability and maintenance of the *status quo,* mean that the dialectic of history can be treated only in an allusive and totally ineffective way.

Studies on urbanization in Latin America come up against this difficulty. Although it is generally admitted that urbanization can be understood only as part of the over-all process of change in society, it is still studied in isolation, and although reference is made to possible connections with other phenomena of change, these phenomena are also studied separately. The admission is, therefore, purely a formal one, and the intention to investigate urbanization from the standpoint of over-all social change is trammelled by the very nature of the reasoning underlying the approaches now in use.

It is, therefore, worth while to explore other possible approaches to urbanization which will make it possible to investigate its formal aspects in the context of the over-all process of change in Latin American societies.

A. *Urbanization in Society or Urbanization of Society?*

The point of departure for this discussion is that there are at least two basic problems in research on urbanization in Latin America which have not yet been sufficiently considered:

(1) Although it is increasingly asserted that urbanization is a multidimensional process—with references to demographic, economic, socio-cultural and other "aspects" —it is not yet clear how these "aspects" are interrelated,

or how, taken as a whole, they are related to the over-all process of change in society;

(2) In practice, the concept is still restricted to a specific phenomenon: the trend towards the predominance of the urban (and particularly city) population over the rural population. At the same time, attention is drawn to the development of a "way of life" in the cities which is different from that of the rural localities and which recently has to some extent been propagated among the rural population itself, although only in certain aspects. This latter phenomenon is frequently equated with "modernization," a concept so ambiguous and ill-defined that it can hardly be used effectively in research.

The shift in the relation between the urban and the rural population and the development of an urban way of life thus appear to be the two most important conceptual elements in the process of urbanization, although it has not yet proved possible to integrate them in one coherent body of theory. The mere superposition of one element on the other, sometimes within the same approach, sheds little light on the nature of the phenomenon. Consequently, research cannot go beyond the analytical; it cannot reconstruct the true place of urbanization in particular within the over-all process of social change, nor can it aspire to explain and interpret the historical significance of urbanization within a society, except allusively.

Starting from an essentially analytical system, the phenomena of change can only be taken in isolation, despite formal recognition that the phenomena of change affecting the basic pattern of social life are essentially interdependent and all have the same type of relationship to society as a whole. Thus, in the prevailing conception, i.e., in the conception which actually guides research, urbanization appears as one process among others, whether it is a question of the trend towards the predominance of urban over rural population or of the development of a way of life, as yet ill-defined, proper to urban settlements, and particularly cities. Urbanization is thus separated from changes in the economic, social, cultural and political structure, although linked to them, and includes only a small proportion of the changes in the ecological and demographic structure. Therefore, it cannot be isolated only from the analytical and methodological standpoint, but also in actual research, i.e., in the systematic reconstruction of its place, characteristics, function and significance in society. In short, urbanization is a process which takes place "in" society, rather than a process "of" society.

The difference between a process which takes place "in" society and one which is "of" society is the difference between: (a) a process which takes place in one of the basic structural orders, which affects society either wholly or in part but which does not necessarily depend on one of the other basic structural orders (in other words, a process which affects one of the urban-rural poles of a society, but with only indirect implications for society as a whole); and (b) a process which takes place in the whole fabric of society, i.e., through each of its basic structural orders, which are broken down into specific sub-dimensions in each case, but which in actual fact constitute a single process.

An example will help to make the distinction clear. If a new technological element is introduced in an area of economic activity, the consequences of this innovation will take the form of changes of greater or lesser importance in the industry in question, which will have repercussions on other spheres of activity and on the social relationships between groups and between individuals. However, changes of this type and dimension do not depend on corresponding alterations in the other basic structural orders, although over the long term an important technological innovation could generate processes of change in the whole fabric of society. In such a case, the changes are changes "in" society as a whole.

Despite its importance and the range of its effects, the

application of a land reform program, however radical it might be, could not be considered as a process "of" society as a whole, unless the dimensions of the reform involved the political, social, cultural, demographic and other orders even though the reform might lead to important changes in society, some of which would be direct effects and others indirect, i.e., linked to land reform only through intermediate processes. Urbanization of the economy, demographic and ecological urbanization, socio-cultural urbanization and political urbanization, on the other hand, are not separate processes, despite the specific form each dimension of urbanization may take, but processes whose elements are key trends and directly interrelated. In other words, it is inconceivable that one dimension of urbanization could take place without the others, whatever the degree and particular features of the process in each dimension.

Starting from the mainly analytical approaches to urbanization, research on the interdependence of urbanization and other specific processes is obliged to consider these processes as "consequences" or "factors" of urbanization, which to some extent presupposes treating the urban phenomenon as social statics rather than as social dynamics. Once again, this is an analytical approach which tends not only to maintain the formal, analytical and methodological isolation of urbanization, but also to transform the historical phenomena practically into fixed data, despite their dynamic character.

It is not easy to find a substitute for this type of conception and research, and the purpose of the present paper is merely to explore other possibilities to the extent allowed by the present development of research.

Nevertheless, even within the limits of the theoretical and methodological model in question, the scope and depth of the traditional field of research is constantly being extended, incorporating problems or phenomena which used to be considered as "consequences" or "factors" external to urbanization itself, and abandoning the narrow limits of the urban sub-society—ecologically and demographically speaking—to study the interdependence of the processes taking place in the city and in the rural areas, within the process of urbanization. In this continually expanding field of research, a number of basic mechanisms relating to the interdependence of the various dimensions of urbanization are now becoming apparent, and it is possible to grasp the nature of the process itself in a way which is more closely integrated with the over-all process of change in society as a whole. It is thus now possible to attempt a reconsideration of urbanization on the basis of society as a whole.

B. *Urbanization and the Over-all Process of Change in Society in Latin America*

There are two fundamental conceptual questions which arise in connection with urbanization in Latin America, from the standpoint of society as a whole: the nature of urbanization and its relationship to the dependent situation of the different Latin American societies.

1. URBANIZATION AND OVER-ALL SOCIAL CHANGE

When attention and research were first directed towards urbanization in Latin America, there was a tendency to explain the process primarily through the high rates of population growth in the societies of the region, and the concept of "super-urbanization" was born to stress the idea that population growth in the urban areas was to a large extent unconnected with changes in the economic structure and, in particular, in the urban economy. It now seems undeniable, however, that the present trends of ecologico-demographic change would have been substantially the same, even if the population growth rates had followed a neutral pattern. In other words, although high population growth rates in the context of a society with a rural economy in a critical state and a slow-growing urban economy help to explain the dramatic and extreme nature of the growth of the urban population in many Latin American countries, the fact remains that the shift in the relationship between the urban and rural population is linked to the changes in the relationship between the urban and rural economies, and that urbanization includes, above and beyond these two specific processes, all the changes in urban-rural relationships and most of the changes taking place at each of these levels or in each of these sectors of society as a whole.

Hence, urbanization should not be considered as merely one of the processes of change in urban-rural relationships, nor as covering only those changes taking place in the strictly urban environment. On the contrary, each of these processes is but one dimension of the general process of the urbanization "of" society as a whole, and it is society as a whole that must be taken as the point of departure in order to explain and interpret the general process of urbanization properly.

From this standpoint, urbanization is not viewed as a specific process which is separate and distinct from the socio-economic, cultural, political, and ecologico-demographic processes, despite their interdependence. It is a dimension of the over-all process of change in society, which is expressed through the processes taking place in each of the various structural orders into which, for analytical purposes, society as a whole can be divided. Society as a whole, for its part, can be thought of as a fabric made up of the different structural orders: the economic, social, cultural, political, and ecologico-demographic. All these basic structural orders are interdependent in relation to each other and to society as a whole, but at the same time they all have a relatively autonomous existence and pattern of change. Hence it is not possible to assume that the different basic structural orders of society are "systematically"—i.e., level by level and element by element—interdependent. In the constitution of each of these orders a part is played not only by functionally necessary elements, but also by elements which have their roots in particular development in the history of the society and which play or may play a decisive role in the actual historical process.

When society as a whole embarks upon a period of historically significant change, the process is channelled through each of its basic structural orders and is affected by the specific characteristics of each of those orders at each moment of the historical process. Over-all change is, therefore, a single process, but one that takes the form of a number of different processes linked together according to the particular circumstances characterizing each of the basic structural orders and the historical circumstances of the society as a whole. This means that the specific processes corresponding to each of these orders may take place at levels very different from those corresponding to the remaining orders.

In this context, if it is accepted that the ecologico-demographic changes implicit in urbanization are related to changes in the urban-rural economic relationships and to shifts in urban-rural relationships in each of the basic structural orders, and also to changes occurring in these orders within the urban and rural sub-societies, it is possible to advance an over-all explanation of the process of urbanization and to check that explanation empirically. Urbanization can thus be viewed as a process "of" society as a whole, taking place through each of its basic structural orders and as a dimension of the process of change occurring in each of those orders.

In other words, in the process of change taking place in the economic structure there is an "urbanization" dimension, just as there is in the processes of change in all the other structural orders. There is, therefore: (1) urbanization of the economic structure; (2) urbanization of the social structure; (3) urbanization of the ecologico-demographic structure; (4) urbanization of the socio-psychological cultural structure; and (5) urbanization of the political structure. In practice, all these dimensions are interrelated to the extent that the basic structural orders of society and their processes of change are interrelated, according to the particular framework of society as a whole and each of its structural orders. The over-all process of urbanization is the result of the specific ways in which the various dimensions of the process in each of these orders are interrelated or linked in practice.

This way of looking at the phenomenon of urbanization in Latin America makes it possible for research to highlight the multidimensional nature of the process, its mechanisms and the specific ways in which the various dimensions are related to each other and, together, to society as a whole. To the extent that the different basic structural orders are relatively autonomous, within this fundamental interdependence, the process of urbanization may take place at very different levels and with different characteristics in each of the structural orders.

In most Latin American countries, for example, the growth of the urban population and its trend towards predominance over the rural population is much more apparent than the growth of the urban economy, and massive inter-urban and rural-urban migration affects the development of an urban, socio-cultural structure. This would seem to indicate that the growth of the urban population bears very little relation to what is happening in the urban economy and in urban and rural society. Nevertheless, a more detailed consideration of the urban population's growth trends and its unequal distribution among the different areas and cities in all Latin American countries immediately reveals that these trends closely follow the growth of the urban economy and the concentration of that economy in certain areas or cities, with the result that the large concentrations of urban population and, consequently, the target of migratory flows, are precisely those areas and cities where the urban economy is growing most rapidly and undergoing the most intensive process of change.

It is evident, therefore, that there is a clear relationship between the processes of growth and change of the urban economy and the rural-urban economic relationships implicit in that process, on the one hand, and the growth of the urban population and the consequent changes in urban-rural ecologico-demographic relationships, on the other. It is clear, however, that in every case the latter process far outstrips the former in scale and pace. This is not because the two processes are not linked historically, but because they take place at different levels according to the particular characteristics and development of each of the respective structural orders.

Thus, because of the progress made in sanitation and medicine, over-all death rates have shown a relative decline in the Latin American countries, but, given the prevalent social and cultural characteristics in most of these countries up to the present—a predominantly rural population, pre-industrial norms and values, the hegemony of catholicism in religion, etc.—there has been no similar trend in the birth rates. Consequently, the over-all population growth rates continue to climb in most of the countries, and particularly in those which embarked relatively late on the path of development of the urban industrial economy.

In most of these countries, moreover, the organization of production and general economic activity in most of the rural areas are, as the result of a number of familiar factors and historical stituations, still at an economic and technological level that is very backward in relation to the economic system of which they form a part. Because of this situation, when a real process of expansion and modification of the urban economy is under way, with its usual tendency towards concentration in certain areas and cities and with the technological and entrepreneurial trends observable of late in industrial development, changes in the economic and non-economic urban-rural relationships are, under present conditions, inevitably weighted in favor of the urban areas. Consequently, the rural population tends to be pushed outside the former economic structure as a result of the impact on the rural areas of the expansion of the urban economy, and large numbers of the rural population seek to become part of the urban economy and society, although only very few succeed in doing so.

Thus, the extremely high over-all population growth rates, together with the effects of the expansion and modification of the urban economy on the rural economy and society, push to a dramatic extreme the growth of the urban population generated by changes in the urban-rural economic relationships in the process of expansion and modification of the urban economy. The growth of the urban population, as such, is a correlative of urban economic growth. The imbalance between the two processes is mainly the result of the factors mentioned above, but this imbalance should not obscure the close relationship between them, and the only way to keep sight of this relationship is not to consider either of them separately. For this purpose, the point of departure must be society as a whole and the over-all process of change in society through each of its basic structural orders.

Naturally, if consciously or unconsciously the traditional functional and structural approach is maintained and society is envisaged as a "systematic" structure, functionally integrated level by level and component by component, the disparities between the dimensions of the same process in each of the basic structural orders will be inexplicable or could only be explained for each one separately.

It is worth noting that urbanization, like many other problems, has gradually become a subject of research because of the striking nature of one of its dimensions, i.e., population growth in the cities, with its present economic, social and political repercussions: the formation of "marginal" populations, unemployment and under-employment, and the provisional political status of the new urban settlers who have no place in the socio-economic structure created by industrial development. Consequently, prime importance in research has been given to this particular aspect of the urban phenomenon. In view of the slight development of the urban economy, particularly of industry, the tendency has been to regard urban population growth as a phenomenon that is apparently unrelated to the urban economy, or to the corresponding changes in the rural economy, the changes in the urban and rural societies, the changes in society as a whole in its relations with other societies, etc. From this standpoint the first and most obvious explanation could only be the huge increase in the growth rates of the total population. Because of certain characteristics of the process, it was forgotten that urban growth had already been a feature of some Latin American societies whose over-all population growth rates were quite low or tending to decline, as in the case of Argentina.

In Argentina, other demographic factors, such as heavy immigration from Europe combined with the particular way in which the country was placed in a dependent situation in the post-colonial era, indicate that this is an exceptional case. Nevertheless, the huge population shift from the interior to Buenos Aires in the period immediately preceding Perón's régime—when the over-all population growth rates remained low—and the subsequent growth of cities such as Córdoba fostered by an intensive process of industrial development (under the national demographic conditions for the country as a whole) show that Argentina's urban population increased in spite of the relatively low rates of total population growth. It was the same in Uruguay.

The huge scale of internal migration, which has led to

an urban population explosion in the Latin American countries, is attributable not only to changes in the structure of urban-rural economic relations, the expansion and modification of the urban economy and the corresponding changes in the rural economy, but also to the high rates of total population growth in the socio-economic framework of under-development. Nevertheless, the present ecologico-demographic process of urbanization in these countries would probably have followed the same pattern even if the over-all population rates had been different—as is shown by Argentina and Uruguay—if the nature of the process and the specific problems encountered had been different, and if some of those problems had never existed.

Urbanization of the economy, in terms of an expansion and modification of the urban economy and an alteration in urban-rural economic relations, is necessarily accompanied by a process of ecologico-demographic urbanization, such as an expansion of the urban population and a change in the urban-rural ecologico-demographic relations. Nevertheless, if the urbanization of the economy coincides with high rates of total population growth, extremely backward rural economies, and rural societies rooted in a pre-industrial and pre-"modern" tradition, the problems and specific characteristics of the urbanization process in the economy, in relation to the demographic characteristics of that society, will be determined by the other factors with which it coincides. It is not the trend in itself—i.e., the direction taken by a particular process—which is different, but its specific forms and manifestations, which in turn are the outcome of the historical framework in which the trend is developing.

Migration will take place whether the population is one hundred or one thousand; but while sixty would migrate in the former case, six hundred would do so in the latter, and the related problems would not only be greater, they would, in all probability, be of a different kind. Let us now consider an advanced rural economy and society. In this case, the migrating population will have different characteristics and different problems, but the urban economy will not be affected by the present-day disparities and problems. If, in addition, this situation arises in an independent country, which can deal with its problems in accordance with its own needs and resources, instead of in a dependent society where the problems have to be handled in accordance with the interests and conditions imposed by its dependent status, the results themselves cannot but be different.

In brief, it is not the nature of the phenomenon which changes, but the historical context and the particular circumstances in which it occurs. In the analysis the necessary distinction must be made between those circumstances and the phenomenon itself.

2. URBANIZATION AND DEPENDENCE

The various structural orders are not only interrelated among themselves, they are also related with and through society as a whole. Hence, a given society must not be studied in isolation but in relation to all the others with which it is linked and which form with it a specific unit within the world system of interdependence that is emerging.

The trend of events in a given society is not merely the product of its own history, but, within its particular context, is shaped by that society's mode of relationship at any given moment with other societies, and more especially those with which it is directly linked. This leads to the second of the key problems that must be considered if an integrated picture of the general process of change, and of urban development in particular, is to be obtained, that is, the relations of one society as a whole with other societies and its place in the nexus of interrelationships.

In Latin America, the national societies comprised in the region are all, in one form or another, dependent societies within the economic and social system of contemporary capitalism, which, in its turn, is part of the world system of interdependence that is now taking shape. In other words, national societies in Latin America are characterized by belonging to a specific interdependent unit and, within that unit, by the fact that they are dependent on other societies. Their very origins and the process by which they have emerged as national entities are bound up with the development of this particular system of interdependence and their history with the history of the whole system, not only in so far as their economic characteristics but also, to an increasing extent—especially since the Second World War—as regards their fundamental structures and processes of development. It is therefore impossible to separate the internal processes of these societies from those that are inherent in their situation within the system of interdependence to which they belong. Consequently, in order to understand the process of urbanization in Latin America, it is essential to start from the idea of independence.

It is not easy nowadays to form a clear idea of the meaning of dependence, since this phenomenon is modifying many of the elements with which it has been and still is associated in Latin American thinking, and an effort is being made to revise and restate it; moreover, this is not the appropriate place for a full examination of the question. For the purposes of the present article, it will be necessary to begin by taking a fresh look at some assumptions which are deeply rooted in Latin American thinking and research, and which make it difficult to appreciate fully the closeness of the ties between dependence and the process of change in Latin American societies.

To begin with, in most studies of Latin American problems and especially those concerned with "development," dependence is considered an external factor. It follows, then, that dependence is the relationship between two independent elements of different kinds. It is only when thus defined that dependence can be regarded as an "external obstacle" to the development of the Latin American societies, in individual cases or in the region as a whole.

It must be remembered, however, in the context of dependence (and with certain reservations) that although the centers of power that hold sway over the dependent societies are geographically outside them, and, in that sense, are external, their interdependence molds and determines existing structures and events within the dependent societies, and the centers of power therefore have interests and support within these societies, and some similarities with them. Hence not all that exists or takes place in a dependent society is simply a reflection of the adjustments and problems that stem from the struggle with external obstacles; it is the direct and indirect result of the dependence manifesting itself from within, with an impact that is "in," not merely "on," the internal organization of the weaker societies. Dependence does not affect a dependent society, only, or even mainly, externally. It acts within, shaping and directing the society's fundamental trends and the nature of its power structures, which thus form part of the pattern of dependence.

Far from being a set of "external factors" blocking the independent development of a society or group of societies, dependence is therefore a nexus of relationships which are established by virtue of the close correspondence between the basic structural orders of the dependent society and the one that has come to dominate it because of circumstances in their past history (which have been or can be determined). More specifically, this means that in its basic traits and outward features, the structure of power and conflict in a dependent society is weaker than that of the dominant society and is also basically derived from and part of the dependent society's relations with the dominant society in the past.

Thus, the economic and social structures that exist in any one of the Latin American countries, whatever the specific differences between them, are so constituted as to conform to the characteristics, requirements and trends of that country's relations with the dominant societies and they change *pari passu* with the changes in those relationships.

The idea of dependence as an external factor would be valid if the relationships in question were those of an independent but undeveloped society with an equally autonomous but powerful society. Cuba's present relationships with other countries are a case in point. The economic blockade of Cuba is an external obstacle to its development, while its current economic and social structure no longer corresponds to such structures in the other countries. Dependence is thus not merely a set of factors external to a particular society, but the whole web of the connections between the basic structure of a weaker society and that of a more powerful society. In this sense it is equally an "internal" phenomenon.

The second point, which is closely linked to the first, is that dependence is usually taken to mean a group of unilateral actions and beliefs or attitudes in one or more powerful societies which exert an influence over other weaker nations. Thus, what is generally understood by the term "economic imperialism" is a body of unilateral actions by virtue of which a powerful society dominates a weaker one. The economic and social systems constituting contemporary capitalism are not only a way of organizing production and social power in general. One of its distinguishing features is precisely the domination—not only in the economic sphere—of the less developed by the more advanced capitalist societies. Viewed from this angle, dependence is a system of "interdependence" between two levels of capitalist societies, in which the more advanced plays the dominant role, and its essence is thus the very system as such of power relationships between the different levels of society and not the unilateral domination of the weak by the powerful.

As in all power relationships, dependence posits an exchange of actions between two end points, the actions of the dominated societies being directly conditioned and controlled by those of the dominant or metropolitan societies. But it also happens that events and developments in the weaker countries have direct or indirect repercussions on the dominant societies themselves, although the latter's independent position prevents such repercussions from having an immediately decisive effect.

If they did not take place within a system of reciprocity and correspondence between the rulers and the ruled, relationships between capitalist societies at different stages of development would not be dependency relationships. They would simply be relationships between two autonomous societies, however incompatible and unequal these might be. The characteristic pattern of the interdependence between a dominating and a dominated body within the same structural unit also presupposes that specific changes at either end of the relationship will be followed by corresponding modifications in the relationship itself. So long as one pole remains supreme, any changes that take place in it will tend to preserve its supremacy throughout the variations in the interrelations of the two. Nevertheless, changes in the dominated society will generally lead to changes in the system of relationships, and may go so far as to end the state of dependence altogether.

When the balance of power between the dominant societies shifts as a result of historical circumstances, or of technological progress and the specific characteristics of the organization of production and social power in each one, the role of the dominated societies in the system of interdependence alters in obedience to the new requirements and patterns. In the same way, the changes that take place in the organization of production and its corollary, social power, in response to modifications in the dominant system alter the weaker societies' mode of participation in the system of dependence.

In Latin America, all the national societies (with the exception of Cuba) form part of the system of interdependence that is characteristic of contemporary capitalism, although in differing ways and degrees. Nevertheless, they do not fit into the system in the same way or at the same level. Hence, each one's mode of participation is contingent not only on the demands of the dominant system, but on its own internal situation, which is a product of its past history and former mode of participation in the system of dependence.

It would be wrong, therefore, to regard dependence as being merely a set of unilateral actions whereby one society dominates another, since that would mean that the dependent society is united in its opposition to the dominating society. This is far from being the case; as the variables and major trends of the dependent society's internal structure are conditioned by its dependent role and the changes that have occurred in this role throughout its history, they embody fundamental conflicts which do not derive solely from the general system of social domination but are inherent in the correspondence between the dominant internal interests and the broad interests of the system of dependence. Thus, the inner tempo of the dependent society parallels that of its relations with the society on which it is dependent, or, in other words, the profile of the dependent society as a whole depends on the profile of its relations with the dominating society or, more specifically, with its centers of power.

Because dependence has been considered an "external factor," the studies that have been made of the basic processes of change in Latin America, and in this particular case, of urbanization, have failed to attach sufficient importance to the system of dependence and the changes in it as one of the main reasons for the trend pursued by the processes of change. It also explains the deep-rooted tendency in Latin American countries to study those changes as if they were taking place in autonomous societies and urbanization had very little to do with their dependent status.

Nevertheless, the increasing complexity of the problem has led to deeper investigation, which has brought to light the fact that the main elements in the trend of change are closely bound up with the changes in the system of dependence in each country and in Latin America as a whole.

In seeking the mechanisms by which the processes of ecologico-demographic urbanization are interwoven with those of economic urbanization, it was found that the latter also were affected by the changes in the relationships of economic dependence. Similarly, the processes of sociocultural urbanization involved in the development and transformation of urban societies and cultures were associated as much with the growing dependence of the Latin American nations on the dominant metropolitan societies as with the increasing correspondence between the dominant culture and social organization in those societies and in Latin America.

Hence, if the processes of change in Latin America are not to be misrepresented by an incomplete and therefore distorted interpretation of the facts, they must necessarily be studied as part of the sociology of dependence. This applies to certain questions of detail as well as to the key factors underlying the specific trends that mark the tide of change. If this is to be done, social research must be constantly aware of the past. To a great extent, the history of the Latin American countries may be regarded as the history of their dependence. This explains why current developments in these countries in terms of the social processes that are taking place are unintelligible without reference to the development of their dependence from past to present.

For instance, one of the main sources of problems in latter-day urban development is the relationship between the growth of the towns and the growth of industry. Although manufacturing industry began to develop towards the end of the nineteenth century in Latin America, it did not get into its full stride until after the First World War, and more particularly in the post-Depression era. Moreover, it did not develop at the same tempo in all the Latin American countries, and its pattern of growth bore little resemblance to the form in which industries are now being established or expanded in those same countries.

What is known as the process of import substitution took place mainly in Argentina, Brazil, Chile, Mexico and Uruguay, though in differing degrees. It was largely due to a deterioration in the economic dependency relationships between those countries and the United States. The sharp contraction in commodity exports to the United States and European markets, as a result of the financial crises there, led to a severe cutback in the consumer manufactures imported for what was already a fairly sizable urban population. The development of the towns in the Latin American countries had formerly been attributable to the development of a commercial urban economy, which was concentrated in a few centers so as to make for the growth of trade with the metropolitan centers—first Europe and then the United States. These trading relations had originated in the pattern of European industrial and financial capitalism at the end of the eighteenth century, and in the special position of the Latin American countries in that system when Spain and Portugal were forced to give up their colonies.

In the last twenty years or so of the eighteenth century, the shifts in the balance of power between the metropolitan capitalist countries of Europe that accompanied the growth and transformation of the capitalist system of production from a mercantile and financial economy to an industrial, financial and mercantile economy weakened and ultimately broke up the colonial system built up by Spain and Portugal and destroyed their trading monopoly in the colonies. Thanks to the changes in the trade routes linking Europe and Latin America and the technical progress of communications and transport, the countries on the Atlantic seaboard and Chile—or, to be more exact, certain centers and areas in those countries—were able to take a more direct and effective part in the new system of dependence that arose out of the decolonization. The countries on the Pacific coast, however, not only lost their hegemony in trade with Europe, but had to remain on the fringes of the new system of dependence until well on into the nineteenth century.

In this context of dependence, the colonial towns that were in direct touch with the trade routes (usually ports, such as Rio de Janeiro and Buenos Aires, or towns such as Santiago that were close to a port) developed economically and demographically as commercial towns and their population was drawn into the consumption pattern of an industrial society and its markets, thus making for the general modernization of those countries, although in an unequal and highly concentrated way. The huge flow of immigrants from Europe to Argentina and Uruguay in particular, and later to Brazil and Chile as well, were a factor in urban development and modernization, and, to a great extent, formed part of the same over-all process.

It thus appears that the post-colonial process of urbanization which first developed in Argentina, Brazil, Chile, Mexico and Uruguay was not shaped by the internal characteristics of those societies considered individually, but by the new dependency relationships they entered into as a result of decolonization and of the subservient position of the metropolitan societies themselves in the context of European capitalism.

As those countries' ties with the metropolitan centers of power became more strained towards 1930, and they already had a fairly large urban population that had become accustomed to certain patterns of consumption based on trade with metropolitan countries, they were compelled to find substitutes for the principal consumer goods imported for their urban population. Import substitution had to be financed almost entirely by national capital, the level of technology was relatively low and the prevailing forms of business organization and management were of the traditional family type, which are reflected in the type of bureaucracy that grew up, the way in which labor relations were handled and production itself organized.

The expansion of industry gave a further impetus to urbanization in those countries, and began, in one degree or another, to transform the economic relations between the towns and the rural areas. The result was that the urban population and the major towns grew far more rapidly than elsewhere in Latin America.

In Ecuador and Peru, for instance, import substitution was later in starting, and took place mainly after the Second World War, although the first plants were set up in the nineteen-thirties. The circumstances were very different too. First, import substitution coincided with a period in which the ties of dependence were becoming stronger rather than weaker, and, for that reason, the substitution process was relatively independent of national capital. Its funds were largely foreign in origin, whether in the form of direct investment capital, loans or financial control. It also had access to a highly-developed technology and a monopolistic type of business organization associated with international consortia, with the kind of labor relations and production processes that are needed for a monopolistic set-up and the demands of an advanced technology. In short, the growth and diversification of manufacturing industry in these countries sprang from certain modifications in their economic dependence and the increasing flow of investment towards the secondary and tertiary sectors of the economy, although the primary sector was not wholly neglected. The ensuing picture is thus one of expansion and consolidation juxtaposed with changes in the system of economic dependence.

This expansion of the urban industrial economy and its far-reaching effects on economic relations between urban and rural areas in these countries have led to the growth of the urban population and, above all, of the major towns, which were strategically placed for developing along modern lines during the previous stage of dependence, or are located in areas that have sprung into prominence as a direct result of the new conditions of dependence, e.g., Guayaquil in Ecuador and Chimbote in Peru. Meanwhile, radical changes have been taking place in the urban-rural ecologico-demographic relationships that are a concomitant of the growth of the urban population and urban economy and of shifts in the economic relationships between the two poles of the national society.

As these countries were at a disadvantage during the first major stage of the post-colonial system of dependence, the factors underlying the economic and social stagnation that was apparent throughout most of their territory were responsible for the economic and social relations and institutional set-up of the colonial era becoming even more firmly entrenched in large areas of those countries. The development of the sectors most closely connected with foreign trade and external financing—particularly in the early stages of industrialization when their dependence was increasing and taking on different forms—was so much greater in the modern and developing areas, both urban and rural, than it was in the backward rural and urban areas that the growth of the urban population was much more rapid in these countries than in those which had undergone the same process earlier. Given the nature of the trends in the growth and change of the urban economy, particularly in the process of industrial development, the growth and change of the urban societies in Peru and Ecuador present a much thornier problem than in the urban societies of the countries where industrial and urban growth began earlier. The form which dependence has taken in the Latin American countries and the changes in this relationship are thus indissolubly linked with each stage and each trend of urban development in every one of these countries at all the decisive moments in their history.

If the urbanization of the economy in Peru (which is a determining factor in ecologico-demographic urban growth) is assumed to stem from the current changes and general increase in the country's dependence, it may be argued that dependence has been a secondary factor in the urbanization of the economies of Argentina and Brazil where urban and industrial development alike have been carried on with national capital and by national enterprises. But in certain cases dependence has continued to play a key role. It has at times prepared the national matrix to take advantage of a turn of events such as a deterioration in its state of dependence to start its industry on the road to development, involving intensive sales to the home market, the existence of already established entrepreneurial groups with the necessary capital and expertise to set up industries, and the formation of large urban centers founded on an urban commercial economy that provided a market for industry and made demands on it. In other instances, dependence has the effect of channelling investment capital into industry, modifying the modest industrial base already in existence, diversifying urban industrial production and stepping up sales, all of which speed up and change the growth trends of the urban population which, habituated to the new industrial patterns of consumption, form a market for the growing output of industry.

Thus, in studying the relationships that make up the state of dependence, it is essential to place them in a historical perspective, to define clearly the different stages of dependence and its social impact on the individual countries at each stage, and to correlate it with the shifts in the balance of power between the metropolitan countries themselves, as a result of changes in the structure of production or of world markets in the capitalist system, to mention only two factors.

As the truth of an actual situation is never abstract it is wholly academic to speak of "the" dependent relationships, "a" process of industrialization, or "a" process of urban development. It is always necessary to state exactly what those relationships are with regard to a particular country and what types of industrial and urban development are under consideration. In short, it is not enough to sketch in the whole historical background; each process must be dealt with factually in relation to a particular time and setting. In other words, a general process must be described in terms of its specific nature and particular history at a given moment in space and time.

It is by no means superfluous to dwell on these problems, since they are not so obvious as they appear to be. If they were, there would not be so many studies on "the" industrialization of Latin America that do little more than record the contrasts and similarities in the industrial growth of the different countries, without relating them to any recognized body of problems and, hence, without mentioning any factor other than quantitative differences in output productivity and investment the magnitude of whose various components may vary without there necessarily being any significant differences in the structure of industrial development.

C. Urbanization as One of the Major Dimensions of the Present Process of Change in the Latin American Societies

Since the urban phenomenon can be traced back in Latin American history to pre-colonial times, it would be well to eliminate the ambiguity implicit in the term "urbanization process." This ambiguity arises from the two different concepts which the term conveys: first, the process whereby towns emerge and develop in a given society, and, second, the process whereby the urbanization of a society has developed and changed in the past.

The Latin American societies are at present undergoing a process of urban expansion and change parallel with a process of contraction and change in rural areas. In the first sense of the term, the assertion that an urbanization process is under way would be valid for a rural locality or a group of rural localities considered separately within a particular national society, and this is undoubtedly occurring. It only occurs, however, as part of the expansion and change of a process which already has a long and eventful history behind it in the national society itself.

Without denying its importance as an academic exercise, it would be unrealistic, therefore, to begin by laying down a universal definition of what is urban and what is rural. It is much more important for the purposes and real possibilities of research to indicate what the present process of urbanization actually involves, and to describe its characteristics and trends, and the factors underlying it, rather than to go into the original meaning of the term. In other words, a scientific theory regarding the present urbanization process in these countries should not be built on the formulation of a general theory of the urbanization of society, because it operates at a different level. The specific purpose of this theory is to present a systematic picture of the elements involved in a specific process, of its changing pattern, its general trends and its implications in an actual society, not in society in the abstract sense. In this context, one of the forms taken by the process of change in the Latin American societies is the expansion and modification of the urbanization process, that is, of a form of social organization which is becoming predominant in some countries and is being consolidated in others.

What distinguishes urban from rural is that they are two different systems of ecological and socio-economic organization of human life, and besides coexisting and being juxtaposed, these systems are permanently interdependent.

This means that they cannot be considered as two extremes in a *continuum*, but rather as two sectors of a single structural unit. Therefore, it is impossible to study what is happening in one of those sectors without first establishing where it coincides and where it conflicts with the other. Expansion and change in one of these systems of organization of human life involve a simultaneous contraction and change in the other. The whole question of urban expansion and change in any society is, first of all, a process of change in the society's urban-rural relationship, giving pre-eminence to the developing urban way of life. That is to say, urbanization is one of the forms taken by the general process of transformation of these societies, and it represents changes in the urban-rural relationships in every basic structural order of society, through expansion of the urban system. If an entirely rural society were being urbanized, the process would primarily involve the emergence and development of urban patterns affecting some portion of the basic structural orders in that society (for example, the emergence of urban-type settlements, secondary and tertiary economic activities, forms of social relationships deriving from these factors, and incipient urban sources of a political power). In the real case of a national society in Latin America or any other part of the present-day world, a developed and consolidated urban organization, actively interdependent with the rural, already exists for each of the basic structural orders of the national society, i.e., it is already one of the basic modes of existence and development of the over-all structure of society. Thus the process directly involves a modification of urban-rural relations in the society, as a consequence of the trends of change and expansion in the urban system of the correlative changes in the rural.

Accordingly, from the standpoint of the dimension of the general process of change in these countries, the present "urbanization process" may be considered as a process of expansion and transformation of the urban systems existing in each of the basic structural orders of the whole society, with, as a part and a result of this process, an alteration of the interdependent rural systems and, consequently, of the entire structure of urban-rural relationships in the society as a whole, all this being largely conditioned by the changes that are taking place in the dependency relationships of the national society as a whole. On this basis, the methodological problem is to differentiate between the dimensions of the processes of change which each basic structural order of society is undergoing, to study the mechanisms of interdependence in each of those dimensions, and to reconstruct the general process in terms of its general trends and its implications for society as a whole.

One of the risks involved in considering the urbanization process as a dimension of the over-all process of change in the Latin American societies seems to be that urbanization might tend to be regarded as synonymous with over-all change. This risk cannot be avoided without first establishing and then working on the basis of the fact that this dimension covers everything in the over-all change which is directly or immediately linked to the alteration of the relations and limits between urban and rural in each major institutional order of society. If this approach is taken as the point of departure, the above-mentioned risks can be reduced or eliminated. To that end, it is necessary to establish what is the nature of this changing trend in urban-rural relations in each basic structural order and what are the factors determining it. The kind of interdependence between the various sub-dimensions of the process depend on the kind of interdependence that exists between the actual orders of each society in each specific historical context, which only specific research can reveal and determine.

1. URBANIZATION OF THE ECONOMIC STRUCTURE

Broadly speaking, this process can be described as the tendency for economic activities in urban centers to pre-

dominate in the over-all structure of economic activity in
society, and the tendency for urbanized forms to become
widespread in the whole structure of economic activity,
particularly the structure of production. In this process,
there is a change in the structure of the previously existing
urban economic activity and, as a result of the impact of
this change on the national economy, a change also takes
place in the rural economic structure itself, all of which
gradually alters the urban-rural economic relationships.

Inasmuch as, in the structure of over-all economic activity in a society, primary activities are mainly a feature of
the rural area, in the present situation urbanization of the
economy means that secondary and tertiary activities are
expanding, becoming more diversified and assuming a key
role in the national economy as a whole. Assuming, further, that the basic secondary and tertiary activities are
located in urban centers, not only those activities but the
urban centers as well will tend to hold economic sway
over the rural localities. For this to come about, it is not
necessary that all the secondary and tertiary activities of
the economy should shift to an urban ecological setting,
since artisan-type activities, for example, and commerce
may be found also in rural areas. It is obvious, however,
that as the urban centers gain and consolidate their economic predominance, the artisan-type activities in those
branches of production which are dominated by the urban
centers will gradually lose their importance and their
ecological and demographic scope, although other rural
artisan-type activities may subsist and even develop for a
time.

If all this is to become possible, the urban economy,
besides expanding, must be technologically diversified and
developed, so that the relations between the actual
branches and levels of urban economic activity will gradually alter in favor of predominance by the technologically more developed branches and levels. This is
perhaps what is happening between manufacturing and

artisan-type activity in urban centers, or between industries manufacturing consumer products and those producing intermediate or capital goods. Moreover, as the urban economy's growth is consolidated during this process, its characteristics will be gradually incorporated even in primary activities, whose functions, technological processes and entrepreneurial organization must be adapted progressively to the requirements and conditions of the urban economy. Thus agriculture becomes more and more mechanized and industrialized to serve the needs of the industrialized urban areas. At a very advanced stage in the urbanization of the economy, primary activities can be considered as rural only in so far as they remain ecologically rural, but in nature they are "urbanized" as a productive process.

While the urbanization of the economy is only just beginning, urban centers at different levels may not be very closely linked and they may enjoy comparative independence, particularly in countries where the population centers are very far apart and the communications and transport systems are little-developed. With the intensification of the process and the definitive predominance of the urban economy, however, an economic system emerges and is consolidated, and the rural area is gradually absorbed into this system as economic urbanization spreads to it. This is normally an uneven and sometimes a discontinuous process in the various countries, and in the various regions of a country.

Similarly, in the initial stages of the urbanization of the economy, the direct day-to-day economic relations between the countryside and the city may be relatively unstable and tangential, although in the over-all historical context the relations between the two must be all-encompassing and continuing, since they both form part of the same structural unit, within which they act upon and are dependent on each other. With the expansion of the urban economy—which also implies urbanization of the economy of rural areas as a result of urban products entering the rural markets and of the technological and functional urbanization of primary activities—the isolation of the city and the countryside from each other in their day-to-day economic relations diminishes and eventually disappears. Thenceforward, the economic relations between town and country, urban and rural, become closer and more direct. The rural economy comes to depend on the urban economy, and urban centers hold economic sway over country towns and villages, just as the urban areas do over the rural areas.

From this standpoint, the urbanization of the economy of a society may also be regarded as a process of homogenization of the whole economic structure and of direct and complete integration of the population in the context of the economy, production, and the urban market. In the long run, this presupposes the disappearance of urban-rural differentiations in the economy, a stage which some modern societies may be about to attain.

In most of the Latin American countries, the process of expansion and change of urban economic activities within the national economy is in full swing, and in some countries urban economic activities are already predominant. Nevertheless urban-type economic activity does not yet seem to have imposed itself on the whole national economy even of those Latin American countries where the process has gone furthest. The trend is probably in this direction, however.

2. URBANIZATION OF THE ECOLOGICO-DEMOGRAPHIC STRUCTURE

This is essentially a process of expansion and modification of the urban ecologico-demographic characteristics of society, with the corresponding modification of urban-rural relations in this structural order, including the changes that take place in each of the terms of this relationship. Since the most visible sign of this process is the growth of the urban section of the society's total population, especially as a result of the growth of the population living in the cities, it is often confused with the process itself, and for many it is still "the process of urbanization of society."

Although this is the most striking feature of the ecologico-demographic urbanization process, it is not the only important one, nor does it occur independently of what is happening in the rest of the ecologico-demographic structure of the society. Urban population growth does not take place in the cities alone, although it is mainly concentrated there in Latin America and the rest of the developing world; to a lesser degree it is also observable in smaller towns and villages. Moreover, the number of cities and smaller towns and villages tends to increase in the course of urban population growth, which implies an expansion of the urban ecological forms of settlement and a relative reduction of the rural, although the latter may increase in absolute terms. The two interconnected processes reveal a change in the balance of the urban-rural relationship in the ecological and demographic structure of society in favor of the urban areas.

In the same process, the urban ecological characteristics gradually change. First, because the cities and minor towns and villages increase in size, in terms not only of the number of inhabitants but also of the ecological space inhabited. Secondly, because a change takes place in the internal ecological structure of the cities and in the smaller towns and villages, which attain the status of cities. Thirdly, because with the increase in the number, size and importance of urban population nuclei, which are relatively scattered throughout the territory of the society concerned, the tendency is for an urban ecological system to become established, together with a network of communications and real and direct interdependent relationships.

The rural ecological and demographic sector cannot remain unaffected in this complex of changes, because it and the urban sector are interdependent within the overall structure of the society. The migration of the rural population to the urban sector is already a tangible sign of change in the rural sector. Furthermore, with the progressive establishment of an urban system, the rural towns and villages are incorporated in the network of communications and interdependent relationships which that implies; consequently, the isolation of the town from the country and of one rural area from another becomes less or disappears.

From a strictly demographic standpoint, the growing urban predominance in the urban-rural demographic relationship is not the only significant change that takes place, although it may be the most obvious and perhaps the most important. Neither can the rural population drain resulting from migration to the cities fail to introduce substantive changes in the rural demographic structure, particularly since most of the migrants are those of the younger sections of the population who are best fitted for urban life, most susceptible to urban influence, best educated, etc. Correlatively, the demographic structure of cities, and to a lesser degree of the smaller urban centers, feels the full impact of the overwhelming influx of a population with very different cultural values and traditions. One of the most obvious results is that the sharp increase in the younger strata in the urban population is accompanied by a parallel reduction in the same strata in the rural population.

To sum up, the trend towards urban ecological and demographic predominance in the society of any of the Latin American countries, but particularly those in which this process is comparatively recent, means not only urban population growth but a whole set of broader and more complex phenomena involving the transformation of all the basic elements of the urban-rural relationship in this structural order. Clearly, rural-urban migration may be a process of urbanization of the population, but not of society. Even so, until such time as other structural orders are incorporated in the process, this is an urbanization of the population only in its ecological sense.

3. URBANIZATION OF THE SOCIAL STRUCTURE

The term social structure is used here in the sense of the structure of social power relationships, i.e., the stratification of basic social groups that constitute the matrix within which exist the many interrelated groups and types of groups that may go to make up a society. From this point of view, the process of urbanization of the social structure consists in the expansion and alteration of the urban patterns of organization of social power existing in the society concerned, and, consequently, in the modification of urban-rural relationships within this basic structural order and of the actual rural patterns of social power structuration which form part of the national society as a whole. The expansion of urban patterns of organization of social power implies an increase in the population incorporated into the society's total system of urban stratification, together with an increase in the population incorporated into each of the classes and strata making up the urban system of social power within the national society.

Since ecologico-demographic urbanization involves the demographic expansion of the urban population, the population drawn into the urban ecological framework likewise joins the whole social order existing within it. Hence, an increase takes place both in the population included in the entire urban system of social power and in the population forming each of its social sectors.

The changes in the patterns governing the urban system of social power in the national society in question—deriving partly from the population increases in the system as a whole and in each of its sectors, and primarily from the alterations brought about in the structure of the urban economy—consist chiefly in modifications of the specific relationships between the various classes and strata forming the urban sub-society and changes in the internal composition of each of those groups. The structural diversification and metamorphosis of urban economic activity gives rise to new occupational and vocational groups and to new sources of status-roles within the economy and correlatively within the social structure. These changes affect the existing sources of power and, to some extent, the specific population groups which control them.

Thus, the urban social power structure changes, gains in flexibility or becomes diversified, when new strata and classes are generated, the internal composition of each of these is altered, and the volume of population comprised in them increases.

The expansion of the demographic framework of the urban system of social power structuration—not so much as a result of the internal increase in the urban population itself, as in consequence of migratory shifts of the society's total population towards the urban ecological framework or of the urbanization of rural localities and areas themselves in the same respect—implies the development of a trend towards the transfer of increasing numbers of the national population to the urban sub-society, with all its inherent consequences. The one of interest here is the progressive incorporation of the country's population into the urban social power system.

This latter process constitutes a mechanism whereby urban-rural relationships are altered within this basic structural order, not only because changes occur in the proportional distribution of the population between the two sub-systems, but also because the dependency relationships between the two forms of organization of social power tend to undergo modification. One of the reasons for this is that the predominance of the urban social power system makes itself felt not only in demographic but also in social terms. If the alteration referred to is really to take place, the rural sub-system of organization of social power must also change. In this case the changes are brought about because forms of economic activity which, historically speaking, are of urban origin infiltrate into the countryside, and because the function and specific nature of rural economic activity in relation to urban activities undergoes modification.

Thus, at the present time, while the urban economy and population are expanding and the urban economy is "in process of change and diversification, under the impact of the widespread introduction of new technologies," the compositions and function of each of the classes and strata in which social power is organized in the urban centers are changing at a pace whose speed varies from one country to another and from one area to another within each country.

In the first place, the traditional ruling classes—mainly landowning bourgeoisies in most of the countries—are gradually altering in content and function with the changes in the economic sources of their social power. Alongside this development, the middle-level groups are expanding, not only demographically but also from the standpoint of their specific functions in society, the scope and range of their influence, and their access to the market and to concrete forms of political power, etc. The working-class population, both industrial and non-industrial, is increasing in number, and while in the urban economy industrial development is taking place and the relative importance of tertiary activities is growing, under each country's specific dependency conditions, a whole stratum of population is emerging which is marginal to the new socio-economic structure associated with industrial expansion.

In the rural sub-society, the composition and specific nature of the ruling social groups is undergoing decisive

modification as more and more products of urban origin
trickle into the market, changes occur in the function of
the crop and livestock farming economy in relation to the
needs of industrial development and of the urban market,
and the former bases of the rural economy gradually disin-
tegrate. A case in point is the decline of the landowning
stratum linked to the "traditional hacienda" system, and
the conversion of part of it into an entrepreneurial sector.
At the same time, the sectors formed by the rural petty
bourgeoisie—which in most of these countries used to constitute a set of relatively scattered and isolated groups—
are expanding, and so is the rural proletariat.

In other words, the structure of social power is changing
not only in the urban sub-society, but also in the rural
areas. In so far as all these internal changes in each of the
sub-societies cannot but affect their interrelationships
within the over-all structure of power, dominance and
conflict in the national society as a whole, the implication
is that the specific patterns and content of the over-all
power structure are tending to change, although not the
basic nature of this structure as a whole.

Thus the urbanization of the social or social power
structure stems from the urbanization of the economic and
ecologico-demographic structures of society, and in its
turn influences each of these processes.

4. URBANIZATION OF THE CULTURAL STRUCTURE

In the abstract, the concept of culture adopted here
covers the whole of the ideological superstructure of a society, together with the symbols, institutions and objects
by which it is served and in which it finds expression. The
term therefore relates both to the images of itself and of
others which the population of a given society entertains
or develops, and to the images of the ruling, subordinate
and alternative nuclei of formal and real axiological orientation. It includes the over-all objectives pursued by the

society or imposed by its ruling groups upon its other members; its systems and levels of aspiration; the formal and informal institutions which symbolize and put into effect its axiologico-normative models, etc. What is more, this interpretation of culture also embraces the perceptive structures and the content of perception of society and nature which exist in a given society at a given time.

Both by its very nature and by virtue of the quality of the scientific instruments at its disposal, culture is one of the most elusive aspects of the historico-social situation. Accordingly, the problem of the urbanization of culture in Latin American societies is considered here mainly with reference to some of its more perceptible dimensions.

Broadly speaking, like all other specific processes or sub-dimensions, the urbanization of culture in existing Latin American societies consists first and foremost in the expansion of the demographic radius of influence of the culture characterizing the urban sub-society of a given national society at a given time, and in the changes brought about in it during the process. This involves both the alteration of urban-rural relationships within the cultural structure of the society, and internal changes in the rural culture predominant in the national society.

In all the countries under discussion, the contents and symbols of urban culture are clearly acquiring or beginning to acquire an increasing radius of influence, not only from the territorial or ecological standpoint, but, to much greater effect, from the demographic angle. Thus, the process under discussion consists in the expansion of the influence of urban culture within a society. Clearly, too, urban culture itself is undergoing constant and increasingly rapid modification. Urban culture nuclei of the past are dwindling and disappearing or gradually changing and adopting different patterns; others that are completely new are being introduced or developing from within, with the ensuing quantitative enrichment of the culture in question. The relations between the axiologico-normative circles co-existing in the society concerned—whether they consist in subordination and conflict or in competition between alternatives—alter likewise as the social groups forming each of these circles change their position and their specific relationships with one another and with the society as a whole.

As the urban ecological and demographic framework broadens, as the urban economy becomes predominant and infiltrates into the countryside itself, and as the structure of social power is urbanized, urban culture too expands, not only inasmuch as its predominance makes it of greater importance within the whole, but also because even the co-existing rural culture is permeated and modified by it in many respects. This spread of urban culture beyond the limits of the town, this tendency for many of its components to spill over into population sectors which are not incorporated in the specifically urban framework, is a phenomenon noted by all students of current change in Latin America, although not much has been written on the subject. Observers are unanimous in pointing out that in each individual country the rural population is subjected to the sectoral influence of contemporary urban culture through many channels and in a variety of ways. This is tantamount to saying that urban-rural relationships within the society's over-all culture are undergoing a vigorous process of change, although it differs in level and intensity among the various regions and localities within a given country, or from one Latin American country to another.

As urbanization of the economy and of the ecologico-demographic structure proceeds, the changes occurring in the actual composition of the rural sub-society show that situations, activities, institutions and symbols of urban origin in that particular national society are making their way into rural areas. With the ground thus prepared, not only the value-normative nuclei, the specific motivations and the content and direction of aspirations, but also the images of society and of nature that stem from the urban world may find fertile soil in which to take root and grow.

Comments on the spread of urban culture in the countryside often give the impression that the process is simply an overflow, as if the contents of one vessel were to be poured into another, without modification of the latter in order to receive it rather than merely on receiving it. Basically, however, the current process of diffusion of elements of urban culture among the rural sectors would not have been possible unless the rural society itself had previously undergone radical modification, or had been passing through a phase of more or less intensive change.

Only in so far as urban society changes does its real culture also change. Similarly, only inasmuch as rural society changes in itself and in respect of its relationships with urban society can its culture veer in the direction of urbanization. As the urban and rural sub-societies are not a continuum, but two interdependent sectors within a single structural unit, it is not only the diffusion of urban culture throughout the countryside that is implied by the modification of urban-rural relationships within the culture of the society as a whole. In addition, in the national society, elements of rural culture are disseminated in the urban culture that has been established and developed as an outcome of the whole urbanization process. This rural-urban diffusion which is effected through the migration of cultural elements from the countryside to the town—a form of migration not necessarily identical with population shifts, although superimposed upon them—is one of the most active processes. The scale on which it takes place depends upon the urban-rural relationships previously existing, upon the degree to which the migrant population was previously influenced or bedazzled by urban culture, upon the cultural disparities existing between the two sectors and upon the types of cultural conflicts by which the total population of a national society is affected.

It is therefore possible that what is called rural culture

in a given country at a given time is the backwash of the urban culture of the past and of its influence on the rural population. By the time migration to the towns takes place, a different urban culture has grown up, and the culture brought in by the migrants is rural only by comparison with the urban culture of the day. This does not apply, however, to countries whose rural sub-cultures are basically different from the prevailing national culture and undergo constant change in the course of history. Argentina and Peru may perhaps serve to exemplify each of the two possibilities.

5. URBANIZATION OF THE POLITICAL STRUCTURE

When urban-rural relationships are examined from the point of view of political structure, it will be noted that in every Latin American country the town has always been the ecological matrix of the principal institutions of political power, despite the fact that town and countryside are relatively cut off from each other as far as direct day-to-day relationships are concerned. Suffice it to recall the real and ideological significance of politico-administrative centralism in the history of Latin America.

This image, however, must be accepted with many reservations if the problem is to be analyzed on a somewhat more concrete basis. From the standpoint of abstract historical relationships, the town has been the dominant sector of society since the very earliest days of colonial capitalism in the Latin American countries. This is true in practice of those societies which were dependent from the outset, where the town was and still is the keystone of dependency relationships. Nevertheless, the political dependency of the rural sector has not unvaryingly existed at the same level or with the same characteristics during each significant historical stage in the development of the Latin American countries.

As long as the structure of production, and the structure

of economic activity in general, were based essentially on primary activities, the rural sector had the upper hand in urban-rural relationships of this kind, notwithstanding the fact that the institutions controlling the society's over-all economy were established in the town, and the latter constituted the mechanism whereby the national economy was linked to the most important international market. As long as the majority of the population was concentrated in the countryside, and the town constituted a relatively isolated entity within the ecologico-demographic structure of the society, there too the rural sector was predominant. As long as the social power structure was based mainly on sources deriving from the primary economy, here again the rural sub-society was preponderant, although the agents of the power institutions lived in the town. Today, in contrast, whatever the specific levels of change reached in the individual Latin American countries, the trends observable are largely favorable to the urban sector in all these spheres.

Against the background of a matrix of rural predominance in the over-all power structure of a society, the political predominance of town over country was more formal and apparent than real in the earlier stages of Latin America's history. While it is true that the most important institutions of the political structure, and often their agents as well, were established in the town, it is equally undeniable that the sources of the power of those institutions and of their agents were to be found not so much in the urban as in the rural areas. Thus, the oligarchical hegemony which was so familiar a feature of the over-all political power structure of the society, and which in recent times is being laboriously reduced and broken down, made use of formal power institutions and mechanisms set up in the town and belonging to a structure whose historical origin was urban—political liberalism, for example; but the access obtained by agents (groups and individuals) to the control of those formal institutions, with the ensuing all-too-well-known distortions, was primarily based on their control of sources of economic and social power which were rural in location and content.

It was by virtue of their ownership of land or their association with the landowning class that the ruling groups in the political structure controlled the political institutions ecologically located in the town. The same thing happened later, in so far as—despite the fact that their power was directly based on secondary or tertiary economic sources—they maintained their social and political ties with the traditional landowning classes. Herein has always lain the reason for the relative autonomy of the rural sector as regards the real effects of the integrating mechanisms of the town-based central political powers, the endemic *caciquismo* (bossism), and the inconsistencies of the process of incorporating the rural population into the political institutions of the Nation-State which are all still to be found in many of the Latin American countries.

Nevertheless, in so far as urban-rural relationships are undergoing intensive change in each of the various structural spheres, the process of political integration of the society as a whole—i.e., the process of incorporating the population into the national political institutions—is gaining strength at all levels and in all parts of the national territory, and in the course of it urban-rural relationships are being modified in the political order of the society. During the process in question, the political hegemony of the town is gradually becoming real instead of merely formal, since the whole of the State machinery pivots upon the political institutions and power mechanisms. Access to the control of these real institutions and mechanisms of political power is becoming mainly the prerogative of agents who are urban by virtue not only of their ecological background but also of their socio-economic sources of power. Even in the countryside itself, it is precisely the groups that are growing up as a result of the urbanization of the rural sector which are becoming the real leading agents of these political institutions.

Thus, as far as the political structure of the society as a whole is concerned, urban-rural relationships have been or are undergoing radical and intensive change, and there is a trend towards the total hegemony of the urban sector in the politico-administrative system nowadays characteristic of these societies. Urban political power is predominant not only in the pattern and location of political institutions, but in the sources from which access can be obtained to control of these, and in the origin and sources of power of their agents as such.

Thus, the urbanization process under way implies the emergence of a new ecological matrix of the structure of political power, rural dependence, and the expansion and alteration of the content and urban patterns of the structural institutions and mechanisms of the Nation-State. The "populistic" phenomenon in Latin America, for example, corresponds to the transitional character of the society, and of its political machinery in particular, as it moves from one period of its history to another. Similarly, the urbanization of the society also finds its own expression in political terms.

II

THE LATIN AMERICAN
CITY IN TRANSITION

CHAPTER FOUR

THE CITY AND POLITICS*

FERNANDO HENRIQUE CARDOSO

The city and politics developed in Western tradition as interrelated concepts and realities. Even etymologically the connection is plain: *Civitas* and *polis* are the roots in different languages to express, simultaneously, a way of life and a form of participation: civics and politics.

The interpretation of those classic writers who studied the city from a sociological point of view was the same. Weber, for example, showed that in the broad meaning of the concept, the city originated as a phenomenon of Western civilization, even though in different civilizations and at various times in history men had built settlements in spatially contiguous areas. But it was only in the Western world that two simultaneous processes occurred that allow a population settlement to be properly described as a *city*: the market (and the regulations of the politics of the urban economy) and the politico-administrative authority that governed the residents of the city, at the same time guaranteeing them (or at least some of them) certain rights relative to their political destiny.

The definition of the city as a *marketplace* seems to be a point of agreement in the literature concerned with the urban phenomenon in Western Europe. Marx concurred on this point, and showed further that the existence of an *urban economy* assumes a long process of social division of

* English translation by Ruth Huseman.

labor and a redefinition of the forms of exploitation of some classes by others, in such a way that the city emerged as the expression of the collapse of the feudal economy and the old manorial regime. Instead of the closed economy of the feudal estate or the system of legal guilds in the population groupings of the Middle Ages— some of which might already appear to be "cities," measured by criteria that do not take into consideration the degree of complexity of the division of labor process between the countryside and the city and among the relationships of labor in the city—there came about a kind of economic organization that encountered, in the existence of a "free and available" labor force and in the concentration of the means of production in the hands of a certain kind of owner, the fundamental and necessary relationship for the appearance of the capitalist means of production.

For Marx, therefore, the city is as essential to the existence of capitalism as the worker is to the profit of the owner. Without the "free and available" labor force and without the owners of the means of production, also "free," there would be no *market*. By "free" Marx meant, first, individuals not formally dependent on the land or on any master and who are, in fact, dispossessed of any means of production of their own; and second, people who must come to the market to exchange their labor for the means of subsistence guaranteed to them by a salary, or, in other words, workers in a city. The owners of the means of production are also classed socially by their position in the relationships of production: In the city they are not personally dependent on any master (although they may pay taxes to the political masters of the city where the market is located), and when they are classified as bourgeois, they have only the wealth that they have been able to accumulate. Their privileged position derives from their ability to control capital (or the means of production and the labor force) rather than from ties of blood or kinship.

Typically, social relations such as these are found only in cities. They occur only in social groupings in which tribal, family, clan, brotherhood, or feudal ties can be broken by the irresistible force of a new type of economy that equalizes all the owners of the means of production, on one hand, and all the nonowners, on the other. By conferring on the men who meet in the market of the urban commune a common, impersonal standing in the face of the impositions and privileges that do not originate in the "rationality" of the market, the capitalist economy creates specific social "extracts": social classes. These, in their usual forms of bourgeoisie and proletariat, are the fruits of capitalism. In the marketplace of the city they find the substantiation of the particular kind of social exploitation that gives them life.

Thus, for Marx the city is both an economic fact and a political relationship. Naturally, the formal equality of the market masks discrimination based on property. But an equalization posited as possible by the "communality" in the city also manifests a contradiction, and so it can nourish, on the subjective level, an aspiration to equality. The bourgeoisie—the privileged sector of the urban classes —articulates as principles "for everyone" its particular group of ideals: liberty, equality, fraternity. In turning the political matters of equality and liberty into an ideology (or making the particular experience of one group a general truth), the bourgeoisie has pointed out at the same time, and contrary to its objective interests, a true aspect of the urban situation: the capitalist market broke through the limitations of the preurban world that represented methods of production predating capitalism. This breakthrough did away, at least on the legal plane, with the inequalities and restrictions that guaranteed the social privileges of the "orders," "feudal estates," "brotherhoods," "clans," and "families" upon which social life was based before the rise to power of the urban bourgeoisie.

The City in the Western World

The relationship between the market and authority (between the methods of production and the expansion of political rule before the advent of the Industrial Revolution), was not a simple one. Let us once again use Weber to illustrate the problems that this relationship poses. To begin with, cities had different historical origins. Some developed within the boundaries of lands in which the prince maintained, in addition to his domestically organized economy (in technical language, organized in the *oikos* manner), a settlement of artisans and merchants. In such cases, even if the purchases of the princely court eventually became important to the economic life of the local population, the city really existed in an economic sense only when a substantial part of the products of its inhabitants and of residents in the vicinity was regularly sold in the local market, which supplied the urban population. The prince guaranteed protection and permitted the market to function in lands under his rule in exchange not only for the regular supply of local products in the market (and of foreign products, when periodic fairs were held), but also for the rights of customs, guards, protection, exchange, justice, and so on, in addition to the taxes levied on the functioning of industries and commercial establishments, and the profits from the rental of land.

Not all cities, however, came into being under the protective (and demanding) custody of the prince or lord. Sometimes the urban cluster originated in the territorial grant of a sovereign who gave space, but not his protection, to the entrepreneurs. And even farther removed from the first kind of city were cities (especially in antiquity and in the first decades of the Middle Ages in the Mediterranean area) that were simple marketplaces. These cities, founded by intruders, pirates, and native or foreign traders, competed with the territorial estates of the nobles and the system of domestic production (*oikos*) that they maintained.

Many cities came into being to supply patrimonial officials or gentlemen whose source of income was outside the urban economy and who were linked to the city only as consumers, as was the case with Peking and Moscow. Cities also arose as centers of export production. This occurred in regions (like Essen) where factories were located that supplied the external market, as well as in localities where extensive artisan activity existed. Some of these cities were later organized into leagues (such as the Hanseatic) to promote the trade of their products more effectively.

In short, cities may have had a predominantly commercial, consumer, or industrial origin. More frequently, cities resulted from a combination of these different forms of economic activity. In any case, markets were established in them, and ecological specialization often led to the appearance of a special business district within the urban area: the *City* for which London was famous, for example, and which under other names existed as an important characteristic of the urban phenomenon.

The relationship beween the countryside and the city, like that between the prince and the market, was not always that of equals. Today it might appear that the city dweller always controlled the wealth and culture of the countryside, but at other periods of time this was not the case. In fact, the opposite was true of the *polis* of antiquity. Ownership of an arable tract of land (*kleros, fundos*) was a requirement for the full exercise of citizenship, unlike the situation of the burgher in the Middle Ages. The full citizen of antiquity, according to Weber (from whose work I have summarized the preceding parts of this article), was a citizen-farmer. In the Middle Ages as well there are several instances of burghers with extensive landed property.

Nevertheless, the complex of phenomena called "the urban economy" is concerned not with how the citizen organized and controlled his agricultural property, but with the interrelationship between the countryside, as supplier of the means of subsistence, and the city, as a place of industry and commerce. As Weber noted:

> It was these naturally given conditions of the urban economy which specifically "urban" economic policy attempted to stabilize by means of economic regulations in the interest of permanency and cheapness of the food supply and of stability of the economic opportunities of artisans and merchants.[1]

Weber emphasized, however, that one cannot generalize the existence of an urban economic policy for all cities.

Similarly, when the politico-administrative peculiarities of cities are analyzed, it can be seen that historically there were countless variations. Although the walled town, the city fortress, was common, there are cases of towns enclosed by palisades that cannot, for this reason alone, be considered cities, since they possessed no market. Certainly the existence of a fortress, a military lord and a social class within the towns—the burghers who had the obligation of military defense of the fortress and construction and repair of its walls, as well as the right of ownership of houses in the burgh—assured the conditions of the bourgeois peace identified with the *pax villae:* The peace of the market was guaranteed by the lord and by the defenses of the town. There are countless historical examples of coexistence of market and fortress: the Bazaar and the Casbah in the Islamic world, the *campus Martius* and the economic *fora* of Rome, etc.

The diversity of economic and politico-administrative characteristics that gave rise to the city led Weber to define it in terms of a set of circumstances necessary for its full development, among which he emphasized the existence of a fortress, a market, a judicial system of its own, an associative relationship among its members, and an at least partial capacity for decision-making and autonomy. Consequently, the city called for administration by authorities in whose selection the burghers (the residents of the towns) had to participate in some way.

The City in Colonial America

Let us now turn from historical digressions on the origins and formation of cities in the Western world. For the immediate purposes of this essay it is important to keep in mind that the city was thought of classically as a socioeconomic phenomena (division of labor, market) and as a political process (relative autonomy of the city in the face of other politico-administrative organizations). The substantiation of these processes called for formalization of certain rules and resulted in the definition of specific kinds of rights (the right of urban ownership, courts for the regulation of economic life, formulas for the definition of power and political participation, etc.).

To what extent does this approach to the urban phenomenon apply to Latin American cities and remain valid in the face of contemporary economic and social changes?

Let us begin with the first question. It is well known that in the colonial period the Latin American city originated and developed under the influence of Iberian commercial capitalism and within the limits of the metropolis-colony relationship. The policy that created it was more the result of Iberian mercantilism than of struggles between the local inhabitants and the lord. Only the prince —no longer as the lord of local domains, but only as sovereign, trusted servant of the Crown and its treasury— counted as a source of power. The city was subordinate to him, as a constituent part of the Empire.

It should be added that the model of political integration of the city that prevailed in the Americas derives from a tradition different from that which distinguished the Hanseatic, Italian, Central European, or English cities. There were indeed cities in Spain that duplicated the patterns of the cities described by Weber and Pirenne, as Morse notes.[2] They were the cities that arose on the route between the Pyrenees and Santiago de Compostela, especially in the Cantabrian region, and were often founded by pilgrims coming from beyond the Pyrenees. These "open" cities (built by the "Franks" from beyond the Pyrenees and *francas* [open] through their "free" legal status) were settlements of merchants and artisans located outside the walled cities. In the central plateau, however, in León and Castilla, the tradition was different. Here, from the tenth to the twelfth centuries, the cities were military-ecclesiastical centers, "with only slight commercial or manufacturing functions."[3]

It was this second kind of Hispanic city that influenced colonization. Politically, as Morse points out, after the reconquest and the royal centralization of the fourteenth century, the city came to depend more and more on the King, and the power of the Crown authorized and granted privileges and rights to the cities. These cities grew politically, not as a means of defense and opposition to feudal or seignorial privileges, but as a department of the state. Local administration was dependent on royal power, and this dependence was welcomed as a means of defense against feudal powers. While the cities of northern Europe joined together in loosely centralized leagues, Castilian cities were united in "brotherhoods" directed by a representative of the Crown. These brotherhoods discharged police and judiciary functions and supplied troops to the King, thereby constituting themselves as parts of the political structure of the state.

From the colonial period on, therefore, there is no possible parallel between Lima and Venice, Buenos Aires and Essen, Bahia and London, and so on. The Latin American city originated as the colonial extension of the King's presence, transferring to the colonial situation the existing relationship between the Hispanic city and the Crown.

Urban colonization in Spanish America was, of course, different from that which prevailed in Portuguese America. Sérgio Buarque de Holanda, in his enlightening chapter on "O Semeador e o Ladrilhador,"[4] pointed out that in the Hispanic conquest the city had its origin under the direct and rigid influence of the regulations written in the *Laws of the Kingdoms of the Indies*. The Spanish desire for dominion, the Castilian tenacity in conferring on nature and conquered peoples the brand of the King, led them to design "abstract cities" in which the central quadrangle of the main plaza and the straight streets leading out of it, strictly conforming to the model in the regulations, stamped local geography with the seal of metropolitan authority. The Portuguese, endowed with greater pragmatism, were less rigid in colonial city planning. They allowed their cities to spread out lazily in the disorder of narrow, twisting little streets that, sometimes level, sometimes uphill, constitute the symbiosis between the variegated and not always easily tamed nature of tropical America and the European conception of an urban settlement. The carelessness of the urban geography of Portuguese America (which gave colonial Bahia and viceregal Rio de Janeiro their appeal) was not enough, however, to reproduce in America the Western organization of the city as a politico-economic phenomenon. During the colonial period the local market did not possess the importance of the bazaars and "cities" of the West and the Mediterranean at the start of commercial capitalism, nor could local authority, represented by municipal councils, oppose the absolutism of the colonial state.

Here again, however, as in the case of the Western city, it is necessary to guard against the temptation to oversimplify. Hardoy has shown in his research that there was also a certain tendency toward adaptation in Iberian colonization. The checkerboard geometry of the cities developed slowly, through trial and error. The choice of location of cities was sometimes influenced by the pre-Columbian urban experience, as witness the cities of Cuzco, Mexico (Tenochtitlán), Bogotá, and Quito, for example.[5]

On the other hand, even the fundamental differences between European and Latin American cities must be carefully analyzed. Actually, if we set aside the fortress cities and the trading posts of the Atlantic Coast (sometimes as amalgamated as the Casbah and the Bazaar), where everything emanated from the King's military might and the external market, the other colonial cities developed for the most part as administrative centers. In this sense they were the Moscows and Pekings of the Americas. They were cities of government officials, and as a result they were tied to the Crown by umbilical cords. This brief typology, however, does not exhaust the varieties of forms of urban clusters in the colonial world.[6] There were periods and regions in which towns and cities drew closer to the Western pattern: markets, autonomy, and courts (although not a separate legal system) continued to exist and have importance in the Americas.

This last process, however, developed more strongly in the poorest and least dynamic regions of the colony. Greater autonomy was possible for an isolated village on the road between Buenos Aires and Lima than for Potosí. On the long and narrow route from Santiago to Lima (and perhaps even in Santiago), the King's commands were less oppressive for the local population than in Quito. And certainly in the south of Brazil, from São Paulo to the vague frontiers with the Hispanic-American world, local town councils were important as a source of power. They were important, however, only up to the point at which the Crown's economic and political interests opposed them. Beginning in the eighteenth century, and especially during the second half of the century, metropolitan government policy was forced to halt inclinations toward autonomy. All that was necessary was for a deposit of gold or some other precious metal to be discovered, whether in the backlands of Goiás in the remote center of Brazil, or in Cuiabá, still farther away (not to speak of the Minas Gerais region, which came to depend directly on Portugal, escaping even the control of the King's representatives in Brazil), and immediately the "city," or rather the town, lost any claim to autonomy.

Except for extreme cases, Ibero-American cities functioned more as components of the imperial system in the colonies than as centers of sovereignty and self-representation. There were *juntas de procuradores* in Cuba, New Granada, Chile, Brazil, and so on. These municipal councils, however, even when they became "heads of government" and addressed the King in the name of other cities, possessed legitimacy only as representatives of the Crown. It was to the Crown that "loyal councils" appealed, and from the Crown emanated the power and authority distinguishing the juntas and councils.

Morse, in the work cited above, accurately describes the relationship between colonial cities and the empire in the dual purpose of the urban pattern: On the one hand, the colonial city was a center for interchange among agrarian producers, producers from small villages, and the kingdom; on the other, it was a "hierarchical linchpin" that organized patrimonially the relationships among the advance posts of the empire, the dependent villages, and the tributary indigenous settlements. Thus the colonial city became "a scene of tension between claims of appropriation and those of accommodation—that is, claims exerted by a tributary hinterland upon those who would appropriate its produce and Indian labor, and claims (sweetened by rewards and franchises) made by church and state accommodating the agro-urban unit to its station in a far-flung patrimonial order."[7] Thus there was a specific calculus of forces and tensions between the lure of agrarian profits in the small villages, and the rewards of status as "part of the empire" guaranteed the cities that had greater available resources as centers of a group of agro-urban satellite villages.

Morse's interpretation permits a more sophisticated view than the simple confirmation of "rural supremacy" in the Ibero-Lusitanian world of the Americas. The dialectic between agricultural village and patrimonial state, between town dweller with rural or commercial interests and Crown official, was the backdrop for political life in the colonial city.

Hemmed in by the Crown's interests and the sea of rural properties organized with a view to the external market, the cities were politically fragile plants in the soil of scant freedom permitted in the colonial Iberian world. When there was anything like a "bourgeoisie" it often developed among a rural aristocracy that lived partly in towns and partly on estates. Otherwise, the typical city dweller was a government official, a soldier, a priest—in other words, a man bound to the bureaucratic organization of a metropolitan state or a Crown, if not that of the King, then that of Christ. Perhaps the only social type that did not fit this pattern was the merchant—not, of course, the merchant employed by the large companies, because the system of chartered companies of the mercantile period gave rise to the figure of the merchant-official —but rather the trader, the dealer, the smuggler who were the "men of the city." Even this social type, however, made a weak foundation for the city: in most cases they were foreigners (even in the nineteenth century, when the colonial pact was broken, the merchants who roamed the Americas from one end to the other were foreigners) who were linked only loosely to the towns. When this was not the case, they were themselves colonists. Portuguese and Spaniards, even in the nineteenth century, controlled a large part of local commerce. But even so, if there did exist in the Americas an urban "estate" or "establishment" not composed of officials, it was based on the merchants, "black marketeers," and shady dealers who, on the fringe of local officialdom, enriched and pressured the town councils. Next to them, although in a subordinate position, the artisans and master craftsmen carried on their battle for survival.

To sum up, the city that dotted the Iberian empire in the Americas, Lusitanian as well as Hispanic, was more a city of officials than a city of burghers. Neither the market nor local councils had the power to oppose the King's courts, colonial regulations, and the interests of the Crown, or to resist the colonial exploitation that cast Iberian royalty and bourgeoisie into the rigid mold of mercantile capitalism. At the opposite pole was the owner of land, Indians, or slaves. The official and the lord were the social types that gave life to the cities.

The city as a forum of liberty for the local inhabitants and as a market that legally equalized the economically unequal had no reason to exist here. The primary function of the colonies was to export the economic end products of a labor force that, if not actually comprised of slaves (as it was in various regions), was subject to the system of landed estates (*encomiendas*), Indian forced labor (*mitas*), and other nonmercantile forms of exploitation; and the colonies' political relationship with the metropolis derived from the complex structure of colonial patrimony.

Did this structure change with independence?

The City in the Independence Period

In the historical periodization of Latin America, the first twenty-five years of the nineteenth century mark the epoch, varying from country to country, during which the nations legally organized themselves as independent states. Economically, however, ties of dependence continued to persist. Beginning at this time, the ascendancy of English over Iberian influence became perceptible in the region. Thus, the continent (in very different degrees from region to region) came to rely more openly on European capitalist penetration for its entry into the international division of labor. The period of Lusitanian or Spanish colonial mercantilism gave way to the *laissez-faire* of British commercial policy. The contradiction between national independence, legally given substance through the existence of a national state, and economic dependence on the capitalism of the dominant countries gave rise to the stage of "national dependence."

From the point of view of the development of cities, without doubt the presence of the "capital city" constituted an important agent of cohesion in national life. In this sense, the change from the colonial condition to formal independence had noticeable impact on urban life. The revival of cities as focal points of political decision-making began in the years just prior to independence, concurrent with what historians have called "the breaking of the colonial pact." The immediate consequence was the strengthening of the markets located in the cities (shown by the presence and activity of English merchants) and the growing role of dominant local classes in the region's political life.

Until the present, the urban nature of some of the independence movements has perhaps been minimized. Nevertheless, it appears that the role of the Cabildo of Buenos Aires or of the Câmara of Rio de Janeiro was decisive in the process of independence. The possibility of more active participation of Latin American cities in politics during this period stemmed from transformations that had been taking place since the eighteenth century, especially since the last quarter of that century. Demographic growth figures indicate that the population of the region as a whole remained stable until 1750, but from then on expanded rapidly. The dissolution of commercial monopolies led to widespread prosperity (Mexico City,

Buenos Aires, Bahia, Rio de Janeiro), strengthening of
local commercial sectors, diversification of elites, and new
alliances and accommodations among the ruling classes, although without shattering the patrimonial "old regime."

Here it is appropriate to point out how urban functions
came to life in Latin American politics, and to describe
them specifically. If in Europe the city gained renown as a
city-state, in America it was the living nerve of the state-
nation. It was not the "bourgeois" in the European sense
of the term who was the agent of political experience, it
was the "native" against the "foreigner." This "native" had
his roots in the rural world and in the bureaucratic patriciate. Furthermore, frequently his first political struggle
was against those who, during the colonial period, had
constituted the foundation of urban life: strictly speaking,
the merchants. The latter continued to find it convenient
to be regarded as "foreigners," since being a "foreigner"
was strategic in bridging both external and internal markets. Thus preindependence patrimony persisted after national autonomy had been won.

Once again, quick generalizations must be avoided. In
some cities, like Buenos Aires, the port not only discharged an important cohesive function, but also grazing
lands were controlled by urban fortunes made in commerce, when not directly under the control of foreign
commercial capital.[8] The symbiosis between colonial trade
interests (later displaced by merchants with English ties)
and cattle interests created an agro-mercantile-export
bourgeoisie, under the hegemony of a unique "oligarchi-
cal-*latifundista*" sector, even though, for example, the
river Plate "oligarch" and the Brazilian *latifundiário* of the
same period had little in common as social types. The
former, despite his rural property, had been linked to the
city since the end of the colonial period. The correspondence between his interests and those of meat industries and exporters was based not only on the ties (which
also existed in other Latin American countries) with

foreign interests—the natives maintained control of production and left commercialization to the foreigners—but also on the interrelationship between urban-mercantile and agrarian capital. The Brazilian *latifundiário*, owner of land and slaves, continued to be a patriarch socially, even when he adopted the ideology of European liberalism in the political dispute under way in the city, and his access to power was determined by the prevailing patrimonialism.

The essence of the urban vitality of Buenos Aires and other Latin American cities (like Montevideo and Santiago) lies in the fact that the national economy, channeled toward the external market through narrow export corridors, was activated by a symbiotic system composed of urban capital and agrarian exploitation. Not irrelevant to this same vitality are the disputes that these cities have had to wage with other urban centers, since colonial times, for primacy in political and economic matters.

Classes and Cities

It is impossible to differentiate the dependent economies of Latin America in terms of the predominance of the external market. Yet, the manner in which social classes and subclasses organized to permit the expansion of exports led to different degrees of urbanization, creating cities as developed as Buenos Aires or as precarious as São Paulo until almost the end of the century (or at least until 1870).

The pattern of economic growth dependent on an external market did not cease to encourage, as a by-product, the formation of some urban centers throughout the region. It should be kept in mind, however, that apart from the "capital cities" (which grew as a direct consequence of the impetus from the national economy, but whose politi-

cal function, as I have pointed out, resembled on a reduced scale the general situation, in which rural life
carried more weight than urban), urban development was
mediocre in the countries in which the *latifundiária* economy grew independently of the cities.

This mediocrity was experienced most strongly in national economies supporting the slave system and other
nonmercantile forms of labor exploitation. The reason is
easy to understand: The city, as we have seen, manifests a
form of social division of labor. The system of agrarian
slavery constituted a fundamental obstacle to urbanization, since it reinforced the tendency in the *latifúndios* to
supply all their own economic needs; the *permanent* availability of the slave, even during the seasonal layoffs from
agricultural labor, led the master to use him in the production of other consumer goods.

Thus during this stage the basic impetus for urban
growth occurred with the introduction and diffusion of
free labor, especially in cases where foreign immigration
took place. Once again, the cities that had consolidated,
since the period of the breaking of the colonial pact, under
the supremacy of social classes tied to urban activities,
took the lead in the impetus supplied by immigration.
They possessed the means to assimilate migrating masses
socially and economically. In the southern part of the continent, beginning in the last third of the nineteenth century, there were cities in which foreigners predominated
over nationals. Even cities established in predominantly
agrarian areas were strengthened by immigration, since it
in itself was already an indicator of the acceleration of the
process of the social division of labor.

In the Brazilian case, it was said that coffee was a "democratic plant," as opposed to sugar cane, which was an
"aristocratic plant." In vegetal silence, coffee and sugar
tolerated these epithets stoically. In "democratic" fact,
coffee production was resorted to when slave labor was
replaced by free immigrant workers. This process, which

interrupted the tendency of the large estates (*fazendas*) toward productive autonomy, increased commercial and artisan functions in many places in the hinterland of the coffee-producing region (São Paulo). It was thanks to this, and not (as some have too quickly concluded) to the immediate and direct increase in the purchasing power of the rural immigrant worker who replaced the slave, that the internal market expanded. In this context, the growth of urban life is a much more reliable indicator of expansion of the internal market than the debatable increase in the rural laborer's consumption. The wages of these laborers were extremely low, and it is a mistake to think that the slaves whom they replaced cost nothing: they had to be fed and clothed. To assume that the rural immigrant exerted greater pressure on consumption, it is necessary to show that he was able to eat and dress better than a slave, and, further, that he could increase his consumption costs. Of course, this process occurred as well, although more slowly, and was less important than the expansion of urban life, or rather of businesses, artisan shops, and small industries of cities in the coffee regions. Simple numerical increase in the labor force played a part, naturally, in the growth of internal consumption, but this was also a direct function of the expansion of exports. In any event, the immigrant who came to carry weight in national life through his economic success was the immigrant who lived in the city, not the poor agricultural worker.

Social changes of the type described above had greatest impact in countries like Argentina, Uruguay, or Chile, where the burden of slavery was absent. In these countries the same process occurred as that described in connection with São Paulo (with countless variations, as, for example, diversification or lack of crops, greater or less access to ownership of land, etc.).

Beginning in this period, the city thus acquired new configurations. Historians have noted that since the end of the nineteenth century, rural landowners have moved to the cities. This process, which occurred over a widespread area—in Caracas as well as in São Paulo, in the Mexico City of Porfirio Díaz and in Santiago—is important not only because it is itself an indicator of urban expansion but also because at this stage the rural landowner was no longer the *senhor,* but an agrarian bourgeois. With the inevitable simplification attending those who must "sum up" in a brief essay great transformations in a region as large and varied as Latin America, it is possible to say that the process of symbiosis between the dominant urban and rural classes of Buenos Aires was widespread by the end of the century. Sometimes, however, the process was reversed: It was the rural bourgeois who moved to the city and began to consume and invest part of his surplus capital there.

In any case, a bourgeoisie existed in the city at that time. Of course, the functions of the bourgeois in this case differed considerably from those of the historical European bourgeois of early capitalism. The Latin American bourgeoisie of this period was a class of regional expression that fought in the city for supremacy of its interests in the nation, warring with other regional sectors of the same agrarian bourgeoisie, or with the mercantile and financial bourgeoisies.

The political system expressing the new harmony between the agrarian classes and the urban sectors closely tied to them was labeled "oligarchical rule" in Latin America. The imprecision of the term masks the reality of multiple alliances among different classes and sectors of classes in the different Latin American countries. Thus, as we have seen, in both Argentina and Uruguay the oligarchy was made up of various interests under the hegemony of the cattle-ranching bourgeoisie tied to exporting interests. In Brazil there were various regional oligarchies with different socioeconomic bases (sometimes purely *latifundiário*-patrimonial, as in the Northeast, sometimes agrarian-mercantile bourgeois, as in São Paulo), which were the backbone of the oligarchy. In Venezuela, before Gómez, the agrarian-*latifundista* base characterized the oligarchy, while in Peru it was determined by the alliance between the bosses (*gamonales*) of the highlands and the coastal planters (allied with the mercantile bourgeoisie).

For the purposes of this essay it is important to emphasize that, in spite of the obvious influence of the agrarian-based system of domination, the role of cities in the political system during the period of expansion of the export economy cannot be underrated. The "calculus of forces and tensions" which, in Morse's words, characterized political life in colonial cities, did not disappear with independence. The "oligarchy" in its urban form had a dual image. On the one hand, the state and the patrimonialism that gave rise to national political institutions continued to give the oligarchy a "cartorial" expression.[9] On the other, one sector of the oligarchy succeeded in adopting "enlightened" attitudes. Almost always there was a "liberal" sector of the oligarchy opposed to the conservative sector. The importance of this sector to the "modernization" occurring at the end of the century must not be minimized, nor is it possible to ignore the relationship that existed between the *city* and oligarchical liberalism.

The sons of *fazendeiros*, the middle class attached to the national bureaucracy and (later) the new immigrant middle class, encountered the seeds of reformist ideas in the schools of the urban centers. The actual course of this process varied enormously from country to country, and a brief summary is impossible. But all movements, whether concerned with social reform (abolition of slavery and peonage), political reform (establishment of the Republic of Brazil, the "liberal" ascendency in Peru or Colombia, the rule of the *científicos* in Mexico, etc.), dynamic economic change (exemplified by the activities of the "generation of '80" in Argentina), or a combination of changes (as with Chilean *Balmacedismo* or, in a different vein,

Uruguayan *Battlismo*), found a home in the cities and a stimulus in such typically urban institutions as schools and universities.

On the other hand, the antioligarchical reaction also received political impetus in the cities. Agrarian movements (of peasants, millenarians, rural "jacqueries," etc.) were the most persistent stimuli in the social struggles of the region, reaching their apogee, for the period under consideration, with the Mexican Revolution. But the political ability to present a threat to the oligarchy almost always depended on the effects in the city of the countryside's social discontent. The Mexican Revolution itself illustrates this point and, sadly enough, the liquidation of the *Zapatistas* shows how deftly the urban sectors were able to pull their chestnuts from the fire. The first thirty years of the twentieth century saw a political attack on the oligarchies. Often still under the leadership of the oligarchy's liberal sectors, the "urban masses" and middle sectors linked to the state, principally the military, began to exert political pressure. Once again it must be kept in mind that in the region as a whole there were many different kinds of social movements. Their political form also varied, from situations in which the party was the organization through which urban politics was expressed, to those in which criticism came either from a sector of the very machinery of the state itself, or through a "mass movement," or from a merger of both with some existing party.

In general, the important thing to keep in mind is that the political axis shifted from the countryside to the city, even though this was not the case with the economic axis of national life. New, ill-defined characters joined the traditional actors on the political stage: the "urban mob" that cheered Irigoyen, for example; the "middle class" parties, represented by Argentine or Chilean radicalism, as well as by the Uruguayan Colorado party; the socialist parties, as in Buenos Aires; the socialist-inclined factions of the Colombian Liberals; and finally the organizations of workers and the Communist parties, as in Peru or Brazil, and the almost universal "workers' parties." There was not always correspondence between party and class, since this politico-organizational structure developed in the context of a patrimonial society in which the "progressive" sector of the ruling classes frequently assumed political roles that corresponded to other less progressive classes. Thus, unintentionally, this "progressive" sector perpetuated enlightened paternalism. In any case, this transformation would have been inconceivable without urbanization of the region.

It should be added that, in relation to the local advance of capitalism and its corresponding social division of labor, the city carried disproportionate weight in the economy and in the political game of "the calculus of forces and tensions." "Urban life" in this sense was historically rooted in the soil of the political centralization of the colonial period and Iberian mercantilism. As a result, urban politics was a kind of ersatz for the real urban struggle: Only on rare occasions did the urban masses actually threaten the oligarchy. Usually, through the process of "expansion and incorporation," it was the social sectors connected to the state, or rural, mercantile, or industrial bourgeoisies, who defined new goals for the political system and undertook to represent the interests of the ruled classes by self-selection. When these sectors were unable to become spokesmen for popular demands, they co-opted or repressed the "pressures from below."

It is of little importance, in this general discussion, to consider the mechanisms by which the "political game" was enlarged and sectors remote from the oligarchy were incorporated into it. In some countries the electoral system of parties facilitated this incorporation. In others, political bossism (*caudillismo*) accomplished the task. In all, "compromise" tended to replace open conflict, covering up brutal social and economic exploitation and an actual political participation that was constantly deferred.

The City and the Masses

After 1930, with the increase of industrialization and the migration from the countryside to the cities, the process took a different shape. Rather than repeat well-known analyses of Latin American populism, it is important to emphasize that the process of politicization of the urban social classes in Latin America cannot be understood in terms of the classical paradigm: There was not in the remote past a struggle between urban privileges and feudalism; nor in the recent past, from the eighteenth century on, did the ideas of individualism, personal rights, representation—in a word, *citizenship*—constitute the core of urban political life in Latin America. In this sense, the peculiar relationship between class and state that characterizes patrimonialism was not dissolved, not even during the populist stage of urban politics in Latin America.

The most plausible hypothesis to characterize populism demonstrates that, as a regime of domination, it assumes an alliance between a sector of the ruling classes (which feels threatened by another sector of the same class and is unable to run the state alone) and certain sectors of the popular masses (more frequently urban rather than rural). Whether this relationship is embodied in a party or an organized movement (as Perón attempted with *justicialismo*), whether it is supported by a diffuse political movement based on labor unions (as in the case of Vargas), or whether it is based on the personal *caudillismo* of some military or civilian leader (as with the populist attempts in Peru, Bolivia, Venezuela, and Colombia at various periods during the present century), the determining factor in Latin American populism seems to have been its ability to define itself structurally by a "downward alliance." This alliance also found its survival mechanism in the state. Manipulation and exchange of benefits (votes or support by the masses vs. wages and participation) depend on control of the state apparatus. Routinization of the populist-state relationship can take place only when populist policy has established a solid union apparatus in the cities (as in Argentina). Even in the case of present-day Argentina, however, what actually exists behind the apparent populism of union policy is the manipulation of populist ritual and symbolism, aimed at a style of politics in which class interests (often in the form of trade unionism) carry more weight than the typical relationship of the populist alliance.

In any event, the political mobilization of the urban masses, in the manner in which it occurred, augmented and reinforced certain characteristics of the patrimonial state. The contract relationship between citizens and legitimation of the state as a "necessary evil" to guard against the *homo hominis lupus* were almost nonexistent in Latin American political ideology. In Latin America, one demands credentials for existence from the individual, not the state.

No doubt this tendency was not alien to the Catholic faith, in contrast with the Protestant ethic. In the latter, as we know, each individual is answerable to God for his errors, without mediators, and receives from the Lord the mark of grace as evidenced by material wealth (at least in the Calvinist ethic). Protestant individualism is so strong in the Anglo-Saxon ethic that even today the New Left emphasizes the guilt of each individual for the excesses of imperialism and of the state, and sees in the "intramundane rejection of the world"—of the Jansenist ideal, of the Catholic Pascalian version—represented by the beatnicks, hippies, and current practitioners of the counterculture, a sign of societal change. "Begin with yourself. First reform yourself, in order to reform the world." The Catholic ethic is, in this sense, more "collectivistic," and as a result less individually "responsible." It is in the bosom of the

Church, in the fusion of the individual with the mystical body of the Sacred Institution—a fusion permitted by confession, repentence, and absolution, diminishing individual guilt, once it is confessed in a whisper to one properly authorized—that salvation is to be found. No one will publicly look with sorrow at errors committed. There is a greater force to whom sins are transferred in the very act of expiation.

Under these conditions it is theoretically understandable that the state can be viewed ideologically as a father—and a benevolent one. The large bureaucratic organizations, the state and the Church, are perceived in a similar manner. An ideological element must thus be added to the description of the sociopolitical structure of Latin America: Catholic partrimonialism.

In the cities the groups that opposed the style of politics engendered by Catholic patrimonialism were for the most part minority sectors of the liberal (generally secular) oligarchy and the common people. Among the latter there was always some degree of anarchic, secular radicalism. The rising tide of urban populism, which frequently generated an alliance between oligarchical conservatism and masses eager for political participation and protection against other sectors of the oligarchy, consolidated in urban political culture a style of participation dependent on the state. It should be reiterated that this style of politics has its roots in Catholic patrimonialism and has little in common with the system of representation and suffrage bequeathed by individualistic European liberalism, even in those Latin American cases in which the "incorporation" of the masses apparently takes place through suffrage.

Parties, representation, contract, and liberalism were persistent aspirations, but not "opposition." The latter, which could not entirely disappear, consisted of some typically urban segments of the Latin American world. Those who made up the "rational legal" liberal opposition

were the middle-class parties of liberal professionals, those
sectors of the civil service appalled by the clientelism of
the state, an occasional industrialist or *fazendeiro* who
believed in the "laws of the market" and was opposed to
interventionism, etc. Often, because of their opposition to
the hybrid relationship between the state and the masses,
these groups ended up being penalized as reactionary and
oligarchical. They were labeled "aristocratic" when they
were actually "democratic," and this singled them out for
electoral defeat before the steam roller of opportunistic
paternalism allied with the impetuous masses. Only in the
countries in which patrimonialism was less deeply rooted
—Argentina, Uruguay, and, to a lesser degree, Chile—did
the parties of the middle class (that is, of the bourgeoisie
allied with the urban middle class, sometimes supported
by working-class sectors) have some chance of survival.
Even in these cases, however, urban populism succeeded
in establishing itself, although it did not do away with
the old party structure as an important political force.

The City and Current Technical-Bureaucratic Domination

The relationship between transformations in the style of
urban politics and socioeconomic changes does not fall
within the scope of this essay. The simple indication of
possible approaches leaves this task to the reader. It is obvious that behind urban populism was growth of the internal market as a focus for economic development, although
without detriment to the export economy. Similarly, the
subsequent break in the populist stage cannot be fully understood without reference to changes in Latin America's
capitalist-dependent means of production. Suffice it to say
that, at the present time, the agrarian economy and industrial enterprise that until most recently guaranteed expansion of the internal market and continuation of the export
trade have come to be influenced by and dependent on

two fundamental economic agents: the "multinational firm" and the state-owned enterprise. Both, together with the enterprises and economic activities existing during the stage prior to national and export development, came to operate within the limitations of a dependent economy ever more closely connected to the dominant centers of capitalism (with the exception of two or three countries in the region), thanks to foreign investment and the pressures of the imperialist states.[10]

The crisis of Latin American populism and the weakness of the party system tied to liberalism gave rise to two new styles of urban politics. Both (one operating in opposition to, the other within the established system) are associated nonetheless with a new order.

In mentioning innovation in the politics of opposition I refer, of course, to the guerrilla. Excluding, as I have done with populism, the current facile characterization of the meaning and scope of this kind of politics, I will limit myself to pointing out two salient features of the relationship between the guerrilla and the old style of politics in Latin America. Inspired by urban success (although he had rural antecedents outside of Cuba), the Latin American guerrilla emerged as a *rural guerrilla*. Debray, in his quasiofficial synthesis of the Left's political style in recent times, *Revolution in the Revolution*, waxes Rousseauesque in pointing out the virtues of struggle in the jungle and the mountains against the evils of the city. Guided by an ill-concealed Cartesianism, Debray begins with a *cogito*: The guerrilla exists, therefore. . . . His principal discussion does not center on the description of the struggle between social forces, the relationship between masses and party, etc., but on the defense of the tactical-strategic military superiority of the rural guerrilla. He does, however, define the advantages of the guerrilla in the political struggle and quotes Fidel Castro: "The city is a cemetery of revolutionaries and resources."[11]

Something similar to the rejection (but not intramundane) of the world and the reform of oneself as the first task of the revolutionary (as with the American New Left) characterizes the writings of Debray:[12]

> In the first stages of life in the mountains, in the seclusion of the so-called virgin forest, life is simply a daily battle in its smallest detail; especially is it a battle within the *guerrillero* himself to overcome his old habits, to erase the marks left on his body by the incubator—his weakness. In the early months the enemy to be conquered is himself, and he does not always emerge victorious from this battle.

When a guerrilla speaks with his contacts in the cities or abroad, he deals with "his" bourgeoisie, always "inclined to make unprincipled alliances."[13]

The importance of this attitude lies in the fact that it is perhaps the first great romantic rejection of the city and, with it, of the "lack of principles" of urban politics, by the Left. It is a kind of unconscious criticism of patrimonialism and its effects on the conduct of popular struggles. However, just as "the city"—an abstraction—was not "to blame" for patrimonialism and populism, "the sierra" cannot be the miraculous cure.

After ten years of guerrilla experience and almost continuous failure there occurred (although without theoretical criticism of the former position) a change of emphasis from the countryside to the city. The urban guerrilla, the Tupamaro and his kind, took center stage and opened up broader political perspectives than the earlier form of Rousseauesque Jansenism preached in the name of Marxism. The appearance of the masses and the Allende electoral victory in Chile in 1970 seem to have altered the guerrilla's initial critical position, which warned against "contamination" by cities and rabble. There still remained, however, the aversion to uncritical acceptance of the traditional style of the politics of compromise, rooted in traditional patrimonialism.

It should be remembered that even before the guerrilla experience there existed a type of massive and spontaneous reaction against the "politics of compromise" by the urban masses. The street riots typical of urban life in Santiago, São Paulo, Rio, or Bogotá were a form of savage protest against the rising cost of living or the violence of the reaction (as with the *Bogotazo* after the assassination of Gaitán or in Brazil after the suicide of Vargas). In a more politicized form, although still in large measure cast in the mold of the spontaneous uprising, the *Cordobazo* of 1968 resurrected in the urban masses the style of "savage protest" which, if it accomplishes nothing else (and I think it does), at least shows the more thoughtful that there exists in the subsoil of Latin American political life the seed of a popular attitude alien to the prevailing political patrimonialism.

The second salient characteristic, from this point of view, of guerrilla politics shows the still-potent force of the earlier historical situation. The guerrilla was conceived of as one of "the handful of men who smash the state." Guevara, through the example set by his conduct, his tenacity in standing by a decision, and his Bolivian quasi-Calvary, attempted more successfully than anyone else to show that the state is "a paper tiger." Guevara understood that the state is a "political actor" and not the mere reflection of the dominant class. Yet at the same time he incorporated into his analysis an unconvincing voluntarism: The determined, exemplary action of a handful of brave men can "smash" the enemy.

Politics, in this field of action, emerges as a relationship with the state, almost without mediation. Political groups, however small they are and however much they are inspired by abstract "class analyses," tend to go directly to the barricades. They want to "smash" the state and put a new state in its place. Often the programs of the groups and movements are plans for government administration. They think of relationships with other groups and classes in terms of the state.

The contrast between this type of attitude and political practice and the activities of U.S. leftist groups (or of national and racial minority groups in the United States) is striking. While in North America movements try to "occupy" a church, a school, or a hospital, or attempt to liberate a city block, in Latin America political imagination induces the leaders to pursue the liberation of an area in order that afterward they may smash the state and reorganize society as a whole. In the Anglo-Saxon countries the political struggle is carried on within the boundaries of "civil society," while in Latin America the privileged circle of political action is limited to the state, or at most extends to the outer periphery of civil society. The fundamental relationships, between group and group, class and class, party and masses, etc., are obscured by that sun that apparently never sets, from West to East, as in bygone days of conquest and empire: the Splendorous State. Paralleling the Left's crucial discovery of the state, there was a rebirth of faith in this irresistible force of "our America" by the bourgeoisie and the international corporations.

To sum up briefly: It would appear that expansion of industrial-financial capitalism under the control of the big corporations caused Latin American history to jump from colonial mercantilism to monopolistic capitalism, without permitting development of the bourgeois competitive capitalism that furnished the soil for the seeds of liberalism and democracy.

In the current phase of monopolistic capitalist development, the large enterprise, varied in its products and markets, geographically dispersed throughout the globe—bringing together, through internationalization, markets formerly "national"—has found its form of expression in bureaucratic administration and the technocratic ethos. To the extent that, for reasons that are not relevant here, the

Latin American national economies resisted internationalization of the market by creating state-owned enterprises and, later, associated these same enterprises with
multinational companies, the public official and the entrepreneur came to don a new uniform common to both: that
of the "technobureaucrat." The bureaucratization of the
business enterprise and the technocratization—as well as
the "entrepreneurization"—of the state are parallel
processes. It remains to be said that both bureaucratization and technocratization exemplify the control of great
capital and do not indicate the disappearance of private
property.

From the political point of view, nevertheless, this
process has relevance. Of course, it has not weakened
special-interest groups nor done away with the differences
and disagreements between the government official (especially the military man) and the businessman (especially
the representative of foreign firms).[14] But in terms of the
political relationship between the bourgeoisie and the
state, between technocratic and professional sectors of the
middle class and entrepreneurs, this transformation en-
ables the interests of those different groups to be recast in
the mold of a new corporatism. From the point of view of
the type of political regime, the old patrimonialism is giving way to governments of the authoritarian type (civil or
military) that find in monopolistic capitalism their vital
nerve.

It is not within the scope of this essay to probe the nature of the political trend in government in those Latin
American countries that have embarked upon the road of
monopolistic capitalist expansion. It is, however, necessary
to point out that this process is not taking full shape in
every country. In some, the previous stage left "demo-
cratic-liberal" aspirations and habits behind (as in Venezuela, Costa Rica, and socialist Chile). In others, the antioligarchical reaction led to noncapitalistic forms of economic
organization, as in Cuba and, embryonically, in Chile. In

all, however, large organizations—bureaucratic, business, state, or party—mark political life. It is not difficult to discern that the colonial past and continuous patrimonialism have bequeathed to Latin American political life a burdensome legacy that filters through the pores of the new society. When new forms of society try to develop as a result of capitalist impetus, it is in the state and the business enterprise (and the interrelation between them) that bureaucratization and the absence of "pressure from below" penetrate most deeply. When the new society tries to prove itself by taking the theoretically more enlightened path of socialism, it is in the party and the labor union that the tendencies toward stagnation, routine, "technicalism," and bureaucratic elitism appear most strongly.

In the context of an "urban civilization" based on "cities without citizenship," characterized by the relationship of "the calculus of forces and tensions," in which the interests of small, organized groups have always prevailed over popular interests, the current tendency toward technobureaucratic rule intensifies the apathy of the "silenced majorities." To the extent that the centrifugal force of urban life did not foster, by increasing the rational awareness of contending social interests, the definition of autonomous interests and organization of dominated groups, the risks of "enlightened autocracy"—summed up in the idea of "national development" as manipulated by the minorities in power—increased considerably.

In the past, the Latin American cultural elite frequently noted the power of patrimonialism and the impotence of liberal democracy. Without denying either tendency, I think that a critical conscience should carry the analysis further. It is necessary to consider not only the political process as it occurs, but also as it appears to us that it must become. In that way identification of potential forces of nonconformity with respect to the "natural" tendency toward bureaucratism and apathy, especially among the urban masses, and reaffirmation of ideals capable of opposing the steam roller of the "lack of urban tradition" or the "tendency toward compromise" become essential for the possible dynamization of political life. Activation of urban-industrial society requires, more than anything else, discarding the ideology of compromise, and substituting for it another, which makes conflict routine and facilitates social justification of the idea that without change, struggle, and tension it will be impossible to implement true political transformation.

In order that social changes do not languish in a pseudo reform of structures controlled by elites who think of themselves as technically and scientifically illuminated (a risk inherent in "bourgeois reforms" but not absent from socialist reforms), it is necessary that "our revolution" come from below, as a Brazilian writer wrote almost forty years ago in analyzing the emerging fascism of that epoch.[15]

Without revitalization of popular support and without an antibureaucratic ideology founded on individual responsibility and awareness of social needs, the leap from patrimonialism to technocratic corporatism could cause the peoples of Latin America to revive in the "jungle of the cities" the barbarism so dreaded by the socialists of the nineteenth century. If society is not revitalized by means of strong social movements to bring about political participation and definition of new forms of control of business, the cities, the state, and basic social institutions, there is the danger of creating a horrible new world in which the city—the ancient forum of liberty—will be replaced by Alphavilles, fully equipped, through the technology of mass communications and apathy, to propagate a kind of "frozen society."

NOTES

1. Max Weber, *Economy and Society: An Outline of Interpretive Sociology*, ed. G. Roth and C. Wittich (New York: Bedminster Press, 1968), Vol. III, pp. 1219–20.

2. Richard Morse, "Trends and Issues in Latin American Urban Research, 1965–70," *Latin American Research Review* VI (1) (Spring 1971), Part 1:3–52; VI (2) (Summer 1971), Part 2:19–75. This is the obligatory reference for anyone wishing to study the urban phenomenon in Latin America. The erudition and sensitivity demonstrated by Morse in his discussion of the process of urbanization lead the reader to see far beyond what the majority of works of this kind permit.

3. Morse, Part 1, p. 15.

4. Sérgio Buarque de Holanda, *Raízes do Brazil* (Rio de Janeiro: Luciano José Olympio Editora, 3d rev. ed., 1965), Chap. IV.

5. Jorge E. Hardoy, "La influencia del urbanismo indígena en la localización y trazado de las ciudades coloniales," *Ciencia e Investigación* XXI (9):386–405, and "El modelo clásico de la ciudad colonial hispanoamericana" (Buenos Aires: CEUR, Instituto Torcuato Di Tella, 1968).

6. In New Spain and Peru, J. M. Houston distinguishes military towns, agricultural centers, mining settlements, administrative centers, and resettled nuclei of Indians (cited in Morse, p. 5). There existed a great variety, then, of types of "cities."

7. Morse, Part 1, p. 11.

8. On this point see Tulio Halperin Donghi, "La expansión ganadera en la compañía de Buenos Aires (1810–1852)," *Desarrollo Económico* (Buenos Aires) III (1–2) (April–Sept. 1963): esp. 73.

9. An adjective derived from the word for "notary's office," given the importance for the ruling classes of requests made of the state and the processing of economic and political concessions by the state.

10. For a discussion of the forms of dependence, see F. H. Cardoso and Enzo Faletto, *Dependencia y Desarrollo* (Mexico: Siglo XXI Editores, 1969).

11. Régis Debray, *Revolution in the Revolution?* (New York: Monthly Review Press, 1967), p. 69.

12. *Ibid.*, p. 71.

13. *Ibid.*, pp. 71–72.

14. For a more detailed discussion of the conflicts and alliances between the state and the corporation, see F. H. Cardoso, "El modelo político brasileño," *Desarrollo Económico* (Buenos Aires) XI (23–44) (July 1971–Mar. 1972):217–47.

15. Sérgio Buarque de Holanda, Chap. VII, *A Nova Revolução*.

CHAPTER FIVE

URBAN SPATIAL STRUCTURE IN LATIN AMERICA[1]

OSCAR YUJNOVSKY

Introduction

The subject of the internal structure of the city has attracted less attention than other themes related to the process of urbanization in Latin America. This is somewhat surprising inasmuch as the spatial organization of cities affects the daily life of the urban population or the capacity of cities to contribute to economic and social development. There are numerous studies of social marginality, squatter settlements, or the social and political role of low-income groups, but they do not deal with the overall context of city structure.

A weak relationship between theoretical and applied research may also be noted. Research has remained mainly academic and divorced from government policy and action in the sphere of urban development planning. On the other hand, housing programs and investments in public utilities or transportation are often carried out without regard to major questions about the formation of the city. The development of urban theory will help to explain the nature of phenomena taking place in Latin American cities and to provide a framework within which policymakers and planners can judge the validity of their actions and the true possibilities of achieving their enunciated goals and objectives. The failures in implementing so many urban development plans in Latin America suggest that those plans did not take into account the sociopolitical context in which they had to be applied.

The objective of this essay is to examine the process of city structuring in Latin America in order that major forces acting upon this process may be defined. For this purpose, a general framework, definitions, and descriptions of important variables are included at the beginning. This exercise must remain a partial effort, and many assertions must be considered only as working hypotheses, because there is no systematic evidence corresponding to an urban typology in this region of the world. In addition, the differences between Latin American countries and between cities of a particular country are so great that careful analysis of specific conditions must be made before reaching general conclusions.

1. *Theoretical Considerations*

THE URBAN SYSTEM AND STRUCTURE

The object of analysis is the city's internal structure, a characteristic of the urban system. The latter is by definition a set of unit elements or components—urban activities—and their interrelationships within a certain geographic space. The actual delimitation depends upon the degree of closure adopted for identification, because the urban system is also a subsystem within higher-level systems of regional, national, and international scope. Three concepts must be distinguished for considering component units according to the different purposes of analysis or action:

a. function, the elementary unit of activity;
b. the establishment of minimum separate physical or technological units, which may or may not encompass more than one function;

c. the decision-making unit, composed of single individuals, families (households), and public or private enterprises producing goods and services (economic firms, units of association, etc.), which are the minimum generators of economic decisions (production, consumption, distribution), personal and social decisions (visits, meetings, participation, family matters, communication), or political decisions (voting, rioting, pressure, danger, etc.).

Decision-making units are minimum components of more complex decision-making subsystems of intermediate levels such as social groups, classes, oligopolies of economic firms, etc. With respect to differentiation of the first and second category, the complexity of functions performed by a single establishment—a supermarket, central department store, or major hospital—may depend upon economies of scale, while an opposite response may be functional specialization, as recent research has discovered.[2]

The urban system comprises many subsystems. When they maintain a certain constancy of their components and interrelationships over time, they are defined as *structures*. The structures are main characteristics of a system by which the latter acquires its basic content. While the urban system may change quantitatively over a certain period of time, structural change implies qualitative transformation of the system and its basic characteristics.[3] The internal spatial structure is a particular structure of the urban system. It is defined as the set of component activities in the city and the relationships they maintain from the point of view of their distribution in geographic space, and the spatial dimension of these relationships.

Different dimensions of the spatial structure may be considered, depending upon the focus of interest. However, this division into social, economic, cultural and ideological, political, military, or physical variables is adopted only for analytical purposes, because the permanent in-

teraction among them within the total urban system, as
well as their nature as components of higher-order supraurban systems, is always recognized.

The urban system is essentially dynamic. The relationships among activities imply movement, and the activities themselves change over time. Thus, formation of
urban spatial structure is a historical process that must be
analyzed by considering the different factors that were operative in the different periods of urban evolution. A his-
torical-structural approach must determine how a city
acquires a given spatial structure at a certain stage. Thus
it is not mere quantitative aggregation of activities in the
short run that should be considered, but the structure
resulting from significant changes in the long run.

ROLE OF THE STATE: DECISION-MAKING SYSTEM

The decision-making system is a basic variable for ex-
plaining urban spatial structure. Although there may be
lags from previous historical periods, each social system
tends to produce urban spatial structures that respond to
its nature and content. This does not mean that within a
certain global society one may not find special cases and
variations of a local nature that yield particular situations.
But, in general, the local case will correspond qualitatively
to that of the society at large. It is important that distinctions among formal methods of social decision-making
such as the market or centralized government do not obscure the true content of a certain social system. The
Marxist concept of the "mode of production" is excellent
in this regard: The decision-making structure of a society
cannot be artificially separated from its other structures
and institutions. The "rules of the game" pertain to certain
structures of production, social relationships, technology,
and cultural values. The field of each decisional unit is
limited by the value system and the legal-institutional
regime—that is, by the social and power structures of the
society.

Development of the internal spatial structure of the city is a process of allocating available land and location resources among activities. This process is determined according to the allocating mechanisms of the mode of production. In the capitalist mode, the basic mechanism in the economic system is the market, which functions on the basis of the decentralized decisions of demanders and suppliers of goods and services, striving to maximize their private benefits. The signals for decision-making are the prices that result from competition, the outcomes varying with the degree of market imperfection, distribution of income, and the power to control those conditions.

In the specific case of urban development, a basic condition is the situation concerning social production relationships in the land market. While landowners can extract surplus created by the society at large in the form of rent, the opportunities for appropriating land and obtaining the best locations and good environmental conditions depend upon the position of the individual decision-making unit in the social structure.

In society an urban development policy always exists, whether in implicit or explicit form. It is determined by the political system—that is, by social classes, groups, individuals, private enterprise, trade unions, professional associations, the Church, the armed forces, political parties, the government and its administrative organs, as well as by foreign interest.[4] The public sector's urban development policy is part of overall policy and is adopted as a result of political control of the state by the dominant groups. The decisions incorporate social and political valuations according to the objectives of the state and those groups in its ultimate control.

The relative autonomy of the modern capitalist state is often discussed in political science.[5] Although the institutionalized political system is the ultimate expression of economic power, it maintains relative autonomy, assuring the necessary cohesion and continuity of the social system, especially in times of acute political conflict. Governmental administration forms a subsystem of decision-making with certain relatively independent powers. Thus it is important that the objectives of the administration be considered, as well as the way its decisions are influenced by other groups in the sociopolitical structure.

The existence of different jurisdictions and levels of government in the urban system also has an impact upon the internal structure. Not only may diverse political issues and conflicts be channeled separately into each jurisdictional sphere, but even in cases of consensus or compromise there may be technical problems of administration and co-ordination. The different jurisdictions may be over areas—municipalities in a metropolitan area—or sectors—different ministries or branches of government.

The government directly influences urban development by means of investments in infrastructure, production of goods and services, and participation in the market as owner of land and buildings. It affects land subdivision and use by means of legal instruments of control and, within limits, it can also induce private action through use of the different tools of socioeconomic policy.

The relationship between private enterprise and state intervention in decision-making may vary according to the specific needs of each national society, but the profit motive and speculation are essential ingredients of the capitalist mode. However, the situation may be that of a transitional state, or one that in fact may have arrived at a qualitatively different sociopolitical system.

This analysis cannot be confined solely within the boundaries of a national society. Consideration of the international framework is particularly important in the case of Latin America, since external dependence plays a large part in shaping internal decisions to objectives of power centers located beyond national frontiers. This is not a simple one-way relationship between foreign powers and a national unit, but a complex network that depends upon the internal structure of power and the joint participation of internal and external forces in control of the system.[6]

The dependent situation strongly affects spatial structure. Cultural and consumption patterns are imported and diffused. Foreign enterprises hold favorable positions in the market due to their scale, technological know-how, financial advantages, and political power to assure preferential situations. Their location, policies, and economic linkages influence the socioeconomic structure and have strong impact upon the territorial distribution of activities.

OTHER SUBSETS OF VARIABLES AFFECTING CITY STRUCTURE

Brief reference will be made to other variables affecting urban structure.[7]

1. *Rank of population and total activity.* Population size, correlated with the number of functions performed by the city, differentiates urban areas. It is involved in the role the city plays in the network of centers and affects the size of the internal market and the structure of spatial requirements of activities: the cost of intensifying the use of land against expansion in area, and incrementing the costs of transportation must be considered with the consequent results of concentration or decentralization processes.

2. *Economic level.* The level of economic development achieved, the general capacity for investment and the amount of surplus obtained, whether internally generated or captured through trade and the balance of payments, conditions the possibilities of expansion or renewal. The overall supply of financial resources affects the total market and the behavior of decision-making units.

3. *Functional composition and socioeconomic structure.* According to its role, a city presents a certain profile of activities with different requirements of location, amount

and quality of space, and communication. For analytical purposes, it is useful to distinguish the following subsets:

a. Activities that produce goods and services. The units pertain to the public or private, national or foreign sectors, and they include economic activities in a restricted sense —manufacturing, commerce, banking, health services—as well as units of social services—clubs and neighborhood associations—with some control of fixed assets, amount of capital, relative access to sources of finance, etc.

b. Households of different social classes, with their demographic and socioeconomic characteristics. In a market system they represent the demand for residential location and space. Analysis must consider characteristics such as family formation and composition, structure of social classes and strata, and income distribution.

4. *Cultural values and ideology.* Values, ideas, and beliefs of individuals and social groups from the preferences of consumers and producers in the economic system and the objectives of participants in the political system. Styles of living are reflected in different concepts of housing design, land occupation, city location, or the use of communications media. Prejudices, social status, subjective valuation of access as compared to environmental quality, and living space enter into the decision functions of individuals, private organizations, and government. Analysis must be made specific to each social class and stratum.

5. *Technology.* This conditions the production functions of firms, the possibilities of changing natural geographic conditions, land occupation and use, or the provision of transport and communication inputs. The relative use of inputs depends upon the technology and opportunity costs determined by the system. Thus technological change may mean changes in factor intensity—the use of land, for example—or location. Technology affects the cost of information-gathering, processing, and transmission, which have an impact upon management techniques and the

relative centralization of firms or governmental administration.

6. *Physical capacity.* The capacity of the urban system is as follows:

a. Natural characteristics. The opportunity cost of land use depends upon such factors as topography, quality of soils, drainage, natural waters, existence of mineral or landscape resources, and climate.

b. Stock of buildings and physical networks of utilities such as water supply, sewerage, or electricity.

c. Networks of transport and communication that condition relative accessibility among points both within and outside of the urban area.

7. *Supraurban systems.* The city's relative position in regional, national, or international systems also affects the internal structure directly in the interurban location of activities according to the relative magnitude and direction of interchanges.

DYNAMICS OF URBAN STRUCTURE

The sets of variables are interrelated, and their concerted action must be considered in dynamic terms. Differences in the rate of growth and changes in the population and socioeconomic structure in relation to processes of investment and adaptation of the physical structure must be examined. Physical elements present some immobility depending on their type, characteristics, and the opportunity cost of their replacement. Given the set of activity requirements and installed capacities, there may be compatibility, deficits, or idle capacity for certain sectors according to the objectives and functioning of the decision-making system. Lack of achievement of a desired level may result in either changes in the pattern of activity requirements or transformation of the physical structure, whether decided centrally or in the market.

Transformation may take place by expansion into new areas of the city or renewal of existing ones. The trend depends upon the general level of the economy, opportunity costs, and the state of sectors involved in the process of transformation. These sectors are influenced by conditions in the construction industry, availability of finance, technological innovation capacity or management know-how, and initiative. The process originates multiple system repercussions. Distribution of activities in terms of land use generates changes in the direction, intensity, and composition of flows of communication and transport. In accordance with available networks and information on them, the flows orient themselves on minimum cost paths. The thresholds of capacity and the appearance of higher costs and congestions, however, influence the search for new paths. On the other hand, the resulting levels in the communication and transportation networks in terms of time-distance, monetary costs, accidents, or comfort, are inputs considered in the location and space-consumption decisions of decentralized units or by governmental administrative and planning bodies.[8]

As noted above, what is important is the consideration of a certain structure that possesses by definition a certain durability, and not the mere summing up of activities and relationships. There are difficulties in the analysis in that there may be long lags before the impact of certain variables. Changes in the decision-making system itself or in technology can be felt.

2. *Latin American City Structure*

HISTORICAL ANTECEDENTS

According to our theoretical framework, analysis of the internal structure of cities must be conducted on the basis of a historical approach. However, this essay will review only briefly certain major factors that affected the development of Latin American cities in the past, so as to concentrate on the present population data.

From the point of view of internal city structure, the usual stages that are considered in a general study of urbanization[9] can be readily compressed into three main categories:[10]

   a. the colonial city (1530–1810);

   b. the city of commercial capitalism (from the second half of the nineteenth century up to 1930);

   c. the city of industrial and financial capitalism (contemporary).

The colonial powers imported to Latin America their contemporary practices of urban form, although they also incorporated the results of experience and contact with New World conditions. The predominant urban form in Spanish America was the regular checkerboard pattern (classical model),[11] which developed in America by evolution. It has been shown that legislation by the Crown—finally codified in the Law of the Indies—was a later event, which supported this development.[12] In the Portuguese colonies, forms similar to the irregular maritime-commercial cities of Portugal were introduced, while the cities under Dutch domination show examples of coastal urban development with canal (as in Recife).[13]

The colonial city is the result of a particular social structure and decision-making system. Society was organized on the basis of rigid stratification in which landowners occupied a privileged position together with high government officials, the clergy, and businessmen connected with external trade. This privileged group was clearly different from the merchants, foremen, craftsmen (*mestizos*), Indians, and black slaves who comprised the labor force for agricultural or manufacturing activities.

In Spanish America the city was structured on the basis

of planned decisions by the original founder and later by the *cabildo* (local municipal council), which was less democratic than its counterpart in Spain and represented the interests of the landed and privileged class. At first, the layout of main buildings was determined and land was given to the early settlers in quantities and locations (with respect to the central plaza) that varied with social rank. Land was granted for private use (*mercedes*), but this was simply a first stage for acquiring legal ownership once the user complied with certain tenure requirements. There were other forms of access to land, such as formal recognition by the *cabildo* of illegal occupation (*confirmaciones*), but the important conclusion is that the land market ultimately functioned through the police power of the *cabildo*, and its direct decisions on general layout, investments in infrastructures and provision of services.[14]

Ownership of land was a basic symbol of social stature, as was central location in the city, considering the high costs of mobility in a horse-powered transportation technology. The result in terms of social ecology was the concentric organization of the city around the segregation of social strata. Residences of the highest stratum occupied a central position, and the poor lived in the periphery.[15]

The period from the second half of the nineteenth century up to approximately 1930 has been designated by many authors as a distinct stage of Latin American development, during which the area became totally dependent on the world capitalist system. Rapid economic growth took place through exports of minerals and agricultural products to expanded European and U.S. markets, while foreign capital was channeled into the Latin American economies for exploitation of natural resources, investments in transportation (railways), and public utilities. The growth process was facilitated by the termination of internal civil wars and the national political organization of the Latin American countries, with the exception of Brazil, where many traits of this period appeared even earlier. Certain countries—the southern cone of South America—also experienced a wave of European-born immigration, which had great impact upon their sociodemographic structures. In general, there was an accelerated process of urbanization and metropolitanization during this period.

Several factors acted upon the city of commercial capitalism:

a. There was little governmental control and total reliance on the capitalist market as the allocating mechanism. Landowners, auctioneers, and subdividers speculated on the basis of individual lots.

b. Technological change in transportation—streetcars and railroads—contributed to the supply of land along axes of development. The private transportation companies—many foreign concerns—also participated in the land market and benefited from the increase in land values along the axes.

c. The new economic structure created new activities with different location requirements—e.g., leading export sectors and linked services, industries, and services oriented to the internal market.

d. Wealth accumulated by absentee rural landowners, mine proprietors, and entrepreneurs connected with the growing economic sectors of international trade caused an increase in the demand for upper-class housing.

e. But demand also shifted through the importation of new values and ways of life, which changed housing and location preferences. The house with a patio gave way to nineteenth-century architecture.

f. The government also adopted the new symbols in public buildings, formal parks, and Haussmanian boulevards and diagonals in general layouts.[16]

g. Increased public-sector budgets permitted higher public-investment capacity and development of urban utilities and services according to new technological possibilities.

Metropolitan areas expanded along major routes and transportation lines. The upper classes moved to new residential districts at the borders of existing urbanized areas, as in the "Barrio Norte" in Buenos Aires, a typical expression of the earnings from Pampean exports—or to detached suburban nuclei located on former vacation sites or new areas with high environmental quality and accessibility, as in the commuter quarters of Belgrano and Flores in Buenos Aires; San Isidro, Miraflores, and Magdalena in Lima;[17] and Copacabana in Rio de Janeiro. "Exclusive" subdivisions were also accompanied by governmental backing and investments in utilities and services.

The decentralized nuclei strengthened development of residential sectors along axes of higher land values. Segregation was assured by the fact that these axes eluded new or already existing groupings of industrial or commercial activities or open land with low environmental conditions.

Other population strata had the following alternatives:

a. occupation by succession of central areas abandoned by the upper classes and initiation of slum areas (Callejones in Lima, Conventillos in Buenos Aires);[18]

b. peripheral location in lower-priced, low-density subdivisions in areas of urban expansion or consolidation;

c. location around old or new decentralized foci or economic activity where the main factors of household location were accessibility to employment and consequent reduction in transport costs, coupled with low land prices.

THE CITY OF DEPENDENT FINANCIAL AND INDUSTRIAL
CAPITALISM

The period of growth on the basis of the external sector ended with the crises suffered by capitalism in this century. The World Wars and the Great Depression paved the way for import substitution of industrial goods in Latin America. In the first phase, industrialization took place as production of goods for final consumption centralized in big cities, especially the capitals. But heavy industry also gave rise to new specialized urban centers and industrial districts within existing cities.

The period shows acceleration of the urbanization process, accentuation of regional inequalities, and concentration of population in large cities. Natural increase and internal migration contribute to urbanization in varying proportions in the different countries. But in discussing their relative weight, the role of factors of "attraction" of big cities vs. factors of "expulsion" due to the structural situation in rural areas, the causes of metropolitan concentration or the size of the tertiary sector, one must keep in mind the extensive literature on the subject.[19] Thus, only certain characteristics of the urbanization process at the local level and their impact upon internal structures will be stressed here.

DECISION-MAKING SYSTEM

The first attempts at urban planning with contemporary criteria took place in this period. After a purely physical planning approach, the stage of interdisciplinary teams was reached, but the majority of proposals were not carried out or were reduced to a timid master plan focused on a zoning ordinance, but lacking adequate instruments for implementation in the financial, administrative, or legal spheres.

There is a disparity of situations in Latin America, running from the total nonexistence of technical planners to those few cities that enjoy well-staffed planning bodies within the municipal machinery. However, even when it exists, local planning is not integrated coherently with other levels of the governmental decision-making system. The municipal government plays a small role in Latin America; the central government and its decentralized agencies control financial resources and are in charge of major public works. The government and these agencies affect the local level directly or indirectly without co-ordination among them or with the municipal level. Metropolitan areas lack an adequate system to co-ordinate the different municipal jurisdictions. In addition to all these difficulties, Latin American political instability conspires against the continuity of technical and administrative action.

The real decision-making mechanism conforms to the sociopolitical regime of dependent capitalism. Foreign interests control key sectors of the economy, which provide high rates of return or growth, or possess strategic characteristics. Control is assured by the size of investment and oligopolistic conditions in the market, but it may also be exercised through the channels of marketing and communications, the financial sector, or by influencing government policy. The latter depends also upon the flow of funds and pressures in the international system of power.

There are differences among the Latin American countries in the degree of state intervention. Although there are interferences such as rent control or direct public-housing investment, resource allocation in real estate is determined in the marketplace. The private sector owns the majority of urban land, and absolute private property rights are not affected by constitutional reforms that specify that property should perform a social function.[20] The proportion of public lands is very small, and zoning and fiscal controls cannot stop land speculation. The problem is aggravated in those countries in which inflation distorts the structure of investment in favor of the real-estate market. This results in excessive subdivision and low density at the urban periphery, as well as more political difficulty in controlling high densities in central areas.

The specific situation of each country must, of course, be considered. The case of Cuba is the exception to the general rule, since the shift in the sociopolitical regime introduced radical changes in the system of urban structuring and growth. The Revolution passed legislation to control the market and eliminated land speculation, especially Law 691 of 1959, which compelled the sale of vacant lots and established a method for determining the price of land. But on October 14, 1960, an urban-reform law was incorporated into the Constitution that entirely eliminated the capitalist market in real estate and assured the viability of the planning process and improvement in living conditions of lower-income groups.[21]

In other countries, like Chile under Allende, the state contributes a substantial proportion of the total production of housing destined for the low-income population, but lack of control over the land market conspires against the reduction of ecologic segregation.[22] In Costa Rica, the Housing Institute has purchased sizable amounts of land on the periphery of main cities, which will facilitate implementation of housing programs, although the same limitation holds with respect to the location of social groups.

SOCIOECONOMIC STRUCTURE

Industrialization changed the "activity mix" of the cities in which it developed, creating different location and space-consumption requirements. In spite of the fact that national capital was the key to development of the manufacturing sector in its first stage, as in Brazil or Argentina, the last phase is the multinational industrial concern in dynamic, capital-intensive sectors using new technology. It contrasts with the small labor-intensive firms in vegetative branches or linked to the dynamic sector. The type of industrialization is a major factor in the failure of the social system to provide the number of jobs demanded in the labor market.[23] Unemployment and underemployment are by no means restricted to the stratum of poor rural migrants.

In some countries, such as Argentina and Uruguay, a process of income distribution and extension of the middle sectors of the population developed; but in others, at a certain stage, distribution is more skewed. Ethnic composition and place of origin must be considered in analyzing the structure of housing and locational demand, in that they help to explain the settlement of poor migrants from border countries in Buenos Aires, or of Sierra *cholos* in Lima vis-à-vis the inhabitants of the coast.

With reference to participation in the housing submarket, the following categories may be considered:

a. Upper- and middle-to-upper-income groups who can save and borrow in the private financial sector.

b. Lower-to-middle-income groups with some saving capacity. In some cases they may receive help from the government in the form of loans or public housing. The purchase of individual lots in the periphery, made possible by the system of installment credit provided by developers, is the most important system of market participation of low-income groups in cities like Buenos Aires or São Paulo, where the level of income permits.[24]

c. Low-income groups in central area slums occupied by processes of ecologic succession (*callejones, conventillos, casas de vecindad,* etc.), and

d. Low-income groups in squatter settlements. The budgetary constraints of these families are such that they must resort to invasions of public or private lands, and their numbers increase proportionately with the decreasing capacity of the city to provide jobs, and the type and characteristics of migrations.[25] But recent research has discovered that the population in squatter settlements also includes old urban dwellers and people with fairly stable jobs, who have previously participated in some other housing submarket. Invasions are organized by people living in central slums or in other squatter settlements in a process of community decision-making and control, as has been analyzed for Santiago de Chile and Lima.[26]

CULTURAL VALUES AND IDEOLOGY

Our analysis cannot be separated from the study of social classes and groups. We want only to refer to the introduction of mass consumption patterns from abroad—values tied to suburbanization and use of the automobile—which have great impact upon housing preferences and the structure of the city.

The apartment building is widely adopted in certain areas of Latin America by middle-to-upper-income groups. Condominium or rental apartments replace old buildings in central areas, prestigious decentralized quarters, or along main radial avenues. The other trend, however, is toward suburban automobile-oriented living. Although no systematic empirical research has been carried out, one is tempted to hypothesize that there is a direct relationship between cultural dependence on the United States and adoption of single-family detached housing in a suburb as a symbol of the "American way of life." The trend can be seen by comparing the situation of countries in Central America with the southern cone of South America, where European living styles present an alternative cultural image. Of course, other variables must be considered, such as distribution of income and the opportunity costs of different housing types in each economic system.

TECHNOLOGY

The transfer of technology in relation to industrialization is a matter of serious research and concern today in Latin America. The impact upon the structure of the economy and the labor market has already been cited. One characteristic that must be emphasized is the role played by motor transportation in the contemporary period. The truck slowly replaces other means of transportation, and the automobile is widely adopted by families with purchasing power. This trend not only derives from the technological comparative advantage of the motor vehicle, but also is sustained by government policy and the interests of car manufacturers. The bitter experience of developed countries is not recognized, and public mass transportation is denied support in favor of freeway construction in the big metropolises.

PHYSICAL CAPACITY

The form of the city and general accessibility depend upon natural geographical characteristics and the transportation systems. Buenos Aires and Rosario, in Argentina, are coastal cities that can expand in all directions into their hinterlands, with limits posed only by lowlands of small rivers and their effluents. This contrasts with cities like Caracas, Bogotá, or Guatemala City, in which urbanized areas must extend narrowly among mountain valleys. Rio de Janeiro or Lima-Callao are also located on the coast, but they are bordered by mountain ranges. While some urban areas are based almost exclusively on motor transportation, like Bogotá or Caracas (in the latter an extended network of freeways has been substituted for the old historical layout), in other cases, suburban commuter trains still exercise a radial influence, as in Buenos Aires.

The internal structure of a city varies with the inclusion of each example in a typology that contemplates the incidence of these different characteristics. Reference will be made here only to cities varying in population rank and according to whether they developed spontaneously or are new towns originated by centralized processes.

1. *Metropolitan areas.* These multifunctional units developed on a great scale, in many cases by conurbation around secondary and tertiary centers. Expansion follows

the direction of main transportation axes, but eventually intermediate areas are also urbanized. Maximum land values are at the city center, which is contiguous but excentric to the old historic core in the direction of the higher-income population. The new high-density centers of office buildings, commercial establishments, and hotels have sprung up through renewal when there is demand for central location and financial resources for investment, as in Buenos Aires (concentration along Santa Fe Avenue), Mexico City (Paseo de la Reforma and Insurgentes), Greater Santiago, São Paulo, or Lima-Callao. In all these cases there also exist secondary decentralized nuclei, in contrast with Guatemala City, where there is almost no renewal, or Caracas, where the new commercial alignment suburbanizes along the "Sabana Grande."

Residential ecology shows sectoral or axial development. Upper strata are located along the northern radius in Buenos Aires and Bogotá; in the east in Greater Santiago (Vitacura and Las Condes) and Caracas; in the south in Lima-Callao (San Isidro-Miraflores), Mexico (Coyoacán, San Angel) and Guatemala City; in the west in Santo Domingo; and in the southwest in São Paulo.[27] Where there is more polarization of classes, ecologic segregation is clearer. While in Caracas the structure tends to a dichotomy between west and east (the *rancheríos* occupy high slopes on the border of the urbanized area), in Buenos Aires, where the middle-income groups comprise a high proportion of the metropolitan population, there is a circumferential gradient from the northern axis toward the south, which is the area of lower income; at the same time, there are "islands" or "interstices" that escape the general trend.

Apart from the upper-class axis, there is also a trend toward low-income groups from the center to the periphery, contrary to the ecology of U.S. cities. This is due to the small size of the central slum area as compared with the number of low-income persons living on small peripheral lots, which they own, or in squatter settlements.

The axis of upper-income groups includes the sites of all kinds of land uses linked to purchasing power—sports clubs, parks, playgrounds—complete provision of services and utilities, and high environment quality in general. The extension of water or sewage systems does not reach low-income areas, where only the main arteries are paved. At the periphery, there is low density, and the borders fade into agricultural uses due to the land's ripening for urban use according to expectations of increases in value.

There are also differences in industrial districts. While small firms locate within the center of the urbanized area, modern manufacturing plants develop in the low-density peripheries that have highway access, as in Lima along the Carretera Panamericana: Rosario, Argentina, along Route 11 to the north; and Buenos Aires on the northern-access freeway (Route 9).

2. *Nonplanned intermediate-size and small cities.* The results of various studies allow certain generalizations[28] for this category of city (below 100,000 in population). Cities that function on the basis of tertiary employment with central location should be treated differently from industrial cities that add other employment foci in peripheral areas. The former are organized according to the classical structure, with decreasing density and rings of residential location following isotransportation cost curves with respect to the city center. The other foci of attraction of the second group introduce alterations into this scheme.

Studies have confirmed the general position of the upper stratum at the city center, surrounded by middle-income groups and finally lower-income strata in a peripheral location at low density. Provision of services and utilities also decreases from the center to the periphery. Thus, the colonial pattern of valuation of accessibility and a prestigious central location is maintained whether the upper strata live in the old patio-houses or in new apartments. However, there are also incipient suburban areas where single-family houses with gardens are located near main-access roads. The centripetal or centrifugal trend of middle and upper strata depends upon city size, the degree of penetration of suburban patterns of life, and relative diffusion through use of the automobile.

3. *Planned cities.* New towns have grown in this period through central decision-making processes. Two commonly cited examples are Brasilia, the new capital of Brazil, and Santo Tome de Guayana in Venezuela.[29] Both cities are successful in terms of their roles in population attraction and regional development, and they both show the potential for developing functionally superior cities by applying urban-planning techniques. These cities were made possible by public control of land through Novacap and the Guayana Development Corporation, in Brasilia and Guayana, respectively. In spite of this, the basic structural characteristics of these urban societies determined different locational and environmental conditions according to class structure and the distribution of income. The physical plan must thus be in accordance with the social regime.

Conclusions

Latin American urban structure reflects the dependent nature of its history. In its last phase of dependent capitalism, the social system shows internal domination by a capitalist class linked to foreign interests. This dominant class controls major fixed assets and resources and state decision-making by means of the political system, which assures full enforcement of the institutionalized market system. This permits the appropriation of urban space—land

and location resources—conquered in the competition with social groups.

The social class structure determines segregation. The city is divided in two: an "urbanized" part inhabited by the dominant upper strata of the society, with a high level of infrastructure services, community facilities, and environmental quality in general; and another in which the dominated social groups are relegated to an inferior position, with lower accessibility, poorer living environments, and deficits of public services and utilities, as well as insecurity of tenure and instability on the land. The urban ecology shows the inability of the social system to integate marginal strata, the differentiated situation of social classes, the general characteristics of underdevelopment, and the problems of the global society.

The system of city structuring adopted in Latin America is reflected in many problems, which are more evident in the growing metropolises. Land is not used efficiently as a resource. Very high densities and congested centers result from competition for accessible locations, while great sections of the city have very low densities and countless vacant lots. The city's expansion takes place in rural areas of high productivity, and urban agglomerations make food supplies more expensive. There is also occupation of flooded or dangerous areas, mixing of incompatible land uses, absence of open space, air and water pollution, and destruction of the natural landscape and the cultural and historical heritage. Transport systems do not take advantage of the possibilities of each transportation mode. What must be stressed is that dominant groups in urban society are also affected by many of these problems merely through living in the city.

Under the present circumstances of increasing urbanization, there is a growing conviction that "laissez faire" cannot be the answer to the problems of Latin American cities. The importance of formulating urbanization and urban development policies at the different levels of government is recognized, as is the urgent need to organize administrative machinery and legislation to assure implementation of plans and programs of urban and metropolitan development. However, it must also be recognized that the results will be disappointing if there are not profound transformations in the social system and methods of resource allocation and decision-making. As we have attempted to point out, the city is structured according to the true socioeconomic forces that shape it and the true "rules of the game" because each urban structure is a reflection of the social regime that generates it.

NOTES

1. This essay draws heavily on my book *La Estructura Interna de la Ciudad: El Caso Latinoamericano* (Buenos Aires: Interamerican Planning Society, 1971).

2. Albert Berry, H. Gardiner Barnum, and Robert Tennant, "Retail Location and Consumer Behavior," *Papers and Proceedings of the Regional Science Association* IX (1962).

3. Maurice Godelier, *Racionalidad e Irracionalidad en la Economía* (Mexico City: Siglo XXI Editores, 1967).

4. Marcos Kaplan, *Aspectos Políticos de la Planificación en América Latina* (Montevideo: Editorial Tierra Nueva, 1972).

5. Nico Poulantzas, *Clases Sociales y Poder Político en el Estado Capitalista*, (Mexico City: Siglo XXI Editores, 1969).

6. Fernando H. Cardoso and Enzo Faletto, *Dependencia y Desarrollo en América Latina*, (Mexico City: Siglo XXI Editores, 1970). See also Aníbal Quijano, "Redefinición de la Dependencia y Proceso de Marginalización en América Latina, (Santiago de Chile: mimeo. UN/Economic Commission for Latin America [ECLA] 1970).

7. A discussion of variables affecting city structure within a different framework is presented by Leo Schnore, "On the Spatial Structure of Cities in the Two Americas," *The Study of Urbanization*, eds. Philip M. Hauser and Leo Schnore (New York: John Wiley & Sons, 1965).

8. This approach is adopted for evaluating short-run changes in city structure in mathematical land use and transportation models. See, for example, Britton Harris (ed.), *Journal of the American Institute of Planners*, Special Issue XXXI (2) (May 1965) and Ira S. Lowry, "Seven Models of Urban Develop-

ment: A Structural Comparison," *Urban Development Models*
Special Report 97, ed. George C. Hemmens (Washington, D.C.:
Highway Research Board, 1968).

9. See, for example, Jorge E. Hardoy's essay included in this
volume.

10. Although the pre-Columbian stage strongly affected the
ecology of later urbanization, it had only slight effect on the internal structure of cities, e.g., location of colonial buildings on
top of native bases or irregular plans where that practice extended to a whole city, as happened in the case of Cuzco. The
settlements established by the Spaniards and Portuguese before
the definitive conquest of the Aztec and Inca empires
(1492–1530) were precarious, although some fairly regular
plans were attempted. On the other hand, development in the
latest period of the colonial regime (second half of the eighteenth century) did not alter city structure substantially. Rather,
changes derived from the weakening of monopoly ties, economic growth, accumulation and greater capacity to invest,
coupled with administrative reforms, which allowed the main
cities to expand, increase their densities, achieve a higher level
of infrastructure and services, and arrive at a state of clearer
differentiation. Finally, the replacement of old colonial institutions brought about by political independence did not affect
city structures until much later, in the second half of the nineteenth century.

11. Jorge E. Hardoy, "El Modelo Clásico de la Ciudad Colonial Hispanoamericana; Un Ensayo sobre la Legislación Urbana
y la Política Urbana de España en América durante las Primeras Décadas del Período Colonial," paper delivered at II
Simposio de Americanistas (Stuttgart: August 1968).

12. Woodrow Borah, "La Influencia Cultural Europea en la
Formación del Primer Plan para Centros Urbanos que Perdura
hasta Nuestros Días," *Revista de la Sociedad Interamericana de
Planificación* 5 (17) (March–June 1971):3–15; also, Jorge
E. Hardoy, works cited.

13. For a typology of colonial physical structures see George
Kubler, "Cities and Culture in the Colonial Period in Latin
America," *Diogenes* 47:53–62, and Jorge E. Hardoy, "La
Forma de las Ciudades Coloniales en Hispanoamérica," (Buenos
Aires: Centro de Estudios Urbanos y Regionales, Instituto Tor-
cuato di Tella, July 1971).

14. Municipal ordinances assured the continuity and width of
streets, maintained land uses within property lines, dispensed
building permits only to registered, authorized builders, and
imposed property taxes according to street frontage for street

maintenance. But there were also zoning controls for assuring that unsanitary or dangerous activities were located in the periphery, or for protection of sources of water supply. See Ralph Gakenheimer, "Decisions of Cabildo on Urban Physical Structure," *Actas y Memorias del XXXVII Congreso de Americanistas* I (Buenos Aires, 1969).

15. This model must consider the specifics of each particular example and the distortion introduced by accessibility costs along the street pattern and main-access roads. The western areas of Caracas were already occupied by the poor at the beginning of the sixteenth century. In Buenos Aires, the upper stratum lived in the area south of the main plaza, while the poor located especially in the western end of the city.

16. Two clear examples are the cities of La Plata, the new capital of the province of Buenos Aires, Argentina (1883), with two diagonals superimposed on a perfect checkerboard pattern, and Belo Horizonte, now capital of the state of Minas Gerais, Brazil (1895), planned with a similar French-inspired layout.

17. Alberto Regal, *Historia de los Ferrocarriles de Lima* (Lima: Universidad Nacional de Ingeniería, Instituto de Vías de Transporte, 1965).

18. In 1909, 10 per cent of the population of Caracas (7,533 inhabitants) lived in *casas de vecindad* or *ciudadelas*, with an average of 18 persons per dwelling. Miguel Acosta Saiques, "La Vivienda de los Pobres," *Estudio de Caracas* (Caracas: Universidad Central de Venezuela, Editorial de la Biblioteca, 1967). The immigration wave into Buenos Aires determined the abrupt growth of population overcrowded in *conventillos:* In 1880 there were 51,915 persons living in 1,770 units, for an average of 29 persons per unit and 2.1 per room. The figures 12 years later were 120,847 persons (20 per cent of the population), with 55.1 persons per unit and 3.8 per room. "Estudio del Plan de Buenos Aires. Evolución de Buenos Aires en el tiempo y en el espacio," *Revista de Arquitectura* 375–76 (Buenos Aires, 1955).

19. Richard M. Morse, *La Investigación Urbana Latinoamericana: Tendencias y Planteos* (Buenos Aires: Ediciones SIAP, 1971); Philip M. Hauser (ed.), *La Urbanización en América Latina* (Santiago de Chile: UNESCO, 1961); Osvaldo Sunkel, "Desarrollo, Subdesarrollo, Dependencia, Marginación y Desigualdades Espaciales: Hacia un enfoque totalizante," *EURE* 1(1) (Oct. 1970):13–49.

20. Jorge E. Hardoy, Raúl Basaldúa, and Oscar Moreno, *Política de la Tierra Urbana y Mecanismos para su Regulación en*

América del Sur (Buenos Aires: Centro de Estudios Urbanos y Regionales, Instituto Torcuato Di Tella, Editorial del Instituto, 1968). See also their essay in this volume.

21. Maruja Acosta and Jorge E. Hardoy, *Reforma Urbana en Cuba Revolucionaria* (Caracas: Editorial Síntesis Dos Mil, 1971).

22. Fernando Kusnetzoff Katz, "Aspectos Espaciales de la Programación de Vivienda y Equipamiento Comunitario en Relación con Santiago Metropolitano," *Seminario sobre Programación de Vivienda y Equipamiento Comunitario*. (Santiago de Chile: PLANDES, May 1967).

23. Mario Robirosa, "Población, Ocupación y Distribución del Ingreso en la Argentina: Un ensayo de investigación," *Revista de la Sociedad Interamericana de Planificación* V (20) (Dec. 1971):25-31.

24. Fernando H. Cardoso, Cândido P. Ferreira de Camargo, and Lucio Kowarick, "Consideraciones sobre el Desarrollo de São Paulo: Cultura y Participación," *EURE* 1(3) (Oct. 1971).

25. The Lima *barriadas* grew after the 1940 earthquake. In 1949, they comprised 25,000 inhabitants, but in 1955 the figure was 120,000 inhabitants (10 per cent of the metropolitan area). In 1961, the proportion had reached 20 per cent, and in 1967 it was 25 per cent of a metropolitan population of 2.6 million inhabitants. Oficina Nacional de Planeamiento y Urbanismo, *Plan de Desarrollo Metropolitano Lima-Callao. Esquema Director 1967-1980*. (Lima, 1967). In 1953, the *rancheríos* of Caracas comprised 310,972 inhabitants, and it was estimated that the proportion was 30 per cent of a total population of 1.7 million in 1966. Richard Morse, "Recent Research in Latin American Urbanization. A Selective Survey with Commentary," *Latin American Research Review* 1(1) (Fall 1965) 35-74. In Buenos Aires, the *villas miseria* comprised 8 per cent of the total metropolitan population in 1968.

26. John Turner, "Uncontrolled Urban Settlements: Problems and Policies," *United Nations Seminar on Development Policies and Planning in Relation to Urbanization*, ed. Tercer Mundo (Bogotá, 1969); United Nations, Department of Economic and Social Affairs, *Improvement of Slums and Uncontrolled Settlements*, Report of the Interregional Seminar (Medellín, Colombia-New York, 1971).

27. Armand Mattelart, "La Morfología Social de una Capital Latinoamericana: Santiago de Chile," *Cuadernos de Economía*, Universidad Católica de Chile 4(11) (1967):15-47; Edmundo Flores, *Tratado de Economía Agrícola*, (Mexico City:

Fondo de Cultura Económica, 1961); Jorge Goldemberg, Joaquín Fisherman, and Horacio Torres, "Déficit Habitacional y Tendencias Ecológicas en la Ciudad de Buenos Aires" (Buenos Aires: *SUMMA*, Aug. 1967), No. 9; Mario Larangeira, "Resumo do Estudio da Estrutura Urbana de São Paulo," *Cuadernos Latinoamericanos de Economía Humana* 1(3) (1958):268–95; Instituto Geográfico Universitario-Universidad Autónoma de Santo Domingo, *Encuestas de Ingresos y Gastos Familiares en la Ciudad de Santo Domingo* (Santo Domingo: 1969).

28. Leo Schnore, op. cit.; Andrew H. Whiteford, *Popayán y Querétaro, Comparación de sus Clases Sociales* (Bogotá: Facultad de Sociología, Universidad Nacional de Colombia, 1963); Floreal H. Forni, "Análisis Ecológico de una Ciudad Media," *Cuadernos del Centro de Estudios Urbanos y Regionales*, 4 (Buenos Aires); Floreal H. Forni and Mario Robirosa, "Estratificación y Distancia Social en Tres Localidades del Centro de la Provincia de Santa Fe," *Desarrollo Económico* 5(20) (Buenos Aires, 1966); Alberto Sireau, *Teoría de la Población, Ecología Urbana y su Aplicación a la Argentina* (Buenos Aires: Ed. Sudamericana 1966).

29. See Corporación Venezolana de Guayana, *Informe Anual* (1963), and Jorge E. Hardoy, "The Planning of New Capital Cities" *Planning of Metropolitan Areas and New Towns* (New York: United Nations, 1967).

CHAPTER SIX

URBAN LAND: POLICIES AND MECHANISMS FOR ITS REGULATION AND TENURE IN SOUTH AMERICA*

JORGE E. HARDOY
RAÚL O. BASALDÚA,
AND OSCAR A. MORENO

I. *General Characteristics of Urbanization in Latin America*

The rate of demographic growth of the population of Latin America, particularly the urban population, is the highest in the world. Within Latin America, the growth rates for South America are slightly lower than those for the area as a whole, but the percentage of urban population is higher. In 1960, according to national censuses undertaken in or near that year, Latin America's total population was 206,560,000 inhabitants, and its urban population was 99,777,000, or 48.6 per cent of the total population.[1] In the same year, South America's total population was 145,003,000 inhabitants, and its urban popu-

* This essay is based on findings derived from research conducted by the authors for the UN Center for Housing, Building, and Planning in 1967–68. Originally published as "La tierra urbana: Políticas y mecanismos para su regulación y tenencia," *Desarrollo Económico* (Buenos Aires) 9 (34) (July–Sept. 1969):163–93. English translation by Felicity M. Trueblood.

lation was 76,774,000, or 52.8 per cent.[2] It is estimated that South America's total population will reach 248,517,-000 inhabitants in 1980, and that its urban population will number nearly 60 per cent of the total population.

Not all South American countries or cities face the same situation relative to their respective processes of urbanization.

Uruguay, for example, which already has an elevated percentage of its population living in cities and high urban concentration, possesses a low rate of demographic growth. It is a small country with limited population, urbanistically stable, and enjoys a national system of centers that has maintained its basic characteristics for decades.

At the other extreme, Brazil is large in area and population, is to a great extent uninhabited, with more than half of its inhabitants still living in rural areas, and has an accelerated rate of demographic growth. Brazil is an example of an extremely unstable country urbanistically, with a system of centers operative only in the nation's peripheral coastal zones, and with incipient penetration of the interiors still lacking well-defined characteristics.

Quantitatively, differences between the two countries are reflected in the following way: Between 1967 and 1980, Uruguay must absorb an urban population estimated at 423,000 persons, while Brazil must absorb 27,655,000 new urban inhabitants. Ecuador, Paraguay, Peru, and Colombia are also examples of highly unstable countries urbanistically; this is a function of their respective percentages of rural population and the rates of growth of their urban and rural populations. Venezuela is urbanistically unstable, too, while Chile and Argentina are moderately stable on the basis of the same indicators.[3]

Annual growth of urban population in Latin America was greater in 1950–60 than in the previous decade, and in Brazil, Chile, Venezuela, and other countries it was double the annual growth rate of total population. Urbanization is so highly accelerated because in almost all

Latin American countries an elevated rate of demographic growth has been combined with massive rural migrations to the cities. High birth rates are maintained in spite of urbanization; on the other hand, there are more and better opportunities to improve the level of sanitation for urban as well as for rural population, thus lowering death rates. The less-developed and -urbanized Latin American countries, such as Bolivia, Paraguay, Ecuador, and Brazil, can achieve the greatest progress in their respective levels of sanitation, with clear consequences for future rates of urbanization.

In addition, internal migrations constitute an aspect of such magnitude that, in certain concrete cases, they have surpassed in importance the natural increase of the population of a particular city. The most accelerated urban increments occurred between 1950 and 1960 in cities of 100,000 inhabitants or more. There are also examples of the highly accelerated urbanization of smaller cities with relation to the exploitation and/or industrialization of natural resources, but, except for purely local reasons, they generally do not have great quantitative weight in the urbanization of a particular country. On the other hand, in some of South America's largest metropolitan areas, like Cali, Caracas, Fortaleza, São Paulo, and Lima, the population has doubled in periods oscillating between 8 and 12 years. In certain countries, with the growth of cities of 100,000 inhabitants or more came the absorption, between 1950 and 1960, of almost 80 per cent of the rural population growth, demonstrating that urbanization has been accompanied by simultaneous urban concentration. In certain less-urbanized countries like Paraguay, within the general framework already explained, cities with 10,000 inhabitants or less grew more rapidly between 1950 and 1960 than in the more urbanized countries, in which this range of cities experienced a decrease comparable to that of rural areas.

Urbanization in South America is occurring without the

minimum necessary investment and with technically inadequate plans or simply without any plans at all.

We estimate that between 1968 and 1980, U.S.
$80,037,000 will have to be invested in South America in
order to settle 55,198,000 new urban inhabitants and
provide them with basic housing levels and water, drainage, electricity, transportation, primary education, and
assistance services.[4] On the average, 51.8 per cent of this
investment should be made in Brazil alone, 13.9 per cent
in Colombia, and 11.6 per cent in Argentina; on the other
hand, barely 1 per cent will be needed in Uruguay. These
estimates do not include the investment necessary to overcome deficits in housing and existing services or to attempt
an annual quota of replacement. Neither do they include
investment necessary to create new sources of rural or
urban employment, or investment in regional infrastructure, housing and social services, higher education,
and scientific, technical, and other research; that is, these
estimates do not include the investment necessary for development. Comparison of the global figure with net annual investment in South America reveals the impossibility
of a short- or medium-term solution if present housing
and urban services standards and criteria continue to be
maintained for low-income sectors. The consequence is an
increase in the housing and urban-services deficit, already
clearly visible.

Urbanization outstrips industrialization—especially heavy
industrialization—as far as sources of employment are concerned. This has caused proportional expansion of the
service sector. In addition, stagnation of the agricultural
sector has demonstrated the structural limitations persisting in rural areas and stimulated the movement of
their population to the cities. This twin situation, the inca-
pability of urban economies to create necessary employment and the inability of the agricultural sector to increase production as well as to create improved living
conditions for rural population, is reflected in the ex-

tremely high rates of internal migration characteristic of the area, and in urban and rural unemployment and underemployment. Migration of rural population to the cities is not only significant in itself but also because it would appear to accelerate in less urbanized countries. In addition, migration across national borders is a relatively new phenomenon, which in large part is carried out clandestinely and which in certain situations tends to increase.

The accelerated growth of cities, investment deficits, and a level of income among important sectors of urban population so low as to impede their access to minimum housing and service programs, combine to create a situation that cannot be confronted by the rigid and limited master plans designed with a predominantly physical orientation. Solutions must be targeted at the national level by means of regionally integrated policies for development of rural and urban areas in more balanced fashion, and through strategies for smaller spaces—for example, a city or metropolitan area and its immediate area of influence—that consider dynamic and changing situations. The existing situation is aggravated by lack of foresight in not taking measures to control land use and to reserve land for future urban and suburban expansion. Uncontrolled growth and subdivision of urban and suburban areas is reflected in increases in investment and operation costs, and in destruction of the natural environment and of excellent agricultural lands. It will be increasingly difficult to provide the most indispensable services to a growing population that naturally tends either to locate on land managed for speculative ends, or to become squatters through lack of broad and flexible locational programs. This complex situation cannot be faced with simple codes and rigid regulations based upon elementary projections.

The three traditional levels of government—national, provincial or state, and municipal—operate with only limited ties among themselves. Decisions and investment at the national and, to a lesser degree, the provincial level, as well as investment by private individuals, define the

characteristics of individual economies and influence rates
of urbanization. The municipalities, with the exception of
a few in large cities and only in the most incomplete way,
cannot provide solutions for budgetary, administrative,
technical, or political reasons. The indifference of national
levels of decision and planning to urban problems coexists
with the municipalities' operational incapacity, and is reflected to a greater or lesser degree in all aspects of urban
life in South American countries.

We believe that urbanization represents a positive tendency in the socioeconomic and political evolution of the
South American countries. Not only can it be converted
into an expansion factor for national economies by creating external economies and internal markets, but it is also
a positive step in the incorporation of masses of population
into more active political and institutional life. For this
reason, the disinterest with which such a complex problem
has been analyzed and treated becomes alarming.

The growing complexity of both contemporary cities
and accelerated urbanization underlines the necessity of
analyzing and guiding their growth with broad spatial criteria, more precise methods, and integrated approaches.
Solutions to a particular city's growth cannot be found in
isolation, but must be an integral element of a network of
centers whose interaction will increase with economic and
technological development.

II. *Planning Systems Adopted. Decision-making Levels.
Regulation of Urban and Suburban Land Use. Zoning.*

1. PLANNING POLICIES OF NATIONAL AND REGIONAL
LEVELS. CO-ORDINATION OF LEVELS. POWERS OF CENTRAL
GOVERNMENTS.

The liberalism that shaped and accompanied the organization of the South American countries that achieved their
independence in the first decades of the nineteenth cen-

tury inspired distrust of strong and centralized state systems. Public administration was underestimated, and the state has been and is still considered by traditional leadership groups as being responsible for the precarious structural situation persisting in the South American countries.

In the case of federal nations, federalism is lax and is slowly losing strength, without resulting in a corresponding rational regional organization programmed at a central level. The absorption by central governments of almost all economic resources caused the growth of certain regional centers without implying the existence of rational regional-development criteria. This policy, far from obeying sane distribution criteria from a territorial point of view, accentuated the marked regional disequilibrium observed today in all South American countries.

As Kaplan and Basaldúa have written,[5] regional isolation, perpetuated by distance or natural barriers, is aggravated by the absence of transportation and communication networks. In each South American country, regions with operational capability and the potential to generate their own growth and exploit national opportunities coexist with other regions that are almost uninhabited and almost incommunicado. In the former areas, regional centers and subcenters arise almost spontaneously, forming networks that serve their territory more or less adequately, and acting as points of interchange with other regions. On the other hand, in little-developed regions, these networks are almost totally absent. Lack of basic territorial integration imposes obvious limits upon the possibilities of national development.

The deficits generated by inadequate national development, the growing and generalized demand that national development be achieved, and the multiple economic, social, and political options that these deficits imply, help to explain why Latin America, like all the "Third World," has come to recognize the need to resort to state intervention and planning as administrative means. Both become especially necessary because the South American countries unlike those of Western Europe and the United States, must accomplish in only a few years the processes and tasks that the developed nations achieved over far more prolonged periods. The South American countries also lack sufficient resources, favorable internal conditions, and world opportunities. They cannot permit themselves an absolute liberalism which, for that matter, was not adopted by the developed nations during their period of formation and growth.

The characteristics of the socioeconomic process indicated herein are reflected in the political and institutional apparatus and the juridical systems accompanying this process. While the state becomes a strategic factor due to its growing interventionism and its attempts at planning, expansion of the services it provides and continual absorption of new tasks, increasingly more complex and technical, are achieved without the South American countries' being able to depend upon a political-administrative machine ready to incorporate and bear this burden. Consequently, the rapid process of transition generates and accentuates contradictions, principally those existing between social and economic reality and ideological and political patterns, and between the requirements of a developing economy and institutional molds that have not been essentially modified. The need for planning in order to induce and accelerate economic and social development is universally recognized, although this recognition exhibits a broad range of hues. The success or failure of a system of planning depends largely upon the rapidity and efficiency with which existing institutions and attitudes can be modified, above all those concerning public administration.

The South American countries have adopted the national planning system in order to give direction to their development. Generally, national plans are characterized by concentration upon a series of sectors and by promotion of certain isolated projects. In none of the South American countries is there an integrated planning system, just as there is no co-ordinated process among the different decision-making levels. The administrative structure does not have access to the technical mechanisms of analysis, programming, and execution that would permit separating national plans into their component parts.

With the exception of Uruguay, all national development plans programmed in the South American countries contain a conceptual error that in our view is basic. We refer to the ignorance of both spatial definitions and, more importantly, of urban planning as a factor of economic, social, and institutional development.

Finally, the characteristics of the process of urbanization, explained in the first section of this essay, determine quantitative and qualitative requirements surpassing the immediate possibilities of any of the South American countries. Responsibility for physical regulation of the land in the hands of municipalities alone, and their well-known technical and budgetary limitations, contradict the dynamism of a process essentially determined at higher decision-making levels.

The conceptual errors noted in preceding paragraphs must be considered along with the lack of harmony between the socioeconomic reality of each country and its institutional and juridical structure, and regional disequilibrium and the power groups interested in limiting the effects of efficient administrative mechanisms capable of absorbing the requirements of a planned system. We believe that these conceptual errors explain the lack of elaboration or implementation of plans programmed or under way in the South American countries. In addition, definition of coherent and implementable regional policies now appears to be a distant goal, in spite of the efforts being undertaken in certain South American countries.

2. URBAN PLANNING POLICIES

Urban plans do not respond to directives or policies established by higher decision-making levels. Such policies generally do not exist, and when they have been delineated their implementation has been hesitating and very partial. Nevertheless, the economic decisions taken by the private sector, and by the public sector at higher decision-making levels, have oriented the urban systems of each South American country toward their present characteristics and defined the structures of metropolitan areas and cities.

A national urbanization policy must be based upon criteria of economic location, at least for the principal urban centers of each region; regarding social and demographic factors, it should be based upon criteria concerning distribution and characteristics of rural and urban population as functions of economic directives; regarding physical factors, it should consider means of determination of urban-regional systems; and regarding institutional factors, it should be based upon organization of mechanisms adequate for supporting previously stated criteria. A national urbanization policy must be concerned with the national and regional dimensions of the urbanization process, since one of South America's main ecological-demographic characteristics is the accelerated growth of centers forming the highest levels of agglomeration, to the detriment of intermediate and small levels of rural population. Even within the highest level, it has been the largest cities or metropolitan areas, or those most important because of their location with respect to industry, that have absorbed the greatest percentages of growth. A national urbanization policy must be the integrating element of future urban-regional systems based upon more efficient regional and national hierarchies, in addition to serving as an instrument of development for new regional poles and sub-poles, and of promotion of rural activity.

The role of central governments is basic to the definition, elaboration, approval, and execution of an urbanization policy. It begins when a country decides to plan its development and to incorporate urbanization as a socio-economic and spatial variable into its projections and investment plans. It continues as territorial space is sub-divided into regions for the purposes of recognizing and focalizing the country's problems, mobilizing its economic and technical support in a co-ordinated way, and giving greater effectiveness to investment programs contemplating the seasonable variables of productivity. Finally, establishment of sectoral-growth goals by region, and of the financial assistance and institutional organization for achievement of these goals, complete the national role in this matter.

In our view, within the general situation of the South American countries, the total concept of the system of regions must be determined at the highest decision-making levels. Nevertheless, it must be recognized that in federal nations, regions are formed with the consent of the provinces. The provinces must decide to group themselves into regions for the purpose of harmonizing their development and avoiding prejudicial competition. In a planned state, the role of the region is the key to analysis, evaluation, and assessment of national, disaggregated development.

To this point, we have defined the components and objectives of an urbanization policy, as well as the level at which it is originated and executed. Consequently, we should now determine the nature of a national urban policy or a national urban order in order to establish its operative framework, which differs from that of an urbanization policy per se. While the latter has total territorial scope as its reference, in which the notion of space is basically related to urban-regional systems and the localization of economic activities in urban as well as in rural areas, an urban policy acts only within urban centers and their immediate areas of influence. Generalizing, it may be said that within the systems of the countries under study, a national urban policy encourages the country's planning apparatus to seek its highest level and its implementation on the basis of persuasion, promotion, and investment. An urbanization policy, on the other hand, is eminently normative and is translated into rules and legal instruments. Even though at the highest governmental levels methods, criteria, and forms of urban planning are formulated only to be overturned by directives that must be carried out by local governments, it is the local governments that plan.

Urban planning norms and directives handed down at the central level to municipalities for their fulfillment, and, basically, for creation of administrative mechanisms in control of such fulfillment, give form to a national urban policy. Differing from an urbanization policy, the normative character of which forces approval or rejection of local plans (even though in exceptional cases this national policy may originate in central planning organs), the management and functioning of a national urban policy must operate through a national organ having executive and decision-making powers. Within the systems in force in South America, planning organs are advisory bodies of the executive power, without decision-making powers of their own. The close interrelationship that must exist in this matter and the co-ordination that must be established among the organs responsible in each case are obvious.

It must be noted that a national urbanization policy, with its regional characteristics, constitutes the frame of reference for an urban regulating plan. The latter's effectiveness depends largely upon the scope and precision with which the former is implemented. In the economic sphere, an urban regulating policy should establish goals for economic activities locating in a metropolitan area or city, and determine in advance that this localization is achieved in the correct sites. In social matters, community equipment and facilities, including housing, must be created, located, and maintained for the fulfillment of economic criteria. Physically, the urban area's internal structure, with its services and land use decided by functions, densities, and the relationship between open and developed space, must be determined in order to assure the effectiveness of economic and social criteria. Institutionally, the operation of minimum- and intermediate-level planning organisms within the national planning system must be assured.

The municipalities, or regional associations of small municipalities, and metropolitan governments, if their scale makes it necessary, must reinforce the technical level of their organisms in order to obtain the best conditions for maximum effectiveness of the socioeconomic objectives of the national plan and of an urbanization policy. With respect to urban development plans, disaggregation of regional plans must maintain a relationship similar to that suggested for disaggregation of the national plan.

Urban master plans must face and anticipate more dynamic and more constant daily problems than do general plans included within an urbanization policy. Thus, organs for the participation of the urban community should be created and adequate integration of the community facilitated. Incorporation of urban development plans into an urbanization policy must be foreseen by the corresponding decision-making organisms. The municipalities, with their problems and limitations, cannot impose policies lying outside the broader frame of reference handed down by higher levels of government.

Urban regulating policies in the South American countries have, in general, been extremely poorly developed, as much in their elaboration as in their implementation. Existing urban planning is the product of the isolated initiatives of a few centers rather than of integrated and well-defined policies. With few exceptions, existing plans correspond to the old concept of master plans and not to the present (and more correct, in our view), concept of integrated local development plans that include all aspects under consideration for the projection of a city or metropolitan area and its area of influence.

Given that, in general, initiative in this matter has originated in local governments, urban plans do not correspond to outlines handed down from a higher level. This causes such plans to be unco-ordinated and totally disconnected from the objectives or goals of central or regional planning. In addition, in cases in which correctly instrumented plans exist in the formal sense, they have not been applied. Plans are only partially fulfilled, and shifted away from problems implying conflicts, whether from purely political motives or because of fear of lengthy judicial proceedings with little possibility of success.

What has been said to this point is valid, as a general rule, in the South American case. However, even at the risk of including experience not yet entirely concrete, we shall now refer to two countries that have put into operation rational policies of control of the urbanization process.

The case of Brazil is highly significant. There, planning is being faced through definition of program regions and socioeconomic development poles. These poles are defined at the political level in three scales: national, regional, and state; that is, studies are oriented toward offering basic socioeconomic directives for local development.[6] These studies are also oriented toward knowledge of each area's economic potential at the level of homogeneous microregions.

Out of the compatibility of the homogeneous region and the sectoral goals of national, regional, and state plans should come the program regions, which will not always coincide with the homogeneous regions. Taking the socioeconomic development plan as a reference point, Brazil is to be regionalized at first in levels of macroregions and systems.

To select each program region's development poles, knowledge of the tertiary equipment of the Brazilian urban network is necessary. In order to gather in this knowledge, studies are being made of the patterns of urbanization in the total context of a development policy. These studies are based upon: (a) the costs of urbanization for different residential densities, defined in turn in terms of different levels of family income; (b) production of household goods and services; (c) the intra- and interurban transportation and communications systems; and (d) potential and prospects of technological evolution. These studies have as their objective the determination of development poles, and produce as an indirect effect an evaluation of the contradictions of federal government housing policy. It was considered necessary in Brazil to relate development poles to housing policy before formulating any kind of recommendation; hence the quantitative goals of the housing sector.

Finally, an evaluation is being carried out of existing institutional instruments at three differentiated levels: (a) direct institutional instruments used for control of urban development; (b) institutional structure in the municipal setting; and (c) evaluation of financial resources applied to the urban development sector.

It should be noted that the Brazilian National Plan of Integrated Local Development is being elaborated in two stages. The first includes study of the natural and human resources of urban centers, together with analysis of the regions in which the centers are located. Once economic and social goals have been established at the regional and national levels, the second stage consists of formulating local economic and social development plans to support the real and objective bases of physical planning.

Once the system described has been institutionalized, the process of its being made operational and concrete is slow. This may be attributed to faulty co-ordination between the Ministry of Planning and Serviço Federal de

Habitação e Urbanismo (SERFHAU), an autarchic organ integrated into the National Housing Bank, which has primary responsibility for local planning. Up to the present, it has not been possible to achieve planning of local units.

Another important case is that of Uruguay, where the National Physical Planning Law (Ley de Acondicionamiento Territorial) is part of the National Development Plan elaborated by the Commission on Investment and Economic Development (CIDE).[7] The law's objective is to establish physical planning at the national, departmental, and local levels as a necessary precondition for a co-ordinated and technical policy. Basic features of the law are: (a) authority of the executive power to regulate the law and provide financial support to its fulfillment; (b) the strengthening of national physical planning policy and creation of interdepartmental committees; and (c) creation of the Directorate-General of Physical Planning as a dependency of the ministry in charge of housing and urbanism.[8]

As we see it, this is an institutional or organizational outline of an urbanization policy, which in general lacks the content we believe such a policy should be given. Nevertheless, it should be noted to its credit that it forms part of a general development plan that is concerned with some of the omissions we have pointed out.

3. REGULATION OF LAND USE IN URBAN AND SUBURBAN AREAS. CONTROLS.

Given the fact that with the advance of the urbanization process, urbanization itself is totally unable to regulate or control land use without adequate planning, everything we say herein must be closely linked to our remarks in the preceding section. In the area under study, there are contradictions at work that may be explained by the structural asynchronisms analyzed in the first section of this essay, which will also appear in section III.

To cite only one example, Brazil, which to date has not structured urban planning[9] (vis-à-vis other countries whose urbanization policies or urban master plans have advanced to a limited extent, as in Chile or Venezuela), is the only South American country to have structured controls at the national level.

The new control in Brazil governs urban subdivision, the responsibility of the subdivider, ceding of air space, and other provisions. It defines as "urban," centers, as well as developed sections adjacent to these centers, which, in the municipalities' judgment, will be occupied by contiguous construction over a ten-year projected period. Basically, this new decree-law (No. 271 of February 28, 1967) is concerned with the imposition of strict norms for subdividers, and gives municipalities the responsibility of seeing that its provisions are fulfilled. We believe that the existence of a law attacking the problem from the national level is of fundamental importance in the Brazilian case. This implies relative control of urban and suburban land use, which, left solely to local regulation, would have meant lack of control over urban fringes and adjacent lands subject to other jurisdictions.

Regarding the regulation of land use, it is clearly useless to create systems that do not enjoy power within the decision-making levels of the vertical hierarchy of administrations, as well as efficient horizontal co-ordination among the different interested departments or offices of the public sector. Nor should one neglect the adaptation of the private sector by means of measures acting as brakes in certain cases or accelerators in others. Basically, these measures are important in regulating capital investment in mechanisms created to fulfill the desired ends. This situation is easily recognized in the model we propose.

In general, and specifically in its zoning provisions, this

mechanism is totally inadequate, not only temporarily, but also until such time as its requirements are fulfilled. In the majority of cases, this is due to the inoperative nature of almost all urban plans in South America.

Zoning may be described as the process of executing regulations through which the municipal government may have adequate control over the use of property units. This brief description summarizes the fundamental characteristics of this institution, such as its quality of being an instrument of legal order appropriate for municipal government, and of serving as a tool to control the use of private property, establishing limitations upon property rights to the benefit of the public interest.

In 1920, a consensus already existed among urban planners regarding the need to instrument controls over land use based upon a new form: zoning. This consensus was consolidated in 1926 with the endorsement of the *Village of Euclid* v. *Ambler Realty Co.* decision, in which the U. S. Supreme Court recognized the timeliness and legality of this solution.[10]

In the 1950s, the distortions produced by zoning at certain stages in the growth of cities began to be evident. Large cities, following the North American example, began to be strangled in certain areas, which became stagnant compartments within the general context of urban area development.

Similarly, one may visualize the financial speculation following on the heels of the levying of corrective zoning measures. Since zoning is a dynamic and flexible instrument, it creates expectations easily exploited by large land companies. This occurs when attempts are made to change the closed system described in the preceding paragraph.

In spite of the difficulties that may result over time from application of this instrument, it is undeniable that in those cases that attempt to regulate a city not subject to previous planning, zoning is the most effective method for determining land use and giving the city a physical form adequate for its development. At the moment, however, technicians, without ceasing to recognize the benefits produced by zoning at determined stages of city development, are cautious and use this solution with reservations:

> It must be emphasized that zoning is not planning, except in the negative sense. Zoning may prevent conditions from becoming worse, but it is improbable that it will have more positive value until its appropriate function as one of the main instruments for implementing a long-term community plan is recognized.[11]

Finally, it may be useful to reproduce an opinion that seems to us highly appropriate in this context:

> . . . zoning as a tool of control should not be presumptuously detailed in premature stages of the city's development, and the emphasis of urban planning in our cities should be dedicated more to establishing the elements permitting growth of development, than to establishing those elements needed to control such development. The advantages emanating from more flexible zoning are enormous in terms of approaching reality, saving in municipal administration, and simplifying the processes of control. Physical ordering of the urban environment cannot be the objective in itself. The urban fabric must rather be the spatial reflection of a vital and dynamic economic and social environment.[12]

We are inclined to consider zoning a useful and necessary means for operationalizing all urban regulating plans. Such plans must acknowledge rational flexibility, and their revision and adjustment must be grounds for special observation on the part of local technical offices.

The financial speculation that zoning may bring can also be produced by not attempting to employ the instrument

it represents. Zoning brings the advantage of rational regulation and location of urban land use, a highly positive
question not to be ignored in studies of local planning.
The possibility of future strangulation in certain areas
does not justify abandonment of this solution. Many measures may be undertaken in order to avoid or minimize the
distorting elements previously described.

It must be emphasized that solution to the problems of
urban land is to be found not in mere control of its use,
but rather in a frontal attack upon the elements governing
its tenure. The difficulties inherent in the practical application of zoning at determined stages of city growth justify this observation. We shall return to this point in the
section devoted to future prospects.

III. *Legislation. Taxes. Urban and Suburban Land Values. Economic Controls. Mechanisms.*

1. RELATIVIZATION OF RIGHTS. ABSOLUTE DOMAIN. EXPROPRIATION.

The legislative structure of South America does not
recognize community supremacy over individual rights,
and admits the existence of absolute rights in personal and
patrimonial spheres. This juridical construction, based
upon *laissez faire* philosophy, has its correlations: in political matters, in the negation of state intervention; and in
economic affairs, in the creation of inductive development
mechanisms.

The static situation created by the system of absolute
rights has undergone modification over the course of his-
toric-social time. This necessitates changing individual and
patrimonial rights to adapt them to the new forms assumed by the socioeconomic structure and the state's political organization. This change or relativization, known in
traditional doctrine as restrictions motivated by the social

interest, does not eliminate rights; rather, it adapts them in order to maintain their operative life. They are transformed into preventatives of conflict that could eliminate their effectiveness.

The right of domain, which may be defined as "the true right, by virtue of which a thing is subject to the will and action of a person,"[13] is the most important of the patrimonial rights; for this reason it is the right most intimately linked to the socioeconomic development model and the political scheme of each national community.

The individualistic criterion of the right to property has as a main characteristic recognition of the right to property in absolute domain or fee simple. Its immediate legislative sources are the North American Constitution of 1789 and the French Code of 1804 in the fields of public and private rights, respectively.

The evolution we noted in the relativization of rights has also occurred in the field of patrimonial rights. Thus, in the specific case of the right to property, it was recognized that the owner of a good cannot have unlimited rights over it if such rights injure the social interest represented by the state.

The general characteristic of the historical development of domain is the guarantee of the right to private property in ideological sections of constitutions, and its definition and characterization in civil codes. The latter definition faithfully follows that set forth in Article 544 of the Napoleonic Code, in which the three kinds of Roman domain appear: absolute, exclusive, and perpetual.

In the process of adapting the existing normative system to changes occurring in the socioeconomic structure, the first limitation upon the code's rigidity is that of expropriation. Expropriation "is the act of occupying and acquiring private property for the purposes of public utility, through just indemnity of its value and damages caused by such expropriation."[14] This institution acquires importance because it is perhaps the only instrument capable of breaking the individualistic molds in which property is cast.

The requirements for expropriation—public utility, legal eligibility, and compensation—arise from its definition. These requirements may be generalized for the South American countries, since to a greater or lesser degree the requirements are respected by general or special norms governing expropriation in the area. Through expropriation the state was able to achieve anticipated, programmed, and localized public works. In the development of the process, the concept of expropriation was broadened, permitting its realization through zoning without the need to specify particular works and limits.[15] Within the scope of this study, with reference to urban and, more specifically, political policies regarding urban and suburban land, the classic system of expropriation is not operative for various reasons, primarily the state's financial difficulties and the slowness of legal proceedings. To expropriate a piece of real property it is necessary to deposit the value of its property tax plus a compensatory percentage.[16] Yet, in addition, in the subsequent expropriation suit, the land's market value is set, which the state in turn must guarantee. Anticipating the amounts to be invested in public works alone, the limitation we pointed out becomes obvious.

In addition, from the legal point of view, the process of expropriation presents the possibility of delays. In all situations, the constitutionality of the expropriation law may be challenged, causing suits in the majority of cases to proceed through all three judicial levels.

Finally, the inflationary process suffered by the majority of the South American countries has caused doctrinaire and judicial discussion of the problem of anticipated dispossession by the state, removing the expropriating entity's haste to possess affected lands, and delaying realization of public works.[17]

In recent years, the majority of the South American

countries have reformed their political constitutions,[18] embracing the criterion of the social function of property.[19] The right to property and its manner of execution is thus limited by a higher interest: that of the public. Social function is the way in which the system "relativizes" the right to property.

The right to property, based upon the idea of subjective, exclusive, and absolute right, is an institution with its own finality. To affirm that it has a social function is to attempt to give it an objective basis, and the more generous we are with this idea, the more we will confuse property with the exploitation of goods.[20] For this reason, we affirm that social function is an ideology characterizing a complex of norms that form a positive system, but is not a positive right.

The social function of property has not been defined either from a legislative or a doctrinal perspective. The first appearance of this concept in the papal encyclical *Rerum Novarum* at the close of the nineteenth century characterizes it as the essence of the right to property and refers to the manner in which it is executed by private interests. This characterization and lack of definition have forced the institution's social evolution to remain in the hands of the legislator, who must interpret the concept in the act of prescribing specific norms, or in the hands of the judge, in the act of applying these norms. The positive right cannot offer to the doctrine of social function the evolutionary strength the latter seeks, because there is no positive right with social function. The latter is incarnate in natural law. Natural law is based upon two principles that are its essence—immutability and identity—thus eliminating its evolutionary possibility.[21]

The legislator must judge the criteria of social function. He does so with his own rules and those offered to him by the system that serves as an institutional framework. Thus, relativization ceases to exist in practice. In addition, in all countries having modern constitutions, there has not been

correlative variation in basic legislation, which continues
to be immutable. As we descend the juridical pyramid, we
find a process of constant Romanization of the right to
property.[22]

In applying the right to property, the courts do not consider the social function ideology inserted in constitutions.
The courts apply the norms of private and administrative
law in conformity with the spirit of their sanction.

To conclude, we may say that the classic conception of
the right to property is alive and well in South America,
inspired by the liberal doctrine championed by all nineteenth-century thought. The relativization of this right
has been attempted in two ways, permitting us to group
the South American countries into the following categories:

a. those that maintain their constitutions without reform, and in which the relativization process arises from
the nonexplanatory interpretation of writers of tracts and
of the law itself, as in Argentina and Uruguay; and

b. those that modified their constitutions in light of the
social function of property and that maintain the Roman
categorization of their legislation.[23]

From the foregoing, we may note that any urban policy,
or specifically any land policy, must exact transformation
in juridical structures to adapt them to the processes of
socioeconomic change.

2. TAXING IN URBAN AND SUBURBAN AREAS. WAYS AND
MEANS OF APPLICATION.

Property tax system. The state is the active subject of
financial activity and exercises taxing power for the immediate and direct purpose of obtaining revenues to satisfy
public expenditure.[24] In accordance with the general norm
previously discussed, we shall consider the problem of this

legal norm's territorial validity. This depends upon
whether the political-institutional system is centralized
(unitary) or decentralized (federal).

In centralized constitutional regimes, such as Uruguay,
Ecuador, and Chile, the problem of local autonomy in the
area of taxation is stated with reference not to the so-
called local or provincial states of federal regimes, but
rather to the departments or municipalities of the communal regime.

The taxing powers of departmental governments are
limited and carefully enumerated by constitutions. Taxation to which local community governments may have
recourse to obtain financial resources is also fixed; the taxing power is delegated by the central government. In accordance with the degree of interest shown, the sources of
important municipal revenues are property taxes and taxes
on idle lands and buildings.[25] On a par with these delegated revenues is the resource offered by national taxes, as
in the co-operative system, which is used when the yield
of tax sources given to municipalities is insufficient for
fulfillment of their responsibilities. Finally, tax collection is
an eminently municipal resource; among the most important taxes we may cite fees for lighting and health services, maintenance of drainage systems, and registration
and licensing of vehicles.

In federal governmental regimes, it falls to the provinces to collect indirect taxes in general, and, in competition with the national government, direct taxes, except
"when the defense, common security, and the general
good of the state" are concerned.[26] Provincial laws institute municipal powers, which include the imposition of
taxes and other contributions to the municipal treasury for
the purpose of paying services and other public expenses
charged to the municipality. As Rafael Bielsa notes, referring to the Argentine case, a typical federal system, "municipal financial power is delegated and limited; in the Argentine system municipalities do not enjoy taxing power in

the constitutional or political sense. They only exercise this power through delegation by provincial or local governments."[27]

From the financial point of view, and in accordance with what has been observed in the South American countries, the traditional property tax system has not had functional utility in urban development because of the following factors:

a. the low and arbitrary assessment of properties, resulting in permanently inoperative property censuses;

b. the lack of mechanisms to adapt property assessment to the tremendous inflationary processes that the South American countries have suffered and are suffering;

c. the ancient and deficient tax-collection system observable in the majority of South American countries;

d. the fact that revenues are not destined for specific uses; and

e. ignorance of the taxing capacity on the part of the urban and suburban population.

The Added-Value Tax. The central property-tax problem is that of recovery of added value. Though this continues to be a problem, even in countries that have already reached a high level of development, it is an exceedingly important question for South America, where investment in public works must necessarily be income-producing, due to chronic scarcity of available resources.

Existing systems, with few exceptions, are limited to simple recovery of the value of public works, without recapturing the greater value produced by the application of public works to private property. The cost of these public works is a burden on the community in the generic sense, since the community pays indirectly through taxes for these works, which, in turn, benefit private individuals who see their fortunes increased accidentally.

The added-value tax is determined by the factors producing financial difficulties in cities undergoing rapid growth, which factors in turn cause an increase in the value of property. By taxing this increase in value, the city can finance the investment required to meet the economic and social costs of growth. There are two aspects of this tax that should be differentiated from a doctrinal point of view:

a. the contribution to the cost of improvements—that is, the cost of public works; and

b. a tax on the highest value acquired by property through the realization of improvements.

We may define and characterize the above tax *b* as "the obligatory compensation paid to a public entity for a public-works project it undertakes for purposes of public use, but which also provides special advantages to particular owners of real property."[28]

The object of this tax, whatever form it acquires, is the highest value received by pieces of property through the application of public works, or, more concretely, the added value. The taxable factor, to be determined by law, is the highest value of property in question.

From the point of view of positive law, the South American country that has developed this tax most fully is Colombia. Its National Property Value Statute (Legislative Decree 1604 of June 24, 1966) has the following characteristics:

a. obligatory contribution is applied to all public works benefiting real property;

b. the work must be in the public interest;

c. all public entities have the power to exact contributions for the work they undertake; and

d. the obligatory nature of contributions to specific investments is established.[29]

Taking into account the limitations of the legislative structure analyzed herein, experience achieved in the different South American countries, and the area's level of socioeconomic development, a tax such as the one analyzed above is beneficial for financing city growth and development.

3. ECONOMIC CONTROLS OVER URBAN AND SUBURBAN LAND

Mechanisms of economic control are those permitting the state to regulate urban and suburban land and to dictate norms limiting speculation, or better, creating a skillful organism permitting the state to enter the land market. So that a mechanism of economic control may operate efficiently, a prior and obligatory requisite is a planning study in which zoning regulations and ordinances clearly indicate zoning areas and their uses.

In this respect, we must remember what was pointed out in an earlier paragraph: Determination of areas in a zoning code is the result of factors influencing a community's internal structure, that is, its physical characteristics, population density, socioeconomic and other organizations, through an integral process of rationalization. In other words, before putting the mechanism into operation, it is necessary to undertake basic studies.

The existence of these economic controls is necessary for economic and political reasons; generalizing, we may say that the following statements are valid for all South American countries:

a. If the state only regulates land use and does not achieve control of urban and suburban land tenure, the state cannot stop speculation, a distorting factor in the land market. The state cannot control speculation because values on the land market depend on the variable income derived not only from land use, but also from land's scarcity and location.

b. Urban land has two different values: real and potential. Real value is derived from present value and is a function of the rental of land. Potential value is related to expectations of change in land use, provoking greater income. In determining both values, the state's action has significant importance because of the work it achieves in equipment and services.

It is strict justice that he who creates wealth may profit thereby; with even greater reason so should the state, which through principles of institutional organization enjoys eminent domain over land. By permitting the state to regulate tenure directly or indirectly, the mechanism of economic control is extremely effective.

In general, mechanisms of economic control do not exist in the South American countries. Some exceptions are the Workers' Bank of Venezuela; the autarchic municipal entity of Curitiba, Brazil; the institution created by the urban renewal law in Bolivia; and the Chilean Urban Improvement Corporation (CORMU).

IV. *Future Prospects*

1. Juridical institutions in South America have never been creations of the legislature, so far as their provisions are concerned, but rather have been charged with regulating real phenomena—that is, legally regulating pre-existing actions. The conception of the right of domain prevailing in South America is the value the legislature attached to the concept of property, as a consequence or reflection of the stage of development of an unmodified juridical-institutional and political model maintained within traditional limits. At this point, it is necessary to formulate certain considerations regarding the basic legislative problem. The planner must face situations by anticipating actions. He must keep in mind, in this case, the characteristics of

the urbanization process and sanction legislation to regulate it. He must abandon the concept previously described —that of sanctioning norms as a consequence of pre-existing actions—and instead exploit planning projections to regulate anticipated situations by means of adequate legislation.

In addition, it should not be forgotten that the city is in a state of permanent activity and that its constant changes respond to stimuli discernible with some precision. It is not possible to delay solutions in the hope of definitive studies that depend upon exhaustive knowledge of the situation. One must begin to act with the knowledge at hand and gradually modify approaches and adjust details as the process develops.

On the basis of the foregoing, we have formulated the following recommendations as possible solutions for adjustment of the institutional machinery guiding and controlling the urban-development process:

a. adaptation of the juridical structure to the processes of socioeconomic change developing in South America;

b. adaptation of basic legislation to the constitutional reforms operative in certain South American countries;

c. conceptual transformation of basic legislation regarding definition and characterization of domain;

d. modification and transformation of the existing system of expropriation;

e. sanction of a national urban-development policy or of certain measures of this policy permitting action to begin at a first stage; and

f. creation of a system of economic control capable of permitting the state to control land tenure and to provide the land it needs for its program of urban development and regulation.

2. The model we propose is a valid alternative for determining in each South American country the mechanism

responsible for elaborating and implementing a policy of urban regulation or development. This policy should include, on the one hand, the form of regulating urban and suburban land, and, on the other, the way in which the state will participate in the tenure system of urban and suburban land. The model does not contemplate an urbanization policy, since this in our view corresponds to the central planning organism of each of the South American countries.

a. The national government has primary responsibility for elaboration and sanction of an urban development policy of national scope, as well as for creation of the appropriate instruments to implement it. The nation is the only institution capable of carrying this task forward, lending in support all of its administrative and technical apparatus. The lack of well-trained human resources in South America and the need to improve use of what exists make this solution necessary.

The function of central governments must be limited to dictating the general outlines of an urban policy of national scale. The central governments should not legislate solution to particular problems from this level; this must be reserved to local governments, which are better qualified as far as their own needs are concerned. Municipal authorities must be in positions to evaluate their own roles within development programming handed down by higher decision-making levels and in which they must be fully integrated.

b. The institutionalization of the mechanism we describe must take place at the central government level. Within central public administration, the mechanism should be located at the national executive cabinet ministry level because of its function.

It should not be a planning organ, since as we have emphasized, such organs are invested only with an advisory capacity within the system existing in the South American area. Rather, because of the nature of the objectives to be fulfilled, it must possess the executive power appropriate to the state's administrative apparatus. The creation of ministries is advisable, which is consistent with antecedents to be observed in South America and also in the United States and Western Europe. Traditionally, the solution to urban problems was entrusted to housing ministries already in existence, which were given powers touching every aspect of urban regulation, without modifying the old name. In these cases, ministries divided their action on the basis of reforming their internal organization. Ministries began to be divided into two large departments or directorates-general, one of urban development and the other of housing. In cases in which this situation obtains, its continuance causes no difficulty. It is obvious, however, that in requiring creation of an administrative instrument having the stated ends, the ministry's name should be clearly demonstrative of its objectives. "Ministry of Urban Development" appears to be the most appropriate name to define its function and field of action.

c. The objectives to be fulfilled by the organ described herein are:

1. Elaboration of a policy of urban regulation and development. This must conform to the urbanization policy for which the central organ of socioeconomic planning is responsible. Even though the former should be integrated into the latter, work must be based upon close coordination and complementarity. Elaboration of an urban policy requires a fixed length of time for its definitive and concrete form. Consequently, until its form is consolidated, regulatory and corrective instruments should be authorized on the condition that such instruments acknowledge sufficient flexibility and are general enough not to distort the process. In addition, they must permit needed readjustments as research and basic studies are completed.

2. Authorization of standards for elaboration of local plans in the hands of municipal governments. These governments should determine the minimum content of such plans, alternative methodologies, and all other elements contributing to rational unification of criteria in this field. The obligatory implementation of local plans by the municipality in all matters within its jurisdiction must be clearly established.

3. Approval of locally drafted plans, anticipating, according to the particular case, intervention by intermediate levels of approval, and control in such plans at the provincial, state, or regional level.

4. Integration of local plans into regional ones for the purpose of consolidating an adequate regional system of centers.

5. Establishment of an operative system of control of urban and suburban land use and anticipation of the creation of mechanisms permitting it to participate in land ownership and management.

6. Provision to the central planning organ of the elements considered necessary for elaboration of an urbanization policy. This should be done through interchange of information and other appropriate means permitting operative interaction.

d. These objectives could be fulfilled by means of the instrumentation of two basic mechanisms: (1) a "Technical Secretariat" responsible for elaboration of a policy of urban regulation and development; and (2) a "National Urban Land Bank" on the basis of which the state could carry forward a policy of land-use control and participation in land ownership.

Natural functions of the "Technical Secretariat" should include:

1. Elaboration of a national policy of urban regulation and development, to be approved and put into operation by the ministry.

2. Dictation of standards to which the municipalities should be subject for the elaboration of local plans.

3. Evaluation of local plans for approval or rejection by the ministry.

4. Control of implementation of local plans.

5. Anticipation of the instrumentation of intermediate decision-making levels (state or regional) for evaluation and control of local plans. Even though technical approval may exist at these levels, it is advisable that formal approval of local plans be undertaken by the central planning organ. This is all subject to the particular criterion followed in each South American country to institutionalize the system.

Resources must be found so that the ministry may assist local governments unable to elaborate their own plans technically and financially. In addition, assistance should be provided for achievement of studies and working papers permitting fulfillment of the system's goals. Consequently, taxes destined for specific applications should be collected, even though they might be imposed as general taxes. There are basically two such taxes: (a) one on real-estate transactions in urban and suburban areas; and (b) a tax on the rise in urban property values deriving from public works. It must be clarified that recovery of the cost of a particular public work is necessarily charged to the organ undertaking it. What would aid the proposed system would be solely the rise in the value of property so improved—that is, the added value deriving from the addition of public works.

The "National Urban Land Bank" would be the autarchic entity through which the state would participate in the land market. Autarchy is basic for fulfillment of the entity's objectives with the required operational freedom. The bank's essential functions are the following:

1. Functioning as an economic and regulating control upon the urban and suburban land market.
2. Permitting the state to intervene in the ownership of urban and suburban land. It has been amply confirmed that without regulation of ownership, the norms of land-use control are insufficient to regulate development.

Basic powers determining the operations of the "National Urban Land Bank" are those of:

1. Buying, selling, and taxing any urban or suburban real property under ministry guidelines, in accordance with local urban development plans.
2. Maintaining offices in the nation's principal cities.
3. Co-operating in financing urban-development programs at local and regional levels, with the ministry's consent.
4. Financing, in necessary cases and on the ministry's express instructions, technical-administrative programs of cadastral surveys and modernization of municipal revenue offices.

The "National Urban Land Bank" should be self-financed. The state should make a considerable contribution to its initial capital formation, either in funds or in titles to real estate. This contribution would permit the bank to begin operations.

Gains appropriate to the urbanization process deriving from transactions in reserve lands would comprise its principal resources. To these funds should be added a sum proportional to the amount collected by the ministry in its recovery of added value. The bank's resources would be completed by sums proceeding from land-use operations or any other operation it realizes with goods and properties under its ownership.

The proposed model is a valid alternative for institutionalizing the mechanisms that must guide and orient the urban development of cities. Obviously, this alternative must be implemented in harmony with the political-institutional characteristics of each South American country.

NOTES

1. Figures presented herein are extracted from *Datos básicos de población de América Latina* (Washington, D.C.: Organization of American States, Department of Social Affairs, 1969).

2. There is a difference among urban population figures generally accepted for the year 1960. This is due to the fact that the figures we include are those of the 1960 censuses in Argentina, Bolivia, Brazil, and Chile, 1961 censuses in Peru and Venezuela, 1962 in Ecuador and Paraguay, 1963 in Uruguay, and 1964 in Colombia. On the other hand, figures for 1960 include estimates for various countries in that year. Total figures are logically somewhat lower.

3. For greater detail see Table 7 in Jorge E. Hardoy, Raúl O. Basaldúa, and Oscar A. Moreno, *Política de la tierra urbana y mecanismos para su regulación* (Buenos Aires: Instituto Torcuato di Tella, 1969).

4. The cost of settling a new urban inhabitant, and providing him with the most economical housing contemplated by public organisms of each South American country and with the indicated urban services, varies in each case. The cost of a Type C housing unit of the VEA Plan of the Argentine National Mortgage Bank (Banco Hipotecario Nacional de la Argentina) is approximately 2,800,000 Argentine *pesos*, or U.S. $8,000. It is a unit of 62 square meters, with two bedrooms, living room, bathroom, kitchen, and a terrace of an additional 6 square meters, and running water, sewage, electricity, and pavement. This amounts to U.S. $2,000 per person for families of four. The cost is similar in the construction of new housing in Ciudad Guayana, Venezuela. It drops to U.S. $1,000 per person in Ecuador and Bolivia. The total estimate is based upon 1967 dollars and real costs of housing under way in the ten South American countries.

5. This paragraph and the two immediately following are drawn from Marcos Kaplan and Raúl C. Basaldúa, *Problemas estructruales de América Latina y planificación para el desarrollo* (Buenos Aires: Ed. Bibliográfica Omeba, 1968).

6. Ministério do Planejamento e Coordenação Econômica, "Plano decenal de desenvolvimento econômico e social," *Desenvolvimento regional e urbano* (*versión preliminar*) VII (March 1967):101.

7. Plan Nacional de Desarrollo Económico y Social (National Economic and Social Development Plan) (1965-74), which has still not been ratified by the legislature. It is contained in two volumes published by CECEA (Montevideo: 1966).

8. The basic objective of the Dirección Nacional de Acondicionamiento Territorial (National Directorate-General of Physical Planning) is co-ordination of physical planning policy applying to all Uruguayan territory and urbanism.

9. In spite of the foregoing, it should not be forgotten that in all matters referring to urbanization policy, Brazil is in the programming stage.

10. *Village of Euclid* v. *Ambler Realty Co.*, U.S.S.Ct. 272-365; S.Ct. 114, 71 L.Ed. 303 (1926).

11. Murling R. Hodgell, "Zoning," *Kansas State College Bulletin* 42 (6) (Apr. 1, 1958):6.

12. Jaime Valenzuela and Reinaldo Posada, *Reglamentos de zonificación y subdivisión de áreas residenciales en América Latina* (Bogotá: Centro Interamericano de Vivienda y Planeamiento, 1968), p. 8.

13. Article 2513 of the Argentine Civil Code, ratified January 1, 1868.

14. This definition is that of Argentine law 13,264, ratified September 17, 1948. It may be generalized as applicable to the other South American countries.

15. Expropriation by zones and with the potential of private sale is alien to Argentine legislation.

16. We stress that our comments upon expropriation are based upon the Argentine legislative model. See Note 14.

17. *Municipality of the City of Buenos Aires* v. *Chukri, Engracia, et al. . . . Expropriation*, Argentine Supreme Court.

18. Chile, constitutional reform ratified by law 16,615 of January 18, 1967; Bolivia, Constitution ratified June 1, 1967; Ecuador, Constitution ratified May 25, 1967; Brazil, March 15, 1967; Colombia, the most recent reform, Legislative Act 4 of 1959; Venezuela, Constitution ratified in 1961.

19. The exception is Uruguay's Constitution, which went into effect February 15, 1967, and which does not take up this principle.

20. R. Rippert, *Aspectos jurídicos del capitalismo moderno* (Madrid: Ed. Aguilar, 1953).

21. José Corts Grau, *Curso de derecho natural*, ed. by Manuel

Laquis, p. 226, and "El abuso del derecho y las nuevas disposiciones del Código Civil," *El derecho* (Buenos Aires), September 19, 1968).

22. Jorge A. Difrieri in Prologue to Hardoy, Basaldúa, and Moreno, op. cit.

23. The countries cited in Note 18.

24. Horacio García Belsunce, "La distribución de los poderes impositivos," *Cuadernos del Centro de Derecho y Ciencias Sociales* (FUBA) (Buenos Aires: Ed. Perrot, 1959).

25. We have followed the legislative example of Uruguay. For more information regarding the example, we recommend Herbert Porro and Mario Grolero, *Tributación inmobiliaria* (Montevideo: Ed. Park S.A., 1966).

26. This is the definition contained in Article 67, inc. 2°, of the Argentine Constitution.

27. Rafael Bielsa, "La noción de autarquía y el régimen municipal," *Anuario del Instituto de Derecho Político de la Facultad de Ciencias Económicas de Rosario* (Rosario, Argentina, 1960).

28. Estéban Jaramillo, *Hacienda pública* (Bogotá: 1953), p. 92.

29. For greater detail and information, we recommend Hardoy, Basaldúa and Moreno, op. cit.

III

THE FUTURE OF THE
LATIN AMERICAN CITY

CHAPTER SEVEN

PHYSICAL SPACE IN
DEVELOPMENT POLICY

CARLOS MATUS ROMO*

My theme refers to regionalization of planning and to
methods of achieving optimum equilibrium between max-
imizing economic growth and minimizing gaps between
different regions. From these remarks may be deduced the
fact that there is a certain incompatibility between aspir-
ing to maximum growth of a particular country and decreasing gaps among different regions, whether measured
by degree of industrialization or income level per inhabitant. I believe that such incompatibility does not exist, and
I wish to demonstrate later in this essay that, on the contrary, if we want to accelerate development of the Latin
American countries, one of the basic ways of doing so is
by decreasing regional disequilibria. I consequently do not
believe that less growth results from decreasing regional
disequilibria. It is exactly the opposite; I believe that elimination of regional disequilibria is precisely the path to accelerating growth.

In the second place, it seems to me that the problem of
regionalizing planning is perhaps too restricted. It also

* The author is an official of the Instituto Latinoamericano de
Planificación Económica y Social (ILPES), but the opinions
expressed herein are solely his own. Reprinted from *Revista de
la Sociedad Interamericana de Planificación* III (12) (Dec.
1969):17–25. English translation by Felicity M. Trueblood.

gives the impression that a national development plan or national development strategy is elaborated first, and that the problem of giving it regional content arises later. I believe that the problem is broader, and that it must be placed on the plane of conceiving a spatial pattern of national development that is part of the essence of the development strategy for a particular country. Thus, simple regionalization of a plan is nothing more than a spatial formality reflecting the substantive content that a development strategy should include.

In the third place, I do not believe in regional planning if it is not part of a national development strategy. The regional dimension cannot generally discover its own potentialities and functions in national development. There is a tendency to search for regional solutions within a country's own borders, even though at times such solutions do not exist. I could in this essay cite various cases of extra-national problem areas of Latin America where vain attempts are made to seek domestic solutions within limited national borders, under circumstances that appear almost obvious. Thus, the restricted concept of regional planning tends to hide, I believe, the main problems of this same regional development, problems that can only be appreciated if one employs the broad perspective of a country's development as a whole.

The ideas I shall expound are not personal; rather, they are the products of the work of a team: the Advisory Division of the Instituto Latinoamericano de Planificación Económica y Social (ILPES). The work of this team is not specifically concerned with regional planning, and has generally collaborated with the Latin American countries in the formulation and definition of national development strategies, whether in a strictly national framework, or whether in the framework of certain schemes of integration (as is the case with the integration of signatory countries to the Declaration of Bogotá). Nevertheless, I believe that it is not disadvantageous that our principal experience has not been expressly in regional planning. On the contrary, I believe that this has opened up for us new prospects for evaluation of regional problems, and new prospects for solutions to those problems. In certain exceptional cases, we have collaborated with a few countries in the analysis of regions, but this has not been, as a general rule, our way of working.

The General Thesis

In order to develop certain theses, I wish to explain a few concepts in the rigorous way I intend to use them during this discussion.

We have become accustomed at ILPES and especially in the Advisory Division to use the concepts of "vertical development" and "horizontal development" where the spatial problem constitutes the difference. This distinction is born as much from observation of economic history "over geography" as from analysis of the development prospects of the Latin American countries. Starting with this concept of purely geographic appearance, and making an abstract synthesis of work experience with the Latin American countries, we have attempted to elaborate aspects of a development thesis that establishes marked distinctions between what we could call a pattern of "vertical development" and a "horizontal" one.

In vertical development it is essential that the country's resources be displaced to the pre-existing location of men. Or, better said, the economic theory we are accustomed to using is based upon the assumption that the external economies already created in zones containing population agglomeration, existing infrastructure, and present-day centers of industrialization, have such advantages that it will always be "economic" to locate a new activity where the old activity already existed. For this reason, each time geographic decentralization of the development process is considered, one hears talk of paying the "cost" of achieving such decentralization. I believe that those concepts are not well-founded in acceptable dynamic economic theory, and later in this essay I shall refer to this in greater depth. In the meantime, I only wish to characterize the concept of vertical development. It is based simply upon assigning spatially the resources of those zones that already present external economies, and, therefore, the greatest advantages. It is curious that although such external economies were created by men, they feel themselves enslaved by their creation when future decisions of major import are considered for a particular country. Horizontal development is exactly the reverse of vertical development. Horizontal development is based upon successive planning of development poles or centers to conquer new space, as a result of which men are displaced to resources. Where the term "vertical" attempts to suggest that expansion of the economic process is achieved in the same concentrated space, building upon what already exists, the term "horizontal" seeks to carry the idea that expansion of production leads to expansion of economic space.

Now that these two development patterns have been established in this extremely schematic way, it would be advisable to give a brief idea of how the structure of Latin American economic space has been formed, and at the same time go more deeply into certain perhaps too easily accepted concepts, as, for example, that of the poorly located natural resources of the interior of Latin America, "artificial development," and certain problems related to analysis of comparative costs of both development patterns.

If one looks at a map of Latin America, seeking to identify the main nuclei of economic activity—the most important conglomerations of population, industrialization, urbanization, and population density—it is obvious that along the coast of Latin America there is a kind of ring (at times lightly submerged in the interior) where the main economic and population centers are located. The latter are directly on the coast or at strategic distances from the coast. In the latter case, different factors have been influential. For example, in the case of Latin American economies of the Andean type there were evidently problems of environmental, plant, animal, and human health that impeded full use of coastal zones for many centuries, and, therefore, indigenous settlements were originally located in the highest but closest areas to the coast. In other cases, location is typically coastal. Thus, we find areas in this development we could call "vertical-coastal" of Latin America, in which there is at times an incredible agglomeration of rural population, revealing an obvious disequilibrium between the quantity and quality of land and the rural population living in those zones. And, closer to the interior of Latin America, there are immense vacant spaces with water resources, energy potential, abundant land in not terribly mild climates but still adequate, mineral resources, etc., that have not been exploited. Latin America's development process is based in general upon attempting to bring those natural resources to already existing population nuclei and to create "supply centers" in the direction of the interior in order to provision large urban nuclei of the vertical-coastal model. And one asks immediately: Why not create new markets and urban nuclei, new industrial nuclei directly linked to those resources? That is, why not displace population to resources instead of continuing the process of displacing resources to population? If there is a surplus of rural population in inhabited zones, why not displace these populations to areas where land is available and where they can create employment opportunities? And, in order to avoid rural dispersion, why not found industrial centers in areas where very little or nothing exists today and create the living conditions that could attract population and build human conglomerations of large dimension?

It is apparently less costly, and this is what I wish to put completely into question, to displace resources to population, and to exploit the external economies already created in Latin America's present development poles.

Naturally, the development process that began with colonial Latin America, favored coastal location of economic activity because it minimized export costs to the dominant center, i.e., to Spain and Portugal. Yet this same coastal location that created the colonial development system created a fact, a coastal export system that the later process of independent development of the Latin American countries respected. Leaping over a large chunk of history in order to approach the import-substitution process of the 1930s, 1940s, and 1950s, we find this latter process called "the drive toward the interior," even though it had a typically coastal location. This occurred because of the need to exploit national markets that already were located on the coast, markets that in turn had been conditioned by geographic concentration of population as a function of the dependent colonial system.

If we think of designing a development strategy, whether for one country or for Latin America as a whole, I believe that we must ask ourselves very seriously whether we must respect locations that originally responded to a totally different historic model, a historical model skewed to the outside, dependent and colonial. And this question is even more pertinent when, the import-substitution process showing signs of exhaustion, our countries began to think of Latin American integration. The latter presupposes, in addition to Latin American coastal communication by sea, interior communication and exploitation of vacant space. It also presupposes exploitation of a healthy proportion of the natural resources which, as a function of the vertical-coastal development pattern, are "mislocated." Naturally, these resources are not "mislocated" in terms of a less-dependent development model, if one thinks of Latin American integration, and if one thinks of exploitation of the Latin American potential internal market. Later in this essay I shall sustain the thesis that expansion of economic space, under definite circumstances, is an indispensable requisite for improved exploitation of Latin America's internal market, reducing marginality and unemployment, and contributing to improvement of income distribution.

Unfortunately, I must make very general statements of problems and theses that require much more detailed grounding than I am able to include herein. Through dialogue or later discussion many of these points can be clarified, but my thesis is not easily accepted. The principal objection refers to costs. These calculations can be analyzed, a procedure that economists are very accustomed to and that they seek to derive from a theory of resource allocation.

If more is invested in industrialization of existing poles, the product-capital relationship is more favorable, the increase in growth rate is greater, etc. Therefore, if a horizontal development pattern is established, in which population displacement to new spaces is indispensable, it will be necessary to create new infrastructure and new dynamic centers, involving extremely long-term investments with a more unfavorable product-capital relationship. This thesis does not appear rational from the point of view of the "economicity" of resources: They are scarce and cannot be employed simply by using this criterion because national product would then grow more slowly and problems would be sharpened.

I believe that these arguments lack solid theoretical grounding, implicitly presuppose a completely static theory of resource allocation, and are based upon more micro- than macroeconomic reasoning. This reasoning does not proceed from an analysis of the whole complex of the economic system's problems and viable roads to their solution, but rather from undue extension of a particular and partial concept, that of "efficiency," to the generality of the social whole. And it appears to me that comparison of costs is, in addition, totally false and inadmissible, even accepting the bases of this static economic theory, because in economics costs have significance such as the efficacy of a means of achieving a like end, and not as something that must be minimized per se. That is to say, costs must be compared in terms of the same objective and not by comparing costs resulting in different ends. Thus, if it can be demonstrated that within the context of a horizontal development pattern it is possible to resolve the problems of employment and marginality, and contribute to resolution of the problems of income distribution, then a goal is defined as an image objective of that horizontal development strategy, having a definite cost. "Economic calculation" could analyze different trajectories or different options for achieving this image objective, and, consequently, if this model of horizontal development has a definite cost, it can only be compared with another option leading to the same objective, so that the analysis may remain within the "economic calculation." In any other way, we simply enter the field of a political decision in which the objective is weakened to reduce its cost. I am not making a comparison of an economic kind that demonstrates that the horizontal development model is inefficient; I am simply making a selection of a political kind, in which I am choosing another image of development. Many of the comparisons of comparative costs of these two development patterns are falsely and simply based upon compromising the image objective that Latin America could pursue.

It is evident that much more rigorous proofs, including mathematical ones, of what I am saying could be presented, but this is not my purpose at the moment. I am simply establishing that, once the image objective pursued by a country or a continent is fixed, the only way to compare costs of alternative development models is to respect this image and not to change it. Upon these legitimate bases of comparison I could demonstrate that the horizontal development model, through expansion of economic space, is more efficient than the vertical development model.[1] On the other hand, it remains contradictory that all of the most-acceptable theses of economic development reject spontaneous resource allocation, and at the same time not only accept without discussion spontaneously generated spatial structure, but also use as its theoretical justification the same theoretical assumptions they reject. I could offer many more technical considerations related to a dynamic theory of resource allocation on which to base my position, but, in the meantime, I ask you to accept these arguments, which have been formulated more precisely in certain studies we have published.

The Different Cases

I do not wish to indulge in a totally global and generic discussion that makes everything vague. Rather, I should now like to discuss these general propositions more concretely, in terms of specific Latin American cases. How is this alternative between vertical and horizontal development in Latin America presented? Does this alternative assume different characteristics according to each country's stage of development? I think these are two questions we should consider and answer through concrete analysis. The Advisory Division of ILPES has been working for four or five years on analysis of national development strategies, and we are therefore familiar with various cases that I shall present to you here, cases in which this alternative between vertical and horizontal development clearly arises. I shall distinguish three typical cases, which may represent caricatures for certain countries, although I will not refer specifically to these countries. A first case, which we shall call A, is characterized by the fact that rural population grows in absolute terms, and what we could call "rural saturation" exists at the national level. Typical examples of Case A are Haiti and El Salvador, with reservations because it has a great growth dynamic beyond its borders. In this case, there are rural populations larger than the quantity and quality of their lands can permit employment at an adequate minimum-income level—that is, these countries have a net surplus of rural population at the national level.

A second case, B, also has a rural population growing in absolute terms, but its rural saturation does not exist at the national level—that is, there is no surplus of rural population at the national level. The quantity and quality of the country's total land permit employment of the present rural population and, even more, employment of the rural population that will exist in the next ten or fifteen years. Yet there are in these countries important "saturated" rural areas or pockets. These zones contain net surpluses of rural population, which weigh heavily on the economies of their country. The majority of the Andean countries—Ecuador, Bolivia, Peru, etc.—are within this category. The fringes of these countries contain net surpluses of rural population. At the same time, however, these countries also possess large vacant spaces within their boundary, unexploited and capable of receiving this rural population. Brazil's case is even more typical of this second category, since it has areas or pockets of important rural saturation; but at the same time no one can doubt that Brazil also has immense vacant spaces with great development potential. Central America, in general, should also be included in this category.

The third case, C, refers to countries in which absolute rural population is decreasing or is stagnating and that in general tend to have a low proportion of rural population. This would be the case with Uruguay, Argentina, Chile, etc., in which rural population is decreasing or has already decreased, or in which the maximum absolute limit has been reached, as reflected in stagnation over various years. At this point, the urbanization process begins to accelerate strongly. It is a process that may be efficient or inefficient, and that may lead to growing urban marginality or to growing incorporation of the population into the socioeconomic system.

Case A: Rural Saturation at the National Level

In this case, a surplus rural population exists at the national level without any possibility of being absorbed either through expansion of rural economic space or through structural reforms—even if reasonable levels of income and productivity per man employed in rural areas are sought. Only an extremely intense process of urbanization and industrialization could constitute a dynamic path to development for these cases. In fact, it is precisely the existence of a large excess of rural population and a proliferation of *minifundios* and subsistence economies that limit the financing capacity and the size of the internal market of those countries. And consequently these limit the countries' ability to undertake a dynamic process of development of urbanization and industrialization. That is to say, rural saturation reached such an extreme in these cases as to limit drastically passage to a succeeding stage, or to a model in which absolute decrease of rural population would be a requirement and in which a major process of urbanization and industrialization could be established on the basis of its development strategy. Unfortunately, this urbanization and industrialization must be based upon a market. If these countries have 60, 70, or 80 per cent of their populations in rural areas, but lack a man-land relationship permitting a sufficient and growing income per man employed, who demands industrial products dynamically, the *minifundio* and the self-sufficient economy proliferate. In addition, having limited total population, these countries maintain it in large part in a marginal position. The magnitude and growth of the internal market make it so difficult as almost to impede the passage to another development pattern in which the natural resource of land is not significant and in which what counts is technological advancement and the process of industrialization and urbanization. It is evident that this analysis presupposes a closed economy, and, therefore, at this point I make the distinction of the case of El Salvador, which has shown great dynamism in the growth of its exports.

In the case of El Salvador, the internal market it lacks is made up for by its relative efficiency in achieving access to the international market. This permits El Salvador to create a small "island of modernity" in the context of its national borders, and to enjoy a certain process of concentrated industrialization. It is an island of modernity, however, that is in contrast to the rest of rural and urban marginality persisting in El Salvador. To modernize the whole country would require unknown rates of growth in exports and internal reforms of great intensity. Since expansion of rural space is impossible in this case and since growth of the internal market, predominantly rural, is linked to such expansion, internal urbanization is a requirement for future development. Nevertheless, urbanization cannot find sufficient employment in the normal prevailing rates of industrialization, and the latter, in turn, cannot find sufficient markets because of unemployment and marginality. In these cases, it cannot be said that problem regions or deprived regions exist; rather, the entire country constitutes a problem area.

Case B: The Contrast Between Vacant Space and Rural Saturation

Case B is perhaps one of the most typical Latin American cases because there are still few countries in which the rate of urbanization is greatly accelerating and absolute rural population is decreasing. We include herein Central America in general, Ecuador, Peru, Bolivia, and Brazil. In all these countries there are important saturated rural areas and important vacant spaces. Nevertheless, in general, spatial development policy does not exist in those countries, and neither is there as a spontaneous tendency, migration of sufficient intensity to drain population from saturated rural areas to vacant or colonization zones. Displacement of man toward resources does not exist in an organic form so as to contribute to solving the problems of rural saturation in these countries. Naturally, inorganic migration occurs from saturated to vacant zones, but such migration, in addition to being insufficient, tends to disperse population and to reproduce the *minifundio* and the subsistence economy in new regions. This evidently causes great contrasts in the regional development of these countries. Let us think, for example, of Ecuador. We see there a highland zone, the Sierra, with great rural saturation —a great surplus of rural population that cannot be productively absorbed within the Sierra zone. Two other zones exist: the coast, with limited exploitation of natural resources, and the eastern zone (Oriente), under a system of exploitation even more inferior to its development potential.

Inefficient distribution of population in space creates well-known contradictions between regional and national development. For example, in the midst of an abundance of land and an abundance of labor, land within the area of influence of the "megalopolis" is governed by an economic system that assumes its scarcity and that tends to emphasize criteria of increasing yields per unit of land to achieve production goals. On the other hand, at the national level, solution to problems of employment, marginality, and income distribution demands a different path: an increase in cultivated land. Consequently, the problems of the megalopolis tend to be resolved in an independent way, almost as if it formed another country and the rest of the nation were its satellite. The example of the increasingly scientific agriculture of São Paulo in the face of Brazil's abundance of land constitutes a typical case of the phenomenon I am attempting to explain. In the same way, in Brazil, in the face of rural saturation of the Northeast, southern Minas Gerais, etc., there are vast extensions of vacant lands.

In these cases, it becomes evident that solution to regional problems cannot be sought within the limited context of the problem region, which in Ecuador's case would be the Sierra. One would search in vain for solution to the economy of Ecuador's Sierra, if the problem was contained solely within the region's borders. Solution to this regional problem can only be found if we think in national terms and if we think in terms of a new Ecuadoran spatial-economic structure. We must also think in terms of displacement of population from areas in which there is no opportunity for employment and from areas in which opportunities to be integrated into the economic system are lacking, to new zones having resources and sufficient land to give employment and income to currently marginal rural population. Thus, the development strategy that arises naturally in these cases implies large displacements of population and clearly typifies a model of horizontal development that cannot be based upon excessive allocation of resources to those poles displaying a certain dynamism at that time. On the contrary, it is necessary to occupy new space. This new space cannot be occupied under the modality of prolonging the rural subsistence economy, or as the prolongation of a typically agrarian economy. This new space can only be occupied with a sense of the future, opening new prospects for development through a combination of industrial and agricultural activities. It is interesting to note that in certain Latin American countries the restructuring of economic space and structural reforms are indissolubly united, and we shall use the case of Ecuador once again in order to visualize this problem.

If agrarian reform were attempted in the Ecuadoran Sierra, it could be argued that if we wish to give the Sierra's rural population an income permitting significant demand for industrial products, the present rural population would exceed the population actually necessary by approximately 600,000 persons. This surplus would tend to be displaced to other zones. Achievement of agrarian reform in this country, as in many other cases, is linked to the expansion of economic space. If the latter does not occur, the economic efficiency of agrarian reform is limited. This does not absolutely signify an argument against agrarian reform; on the contrary, it is an argument for couching it in the exact terms to assure its positive role in the development of a particular country.

On the other hand, because many so-called vacant lands actually have owners, neither is expansion of economic space feasible if the lend-tenure system is not reformed. Thus, expansion of economic space also requires agrarian reform, and consequently restructuring economic space and agrarian reform go hand in hand in this second case (B) under analysis. Yet there is another extremely important fact that determines the agricultural strategy arising naturally within the context of these groups of countries. We have become accustomed to hearing many agronomists expressing their worry over land yields. Generally, in all agricultural planning, great emphasis is placed upon scientific agriculture and an increase in yields per hectare on the assumption that this will contribute to raising income per man employed for the whole agricultural sector. Is this, then, an adequate policy for the countries represented by this case? On the contrary, I believe that it can be demonstrated that emphasis should not be placed upon yields per hectare to achieve agricultural production goals. What must be dominant is expansion of economic space. Increases in yields per hectare must be subordinate to the

objectives of the general strategy of national development
and to the strategy of agricultural development as the only
way to make the latter consistent with the general goals of
employment and reducing marginality. For example, considering only the objective of increasing agricultural production, the latter could be achieved in smaller spaces and
with great increases in yields per hectare. This would
increase surplus rural population and concentrate income
even more, leaving the problem of saturated rural areas
intact.

I shall give certain figures to exemplify better Ecuador's
case. The Sierra has approximately 1,850,000 persons in
rural areas; the coast, approximately 1,480,000 persons;
and the Oriente, a total of approximately 84,000 persons.
According to 1966 figures, there is a total of about
3,500,000 persons living in rural areas. Nevertheless, in
each of these zones a different relationship exists between
present rural population and the available land quantity
and quality that it can absorb. For example, in the Sierra,
there would be a surplus of some 650,000 rural inhabitants, more or less, if certain goals of income per man
employed in agriculture are attempted. I shall discuss this
matter specifically later in this essay. The coast, on the
other hand, could absorb some 370,000 additional persons,
in addition to absorption of those in the underemployment
category in the area. In the Oriente, there could be some
450,000 or 460,000 additional persons in relation to the
some 84,000 persons already there. How, then, are these
population surpluses and deficits in the different regions of
Ecuador produced? The answer lies in different causes,
which would require lengthy explanation. Simplifying the
problem, however, I shall attempt to analyze the situation,
referring to certain typical coefficients we use in studies of
this kind.

In these zones, only a certain proportion of the land is
used; even in the Sierra, with its great surplus of rural
population, less than the total is used. Only 74 per cent of

the land in the Ecuadoran Sierra is being used, only 36
per cent of the coast, and only 7 per cent in the Oriente,
giving a mean for the entire country of land under exploitation of approximately 45 per cent. And on this 45 per
cent (of land currently under cultivation) live 2.12 times
the rural population that could be supported if it were
desired to give the man employed in agriculture an adequate income. More than double the population necessary
to achieve certain income goals per man employed in
agriculture lives in less than half of Ecuador's exploitable
rural space. And, strangely enough, this population excess
is the same in terms of an "excess labor coefficient" for
the Sierra, coast, and Oriente. In other words, the limited
colonization carried out in the Oriente, using only 7 per
cent of the land, involves 2.2 times more rural population
than the already incorporated colonization area can support. Colonization is thus repeating the scheme of an economy of self-sufficiency and repeating the scheme of rural
saturation. On the coast live 2.3 times the rural population that the 36 per cent of the land under present cultivation could support, and in the Sierra live almost 2.1 times
the population that could reside on the 74 per cent of the
land under exploitation. This gives, for the country as a
whole, a saturation coefficient of 0.96, less than unity.[2]
That is to say, the country can still absorb additional
rural settlement within available known rural space, but
its margin of additional rural employment is low, because
only a little remains to reach a saturation coefficient of 1.
This coefficient 1 would represent more or less the man-
land relationship permitting elimination of rural underemployment. At present, there is a large mass of marginal
rural population, which has an income per rural inhabitant
of $42 per year more or less. (The latter sum counts for
nothing in terms of demand for industrial products and
from the point of view of demand for agricultural products.) If, in order to overcome this situation, the goal is
established of giving this marginal group an income of

$200 per man per year within the next twenty years, the only way to achieve this goal is by growing horizontally through occupation of this economic space and through change in the land-tenure system. In addition, stabilizing rural population is a requirement. In Ecuador's case, the goal of $200 per inhabitant per year is only compatible with a rural population fluctuating between 4 million and 4.2 million inhabitants. If Ecuador's rural population were to reach 5 million, this goal could not be achieved, and instead of $200 per year, the result would be a reduction to some $165 per year for forgotten agricultural groups.

One might ask: Why invest in expanding rural space and in displacing rural population from saturated to vacant zones? Why not absorb surplus rural population in a smaller space, transferring it more rapidly to the urban economy through concentration of investment in the industrial-development process? My answer to these questions would be the following. Within the previously noted context, such a solution would only be possible on paper, for these systems, by maintaining a great proportion of the population in the countryside and in a largely marginal condition, are not capable of motivating great industrialization. This is because of the weak growth of their internal market. They cannot conceive of extremely high rates of industrialization if demand for industrial products grows slowly. This is not the only reason; in many cases, the future existence of an efficient agricultural sector, even with a much smaller total rural population, is conditioned upon expansion of rural space.

A case is then stated herein in which definition of a spatial policy for the country exceeds in many respects the "regionalization of a development plan" and constitutes the essence of the country's development strategy, because the way of materializing its internal market, absorbing marginality, and giving income to the rural population so that it may demand industrial products, requires expansion of economic space on a par with structural reforms in agriculture. This should be done in such a way as to place the problem of the spatial policy of development, or of regional policy broadly understood, at the highest possible level in order to define a development strategy, and not in the subordinate context of regionalizing a previously conceived plan.

Case C: Singular or Plural Spatial Concentration of Urbanization and Industry

Those groups of countries in which rural population is decreasing and losing importance in occupational terms constitute examples of this case (Argentina, Chile, Uruguay, and Venezuela). For these countries, agricultural growth through expansion of space is in some cases not possible, and, in others, is not the most economic and efficient method. Scientific agriculture and increase in yields per hectare are the most adequate means to achieve the goals of agricultural development. Thus the process indicated for the preceding group is reversed. In the previous case, because total rural population was growing, it was more efficient from the point of view of the juxtaposition of national objectives that idle labor flow toward idle lands, producing an expansion of total economic space, and only to a lesser degree an increase in yields per hectare.

This does not mean that in certain situations in these countries there are not reasons to expand economic space. If there is a very low figure of land cultivated per man—for example, in the case of Venezuela, land area cultivated per man is much lower than in the United States—this could justify expansion of economic space for two reasons: first, to increase the general endowment of land per man and fix it at an adequate level, and, second, to eliminate certain pockets of rural saturation that also exist in Venezuela, primarily in mountainous regions. In the case of

Uruguay, which I do not know well, it appears to me that expansion of economic space is physically impossible and that increase in yields per hectare is the only path. The most general case of this group of countries is that when rural population begins to become a scarce resource—that is, when total rural population begins to decrease—the functioning of the most efficient production within the strategy of agricultural development must change. At this stage, this causes increasing yields per hectare to begin to assume clear preponderance. Horizontal development is not valid here for the agricultural sector, and expansion of space and elimination of marginality are suggested simply for other reasons, much more closely linked to urban-industrial problems. The rise of an adequate group of growth poles giving an "urban cover" to the entire country —that is, without leaving important zones on the margin of the influence of urban culture—sums up the problem for this case. Horizontal development must be industrial in this case to permit, among other reasons, vertical economic development of agriculture. Vertical application of technology to agriculture would thus be achieved around agricultural belts surrounding various industrial poles, which would not leave important areas on the margin of technology. Naturally, it is this case in which the problem of costs and external economies is posed most emphatically, because the problem arises of deciding whether to continue investing in the industrial development of an existing pole that has already attained a certain size, or to begin diverting resources to the creation of new industrial centers. We must, therefore, at this stage analyze in depth the problem of costs and external economies, and what they mean from the point of view of horizontal development.

Certain other arguments should now be added to my initial position regarding costs. I have often heard people, economists in particular, speak of "artificial development" and other similar concepts when new zones are concerned.

I suppose this arises from the opinion that it is not economic to create productive activity where nothing exists, where the present market does not justify it, etc. Exaggerating this concept, since external economies were in Europe, Latin America's entire development was artificial. The problem of the "artificial" is clearly temporary; what some refer to as "artificial" today ceases totally to be so twenty years later if an urban conglomerate and a population mass in a completely new center have been created, and if this zone achieves self-sufficiency through the dynamic force of the weight of its own market and through the external economies it creates by means of the mechanisms called artificial. It does not constitute, therefore, a definitive argument in favor of rejecting the thesis of spatial expansion via the creation of new industrial poles as against excessive strengthening of existing ones. I wish to avoid confusion at the outset by placing the horizontal development pattern adequately in the context of this case, in which the problem is typically urban-industrial. We must distinguish different sizes of poles and different development models that may be involved within this same case.

In countries in which relatively incipient urban-industrial poles still exist, it may be convenient to consolidate these poles before beginning the successive process of creating new centers. If we analyze the problem in greater depth, however, circumstances may be involved in which it is even preferable at this incipient stage to begin creating other centers.

I am going to add other, more qualitative, arguments to those I mentioned earlier regarding the problem of comparing costs involved in both models. We must ask ourselves whether a certain succession in the creation of poles does not underlie the maintenance of the growth dynamic of a country or region whose central motive force is the internal market. This succession departs from the problem of designing a development strategy that does not simply monitor the point at which it is no longer convenient to continue investing in existing poles, but also suggests opportune times for investment in new dynamic development centers. I state this for two reasons. In the first place, diffusion of the benefits of development tends to be confined to a "geographic area of influence." This may be argued theoretically, and empirical evidence may be presented from Latin American reality. The benefits of development appear to have a certain boundary, and beyond a certain radius of the physical-spatial action of dynamic centers the effects of development disappear.

In the second place, social agglomeration has both economies and diseconomies of scale, although I do not believe that a horizontal development pattern can be established that would lead to diseconomies of scale for certain development poles. The latter is a concept that has always been stated entirely too vaguely and imprecisely, and that has served to justify many different things. I believe that the problem does not consist in the fact that once a development pole has achieved a more or less precise size (and under certain circumstances), certain diseconomies of scale necessarily occur. I should say, on the other hand, that the problem is valid in terms of national and spatial allocation of resources, whether or not existing poles have diseconomies of scale.

The problem's central theme is whether, by means of concentrating investment in existing poles or, on the contrary, in new, progressively arising centers, the chosen image objective is achieved in less time and at lower cost. "Economies of scale" cannot be measured in terms of a development pole's efficiency per se, but rather in relation to the particular development strategy's objectives.

I believe that we would choose a sterile path indeed if we set ourselves to isolated investigation of when a pole arrives at optimum size and when it begins to suffer certain diseconomies of scale. For this reason, I refer in this statement to the fact that "social agglomeration" has certain economies of scale; I am not referring to strictly economic problems, but rather to the way of life originating in the size of certain cities and the possibilities of achieving active participation by members of the population and their self-realization as human beings when urban-industrial centers surpass a certain size. In addition, spontaneous spatial economic concentration does not permit the distribution of man in space that would achieve the best standards of living and employment opportunities. This would have to be the objective of spatial occupation planning, since the advantages already created in existing poles lead spontaneously to their reinforcement. If we accept these tendencies, we are tacitly accepting the fact that we are not moving toward the objectives we desire; in fact, we are guided by the "implicit objectives" to which spontaneous development leads us.

Vertical development also leads to "premature concentration" in islands of modernity, an extremely clear phenomenon in Latin America's case: large centers with all the "appearances" of development, in contrast to the marginality of the great masses. In this model of premature concentration in islands of modernity, the dynamism of those development centers does not reside in the masses' incorporation into the consumer market, but rather in the growing "diversification" of consumer goods to satisfy a luxury market.[3] The system increasingly tends to be based upon the importing of foreign technology, introducing the latest goods produced in the developed countries, permanently diversifying the market basket of goods, and substituting the dynamism proceeding from diversification of the market-basket goods of minority groups for the dynamism that this tight market cannot provide to mass consumer-goods industries.

This development model, in "islands of modernity," neither tends to resolve the problems of marginality nor needs to resolve them to have a certain dynamism. Of this we must be conscious; there is no serious contradiction within this model that could destroy its own dynamism within a foreseeable period of time. Therefore, the market's internal dynamic in this vertical-urban development scheme tends to be minor because, among other reasons, growth of the internal market is only necessary for the vitality of this development model. Growth of the internal market is only necessary in a development model based upon industrialization for the masses. Yet it is possible to conceive of another "vertical" and "diversification" model of industrialization, oriented toward a luxury market. Incorporation of the great masses who find themselves on the margin of the market is not necessary for this model, and, therefore, the latter tends to be inefficient from the point of view of the image objective we are pursuing, even though it is efficient on its "own terms."

Thus, in these cases in which "islands of modernity" tend to be produced, contrasting enormously with the system, we must ask ourselves whether this radiating capacity is of such a magnitude that it is gradually able to absorb the marginal population. Actually, except in very special cases, this radiating capacity does not exist and only causes a "spillage" of limited benefit to the great masses. I believe that we can also demonstrate very clearly that marginality tends to grow in relative terms under this system of islands of modernity. To put it another way, it is not a question of impatience in resolving Latin America's problems, but rather that this model simply does not tend to resolve them, in any time period. Therefore, if this insular radiating capacity is insufficient, what is necessary is the direst transformation of what we might call the "nonmodern" sector, moving directly to incorporate this sector, which is on the margin of the economic system and on the margin of the system's modernity. The direct transformation of this nonmodern sector implies a horizontal development pattern. It implies, if rural saturation exists, giving land to these people in new economic space, reform of systems of land ownership, and creation of new urban-industrial centers to give an urban spread to the entire system and incorporate the population into higher standards of living. Horizontal development also provides, among other things, a most important orientation toward planning: We cannot plan only the islands of modernity that tend to monopolize the bulk of the investment; we must also be directly preoccupied with transformation of deprived zones, because they do not tend to be influenced by the process of spontaneous development.

Conclusions

To end this essay, I should like to present the following main conclusions:

1. In the last two cases analyzed (B and C), horizontal development is a requirement for incorporating the population into the development process. In B, what is essential is a rural economy with a growing rural population, and in C, an urban economy. Yet, in both cases, the essential ingredient for producing direct transformation of the nonmodern sector is expansion of economic space.

2. Horizontal development, in Case B, rejects the thesis of agricultural growth with emphasis on yield per hectare, for the reasons noted, and Case C rejects the thesis of the radiating capacity of the center's macrocephalia toward the internal periphery; in the great majority of cases such radiating capacity does not exist in terms significant enough to achieve certain development objectives spontaneously. Thus it is necessary to seek direct transformation of the "nonmodern" sector, expanding economic space and creating new dynamic centers.

3. Costs of horizontal development may only be measured in terms of an image objective and not in terms of the cost of the existing development pattern. The existing development pattern does not lead to a desirable image

objective. It therefore has a lower coefficient of investment and requires a lower total amount of investment, and does not lead to an adequate solution.

4. A spatial-development policy becomes vital to economies searching for dynamism primarily in the internal market, because exploitation of the potential internal market of the Latin American countries, a potential that remains unexploited because of the marginality of the population (probably more than 50 per cent of Latin America's population is marginal), depends upon expansion of economic space. Half of the Latin American market remains unexploited. If the vitalization of internal markets is essential for certain countries because they do not enjoy the possibility of growing dynamically toward international markets, their great paths to development lie in the search for a new internal dynamic in which a spatial-development policy is vital to the definition of development strategy.

5. To conclude, this entire problem totally surpasses the matter of regionalizing a development plan, and constitutes in practice a challenge to the theories of growth of underdeveloped areas that suggest planning for allocation of resources and distribution of the benefits of development, but that unconsciously accept "laissez faire" in spatial structure. Such a contradiction reveals the weakness of the theoretical framework on which policies to combat underdevelopment are generally based.

NOTES

1. See Instituto Latinoamericano de Planificación Económica y Social (ILPES), "Polémica sobre el desarrollo del interior de América Latina," mimeo., 1967.

2. The coefficient of saturation is equal to the product of the coefficient of land use (0.45) times the coefficient of surplus labor (2.12).

3. See Matus Romo, *Algunas cuestiones básicas para la discusión de una estrategia de desarrollo latinoamericano* (Sept. 1968).

CHAPTER EIGHT

URBANIZATION AND DEVELOPMENT*

LUIS LANDER AND JULIO CÉSAR FUNES

There can be no doubt that in the end urbanism will
be victorious. . . . The last phase has not been
reached but it is clearly in sight. Urbanism will no
longer be confined to the cities; it will replace the
traditional folk societies. Farmers will live in less
densely populated settlements but farming will indicate only an occupational difference. As such it
will be carried out like any enterprise in the city.
The urban way of life will finally be the only mode of
living.

Egon Ernest Bergel

1. *Demographic Evolution*

Investigations carried out on prehistoric and protohistoric times (based on traditions and legends) show that
man has inhabited the earth and made use of tools for
more than 100,000 years and possibly for more than 1
million years.

During the Paleolithic and up through the middle of the
Mesolithic, population growth was, perforce, insignificant.
The United Nations has stated, "with an annual and con-
tinuous average growth of slightly less than 0.02 per cent,

* Reprinted from Documento URVEN 8 (Urbanización en Venezuela) (Caracas: Centro de Estudios Nacionales del Desarrollo—CENDES, 1965). English translation by Charles J.
Savio.

the descendants of only two dozen individuals would have reached 100,000 years ago the same figure that the world presently contains."[1]

In the Neolithic period subsistence agriculture accompanied the appearance of small villages, which continually changed sites because of soil exhaustion.

The appearance in the Nile region and in Mesopotamia, four thousand years before Christ, of collective labor, dike construction to contain flooding, irrigation ditches, etc., marked another important step in world population growth.

With respect to the above UN document, what we know about prehistoric and protohistoric times permits us to form only a very general idea of the changes undergone and allows formulation of the following principal types of demographic regions:

a. a region of civilizations linked to one another, centralized in agrarian and commercial cities, around the Mediterranean, and in the southern, southwestern, and eastern parts of Asia, as well as in an independent zone of similar nature in Mesoamerica;

b. peripheral frontier regions and isolated regions, with village and tribal economies in northern Europe, the northern part of Asia, sub-Saharan Africa, Oceania, and the greater parts of North and South America; and

c. regions of nomads, especially in southwestern Asia and embracing the horsemen-shepherds of central Asia.

With respect to the ancient world—even though we know that an increasing population in some form resulted —quantification of the population can be based only on indirect and not very reliable means. It is therefore estimated that the world population, at the dawn of the Christian era, oscillated between 200 million and 300 million inhabitants.

Growth of world population during the Middle Ages appears to have developed in the following form:

1. wide fluctuations, with a relatively small net growth rate and in some cases a net decrease, in the ancient centers of large population; China, India, Mesopotamia, the Near East, and Egypt;

2. similar but less violent fluctuations with an incipient tendency toward population increase in the South and West of Europe, with noticeable decreases at different times in Greece, Spain, and the Danube region;

3. accentuated increases in the "frontier regions" of central and eastern Europe. Information on population growth in frontier regions of other continents during this period is very limited.[2]

Serious doubts about world population growth also exist with regard to the beginnings of the Modern Age, but various estimates exist from 1650 on, as may be seen in Table 1.

Table 1
World Population Estimates by Regions, 1650-1950

Estimates and Dates	World Total	Africa	North America	Latin America	Asia Except U.S.S.R.	Europe and Asiatic U.S.S.R.	Oceania	Area of European Colonization
Estimates by Willcox:[a]	470	100	1	7	327	103	2	118
1650	470	100	1	7	327	103	2	118
1750	694	100	1	10	475	144	2	158
1800	919	100	6	23	597	192	2	219
1850	1,091	100	26	33	741	274	2	335
1900	1,571	141	81	63	915	423	6	573
Estimates by Carr-Saunders:[b]								
1650	545	100	1	12	257	103	2	113
1750	728	95	1	11	437	144	2	157
1800	906	90	6	19	595	193	2	224
1850	1,171	95	26	33	656	274	2	335
1900	1,608	120	81	63	857	423	6	573
Estimates by United Nations:[c]								
1920	1,834	136	115	92	997	485	9	701
1930	2,008	155	134	110	1,069	530	10	784
1940	2,216	177	144	132	1,173	579	11	866
1950	2,406	199	166	162	1,272	594	13	935

[a] Willcox, *Studies in American Demography* (1940), p. 45. The estimates with regard to the Americas are divided between those which correspond to North America and Latin America according to the figures which appear in pp. 37-44 of the cited work.

[b] Carr-Saunders, *World population* (1936), p. 42.

[c] United Nations, *Demographic Yearbook* 1949-50, (1950), p. 10; and United Nations, "The past and future growth of world population" (1951), Table II; the figures for 1940 correspond to unpublished estimates of the U.N.

[d] U.S.A., Canada, Alaska, St. Pierre, and Miquelon.

[e] Central and South America and the Caribbean Islands.

[f] Estimates on Asia and Europe which appear in the Willcox and Carr-Saunders series have been readjusted to include the Asiatic population of the U.S.S.R. in that of Europe rather than in that of Asia. The following approximate figures were used for the population of Asiatic U.S.S.R.: 1650, 3,000,000; 1750, 4,000,000; 1800, 5,000,000; 1850, 8,000,000; 1900, 22,000,000.

[g] Includes North America, Latin America, Europe with Asiatic U.S.S.R. and Oceania.

Source: United Nations, *Factors, Determinants and Consequences of Demographic Trends*, New York, 1953.

Annual rates of population growth, based on the preceding estimates, are as follows:

Table 2

Average Annual Rate of Growth of World Population
1650-1950

| | Annual Growth Expressed in % of | |
| | Total | World |
Era	Willcox Data from U.N.[a]	Carr-Saunders Data from U.N.[b]
1650-1950	0.5	0.5
1650-1750	0.4	0.3
1750-1800	0.6	0.4
1800-1850	0.3	0.5
1850-1900	0.7	0.6
1900-1950	0.9	0.8
1900-1920	0.8	0.7
1920-1930	0.9	0.9
1930-1940	1.0	1.0
1940-1950	0.8	0.8

[a]Computations based on the Willcox estimates for the years 1650-1900 in *Studies in American Demography* (1940), p. 45, and on U.N. estimates for the years 1920-1950 in *Demographic Yearbook* (1949-50), p. 10.

[b]Computations based on estimates of Carr-Saunders for the years 1650-1900 in *World Population* (1936), p. 42, and on U.N. estimates for the years 1920-1950 in *Demographic Yearbook 1949-1950* (1950), p. 10.

Source: United Nations, *op. cit.*, p. 13.

A tendency toward an increase in the growth rate can be seen from 1850 on; nevertheless, unreliability of data cautions against unreserved acceptance.

At any rate, between 1650 and 1950, three centuries, world population quadrupled or quintupled, depending on the source used, and the cumulative annual growth rate reached 1 per cent in the 1930–40 decade, although it fell for a time to 0.8 per cent in the following decade as a consequence of the devastation of World War II.

It is important to point out that the tendency of an increasing population growth rate, together with the growing tendency toward spatial concentration, on which we will elaborate below, calls for a more thorough knowledge of these phenomena. A growing number of investigators are trying to formulate a theoretical framework that can explain these facts and offer a guide to the solution of these problems, whose complexities increase day by day.

Insofar as Latin America is concerned, its population growth shows an even greater increase, reaching higher levels than all the other regions of the world in the past few decades. This tendency, which was incipient in certain countries during the nineteenth century, became generalized throughout practically the entire region in the twentieth century. A high birth rate, a constantly diminishing death rate, and high immigration rates from the exterior are the reasons for this phenomenon.

Argentina and Brazil are the Latin American countries whose populations grew most in the past century. Mortara's estimates for Brazil show that the increase for 1840–90 was 131 per cent and for 1890–1940 was 190 per cent, which means that the cumulative annual growth rate for this latter period was 1.69 per cent.[3] The increase for the entire region in the past few decades is even greater. Increase in Latin America's population for the years 1920–50, according to ECLA estimates, shows, on the basis of questionable statistics, an annual rate of 1.9 per cent. But the levels of the figures after 1950, which are much more reliable, are even higher. Table 3 shows population estimates and projections of the 20 Latin American countries and, separately, those of other countries and territories of the region for 1925–80.

In the 40 years 1925–65, the population of the 20 Latin American nations went from 92,852,000 to 236,852,000 inhabitants, equivalent to an annual growth rate of 2.4 per cent. The other countries and territories in the region went from 4,214,000 in 1925 to 8,190,000 in 1965, for an annual rate of 1.7 per cent. Total population of the region increased from 97,066,000 in 1925 to 245,042,000 in 1965, giving an annual rate of increase of 2.4 per cent.

Table 3

Population Totals, 1925-1980

(Mid-Year Estimates and Projections)
(Thousands of Persons)

The 20 Latin American Nations and Other Countries
and Territories of the Region

Year	Latin America (20 Nations)	Other Countries and Territories of the Region	Total
1925	92,852	4,214	97,066
1930	102,613	4,519	107,132
1935	112,727	4,932	117,659
1940	124,143	5,392	129,538
1945	137,879	5,867	143,746
1950	155,973	6,378	162,351
1955	178,731	6,881	185,612
1960	205,787	7,413	213,200
1965	236,852	8,190	245,042
1970	272,912	9,031	281,943
1975	314,990	9,923	324,913
1980	363,802	10,874	374,668

Source: Boletín Estadístico de América Latina, Vol. III, No. 1,
United Nations, February 1966.

Projections for the year 1980 show a population for
the 20 Latin American nations of 363,802,000; for other
countries and territories of the region, 10,874,000, and a
total for the region of 374,668,000 inhabitants. These
projections were figured using annual rates of growth of
2.9 per cent for the 20 nations and of 1.9 per cent for
the other countries and territories.

In order to present with greater clarity the situation
that the region will face in the present stage of the
"demographic explosion," estimates and projections of population for the decades 1930–80 and the average annual
growth are presented in Table 4.

The different zones that make up the region exhibit
different rates of growth. The temperate zone, composed
of Argentina, Chile, Uruguay, Paraguay, and the Falk-
land Islands, has the lowest rates—approximately 1.9 per
cent annually for the past decade—while the tropical
zones and continental Mesoamerica reach rates that ex-

Table 4
Total Population, 1930-1980
(Mid-Year Estimates and Projections)

	1930	1940	1950	1960	1970	1980
Latin America (thousands of persons) 20 countries	102,613	124,143	155,973	205,787	272,912	363,802
Average annual increase		1.9	2.3	2.8	2.9	2.9
Other countries and territories (thousands of persons)	4,519	5,395	6,378	7,413	9,031	10,874
Average annual rate of increase		1.8	1.8	1.5	2.0	1.9
Total (thousands of persons)	107,132	129,538	162,351	213,200	281,943	374,668
Average annual rate of increase		1.9	2.3	2.8	2.9	2.9

Source: United Nations, *Boletín Estadístico de América Latina*, Vol. III, No. 1, February 1966.

ceed 3.00 per cent annually and show signs of exceeding even that figure in the immediate future.

With regard to Venezuela, gains realized in this century show a marked tendency toward constant increase. Figures in Table 5 reflect estimates and projections for the Venezuelan population and cumulative annual growth rates during the decades 1930–80. Even though the rate

Table 5
VENEZUELA
Total Population, 1930-1980
(Mid-Year Estimates and Projections)

	1930	1940	1950	1960	1970	1980
Thousands of persons	2,950	3,710	4,974	7,331	10,399	14,827
Average annual increase		2.3	3.0	3.9	3.6	3.6

Source: United Nations, *Boletín Estadístico de América Latina*, Vol. III, No. 1, February 1966.

of 3.9 per cent for the decade 1950–60 reflects a slight decrease, it is not unreasonable to predict that the Venezuelan population will double in the 20 years 1960–80.

Before drawing conclusions from the facts presented and probable future tendencies, it is necessary to introduce a very important variable: urbanization.

2. The Process of Urbanization

In man's long history (100,000 or 1 million years) the appearance of cities and urbanization is relatively recent:

7,000–10,000 years. Nevertheless, the forms that urbanization has taken in our time have a much more recent history. It is evident that the Industrial Revolution, which began in England, is the fundamental reason for the unprecedented concentration of human beings in space. But before presenting data that show the tendency toward concentration, it is necessary to explain what is meant by urban and rural, because conclusions drawn will depend to a large degree on the definitions used.

The examples offered by various investigations of the topic, whether conducted by international organizations, universities, or other national agencies, have not clarified the situation. Social investigations have defined "urban" and "rural" in an arbitrary manner usually governed by the specific needs of the project under study. This is one of the reasons that the term "urbanization" means different things to the various scientific disciplines. Thus, urbanization to the demographer is the process of population growth; to the sociologist, a process in which a change of life style occurs; to the engineer or architect, a physical process; to the economist, a process involving changing forms of production; to the political scientist, an institutional-legal process, etc.; but these changes do not take place simultaneously in today's rapidly changing societies.

A hazy region lies between clear-cut examples of rural and urban, where the definitions of the different disciplines do not coincide. It is in these ambiguous zones, where, for example, a demographer might tell us that an agglomeration of 6,000 inhabitants is an urban population but a sociologist would object, saying:

Keeping in mind population and occupational figures, we must recognize that before calling a person or an aggregate of individuals "urban" or not, we have to take their attitudes and behavior into account because these could vary along the urban-rural continuum. In the majority of countries there is a tendency of the rural areas to adopt an urban life style. Such an urbanization process is quite noticeable, as Nelson has observed in certain isolated Mormon communities: "Urbanization or, as some sociologists label it, the secularization of life, is proceeding with giant strides. The communications and transport networks so characteristic of contemporary life bring even the most remote areas into instant contact with the rest of the world. The diffusion of urban habits in the countryside is unmistakable everywhere. The number of farmers diminishes while the size of the farms increase. Life becomes more impersonal, mutual help becomes less frequent and contractual forms of association increase in number. Formal organizations increase simultaneously with new interests—economic, social, recreative, educative. New occupations are created as specialization and division of labor become more elaborate. Population homogeneity gives way to a growing heterogeneity. Attitudes change. The feeling of community declines in conjunction with the development on all sides of special interests. These developments can clearly be seen in today's Mormon village as well as in all U.S. communities."[4]

From the above may be seen that the concept of urbanization is more complicated than a mere demographic definition. Furthermore, as Hope Tisdale Eldridge tells us: "Urbanization as a process of population concentration involves two elements: (a) multiplication of contact points, and (b) increase in the size of individual concentrations. As a result, the proportion of the population living in urban places increases."[5]

After pointing to the criteria that the UN presented in its 1955 *Demographic Yearbook,* Philip Hauser affirms that "even for census purposes, the definition of 'urban' involves more than one dimension and the establishing of an arbitrary cutting point between urban and rural. . . ."

In practice, many international studies consider populations greater than 20,000 as "urban" because data are usually presented that way and because an agglomeration of that size exhibits no rural characteristics.[6]

As a consequence of this arbitrary cut-off point, different nations' censuses use other idiosyncratic figures. In Ireland, "urban" refers to centers populated with 1,500 or more inhabitants, while in Mexico the figure is 2,000 or more. In Venezuela, three divisions were established for purposes of the 1961 General Census of Population: an "urban" area to refer to population centers with more than 2,500 inhabitants, an "intermediate" area to those centers with between 1,000 and 2,500 inhabitants, and a "rural" area for places with less than 1,000 inhabitants. In the United States, "urban" means places with 2,500 or more inhabitants, but, in addition, there are three other forms of population concentration that come under that classification: "Urbanized Areas," which include a central city and all contiguous territory in which the population density equals 2,000 per square mile, political boundaries notwithstanding; Standard Metropolitan Statistical Area (SMSAs), which include a city (or cities) of more than 50,000 inhabitants, the county in which it (they) is located, and contiguous counties that are socially and economically tied to the city (cities); and Urban Regions, which are made up of contiguous SMSAs.[7]

Finally, Bergel states:

> It is evident that a place does not become urban when it goes from 2,499 to 2,500 inhabitants; it is equally obvious that a place with 2,500 and one with more than 1,000,000 inhabitants have to have more in common than just being above a certain boundary line in order to justify their being lumped together and distinguished from rural areas.[8]

Some efforts have been made to define exactly what is urban, trying to keep in mind the numerous factors involved in the process. Sorokin and Zimmerman, for example, list eight characteristics that allow differentiation between urban and rural: (1) occupations; (2) environment; (3) community size; (4) population density; (5) heterogeneity or homogeneity of the population; (6) social differentiation or stratification; (7) mobility; and (8) the system of interaction (number and type of contacts).[9] This greatly complicates the picture because the functions of urban nuclei vary greatly in form, depending on time and place.

In a study recently begun by CENDES in collaboration with the United Nations, it was necessary to define urban and rural population while keeping in mind the complexity of the problem—that is, all of the different elements bearing on the process.[10] One of the most important objectives of that study was to arrive at specific recommendations for solution of present and future urban problems and to establish *a policy for distribution of population and factors of production within the context of a national development policy.* This objective demands clear definition, which can be adjusted to Venezuela's present realities and classification of all population centers that are attracting waves of migrants. It is in these centers that the bulk of rapid growth and problems associated with such growth are expected to appear.

For this reason, the variables judged most important in influencing the process were considered very carefully to promote uniform utilization. As a first approximation, the elements considered in their different aspects were the following:

With regard to the *demographic aspect,* the patterns of migratory currents were studied, keeping in mind the size of populated centers and their absorption of migration. With these factors it was possible to set a limit to what we will consider "urban" for the purposes of this study. Table 6 presents the populated centers of Venezuela according to the censuses of 1920, 1950, and 1961.

Table 6
Classification of Venezuela's Population Centers
According to Size for Censuses of 1920, 1950, 1961

Size of the Population Centers	1920		1950		1961		% of Population		
	Pop. Ctrs.	Pop.	Pop. Ctrs.	Pop.	Pop. Ctrs.	Pop.	1920	1950	1961
100,000 and more	1	107,236	3	1,034,754	5	2,256,892	4.5	20.5	30.0
50,000-99,999	—	—	3	207,169	9	621,171	—	4.1	8.2
20,000-49,999	1	46,099	12	376,730	22	675,371	2.0	7.5	9.0
10,000-19,999	5	68,718	16	229,754	33	437,749	2.9	4.6	5.8
5,000-9,999	11	76,179	41	272,606	51	352,603	3.2	5.4	4.7
2,500-4,999	28	90,694	88	298,431	102	361,500	3.8	5.9	4.8
1,000-2,499	101	158,270	198	291,587	256	373,336	6.7	5.8	5.0
Less than 1,000	10,472	1,817,902	40,088	2,323,805	23,694	2,445,375	76.9	46.2	32.5
Total.	10,619	2,365,098		5,034,836		7,523,999	100.0	100.0	100.0

Source: Dirección General de Estadísticas y Censos Nacionales de Venezuela, p. 72.

The figures in Table 6 demonstrate the tendency of the Venezuelan population to concentrate in the larger populated centers. This tendency is clearest in the lower ranges of the 10,000–19,999 class. One difficulty, and the reason that data cannot be strictly adhered to, is that certain changes in size can move a populated center from one class to another. This means that classes are not strictly comparable over time.

Comparing the corresponding data for the censuses of 1950 and 1961, the following class changes are presented:

Table 7

Class	No. of Population Centers in 1961 Which Changed Class Since 1950 Census	% of Total Number of Centers Presently in Class
100,000 and above	2	40.0
50,000-99,999	6	66.6
20,000-49,999	16	72.7
10,000-19,999	31	93.9
5,000- 9,999	30	58.8
1,000- 4,999	144	40.2

Table 7, in addition to showing the accelerated growth of population centers, shows the relationship between the intensity of that phenomenon and the size of centers. The group that exhibited the most change was precisely that comprising 10,000–19,999 inhabitants. This is evidently a crucial category; the almost complete transformation of this group (93.9 per cent were in a different class in 1950) as well as of the 5,000–9,999 group shows that the most accentuated growth took place in these classes. Using hypothetical rates of normal growth, based on their weighted means as equal to the nation's total population, the following table of migration totals was obtained:

Table 8

Classes	Migration Levels	Population Data Start 1950	Finish 1961	Rate[b]
100,000 and above	684,000	1,187,990	2,256,892	39.7
50,000–99,999	209,000	304,443	621,171	45.2
20,000–49,999	231,000	328,088	675,371	46.0
10,000–19,999	147,000	214,989	437,749	45.0
5,000– 9,999	67,000	210,280	352,600	23.8
1,000– 4,999	75,000	473,830	734,836	12.4
Less than 1,000[a]	−790,000	2,323,805	2,445,375	−34.0

[a]Calculation based on population centers with less than 1,000 inhabitants in 1950.
[b]Derived by dividing the migration level by the average population during that period.

Migration levels for each class were obtained by using data from populated centers within those classes from the 1961 census. Migration levels show the tendency of the population to concentrate in population centers according to size. It is again evident that the power of attraction is close to a maximum with the 10,000–19,999 class, and then drops off sharply. This would seem to indicate agreement with the working hypothesis that 10,000 inhabitants is a meaningful boundary for urban population centers; nevertheless, keeping in mind the fact that this has been the group that has had its component centers change most significantly—that is, that the great majority of the centers that fell in this category for 1961 were in the next lower category (5,000–9,999) in 1950, it was decided to lower the dividing line to 5,000 inhabitants.

As far as the *sociological aspect* is concerned, the

scheme is based to a great degree on the well-documented premise that important differences exist between rural and urban life styles. For example, by focusing attention on the cultural system, one would expect to find the incidence of modern attitudes much greater in urban areas than in rural.

Therefore, it is possible to establish a threshold between urban and rural by investigating the attitudes held by various groups along the continuum which, at the same time it considers traditional-modern extremes, takes into account the size of population centers. Based on this premise, the attitudes of 28 sample groups were analyzed.[11] In the preliminary analysis, it was observed that in addition to the number of inhabitants of a particular place, other variables, such its economic status and the occupational profile of its inhabitants, exerted a decisive influence on the degree of modernism exhibited.

In order to determine the threshold, then, it was necessary to control the effect of these variables. From the analysis it could be seen that the normative orientations of three groups living in centers with less than 10,000 inhabitants, which formed part of the economic occupational sphere and which could be classified as of low socioeconomic status, consistently occupied the lowest ranks in the attitudinal modernism scales.

It was also observed that significant differences existed between these groups and those of similar status and economic activity, who lived for the most part in population centers of 20,000 to 100,000 inhabitants. Of course, these latter groups showed a low level of modernization, and a certain heterogeneity existed among them, indicating that the people who made up those groups were undergoing a process of transition; in other words, the internalization of all aspects of urban values had not been equally achieved by the groups.

From the above, it can be concluded that, given homogeneous levels of socioeconomic status and occupation, it is possible to identify important differences in the attitudes of groups, depending on the size of population centers in which they reside.

It was noted that if a population concentration of less than 10,000 inhabitants was used to define a rural population, the most traditional sectors of the population would fall within this rural zone; but if this limit is set too low—for example, 1,000 or less inhabitants—there is risk of excluding some traditional groups with very rural attitudes from that classification. A further problem is that, on passing into the urban category, these people will make urban population centers appear less modern attitudinally. On the other hand, if population centers with more than 10,000 inhabitants are considered as rural zones, there is the possibility of the opposite problem: Groups with modern orientations would be considered as rural, thereby distorting the life-style image within that sector. For the reasons mentioned, the figure of 10,000 inhabitants was chosen as most recommendable from the sociological point of view for distinguishing between urban and rural sectors in present-day Venezuela.[12]

With regard to the *physical aspect*, the fact that population is grouped with varying degrees of density had to be kept in mind. In population aggroupations there is a tendency of housing distribution to follow a certain pattern in order to facilitate traffic, both of persons and vehicles, for better internal and external communications. Moreover, whenever it is realized in these population concentrations that new activities are needed, the necessity of allocating them physical space contributes to creating an area or neighborhood which, however small, is made up of buildings and streets with an increasingly urban appearance.

In this process, from the physical point of view, it is extremely difficult to establish what was earlier called a "threshold" between the rural and the urban. The concept of density is of no use here because, aside from being quite relative, it is possible to imagine a typically rural agglomeration with high population density; and, on the other hand, it is also possible to conceive of a typical urban concentration with a low density. Nevertheless, by analyzing extreme cases where there is no doubt about whether a center is urban or rural, there are still profound differences that have to be taken into consideration when it becomes time to establish the dividing line.

In keeping with this notion, the principal characteristics of the two extremes were taken into consideration, remembering all the while the declared goal and one of the most fundamental purposes of this study: arriving at specific recommendations for solution of present and future urban problems.

Characteristics of the population centers toward the rural end of the continuum were defined as follows:

a. All have more or less equal accessibility and therefore are not subject to increasing demand for the area or to rapid appreciation of the land.

b. Different land uses are rather haphazard, even though a tendency of several different uses to congregate in one center can be noticed.

c. Vital necessities are reduced to providing indispensable services, such as water, light, sewers, paved streets, schools, dispensaries, and so forth.

d. In order to guide their growth, given the rudimentary nature of the needs and the stage of development, all that is required are a few general norms, somewhat like the *Leyes de Indias,* and simple programs of public works.

At the other extreme, the principal characteristics of typically urban centers were defined as follows:

a. Interurban transport is a patent necessity because distances are now too long to be covered on foot;

b. Land uses reach a certain level of specialization, and

the competition for land creates rapid appreciation in the value of real estate;

c. Definition of a center and periphery;

d. Appearance of congestion, noise, and change of land use with concomitant deterioration of physical structures;

e. Congestion and the increase of vehicles require more complex organizing of traffic, including the establishment of vehicle parking, especially in the city center;

f. Juxtaposition of incompatible activities, competition for space, and rapid changes in physical structure point to the necessity of zoning the city into specialized sections in such a way as to minimize inefficiency and conflict.

As mentioned above, identification, quantification, and solution of these problems are some of the basic objectives of this study of the phenomenon of urbanization. To those ends, the line between urban and rural will be taken to be the area in which problems begin to become noticeable.

Past studies and experience through direct contact with Venezuela's population centers permit the following observations:

1. In population centers of less than 10,000 inhabitants, problems are of a primitive type.

2. In centers of from 10,000–20,000 urban problems are quite noticeable but not complex.

3. Where the elements that complicate the urban structure as well as the characteristics and problems that have been outlined above begin to acquire more and more relevance and complexity is in the area of greater than 20,000 inhabitants. For the above reasons, from a purely physical point of view, the 20,000-inhabitant level is considered the limit sought.

Considering *economic aspects* in order to distinguish urban-rural categories, studies of the economic base of populated centers show important differences according to size.

The most significant item in this sense is the employment distribution structure according to branches of economic activity. Another important classification for pointing out economic differences is the level and type of industrial development of these population concentrations. The censuses that have been carried out in Venezuela lack this information at the level at which it is most needed, and therefore some indirect indicators are taken as rough approximations on the assumption that certain economic activities cannot be pursued without the presence of other factors such as economic institutions, public services, means of communication, and so forth. These indirect measures, which can be easily obtained, allow the drawing of conclusions that can be checked against the behavior of other factors, which, like the structure of employment or of industrialization, will lead to knowledge of the economic bases of urban centers.

Three items were considered capable of shedding light on urban-rural classification: economic institutions, provision of public services, and communications and transportation facilities. Different measures were considered for these three items, and, noting their stability or complete absence in populated centers, an urban-rural boundary was established at 5,000 inhabitants, as well as values for differing degrees of urbanization.

It can be concluded from this lengthy exposition that serious difficulties lie in the way of interdisciplinary acceptance of the concept of urbanization and, therefore, of what constitutes urban and rural populations.

Nevertheless, taking into account all the aspects involved in the phenomenon, the following distributions were used for purposes of the study:

Rural population: Groupings in centers of 4,999 or less inhabitants.

Urban population: Groupings in centers of 5,000 or more inhabitants.

In addition, the following degrees of urbanization were designated:

Level of Urbanization	Inhabitants
First	5,000 – 19,999
Second	20,000 – 49,999
Third	50,000 – 99,999
Fourth	100,000 and more

We can now discuss urbanization and its consequences in the world, in Latin America, and in Venezuela. As was stated earlier, the process of urbanization, with the appearance of cities, is a relatively recent phenomenon in the history of mankind. Serious difficulties arise in trying to estimate the per cent of world population that lives in urban centers, but it is clear that in the first thousands of years the process was very slow. As Lampard states:

Human populations have been integrated into "cities" for almost 7,000 years. For most of this time, however, urban settlements were scarcely recognizable and, when in the course of a little more than 5,000 years, the first ones became definitive, they were limited—due to restrictions placed on them by the immediate environment —to a few scattered areas. Never did these urban areas contain more than a small fraction of the total population; perhaps they attained levels of 15–20 per cent of a localized population but never more than 5 per cent of a larger regional base. After thousands of years of such relatively stable levels of urbanization, the past two or three centuries witnessed an unprecedented increase in the rates and levels of urbanization with the repercussions and ramifications which distinguish the period A.D. 1750–1850 as a crucial period in the history of human society. The impediments which had moderated human growth and redistribution until that time were rapidly reduced. The emergence of societies due to rapid urbanization with more than 50 per cent of their population growth residing in cities represents one of the most drastic changes in the human capacity for social organization since the agricultural and urban revolutions which took place 6,000–10,000 years before.[13]

Table 9 presents data giving some idea of the urbanization process after 1800.

Table 9

Population: World and Urban

1800-1960

Year	World Population (millions)	Population in Cities Greater Than 5,000 Inhabitants (millions)	Per Cent in Cities	
			5,000 and Above	100,000 and Above
1800	906	27,2	3.0	1.7
1850	1,171	74,9	6.4	2.3
1900	1,608	218,7	13.6	5.5
1950	2,400	716,7	29.8	13.1
1960	2,995	948,4	31.6	20.1

Source: Eric E. Lampard, "Historical Aspects of Urbanization," *The Study of Urbanization.*

It should be noted that if we consider the population living in centers of more than 5,000 inhabitants as urban, only 3 per cent of the world population in 1800 was urban. This figure had increased to 31.6 per cent in 1960.

The tendency of the population to concentrate in urban centers at the same time as population was increasing first took place in those countries where the Industrial Revolution succeeded in raising them from backwardness and transforming them into developed countries:

The last two centuries (1750–1950) have been witness to an unprecedented concentration in urban areas of people and economic activity due to the Industrial Revolution. During this brief period many villages and towns in Europe and North America ceased to be regional markets of farmers and artisans and were converted into throbbing centers of all types of manufacturing, services and distribution activities, characteristic of an expanding economy.[14]

Nevertheless, although this may have been the tendency of the now developed countries, study of these same vari-

Table 10

Indices of Urbanization in Latin America

| Country | Year of Census | Percentage of Total Population Which Lives in Localities of More Than: | |
		20,000 Inhabitants	100,000 Inhabitants
Central America and the Antilles			
Costa Rica	1950	17.5	17.5
Cuba	1953	36.5	21.9
El Salvador	1950	13.0	8.7
Guatemala	1950	11.2	10.2
Haiti	1950	5.1	4.3
Honduras	1950	6.8	0.0
Mexico	1950	24.1	15.1
Nicaragua	1950	15.2	10.3
Dominican Republic	1950	22.4	15.9
Panama	1950	11.1	8.5
South America			
Argentina	1947	48.3	37.2
Bolivia	1950	19.7	10.6
Brazil	1950	20.2	13.2
Colombia	1951	22.3	14.7
Chile	1952	42.9	28.5
Ecuador	1950	17.8	14.6
Paraguay	1950	15.2	15.2
Peru	1940	13.9	8.4
Uruguay	1950[b]	36.2	32.6
Venezuela	1950	31.0	16.6

[a]The data for Panama and Colombia include Indian populations organized in tribes.

[b]Estimates from "The World Distribution of Urbanization" by Kingsley Davis and Hilda Hertz, *Bulletin of the International Statistical Institute*, Vol. XXXIII, Part IV, p. 237.

Source: United Nations, *Demographic Aspects of Urbanization in Latin America.*

ables in today's underdeveloped areas of the world seems to indicate that increase and concentration of population may be necessary but not sufficient conditions for industrial development.

We turn now to the phenomenon of urbanization in Latin America, and in Venezuela in particular. The process of urbanization began intensively in Latin America in the nineteenth century for a few countries and for almost the whole continent in this century. Data from Table 10 show the degree of urbanization attained.

The data show notable differences among the countries that make up the area. Even as early as 1950 the continent as a whole exhibited an index of urbanization greater than the world average, and three countries—Argentina, Chile, and Uruguay—were among the fifteen most urbanized countries of the world, as may be noted in Table 11.

Table 11

Per Cent of Population Living in Cities of Principal World Regions, 1950

Region	Per Cent of Population in Cities		Index of Concentration in Large Cities 100 × (2) / 1
	20,000 and More Inhabitants	100,000 and More Inhabitants	
	(1)	(2)	(3)
World	21	13	62
Oceania	47	41	87
North America[a]	42	29	69
Europe	35	21	60
U.S.S.R.	31	18	58
Latin America	25	17	68
South America	26	18	69
Central America and the Antilles	21	14	64
Asia[b]	13	8	63
Africa	9	5	51

[a]Includes U.S.A. and Canada.
[b]Excludes U.S.S.R.

Source: United Nations, *Demographic Aspects of Urbanization in Latin America.*

Accelerated urbanization began in Venezuela in the past few decades, but the change from a backward agricultural country to an industrial and modern one has been so abrupt that the transition, still in process, has created a complex of problems which, as of this writing, have proved insoluble.

Table 12 shows the situation for different years.

Table 12

VENEZUELA

Per Cent of Total Population Living in Centers of
Population Greater Than 20,000 and 100,000 Inhabitants

Census Year	% Centers Greater Than 100,000	% Centers Greater Than 20,000
1936	10.4	19.1
1941	11.6	21.1
1950	16.6	31.0
1961	29.9	47.2

Source: United Nations, *Demographic Aspects of Urbanization in Latin America.*

The average annual rate of growth of the population living in centers of 20,000 and above or in those of 100,000 and above, and the total population of the country, are shown in Table 13.

Table 13

VENEZUELA

Average Annual Rate of Growth of Population
Living in Selected Areas and of Total Population

Intercensal Period	Localities with More Than 100,000 Inhabitants	Localities with More Than 20,000 Inhabitants	Total Population
1936-41	4.8	4.7	2.7
1941-50	6.8	1.0	3.0
1950-61	7.5	7.1	3.6

a. The average annual rate of growth is calculated by dividing the intercensal growth by the average population for that period (defined as the average of initial and final censused populations for each period) and by the number of years in the intercensal period.

3. *Evolution of Socioeconomic Development*

We will put aside for the moment the population situation in order to consider economic and social development and eventually whatever relations may exist between the two. The existence of countries more developed than others has always been with us. In the history of mankind various peoples have been found—for whatever reasons—to be in the forefront of the known world.

Nevertheless, the past 250 years have witnessed spectacular advances in certain areas, while improvements were much more modest in remaining parts of the globe. This gave rise to the dual situation in which one third of the world's population—in which the people of the U.S.A., the U.S.S.R., northwestern Europe, Canada, Australia, New Zealand, and other small areas are included—makes up an "upper class of nations" and, on the other hand, the remaining two thirds of the population constitute the lower class of nations, whose most striking characteristic is an income level much lower than the members of the first group. In this bottom stratum are to be found the Latin American nations as well as African, non-Soviet Asian, and even a few European ones.

The "upper class of nations," which is the most industrialized, exhibits a constant tendency toward improving its situation due primarily to the favorable circumstances of high levels of saving, high level of technology, an elevated level of training, and economic relations with countries from the other "class."

The "lower class of nations," with its hitherto insoluble

problems, is mired in ignorance, misery, and bad health. In comparison with the privileged one third of the world's population, their plight seems to be deteriorating.

The favorable elements that preceded the evolution of the past 2½ centuries included the great geographical discoveries of the Europeans, and a series of technological inventions that revolutionized agriculture and transportation, made possible the generation of economic surpluses, and enhanced the feasibility of investing overseas. The beginning of this type of economy can be fixed approximately at the end of the fifteenth century, when the Portuguese Vasco da Gama united the European markets with those of the Spice Islands after rounding the Cape of Good Hope and crossing the Indian Ocean. Cloves, nuts, and peppers were thus the first items in a process that could be called an economy of exportation of primary products. In this first epoch, specialization was the watchword. Elizabeth I of England, in a speech to the directors of the British East India Company, voiced the reigning philosophy: "God has disposed that no nation have all that man can use but rather that nations have need of one another."

A rapid expansion of channels bringing primary materials to Europe was produced through different means, and in the course of a few decades they practically covered the globe. In such a manner, the economic system, along with the political and social implications that it involved, was born. It was maintained practically immobile until the twentieth century. Gold and silver from Peru, tobacco and cotton from Brazil and the United States, and sugar from the Caribbean Sea and the Indian and Pacific oceans became familiar items in international commerce. From 1870 on, with the opening of the Suez Canal by the French, one of the strongest imperialist powers, new rich lands that were particularly apt for this type of trade were incorporated into the system of exportation of primary products.

We do not here intend to examine the implications and the positive or negative influences that subjugation to imperialist metropolises had for the weaker countries, but rather to show some of the consequences. For a few countries, like the United States, for example, this international commerce represented a transitional period that was astutely exploited. Within a short time, by copying the Europeans, the Americans ended with genuine economic and social development as well as powerful military forces, and reached a position of leadership with regard to future decisions concerning the division of colonial wealth.

Table 14

Income Distribution for World Population by Regions and Level of Income Per Capita, 1966

	% of World GNP Expressed in Real Terms	% of World Population	GNP Per Capita Expressed in Real Terms (U.S. dollars)
Developed Countries	58.7	19.7	1 744
Western Europe	22.0	8.7	1 472
U.S.A.	29,4	6.2	2 790
Oceania	1.4	0.5	1 513
Canada	2.1	0.6	2 048
Japan	3.3	3.2	613
South Africa	0.5	0.5	598
Socialist Countries	23.7	34.6	401
U.S.S.R.	12.1	7.2	986
Eastern Europe	4.7	3.3	825
China	6.6	23.2	167
North Korea	0.1	0.3	211
North Vietnam	0.2	0.6	199
Underdeveloped Countries	17.5	45.7	223
Africa	1.9	6.9	164
Latin America	4.9	6.8	421
Asia	6.8	26.1	154
Southern Europe	1.9	2.2	501
Near East	1.7	3.5	257
WORLD TOTAL	100.0	100.0	585

Source: P. N. Rosenstein-Rodan, "International Aid for Underdevelopment Countries," *The Review of Economics and Statistics,* May 1961, cited by ECLA, *El Desarrollo de América Latina en la Post-guerra.*

Nevertheless, this international commerce seems to have been one of the principal reasons for the stagnation of the majority of countries and colonies, many of them forced into it against their will. The Industrial Revolution thus permitted a handful of countries to climb out of backwardness. Since it could not be utilized by the colonial areas, a growing gap of economic and social welfare between the two groups began to be noticed. Immediately following the Second World War, what some authors call the "modernization rebellion" or the "revolution of the exportation economies" took place. This "revolution" sought as a basic objective to end the overt and/or masked colonialism that had endured for four centuries and to embark on a process of self-sustained development. Table 14 supports the contention of a dual world society.

It is clear that the average product or income figures are not without problems of accurate measurement, but they are still the best indicators available. The GNP per capita of Latin America in 1961 is shown to be U.S. $421 in real terms. Our continent is not even close to the world average, U.S. $585. Moreover, Latin America's income is less than a third of what Western Europe receives, less than a sixth of the U.S.A.'s share, less than half of the U.S.S.R.'s, and is even lower than that of southern Europe, that continent's most backward zone.

Nevertheless, the average figure for Latin America hides some important differences among countries, as Table 15 illustrates.

The data of Table 15 show us that the average figure of $421 includes Argentina, with $799, followed by Venezuela, with $644.50, at one end of the spectrum, and Bolivia, with $122.30 at the other.[15] While there are some countries that approach the European levels or hover around or above the world average—Argentina, Venezuela, and Uruguay—the majority are closer to African and Asian levels. Moreover, only five countries, with a population that contains a little less than 20 per cent of the Latin

Table 15

LATIN AMERICA

Level of Income Per Capita and 1961 Population

Countries	Level of Real Income Per Inhabitant	Percent of Regional Population
Argentina	799.00	10.1
Venezuela	644.50	3.6
Uruguay	560.90	1.2
Cuba	516.00	3.3
Chile	452.9	3.7
Mexico	415.4	17.0
Brazil	374.6	34.4
Colombia	373.4	7.5
Panama	371.0	0.5
Costa Rica	361.6	0.6
Dominican Republic	313.2	1.5
Nicaragua	288.4	0.7
Peru	268.5	5.3
El Salvador	267.5	1.2
Guatemala	257.7	1.8
Honduras	251.7	0.9
Ecuador	222.7	2.1
Paraguay	193.2	0.8
Haiti	149.2	2.0
Bolivia	122.3	1.8
Latin America	420.7	100.0

Source: P. N. Rosenstein-Rodan, "International Aid for Under-development Countries," *The Review of Economics and Statistics*, May 1961, cited by ECLA, *op. cit.*

American total, receive a greater than average income for the region, and there are nine countries with per capita income less than $300.

The growth of Latin America during the postwar years signified an increase of gross internal product per capita from $220, at market prices, to a little bit more than $300 in 1960.

The various countries experienced different fortunes during this period of growth, and their evolution can be classified according to three main situations: (a) countries that underwent a diminution of their GNP/per capita (for example, Haiti), (b) countries that remained practically at the same level (for example, Argentina and Honduras), and (c) countries with high levels of growth (for example, Venezuela and Brazil).

During the first years of the postwar period, Latin America experienced an acceptable level of growth. Afterward, a period of decay set in and tended to become generalized throughout the area by 1955. Table 16 supports this view.

Table 16

LATIN AMERICA

Rates of Growth of Population, Gross Internal Product and Real Income Total and Per Capita

Period	Popula-tion	Per Capita Gross Product	Per Capita Real Income	Per Capita Gross Product	Per Capita Real Income
1945-50	2.3	5.8	7.1	2.3	4.5
1950-55	2.7	4.8	4.6	2.0	1.8
1955-60	2.9	4.0	3.6	1.0	0.7

Source: ECLA, *op. cit.*

The data illustrate clearly the deterioration of the past few years, certainly a far cry from the growing expectations of the Latin American peoples and also well below the growth rate postulated by the Alliance for Progress, which rate "should not be less than 2.5 per cent annually per capita."

Even Venezuela, the Latin American country with the highest rate of growth in the postwar years, did not escape the general tendency toward weaker growth rates in the past few years. The long-term tendency from 1945–1960 shows a cumulative annual increase in the gross internal product of 8.3 per cent. Nevertheless, disaggregating the data into five-year periods, as in Table 17, clearly shows a large and continuing drop.

The tendencies of sectoral growth during the postwar period are presented by the data in Table 18.

Table 17

VENEZUELA

Evolution of Gross Product and Real Income, Total and
Per Capita. Cumulative Annual Rates by Period (%)

Period	Popula-tion	Total		Per Capita	
		Gross Product	Real Income	Gross Product	Real Income
1945-50	3.1	10.6	14.2	7.3	10.7
1950-55	4.0	8.7	8.5	4.6	4.3
1955-60	3.9	6.5	5.2	2.5	1.2

Source: ECLA, *op. cit.*

Unfortunately, very few investigations on income distribution in Latin America exist. Very few countries have undertaken such studies, and those studies that exist have usually been compiled by investigators working independently. It is one of the areas that requires attention by social scientists. For this reason, we will look at conjectural income distribution for Latin America undertaken by ECLA in which extant data on five countries of Latin America were used. Afterward, in keeping with the above pattern, we will consider the Venezuelan situation.

Table 18

LATIN AMERICA

Tendencies of Sectoral Growth for 1945-59 to 1955-60

(Rates of cumulative annual growth)

	Total Growth	Per Capita
Agriculture, livestock raising, hunting and fishing	3.5	0.7
Mining and Quarries	7.3	4.4
Manufacturing industries	6.1	3.2
Construction	4.9	2.0
Transportation and communications	5.7	2.7
Commerce and finance	5.2	2.3
Government	4.2	1.3
Other services	4.6	1.7
All Sectors	5.0	2.0

Source: ECLA, *op. cit.*

It is well known that the average income figures do not reflect the true life conditions in the underdeveloped countries because of the high inequality of distribution, one of the sad realities of life in our continent. Just as with the regional inequalities, a topic that we will treat in a later study, it is evident that economic development, social integration, improvement in education levels and training and, in general, the whole array of modernizing aspects that a society in transition from traditional to industrial must pass through, are seriously affected by deep-seated inequalities that permit a small number of citizens to enjoy high standards of living while the majority of the population lives in misery (without shelter, without a minimal level of nutrition, and, in many cases, without steady work), poor sanitation, and illiteracy.

On the other hand, the situation in the developed countries is quite different. People with higher levels of income receive a lower percentage of the total, and those with low levels of income receive a higher percentage. Since the amount of shared income is high, the benefits of development are extended to all the population, and consequently everyone can enjoy high mass consumption.

Table 19
Income Distribution by Levels for Selected Countries

Country	Year	Upper Levels of Income		Lower Levels of Income	
		% of Persons or Families	% of Total Personal Income	% of Persons or Families	% of Total Personal Income
Chile	1960	10.0	37.5	60.0	24.0
Denmark	1952	10.0	30.7	60.0	29.5
Ecuador	1957	10.0	30.0	60.0	36.0
U.S.A.	1952	10.0	31.0	60.0	32.0
Italy	1948	10.0	34.1	60.0	31.1
Mexico	1957	10.0	45.0	60.0	24.0
Netherlands	1950	10.0	35.0	60.0	29.5
Puerto Rico	1946-47	10.0	40.8	60.0	23.6
United Kingdom	1952	10.0	30.0	60.0	34.0
German Fed. Republic	1950	10.0	34.0	60.0	29.0
Sweden	1948	10.0	30.3	60.0	29.1
Venezuela	1957	10.0	45.0	60.0	16.0

Source: ECLA, *op. cit.*

If we examine the influence that direct taxes have on income distribution, we can see that whereas in the developed countries the taxing policy strongly exhibits an equalizing tendency, in the underdeveloped countries the taxing incidence is so weak as to be practically equivalent to having no policy at all.

ECLA has come up with a conjectural income distribution, taking as a base the extant studies on Chile, Ecuador, Mexico, and Venezuela. A level of gross internal product equal to $450 for 1962 was used, and a personal income of $370 per capita was arrived at, as shown in Table 20.

Table 20
Conjectural Income Distribution Prevalent in Latin American Countries[a]

Category	Proportion of Pop. Within the Category (%)	Proportion of Total Personal Income Received by the Category (%)	Annual Average of Per Capita Personal Income Percentage Relative to General Avg.	Dollars	Mean	Monthly Income Per Family (dollars) Range Low	High
I	50	16	120		55	0	100
II	45	51	400		190	100	500
III	3	14	1750		800	500	1300
IV	2	19	3500		1600	1300	
Total	100	100	370		170		

[a]Percentages and absolute figures in this table have been rounded off.
Source: ECLA, *op. cit.*

If we now consider the situation prevalent in the developed countries, important differences with regard to the fact that concentration of wealth is much less there than in Latin America can be noted and, furthermore, the lower levels that encompass half of the population are living at subsistence levels ($120 per capita per year).

The principal differences between the form of distribution operative in Latin America, on the one hand, and in Western Europe and the United States, on the other, according to the cited ECLA report, are the following:

a. "In the Latin American countries there is a greater concentration of income in a reduced percentage of the population, which is the social stratum capturing the highest incomes for itself. In effect, whereas in Latin America a third of the income is concentrated in about 5 per cent of the population, in the industrial countries of Western Europe and in the U.S.A. a much smaller proportion of the total income (22 per cent and 20 per cent, respectively) goes to the social strata in the upper brackets even though they represent the same proportion of the total population."

b. "The social sectors in the lower levels which represent half of the population receive only 16 per cent of the total income in Latin America. In the European countries and in the United States, on the other hand, the same sectors which also represent about half of the population, receive a markedly larger share of the total income (22 per cent and 23 per cent, respectively)."

c. "A comparison of the levels corresponding to high-income groups with the average also exhibits substantial differences. Thus, in Latin America the corresponding index is 6.5 times greater than the figure for the region taken as a whole, while in industrialized Western Europe it is only 4.4 times greater, and in the United States 4 times the average figure."

d. "Comparing the lowest income groups with the regional average gives an index of 32 per cent in Latin America, 44 per cent in the European countries, and 46 per cent in the United States."

e. "This characterization of the income distribution can afford even more insights by observing the difference between the average incomes of the two extremes: In Latin America, the upper average is 20 times greater than the lower, while in the more economically developed countries of Europe, the difference is half that, and in the United States even less."

With regard to Venezuela, Carl S. Shoup et al. undertook a study in 1957 on income distribution. This was one of the four studies that ECLA used for its conjectural distribution. Table 21 shows that Venezuela is a country with one of the most unequal income distributions in Latin America.

Table 21

VENEZUELA

Distribution of Personal Income (1957)

(%)

	Proportion of Country's Units in Category	Proportion of Total Personal Income Received by Category	Relative Proportions Received by Each Group Unit
Category I	50	11.0	22
Sub-category IA	35.5	6.0	17
Sub-category IB	14.5	5.0	34
Category II			
Sub-category IIA	18.0	11.7	65
Sub-category IIB	11.0	12.2	111
Sub-category IIC	16.0	34.6	216
Category III	3	12.8	427
Category IV	2	17.7	885
	100	100	

Source: Carl Shoup, *The Fiscal System of Venezuela,* Caracas, 1960, cited by ECLA, *op. cit.*

The same problem of inequality can be seen, as might be expected, by studying our continental situation in the light of other socioeconomic indicators. Thus, large sectors of population have caloric intakes greatly exceeding the average figure; large segments of the population are illiterate; whereas the mean educative level of the continent was 2.2 years in 1950, that of the U.S.A. was 9 years, and Japan's was 7.2 years.

4. *Accelerated Urbanization and Underdevelopment*

Concentrating on Latin America, we can point out the following from the above discussion:

a. The Latin American countries have, in the past few years, been responsible for placing their continent among the world's leaders both in population growth and in urban concentration.

b. At the same time, the rate of economic growth has not only failed to keep up with this population growth and concentration, but it has also exhibited the sorry spectacle of deterioration.

c. To make matters worse, the few studies that exist on the subject show an extremely unequal distribution of wealth and income in which small minorities get the lion's share while the overwhelming majority barely gets enough on which to subsist.

d. As a background to the serious situation described above, stands a dualistic world society with its "upper class" and "lower class" of nations. The Latin American nations are an integral part of this latter category.

e. To synthesize: The complex problems that the Latin American countries suffer are a reflection of the tragic coexistence of an accelerated urbanization process and economic underdevelopment.

We should add, although it may be obvious, that the absence of a coherent and rational strategy, when combined with the feeble negotiating power vis-à-vis the international powers, puts Latin America in a desperate plight, from which it is struggling to escape.

One of the most important causes of the present problems linked with urban development is the insistence on adhering to outmoded institutions and systems, many of them imported from other areas and never conscientiously evaluated. In light of the results obtained, it would seem evident that careful analysis enabling adaptation of these countries to the imperatives of change is essential. Unless this happens, this process of change will be very painful and exact a great social cost.

Among these institutions the laws regarding land use and occupation and the complex of problems that attend them are among the most salient. One of the consequences of such a system is the soaring cost of land. This constitutes an important impediment to urban development because it leads to a demand for investment that the present rate of economic development is unable to support.

To complicate the problem, the inequality of distribution means that large numbers of the population remain on the fringes of the market. Their inability to save is the prime reason for the cost of urban land to be out of reach.

As an example, if we study the rises in price in Caracas for the 13-year period 1938–51, we soon appreciate clearly that the increases are disproportionate to improvements in services and other embellishments. Essentially, there has been an increase over original value of from four- to eighteenfold.

The total value of the central part of the city in 1938 was Bs.56,810,625 for an area of 5,429,750 square meters with an average value of Bs.104.63/m^2. In 1951 the value increased to Bs.2,252,703,750, with an average value of Bs.414.88/m^2—on the average, a fourfold increase. In the heart of the city some sites actually went from Bs.50/m^2 to Bs.900/m^2.

From 1938 on, the value of land outside of the city center became more appreciated, and at the same time all values in general rose disproportionately. Lands that sold for less than Bs.10/m^2 in 1938 rose to Bs.30-, 40-, and 50/m^2 once they were provided with utilities, either through private or public initiative. But by 1951 these same lands, without any additional improvements, were worth Bs.95/m^2, and in some cases reached values of Bs.185/m^2 and Bs.250/m^2—that is, seven times their value once they had been provided with utilities. On main thoroughfares outside of the center, 1951 values reached averages of Bs.300-, 475-, and 750/m^2, and sometimes went as high as Bs.900/m^2. We can thus say that increases up to fifteen times the value of improved land were not unknown. Some prices became higher than many of the different lots in the central area of the city.

From that time till now, increases have continued at a rapid rate, until today we encounter prices of Bs.200/m^2 for residential zones that in 1951 were only Bs.70/m^2— that is, three times less.

In the center of the city, values have continued to rise, but at a slower rate than in the previous period. Some values have gone from 750 to 2,388; from 1,200 to 2,939; from 300 to 418; that is to say, to a maximum of about triple their value in fifteen years. The larger the values become, of course, the slower the rate of growth becomes until stabilization occurs. The maximum values in the center have stayed more or less the same or have risen slightly. The growth has been greatest in those below a certain range.

Outside of the center, as we have already mentioned, some values have exceeded those inside of it; there are now figures of around Bs.1,000/m² in commercial sub-centers, of Bs.400-, 500-, and 600/m² near main thoroughfares and high-rise areas, and of Bs.120–200/m² in quiet residential zones. By 1966 the prices were four times what they were in 1951. In general, the values have risen fourfold in fifteen years outside of the city center. Certain places exist where rises of six and seven times the value have occurred.

The factors that can be designated immediate causes of the rise of land costs are five: (1) zoning, (2) changes in zoning or rezoning, (3) installation of services, (4) construction of roads or other works, and (5) demand.

The first factor, when it deals with the transition to urban use of what was once virgin land or used only for agriculture, grazing, etc., is one of the most serious causes of the increase of price of land, especially of speculation. Agricultural lands priced at Bs.5,000 or Bs.10,000 per hectare—by merely becoming zoned through a simple governmental decree—have immediately increased their value tenfold, to about Bs.50,000 or Bs.100,000/ha. There have been cases in which agricultural lands, without a single centimo spent on improvement, have gone up to Bs.20/m² or Bs.200,000/ha in the course of a few years because of a zoning decree.

Often land is subdivided, sold at a high price, and then occupied by squatters, leaving the government to pay for the costs of providing services.

It should also be mentioned that sometimes the government pays an inordinate price for land in order to effect public works, a price that it, itself, had some control over.

The second factor consists in a change of zoning—that is, in a variation of the population density in order to permit a greater amount of construction in the same area, or also in a change of the type of use permitted (residential, commercial). Once the changes are made in the zoning, prices of the land automatically rise because of the potential rent available with the built-up land.

Calculations that we have made but omitted for the sake of brevity allow us to state that when a lot of 2,000m², zoned as Residential 5 (R5) and whose area of permissible construction is 100 per cent of the land's area is changed to Residential 6 (R6), where permissible construction is 160 per cent, it automatically acquires an additional value of Bs.270/m². This means that as a consequence of a zoning change, a lot of 2,000m² that was worth Bs.900,000 increases in value to Bs.1,440,000, and its owner makes a net profit, with no expenditure of energy on his part, of Bs.540,000.

The third factor corresponds to the installation of services where two alternatives should be considered: (a) when the services are installed by private enterprise, lands are increased in value by it and a profit is made, and (b) when the services are installed by the public sector, and the total value benefits the owner of the land without any investment on his part. In the first case, when the profit obtained is reasonable, the deed can be considered acceptable; but when the installation of the services has been done by the state, it is not fair that the increased value of the property should accrue to the landlord. Commonly many landowners leave their lots idle in the hope that services will be installed nearby, thus raising the value of their land.

The fourth factor that we consider important in raising the value of land is the construction of important roads or other works by the state. Such is what happens to lots near freeways, near large educational centers, markets, etc. Immediately a price rise is produced and usually taken advantage of by the landowner. Of course, in Venezuela there are legal means by which the state can recoup some of the added value (*plusvalía*) caused by its public works, but serious defects exist insofar as determining the areas exposed to the upward valorization as well as little experience in the proceedings necessary to obtain whatever the added value amounts to.

The fifth factor is the demand—that is, the existence of an oligopolistic market that allows unilateral price fixing, thereby producing a freeze on extensive areas of improved land and distorting the free play of supply and demand. We know of cases of large improved land areas that have quadrupled in value over a few years without any additional investment being made in them, without any improvement in services or construction of roads or important works nearby. In Caracas, residential lands intended for single-family living that originally sold for Bs.14/m^2 have risen to Bs.200 without any modifications or zoning changes to increase the value having taken place.

Such a situation of inordinate increase in land values as a consequence of factors whose manipulation is largely under state control—for example, zoning, development, construction of important works, and the provision of services—has become extremely significant, especially in Caracas. Today no improved land lies within reach of middle- and low-income people in Caracas, and even the prices of unimproved land are at a level too prohibitive to be used for housing in the public interest. This fact constitutes a serious problem standing in the way of urban development plans.

The situation with regard to urban land valorization in the cities in the republic's interior is not quite as serious as in the capital for the following reasons: (a) the great bulk of migration moves toward Caracas—about 40,000 persons per year; (b) topographical conditions of Caracas—a narrow valley of limited areas; and (c) greater intensity of use because of (a) and (b).

However, in the near future, unless there are some structural changes to prevent them, similar processes as those currently at work in Caracas will take place in the other cities as soon as those cities reach a certain stage of their development.

In any case, it is a fact that even when the conditions that lead to disproportionate increases in the cost of urban development are absent, it can be presumed from the preceding analysis that the degree of economic development attained in Latin America as well as of its rate and orientation is not sufficient to cope with the day-to-day necessities that accelerated urbanization imposes.

Such a situation has as a concomitant an increasingly growing deficit in the provision of basic services and the creation of an infrastructure adequate for the proper functioning of urban life. It is imperative that attention be paid to the deficits of education, health, public services, housing, urban thoroughfares, etc., in all the Latin American nations.

To take only one example, we will present some figures dealing with the housing sector. In Table 22 estimates made by the Organization of American States (OAS) with regard to the Latin American housing deficits for selected years are presented.

The OAS admits that a certain margin of error is present in the data but that "it can be seen that in order to resolve the current problems—and using a very conservative figure of $1,500 per constructed unit—an investment of at least $23,500 million will be needed. To this figure should be added a considerable additional sum in order to handle to necessities due to the normal annual growth of the region. Moreover, if an average Latin Amer-

ican family is assumed to contain 4.5 persons, it is calculated that at least 34 per cent of the area's families are
bearing the brunt of the quantitative and qualitative
deficit of housing."[16]

Table 22
Approximate Housing Deficit in Latin America

Country	Population (thousands of inhabitants) 1962	Deficit	Observations
Argentina	20,600	1,600,000	for 1962
Bolivia	3,900	384,000	for 1961
Brazil	74,300	8,000,000	for 1962
Colombia	15,600	300,000	urban only, 1963
Costa Rica	1,300	86,000	for 1963
Chile	8,100	454,000	for 1960
Ecuador	4,600	480,000	for 1960
El Salvador	2,600	60,000	urban only
Guatemala	4,000	558,000	for 1962
Haiti	4,300	—	unknown
Honduras	2,000	200,000	for 1961
Mexico	36,800	1,200,000	for 1962
Nicaragua	1,600	158,000	for 1960
Panama	1,100	118,000	for 1960
Paraguay	1,900	160,000	for 1962
Peru	11,200	825,000	for 1961
Dominican Republic	3,200	206,000	for 1962
Uruguay	2,900	100,000	for 1963
Venezuela	7,900	675,000	for 1963
TOTAL	207,900	15,664,000	

Source: O.A.S., *Study of the Social Situation in Latin America: 1963-64.*

But since the population is continuing to grow and also
to become more concentrated, the deterioration and consequent improvement and substitution of housing have to be
taken into account. In order to gain an idea of the
problem's magnitude, data referring to the necessary
levels of housing for the next few years are indispensable.
From a UN study we have taken the following: Tables 23,
24, and 25.[17]

Table 23

Quantity of Necessary Additional Housing in Urban Areas of Latin America
1960-1975

| | Average of Annual Needs | | | Total Needs |
	1960-65	1965-70	1970-75	1960-75[d]
	Housing units (millions)			
Housing necessary for population increase[a]	0.9	1.3	1.5	18.7
Housing necessary to replace uninhabitable dwellings[b]	0.3	0.3	0.3	4.1
Housing necessary to keep up with annual deficit[c]	0.2	0.2	0.2	3.4
TOTAL	1.4	1.8	2.0	26.2

[a]Calculated by dividing the annual average of population increase by a value per home of 4.7 persons.
[b]Based on the assumption that the housing of 55% of the 1960 urban population will have to be replaced in 30 years.
[c]Based on the assumption that housing sufficient to lodge 45% of the 1960 population will have to be built.
[d]Figures are rounded.

Source: United Nations, *World Housing Situation and Estimates of Housing Needs,* New York, 1965.

Table 24

Quantity of Necessary Additional Housing in Rural Areas of Latin America
1960-1975

| | Average of Annual Needs | | | Total Needs |
	1960-65	1965-70	1970-75	1960-75[d]
	Units of housing (millions)			
Housing necessary for population increase[a]	0.4	0.3	0.3	4.8
Housing necessary to replace uninhabitable dwellings[b]	0.7	0.7	0.7	10.3
Housing necessary to keep up with annual deficit[c]	0.5	0.5	0.5	6.9

[a]Calculated by dividing the annual average of population increase by a value per home of 5.2 persons.
[b]Based on the assumption that the housing of 50% of the rural population will have to be replaced in 20 years.
[c]Based on the assumption that housing sufficient to lodge 50% of the 1960 population will be needed in 20 years.
[d]Figures are not rounded off.

Source: United Nations, *op. cit.*

Table 25

Quantity of Additional Housing Necessary in
Urban and Rural Latin America, 1960-1975

| | Average Annual Needs | | | Total Needs |
	1960-65	1965-70	1970-75	1960-75[a]
	Units of housing (millions)			
Urban areas	1.4	1.8	2.0	26.2
Rural areas	1.6	1.5	1.5	21.9
TOTAL	3.0	3.3	3.5	48.1

[a]Not rounded off.

Source: United Nations, *op. cit.*

Between 1960 and 1975, therefore, it would be necessary to produce 48.1 million housing units, 26.2 million
units in the urban areas, and 21.9 million units in the rural

areas, which means an annual construction rate per 1,000 inhabitants increasing from "14.1 in 1960 to 10.8 in 1975, a figure much higher than has ever been attained by any country in the hemisphere."

With regard to Venezuela, the urban deficit increased in the past few years to a figure equaling that of all the other Latin American countries together. A report published in 1964 calculated that there was a housing deficit of 800,000 units, of which 50 per cent, or 400,000 units, were in population centers of 1,000 and more inhabitants.[18]

The report, produced by a commission appointed by the President of Venezuela, not only estimated the housing deficit but also calculated the infrastructure necessary for normal functioning. We consider it worthwhile to present some of the results of that study, changing only the bolívar figures to dollars in order to facilitate the analysis.

The commission divided the heading "Urban Development" into four basic subheadings and made the assumption that 25 per cent of the housing, or 100,000 out of 400,000 dwellings, had problems of insufficient land. Moreover, an average density of 100 persons/ha was

Table 26
Urban Development Deficit

a) Acquisition of land and payment for improvements, 5,400 Hectares at $11,111.11/Ha. (average)[a]	$ 59,999,994
b) Provision of Public Services	
(1) Aqueducts. 1,720,231 at $60.00/person $103,213,860	
(2) Sewers. 4,384,539 persons at $48.9/person $214,403,957	
(3) Electricity. 240,000 families at $77.8 each $18,672,000	
(4) Local thoroughfares. 50% of the housing is not served by adequate roads, etc. Taking 21,600 hectares as a base figure and the cost of road-building as 8,888.9/Ha. $192,000,240	
TOTAL PUBLIC SERVICES	$ 528,235,766
c) Housing. Figuring that the greatest deficit is concentrated in low income sectors and that a large share of the expenditure is in the form of credits, materials, and technical assistance for improving housing, the average cost is estimated to be $1,111.11 each. 400,000 dwellings at $1,111.11 each	$ 444,444,444
(1) Social Care (a) Hospitals 14,000 beds at $8,888.9 each. $124,444,600	
(2) Educational (a) Primary. 4,300 classrooms at $11,111.11 each. $47,777,778	
(b) Middle. (60 buildings) $13,333,333	
TOTAL COMMUNITY SERVICES	$ 185,555,711
TOTAL	$1,218,235,915

[a] A relatively moderate cost which presupposes measures taken against speculation.
Source: Commission for Urban Development and Housing, Caracas, 1964.

adopted, which meant that 5,400 hectares had to be acquired in order to satisfy the demand for land. With these assumptions the cost of the urban deficit was calculated, as illustrated in Table 26.

The total investment, then, needed to make up for the Urban Development deficit in 1964 reached the level of $1,218,000,000. If, as the commission estimated, seventeen years to solve the problem are allotted, an annual investment of $71,800,000 will be required.

Table 27
Projections of Urban Development Problems

a) Acquisition of lands (with help of a land policy) 46,300 Has. at $5,555.55 per hectare		$ 257,222,222[a]
b) Provision of Public Services		
(1) Aqueducts ($60 per person)	$ 397,800,000	
(2) Sewers ($48.9 per person)	$ 324,133,333	
(3) Electricity ($77.8 per family)	$ 95,666,666	
(4) Thoroughfares ($8,888.9/Ha., assuming 66,300 Has. needed)	$ 589,333,333	
TOTAL PUBLIC SERVICES		$1,406,933,333[a]
c) Housing		
(1) Group of 222 at $666.6/month. (State aid to Savings and Loan System)	$ 844,444,444	
(2) Group of 66.6 at $222/mo. (46.51% of 1,230,000 families) $72,073 at $2,222/unit	$1,271,273,333	
(3) Group of less than $66.6/mo. Help with materials and technical assistance 233,000 families at $1,111	258,888,888	
TOTAL HOUSING		$2,374,606,666[a]
d) Communal Services		
(1) Social Care		
(a) Hospitals, calculating 4 beds per 1,000 inhabitants. 26,520 beds at $8,888.9	$ 235,733,333	
(b) Health Centers	$ 22,222,222	
(2) Educational		
(a) Primary, 25% of the population, $222.2 per student. 1,657,500 X 222.2	$ 368,333,333	
(b) Middles, 5% of the population, $444.44 per student. 331,500 X 444.44	$ 147,333,333	
TOTAL COMMUNAL SERVICES		$ 773,622,222[a]
TOTAL		$4,812,384,443[b]

[a]Figures are rounded off.
[b]Original figure was given as $4,821,384,444.
Source: Commission for Urban Development and Housing, Caracas, 1964.

The population increase in places of 1,000 and more inhabitants during these seventeen years was also taken into account and, again, calculations were made for the four main subheadings. The amount of investment needed for the increase of 6,630,000 new inhabitants is presented in Table 27.

Adding the deficit from Table 26 to these figures, we arrive at a figure of $6,030,000,000, which, over a period of seventeen years, comes to an annual average of $356,-200,000.

The commission noted the actual amounts of investment for 1963 and 1964 in the four basic subheadings $129,000,000 and $73,700,000 respectively, figures that are quite distant from the sums needed to cover the necessities of urban development.

The object of this exposition on the social costs of urbanization is to point out their magnitude and complexity as well as to call attention to the seriousness of the process and to the urgency of finding solutions.

What to do?

From the above it can be gathered that a strategy for accelerating economic development is of the utmost urgency. Simultaneously, channeling of the urbanization process through policies of land use that will help to diminish the urban centers' growth rates and permit them to absorb the large waves of migrants coming from the countryside is equally necessary.

In order to achieve the first goal it would seem indispensable to think less in national terms and more, a great deal more, in Latin American regional terms. Accelerating the process of integration would help bring into play two powerful levers for promoting development: one, of an economic nature, would be the potential market available, already more than 200,000,000 consumers; another, of a more political nature, would be the ability to act as a unified and homogeneous entity, taking advantage of the newfound power to question the terms of exchange in this dualistic world to which we have already made reference.

In order to achieve the second goal it is indispensable to become more knowledgeable about the process and attempt to orient it. A change of attitude representing a willingness to introduce the political and institutional changes indicated by the newly acquired knowledge will be necessary.

Urbanization is, or should be, one aspect of the change process through which a rural society is transformed into a modern industrialized society. In our time a whole complex of frictions and maladjustments has arisen due to the process, but it is evident that urbanization is necessary for development and, therefore, if the process is better understood than presently, it will be possible to minimize the negative aspects and take advantage of its boons.

Recognizing, then, the complexity of the urbanization phenomenon, it will be necessary to familiarize ourselves with its component elements, be they demographic, sociological, economic, physical, institutional, or political. Once the problem is understood in all its ramifications, it can be best understood in its particular incidence, whether regional or national.

So far we know of no studies with the orientation that we have proposed. Nevertheless, this year a joint project between CENDES and the UN has begun in Venezuela; that project will attempt to study all of these aspects.[19]

The principal objectives are the following:

a. Identify the important aspects of the urbanization phenomenon in Venezuela.

b. Determine the causes and consequences of the phenomenon.

c. Try to predict the future problems associated with urban development in the country.

d. Arrive at specific recommendations for the solution of present and future problems and for establishing a policy of population distribution as well as of distribution of means of production within a national context of development.

e. Devise a theoretical framework and secure the necessary data for an analysis of the market mechanism and other studies that should precede investment. Establish the necessary conditions for rational placement of economic activity, for both public and private sectors and with regard to the designation and distribution of social and other basic capital investments.

In order to reach these objectives, the following set of hypotheses have been devised:

a. The process of urbanization will continue for the foreseeable future in the same direction as at present, but with greater intensity.

b. The principal causes will continue to the high rate of population increase and the limited capacity of the rural areas to absorb additional populations. The less prosperous and attractive the rural areas are, the greater will be the push to the city.

c. Until a high level of urbanization is reached and other factors begin to impinge on the birthrate, the increase of population in Venezuela will continue to be one of the highest in the world, and the next few years will be particularly difficult because of a veritable population "explosion."

d. The bulk of future migrations will be toward the large cities because of their relative advantage with respect to work opportunities. Future development of the economy—including sectoral changes—will favor the larger cities regarding the creation of employment.

e. As a consequence of the preceding points, the problems that are produced by urbanization will be exacerbated in the future.

1. Problems of unemployment and underemployment.
2. Problems of extremely unequal income distribution and the social tensions that those involve.
3. Problems of inadequate housing and public services and the high costs of providing them.

4. Problems of marginalization and social disorganization.
5. Problems due to financial resources insufficient to meet the above problems, due primarily to an inadequate taxing system and generally to the inefficiency of municipal governments.

f. The process of rapid urbanization is irreversible; its direction and rate can be influenced only in a very limited manner.

g. In order to ease the problems arising from rapid urbanization, public policy can indirectly influence a few selected factors and directly influence development within the urban communities.

The indirect effects can be achieved through:

1. A population policy.
2. Strengthening the rural economic base (agriculture, animal husbandry, forestry, fishing, and mining).
3. Increasing the attractiveness of rural areas.
4. Creation of new development poles.
5. Programs for intraregional development in order to achieve better urban-rural relations and a hierarchy of different-sized cities.

The direct effects can be achieved through:

1. Preparation of the cities for the anticipated rapid growth.
2. Training of rural migrants for city life.
3. Discouragement of speculative investments, and channeling of investment capital toward productive industries and other sources of employment.
4. Development of better fiscal policy and more equitable distribution of services in order to achieve better distribution of "real" income.
5. Reduction of the price of land.
6. Provision at realistic levels of necessary services and installations through means consonant with the degree of development reached.

7. Achieving rational patterns of land use that will take into account consideration of traffic generation.
8. Improving municipal government.

We feel that an integral and multidisciplinary study of the kind of urbanization process described is indispensable for rational decision-making both by the private and public sectors. Errors are too costly in this field, especially if we keep in mind the social and economic costs of development with rapid urbanization.

Finally, given the scarcity of resources, systematic and careful planning techniques should be integrally applied. Not only should they cover all sectors, but they should also encompass the urban, rural, regional, and national arenas.

Planning experiences in Latin America have traditionally focused on national concerns and done so only in terms of economic variables. Little has been done with political and social variables, nor, for that matter, on regional and urban aspects. Thus, most of the countries on this continent have plans for economic development, but none have taken into account the political means necessary for the community willingness available to translate plans into action.

In the past few years, work has begun on the regional level, and some successes have been obtained. Latin America now has the experience with SUDENE in Brazil, the "world's biggest laboratory," from which Latin America can learn much about regional planning. Within the area of planning, the investigations begun by CENDES and others, which have included some politico-social variables, can be considered as pioneering efforts.

Very little has been done up to the present about integrating urban planning into the whole picture of national planning. From the situation as described above, it should be clear that the problem of urban development is of such import that immediate action is necessary. However, just as bad or worse a situation exists in rural areas, and the urban problems cannot be treated while ignoring the countryside's miserable plight. It should be evident that neither urban nor rural development can take place without an attack on the impediments at three levels—national, regional, and urban-rural—and, we are positive, without an awareness of the historical necessity of Latin American integration.

NOTE: The authors have been working for some time on a study of the phenomenon of urbanization in Venezuela, a joint project being carried out by CENDES and the UN. Luis Lander is national director and Julio César Funes is project coordinator. Some of the project's findings have been included in this essay, and the authors wish to acknowledge the collaboration of the entire research team, especially Drs. Julio Páez Celli (demography), Gabriela Bronfenmajer and Josefina Hernández (sociology), Luis Mata M. (economics), Fernando Travieso (physical planning), and Alberto Urdaneta (urban planning), who are in charge of the various subprojects that make up the investigation. However, the authors take exclusive responsibility for errors of fact and interpretation.

NOTES

1. UN, *Factors, Determinants, and Consequences of Demographic Tendencies* (New York, 1953).

2. Ibid., p. 10.

3. Ibid., p. 16.

4. Nels Anderson, *The Urban Community: A World Perspective* (New York: Holt, Rinehart & Winston, 1959), p. 7.

5. Cited by Hauser and Schnore in *The Study of Urbanization*, p. 9.

6. Hauser and Schnore, p. 9.

7. Only the "urban regions" from the 1960 census were considered: "New York-Northeast New Jersey" and "Chicago-Northeast Indiana." (See Philip Hauser, op. cit., with regard to the concept of "megalopolis," which refers to the union of several metropolitan areas, for example, the eastern seaboard of the United States from Boston to Washington, D.C.)

8. Egon Ernest Bergel, *Urban Sociology* (Buenos Aires: Editorial Bibl. Argentina), p. 19.

9. See Bergel, p. 21. The author refers to the position taken by Sorokin and Zimmerman and comments on it, concluding that "we will call a city all those population concentrations where the majority of the occupants pursue non-agricultural activities." "For purposes of our discussion, we will consider 'urbanization' as a process and 'urbanism' as a condition or a series of circumstances. Therefore we will differentiate between dynamic and static urbanization." (The three definitions are admittedly not above debate.)

10. This project was called "The Phenomenon of Urbanization in Venezuela" (URVEN).

11. CENDES, "Conflictos y Consenso de la Sociedad Venezolana."

12. It should be pointed out that the size of the sample does not permit attaching much significance to the figure.

13. Eric E. Lampard, "Historical Aspects of Urbanization," *The Study of Urbanization*, pp. 522–23.

14. Eric E. Lampard, "Historia de las Ciudades en los Países de Economía Avanzada," *Cuadernos de la Sociedad Venezolana de Planificación*, Vol. III, No. 7–8 (June–July 1964).

15. The United Nations puts Venezuela in first place in its estimates of levels of income for Latin America. A difference in methodology used by the M.I.T. group accounts for the discrepancy. With regard to the methodology, see P. N. Rosenstein-Rodan, "International Aid for Underdeveloped Countries," *The Review of Economics and Statistics* (May 1961).

16. OAS, *Study of the Social Situation in Latin America: 1963–64*, p. 111.

17. UN, *World Housing Situation and Estimates of Housing Needs* (New York, 1965).

18. Commission for Urban Development and Housing, Caracas (1964).

19. See the URVEN 8 study, from which the working hypothesis' objectives have been taken.

CHAPTER NINE

THE UNDERDEVELOPED CITY*

VÍCTOR L. URQUIDI

Contemporary cities belong to poor people.

—J. F. C. Turner, at UN Interregional Seminar
on Urban Development Planning and Policy,
Pittsburgh, 1966.

The disintegration of Rome was the ultimate result of
its overgrowth . . . a menacing example of uncontrolled expansion, unscrupulous exploitation, and ma-
terialistic repletion.

—Lewis Mumford, *The City in History*, 1961.

Contener el problema, evitando así que empeore.

—From a report, Inter-American Development
Bank, 1965

I.

Urban growth, occurring at a considerably higher rate
than over-all population growth, is rapidly gaining importance in the list of unsolved, and perhaps insoluble, social

* Originally published in Spanish, "La Ciudad Subdesarrollada," *Demografiá y Economiá* III (2) (1969), publication
of El Colegio de México, Mexico City.

and economic problems of the less-developed countries of the world. Although in some of these nations there were clear signs of accelerated urbanization during the forties, particularly under the impact of World War II and its consequences, it is since 1950, approximately, that the process has gathered speed. But this process is still largely urban growth and not urban development, if the latter term is taken to mean an organic, purposeful pattern of change that may contribute to solid economic advance and greater well-being without creating painful imbalances or producing new forms of social ills. Cities, of different sizes and conditions, are growing. They hold more people, expand horizontally and vertically, concentrate more industrial and commercial activity in their midst, attract the major shares of investment and services, and benefit proportionately more than rural areas from educational and general cultural advancement. But growth of the cities in the poorer countries, unforeseen on its current scale, has brought a new dimension to social and economic development—the requirement that, somehow, economic growth, difficult in itself, be made compatible with desirable standards of urban life and take into account the many complex forces that shape the city and the behavior of its inhabitants.

The problems of urbanization are, of course, worldwide. The city is of great concern to sociologists, planners, statesmen and politicians, the news media, and ordinary people in the industrially developed nations of the world. Although the lurid descriptions of the industrial towns of the nineteenth century are largely a matter of history, today's economic wealth in the more advanced nations has not led to socially satisfactory solutions. Almost measureless contrasts remain between the living and housing conditions of the families in the upper income brackets and those in the underprivileged layers. Recent and sudden realization of those differences is demanding a serious reappraisal of urban development policies, and the consideration not only of the internal problems of each city, but of the interrelationships of urban centers among themselves and the ultimate meaning of urbanization for a nation as whole.

The gravity of these problems in the developed countries of the Western world, and the almost frightening implications of the vast future megalopolitan conurbations in prospect, cannot be underestimated. However, most of the literature on the subject, whether gloomy or Utopian, treats the city, or the chain of cities, as amenable to some sort of concerted effort on the part of planners and authorities at local and national levels: resources are potentially available and what is needed, broadly, is decision in terms of social and political priority (aside from certain controversies between different exponents of town planning). In the less-developed parts of the world—where, it should not be forgotten, average per capita incomes vary in different regions from one-twentieth to one-fourth of the average incomes in the industrially advanced nations —the problem is one of virtual unavailability of resources, in addition to the far from simple decision-making aspect (on which the prospects may be incomparably less encouraging). Urbanization in the less-developed countries is necessary for modern development, but it is assuming some of the worst features of the growth of cities in the industrial nations and is being compounded by unprecedented social change stemming from high rates of population growth and massive movements of people from rural to urban areas.

All these circumstances are producing the *underdeveloped city*—the city of the underdeveloped nations. Because of the economic and political context in which it is evolving, this kind of city may well become the permanently underdeveloped city. The following is an attempt to survey the broad conditions surrounding this particular facet of the "Development Decade" and some of the lines of approach that may help to contain the problem, at

least. I have drawn largely on recent literature on demographic change and urban development.[1] I cannot claim
any specialized knowledge—which may be an advantage
—but try to view the problem more generally, as a development economist may be likely to, though not to the
point of allowing the whole picture to become blurred and
dissolved in platitudes. I shall, inevitably, draw mainly on
Latin American data and experience, but much of what
emerges from this picture is probably applicable to urban
growth in Asia and parts of Africa.

II.

Over 2.2 billion people inhabit the underdeveloped
world, as against about one billion in the more economically fortunate countries. A common measure of the level
of urbanization is the percentage of population living in
towns of more than 20,000 inhabitants. This was 14 per
cent in 1920, 19 per cent in 1940, and 25 per cent in 1960
for the world as a whole; that is fully 753 million people
in 1960.[2] Of this amount, over one-half, some 380 million,
lived in the less-developed areas: southern and eastern
Asia, Latin America, and Africa.[3] In Latin America, the
ratio inhabiting towns 20,000 and over in 1960 was 32 per
cent, whereas it was only 14 per cent in southern Asia; in
North America, it was 57 per cent, in Europe 41 per cent,
and in the Soviet Union 36 per cent.[4] During 1940–1960,
the number of inhabitants in such towns more than doubled in the less-developed areas: in Latin America, it rose
by 170 per cent, in Africa by 164 per cent, in southern
Asia by 130 per cent, and in eastern Asia by 96 per cent.[5]
In the developed areas, these increases ranged from 24 to
76 per cent.

However, towns containing from 20,000 to 100,000 people cannot be taken as cities in the ordinary sense of the
word. If cities holding 100,000 and over are taken as in-

dicators of urbanization, the percentage of world population living in them rose from 8.6 per cent in 1920 to 12.6 per cent in 1940 and 17.5 per cent in 1960; there was a rise of 82 per cent from 1940 to 1960.[6] At present some 600 million persons live in cities this size, and perhaps one-half of them are in the less-developed countries, where rates of increase are generally higher.

Yet another convenient cut-off point is the 500,000 limit, which distinguishes large cities from mere cities and towns. By 1960, almost 12 per cent of the world's population, or 352 million people, inhabited such large cities, as against 5 per cent in 1920. In southern Asia, Latin America, and Africa, the number of inhabitants in cities of this rank more than tripled between 1940 and 1960 and rose by almost that rate in eastern Asia; it doubled in North America and the Soviet Union and went up only by one-fifth in Europe. The decade of the fifties, in particular, witnessed a more rapid expansion of the large towns and the metropolises than of the smaller cities. Urban concentration increased, especially in the Soviet Union and in the less-developed areas. In the latter regions, 46 per cent of the urban population in 1960 was already living in cities of 500,000 or more people. The rapidity with which this occurred in these regions does not, of course, mean that the levels of urbanization of the industrial countries were being reached, but it is significant that almost as many people lived in cities above 500,000 inhabitants in the poorer countries as in the richer.[7] In Latin America alone, 17 per cent of its total population in 1960 was in this type of city, a ratio higher than that of the other less-developed regions, equal to the European, and above the world average.[8]

Given differential rates of population increase between the developed and the underdeveloped areas, the latter (excluding Japan) are expected to account for over three-fourths of world population by the year 2000, assuming a total of 6.13 billion inhabitants.[9] It is estimated, in fact, that over 85 per cent of the increase in world population between 1965 and the year 2000 will take place in the less-developed areas,[10] owing to the expectation of high birth rates in these areas, assisted by declining mortality, as against the lower population growth trends prevailing in the industrial countries. Judging from recent trends and experience, and the many factors attracting people to the cities and inducing them to migrate from rural areas and small towns, it may be that by the year 2000 close to one-fourth of the world's total population will inhabit cities of 500,000 people and over; of these 1.5 billion persons, perhaps as many as two-thirds, or nearly one billion, will be in the less-developed regions. Out of this billion or so people, easily 300 million will be in Latin America. If the dividing line is put at 100,000, the less-developed areas may contain more than 1.8 billion inhabitants in cities of that size and over, of which some 400 million will be in Latin America.

Latin America seems to be taking the lead insofar as rates of increase are concerned, for nearly 47 per cent of its population may be living by the year 2000 in cities of 500,000 inhabitants and over, which would be almost twice the ratio for the world as a whole. And approximately 60 per cent of Latin America's future population is likely to inhabit cities with more than 100,000 inhabitants each. In 1960, already 19 Latin American cities had over half a million people; today there are at least 22 such cities, and there will be many more in the future as rural-urban migration continues and people flow from smaller to medium-sized towns and thence to the larger ones.

Rapid urbanization is evident throughout Latin America. Using the standard definition, for international comparisons, of 20,000 inhabitants and over as urban, Latin America's urban population expanded at an average annual rate of 5.1 per cent between 1940 and 1960. This rate was at least 5.3 per cent in 1950–1960. In this decade, in the two most populous countries, Brazil and Mexico, the rate was 6.5 and 5.2 per cent, respectively. In Venezuela, it was 8.2 per cent; in the Dominican Republic, a small country, it was 9.0 per cent; in Panama, 5.1 per cent. In Mexico, the growth rate of urban population in cities of 100,000 inhabitants and over, during 1950–1960, was 5.3 per cent; these cities accounted for two-thirds of all urban population in 1960. The corresponding rates in Venezuela and Brazil were 8.1 and 5.5 per cent.[11] In Venezuela, the number of people in cities having more than 100,000 inhabitants was only 10 per cent of total population in 1940, but this share had risen to 30 per cent by 1961.[12]

Some of the larger cities of Latin America increased their population during the 1950's by 60 to 70 per cent; for example, Mexico City, São Paulo, Bogotá, Guayaquil, Quito; and some almost doubled it or more, such as Caracas, Lima, Cali, Santo Domingo, Monterrey, Belo Horizonte, Guadalajara. Even higher rates of increase were recorded in certain smaller cities. Expansion was less rapid in Buenos Aires, the largest capital in Latin America, and Rio de Janeiro, former capital of Brazil, but in these two cities size itself is already significant, so that even a 3 per cent annual growth is important to reckon with.

Present trends in Latin America are likely to continue generally, although rates of urbanization may slow down in some of the larger countries as well as in the larger capitals. Rural-urban migration is not likely to abate, but may be directed increasingly to the medium-sized cities as industrial and commercial development spreads to them. A doubling of urban population as a whole every fifteen years is the minimum outlook, whereas rural population in the same time-span may rise by only 40 per cent (which in itself is disquieting). In countries such as Ecuador, Colombia, and some of the Central American nations, expansion will be threefold every fifteen years, and in others, such as the Dominican Republic and Venezuela, four- to fivefold, if present trends continue.[13]

Data on world population, especially for the less-developed areas, are subject to revision and should, of course, be taken as estimates. Approximations are even larger in the case of urban population, for which there are different definitions, and a given-sized town in terms of number of inhabitants obviously has quite a different meaning in Africa than in Latin America. Projections to the year 2000 are, furthermore, no better than the assumptions on which they are based. Nevertheless, it seems necessary to have some idea of magnitudes, not only important in themselves but also as background to other considerations affecting urban growth and giving it peculiar features in our time.

III.

The rapidly growing Latin American cities—and the same is broadly true in the other less-developed areas—are not the product of highly productive agricultural and industrial societies, but are associated with conditions where rural productivity is usually low, manufacturing is only partially developed, the levels of education, skills, health, and welfare are still grossly inadequate, and income and property are highly concentrated. Latin America's cities—even the larger ones of European vintage—are poor; poor and partially run-down, or poor and backward, or poor on the average with splashes of wealth interspersed in shockingly grim slums and ugly surroundings, held together by increasingly inadequate transportation and other services. Latin American nations are beset with the "premature city"—a preview of a future "noncity" if current development prospects remain unchanged.

It is common knowledge that in almost every large city

of Latin America, so-called "marginal" communities have sprung up around it, or have sometimes penetrated into its heart. They vary from shantytowns to squatter settlements and clandestine subdivisions, and constitute what one author terms uncontrolled urban settlements, largely inevitable.[14] These settlements are or have been the "reception centers," by and large, for the poor and unskilled migrants from the rural areas and the lesser urban zones. The expansion of these communities has been so rapid and unexpected that it has been impossible to supply them with essential services—water, sewerage, light, and the other usual municipal services; they lack schools, health units, protection, and amenities; the land on which they are settled is frequently subject to flooding and erosion; their housing consists largely of hovels ingeniously contrived from waste metal, wood, stone, or board; they sometimes have a "civic" organization of their own, but they also all too frequently harbor the habitual criminals and breed violence, theft, and vice. To these areas must be added the traditional hard-core city slums, perhaps worsened today. Slum dwellers and marginal community dwellers may number from one-quarter to one-half or more of the population of the larger cities in India, Turkey, Peru, Venezuela, Iraq, Senegal, and many other countries.

These squatter subcities of squalor are the result of two main difficulties: on the one hand, the inability of rural areas to provide a living to a rapidly increasing population; on the other, the incapacity of the economic system to absorb urban dwellers sufficiently into industrial employment.[15] Both sets of problems require some elaboration, and through them runs a third factor, namely, relatively high levels of fertility combined with declining general and child mortality, which for the time being means unprecedented rates of growth of population that are likely to be sustained for a long period of time.[16]

Rural conditions are in most countries responsible for a large share of the migration to squatters' settlements in the

larger towns. In spite of progress in many areas, the land
tenure systems are inadequate and frequently socially
unjust. Most farmers do not own land, or they have such
small plots, freehold or in rental, that they cannot make a
living. Programs to improve farming methods and raise
yields, to broaden markets, and otherwise to provide incentives have been insufficient. People move to urban
centers not because new techniques have made them
redundant on the farms, as in the advanced countries, but
because the land cannot feed them. They go in search of
better-paid occupations, new opportunities or the apparent
security—or even the "lure"—of the city. It would not be
possible here to analyze these problems in detail. There is
a growing awareness of them, and many agrarian and
farm development programs are under way in Latin
America, India, Pakistan, and elsewhere. But it is doubtful
that the scale of these programs is large enough. And it
must be admitted that, insofar as they succeed, the logical
conclusion, as productivity and incomes rise, would be for
more people to move to nonagricultural occupations. It
would help if new manufacturing industries were established in areas where there is a surplus farm population, around the smaller towns.

Industrial development, largely and necessarily confined
to the cities, has not yet reached a stage where it is
broadly enough based to cope with the potential additions
to the industrial labor force arising from migration into
the cities, or even to absorb the natural growth of urban
population in the working ages. It has been found that in
1960 the share of manufacturing employment in total
nonagricultural employment in Latin America was 27 per
cent as against 35 per cent twenty years earlier, and that
employment in tertiary activities is relatively higher in the
region than it was in Europe or the United States at a similar stage of industrialization.[17] This means that employment in trade and services and the many lesser occupations has increased in Latin America more rapidly than in

industry, thus suggesting that the flow of migrants into the cities has resulted in a spread of urban underemployment. One estimate indicates that as many as 8.2 million people —12 per cent of the labor force—were in a condition of "disguised unemployment" in Latin America in 1960, and that instead of diminishing, this unproductive and subsistence-income sector or urban life may be expected to reach close to 11 million people by 1970.[18] In some countries, underemployment is estimated to be as high as 25 per cent of total employment in "miscellaneous services," which comprise a considerable slice of tertiary activity.[19]

Industrial development, despite high rates and spectacular advances in certain branches in the Latin American countries, is not yet rapid or diverse enough, nor are the supporting educational and training services in turn expanding adequately to absorb into steady and productive employment the additions to urban population in the working ages. Particularly, there are large surpluses of unskilled labor, including potentially employable female workers. Modern technological developments tend furthermore, in many cases, to increase the capital/labor ratios and, in any event, to require highly skilled personnel. Again, it would not be possible here to attempt any further analysis of the industrial development picture, except to say that in addition to the limited domestic markets, largely resulting from low farm productivity, there are numerous other problems connected with industrial and trade conditions, and generally, with the patterns and fluctuations of world trade, which affect unfavorably the development programs and policies of the poorer nations.

The imbalance between agricultural and industrial productivity and the difficulty in pursuing both adequate agricultural development and more rapid industrial growth are thus at the heart of the expansion of marginal and squatter communities in the Latin American cities. These people are there and they are increasing in numbers. According to one estimate, such "marginal groups" grow at rates of as much as 15 per cent annually in some places.[20] This creates pressure not only on employment but on wages, and tends to cheapen labor below subsistence levels. It further establishes an impossible burden on urban facilities, and constitutes an increasing source of political instability. Thus living conditions in the cities reflect —and will long continue to do so—the economic plight not only of their inhabitants but of the underdeveloped economies as a whole.

Adequate city growth, housing, and services can only be the product of high productivity and rapidly rising output combined with an efficient educational system, an equitable tax structure, better income distribution, a less rigid social structure, and a careful awareness of the totality of factors affecting the city. The expansion of the middle-income strata in the developing countries, though it creates a demand for much of what a modern city should be, hardly offsets the growing weight of the supply of entrants into the marginal communities. Thus for every middle-class apartment building or office skyscraper, there may arise overnight thousands of hovels inhabited by five, six, or more persons per room. These are uneducated, hungry, unhealthy and needy persons, who have few opportunities for social and economic advancement. According to one study, 90 per cent of migrants into Santiago, Chile, fail to develop any upward mobility.[21] Innumerable examples may be given of unemployment, low income, and appalling living conditions in squatter settlements in Latin America and elsewhere.[22]

IV.

Apart from the increasing sprawl of the underdeveloped city, the grotesque transportation systems, the noise and the now rapidly spreading air pollution, the lack of water, the flooding, the almost totally absent police, the filth, and the unsightly, unplanned building agglomerations, one major problem stands out: housing. It has been argued that the urban housing problem in the less developed countries is insoluble. This is easily an intuitive and *a priori* statement that many would question. However, it may be not far off the mark. Recent estimates for Latin America—and no doubt similar calculations have been made for other areas—indicate that the approximately seven-million-unit shortage in urban housing, even in terms of the presently inadequate definitions, could be proportionately reduced —that is, in relation to total housing needs—within this century, but not eliminated.[23]

Present rates of construction of dwellings are on the whole low. In 1964, one estimate indicated construction of slightly over 400,000 units, urban and rural, which is two new dwelling units per thousand inhabitants. Another estimate suggests the ratio might have been three.[24] Mexico, Venezuela, and Brazil are particularly lagging in meeting new annual housing needs. Chile, Costa Rica, and Columbia may be near to facing the yearly increase in requirements. It is unlikely that, despite new programs and new domestic and external sources of finance, much headway has been made beyond the 1964 rates. It is therefore doubtful that the shortage is being reduced. To merely keep the deficit from rising, assuming minimal average space per dwelling unit, Latin America would have to build annually several times as many units as at present; perhaps some six times the present rate of construction, resulting in a ratio of ten units per thousand inhabitants. To do this, the annual investment cost, conservatively estimated (including utilities and basic facilities), would equal almost 40 per cent of the present rate of aggregate gross investment (which is about 16 per cent of GNP).[25] Given certain conditions, this might not be out of the question, but certainly extremely difficult. It would still mean carrying forward indefinitely the seven-million urban deficit, as well as the rural shortage (variously es-

timated between 8 and 14 million units). To actually
reduce the deficit, at least that in cities, would of course
require a much greater effort and a larger share of gross
investment annually.[26] One could speculate about various
financial possibilities and assumptions about growth rates,
saving ratios, tax burdens, housing specifications, and so
forth. But it is only necessary to recall that besides urban
housing (and rural), there are other tasks to be performed
—in education, land tenure, agricultural development,
health and welfare, and other urgent social and economic
needs in Latin America and elsewhere.

The problem, obviously, is not one of financial or even
real resources only, much less one that can be helped
much by international financial cooperation. It is also one
of basic concepts. "A passive attitude is generally adopted
in the face of the progressive aggravation of the shortage
of housing and community services, and there is a tendency to concentrate on the ornamental aspects of town
planning."[27] But town planning itself, in the sense of
operating plans rather than architects' dreams, is almost
nonexistent. Where a city has been planned and developed
from scratch, as in the case of Brasilia, it has solved little
or nothing. Housing development suffers, in consequence,
from the inadequacy of overall planning. Ad hoc solutions
prevail, and even the best housing programs run into
difficulties and prove inadequate to the scale of the city's
problems.

For these reasons also, the design of housing and urban
community programs is unrealistic in terms of the forces
influencing urban development. Most public and other
housing programs in the less-developed countries are in
effect attempting to meet, at best, the requirements of certain types of middle-class demand, and even in the lower
middle strata the standards and materials used tend to be
those of the richer countries. Housing costs are high in
relation to the level of development and purchasing
power. A mere comparison of labor and materials costs be-

tween, say, California and Asunción, Paraguay, is simply
beside the point, for in fact in the latter country such
costs, though lower, may be higher in terms of wage-in-
come and of prospective real income. Interest on housing
loans is generally higher in the less-developed countries,
both absolutely and relatively.

Closely related to this is the question of land values.
The estimates for the cost of housing programs in Latin
America, merely to contain the problem, make little allow-
ance for the actual cost of land. In the case of a minimal
housing unit, in a multifamily four-storied building, with
an average of 80 square meters of land per unit of 70
square meters of floor-space, the cost of land and basic
services would be at least 9 per cent of the total unit-cost;
for a middle-income family, it would vary from one-tenth
for 80 square meters of floor-space to one-fifth for twice
that amount of construction per unit.[28] Land values in
Latin American cities are notoriously high, as a result of
speculation, investment preferences, lack of regulation,
and general economic factors. In one Latin American capital, Caracas, site values in different parts of the city
increased from 4 to 18 times in a thirteen-year period.[29]
"There is today no supply of land in Caracas within the
reach of low- and middle-income families, and even undeveloped land prices are so high that they have become
prohibitive for utilization in low-cost housing."[30] It is
common in Latin American cities for middle- and low-income families to have to pay more for the site than for the
dwelling-unit built on it. In most Latin American countries, according to the Inter-American Development Bank,
there are considerable legal and other difficulties in purchasing land for housing projects, aside from the cost.

Public housing programs should imply adequate institutional arrangements, ranging from a basic law, research
services, and coordination of the work of the various agencies within an overall plan, to appropriate relationships to
other aspects of urban and regional development. In most

Latin American countries, such arrangements are seriously deficient. Merely on the side of efficiency in construction and research on new materials and cost-reducing methods, the situation is poor. Except for seven or eight countries undertaking such research, the rest of the Latin American countries continue to build with old-fashioned methods.[81]

Given the prevailing income-distribution in most less-developed countries, a large majority of potential house-holders would in any event be unable to pay, within a reasonable period, for both house and land, or even for construction alone. It is not clear to what extent efforts to reduce the cost per dwelling-unit would actually meet the weak levels of demand at market prices and under ordinary financing conditions. Low-cost housing projects frequently suffer from rapid turnover in occupancy because of nonpayment, and owners or tenants are apt to overcrowd their dwellings and turn them partly to commercial uses.

An adequate consideration of the housing problem cannot, therefore, abstract from general economic conditions or from the social, cultural, and technological framework. A merely quantitative approach is insufficient, however attainable the quantitative goals may appear to be. The housing problem seems to raise serious doubts about urban life in general, but the latter is in turn largely a reflection of inadequate economic development coupled with unduly high population growth. The answer to urban development, and the future of the presently underdeveloped city, must be sought, consequently, in the broader context of economic growth and social change, rather than in the city itself or in its structure.

V.

In the industrially advanced nations there is a fairly purposeful and concentrated effort to apply knowledge and organizational ability to the expansion of output and to the extension of the benefits of productivity to the mass consumer; this is true under different social systems, including the Soviet. The less-developed nations as a whole do not appear to be catching up with the industrial countries. They are induced by modern communications—advertising, radio and TV, cinema, and periodicals—to adopt the aspirations and the consumption patterns of the high-income countries. They also partially incorporate up-to-date technology into many activities, all too often without regard for local conditions in the labor market that favor labor-intensive rather than capital-intensive industry. Within fragmented and discontinuous domestic markets, frequently small, they permit unhampered and irrational private investment decisions to be made that lead to high-cost manufacturing and low manpower absorption. Educational and other social programs are inadequate and are held back by economic progress itself. World trade conditions are not favorable to the less-developed countries, and international attitudes to development, in spite of much good talk—for instance, at the United Nations, at regional summit meetings, and other gatherings—can only be called begrudging at best. The international political situation is no less discouraging as the nuclear and space-age powers involve the poorer nations in their rivalries. Development under these conditions will be a miracle indeed. And the cities can only be a part of that whole, not a separate entity. Urban development can only begin to be rational in response to an improvement in the general conditions favoring growth and social change.

It is said that most so-called solutions to the urban development problems are not more than short-term partial answers to inadequately defined issues. Much research is needed to help achieve better evaluations on which to base policies. But, as in most other aspects of development, policies have to be established even in the absence of full and adequate information and analysis. Above all, as many have pointed out, a "strategy" needs to be adopted. There cannot be partial answers, nor can successful projects of a particular country be transplanted wholesale to another. It is often the planner—using this term in a broad sense—who makes attainment of a plan impossible, because he sets his aim too high or tries to reach too many objectives at the same time. This is particularly the case with urban planning, where social and even aesthetic considerations may cloud the economic reality. But it is also the lack of overall vision that repeatedly prevents individual programs from succeeding or from leading the way to broader solutions.

It seems necessary, in the underdeveloped countries, to recognize certain conditioning factors that are not likely to change for some time. Thus any policies adopted should duly take them into account. Population growth, even with intensified family planning programs, is bound to continue at a high rate, and rural-urban migration can be expected to put increasing pressure on urban facilities. The expansion of cities is unquestionably a necessary condition of industrialization, and industrial growth is the main instrument by which development can be accelerated and social mobility increased. But given the nature and level of the physical and human resources of a less-developed country and the effective educational opportunities likely to arise, a broad policy should set out to impede the sort of concentration that is now taking place in the larger cities. The poorer countries are economically and institutionally unprepared for such concentration. An essential piece of the strategy should thus be to encourage the growth of the smaller cities through the spread of manufacturing and other modern activities by means of appropriate incentives and suitable regional planning. Until recently, inadequate communications were a potent force tending to concentrate industry in the capital cities or other large towns. But modern methods of transportation are bringing about new location patterns. This process needs to be stimulated, as a means of slowing down or spreading out the rural-urban migration and avoiding the high social costs of excessive urbanization, and also of raising incomes in the smaller urban centers to the level where housing and other improvements can come within partial reach of the local market. Such a policy will not slow down urbanization as a whole, but will at least avoid high concentration.

Meanwhile, given certain perhaps unduly skeptical assumptions about present trends in social progress in the less-developed countries, some aspects of urban reality must be faced squarely. Marginal low-income groups will exist for a long time; they will be increased by rural-urban migration and by high birth-rates; they cannot be regarded as temporary or as if they were about to become conventional middle-class strata. Urban development plans must therefore allow for their gradual and selective improvement and incorporation. This part of the strategy is beginning to be recognized in many quarters and has in some countries become explicit. There are various means of giving it content. Slum clearance, as in the industrially advanced countries, is only applicable in the hard-core poorer areas of the large cities, but not in the so-called uncontrolled urban settlements or marginal communities. The existence of the latter and of the conditions creating them cannot be ignored. It therefore seems necessary to adapt certain institutions to their existence and to introduce in those settlements important elements of improvement in which the settlers may actively participate.

In many cases, it would be advisable to legalize "squatters' rights," particularly where the settlement is more than a place of temporary abode and shows clear symptoms of "progressiveness," as measured by occupational characteristics of its inhabitants, attitudes to ownership, and participation in community activity. Establishment of legal ownership should be accompanied by the subsidized introduction of basic municipal services, frequently with local participation in their construction through voluntary work. Subsidized cooperative programs for the sale of

materials, free technical advice on building, and assistance
in bettering conditions in the home and in family life are
essential requirements of such programs. There have been
many such experiments in Latin America, Africa, and
Asia, including some in which "core houses" are provided
to be expanded gradually. The "roof-loan" scheme in
Ghana, the self-help projects in Santiago and Bogotá, and
many others of a related nature seem to be steps in the
right direction. All assume that the squatter is capable of
organized activity and of a good measure of responsible
behavior. "Squatting . . . is not to be understood as a totally lamentable phenomenon. . . . In some respects . . .
the squatter enterprise is probably the most significant
form of home-building taking place in the world today."[32]
There thus seems to be a large volume of untapped sav-
ings, in the sense of potential effort, among the squatters,
so that public resources may properly be put to work in
that area.[33]

Legalization of squatters' rights may frequently require
outright purchase of the land by a local authority, through
a nationally financed program, in order to grant it to the
squatter. In some cases, a subsidized sale would be preferable, or a combination of tenancy and sale over a given
period of time. Each scheme would have to adapt to the
particular characteristics of the settlement. A slightly
different situation arises where the marginal community
dwellers actually own, or have begun to pay for, the land
they occupy and have started building on it. The need
here would be for introduction of utilities and help in ra-
tionalizing the process of construction and development,
and especially for replacement of onerous or inadequate
financing by a suitable subsidized scheme, adapted to the
actual and prospective income levels of the dwellers.

A strategy must also include consideration of the broad
problem of land values, the incidence of which, even on
the middle-income groups, is unduly unfavorable. The
shift from run-down housing or a hovel into a better

neighborhood or a moderate-income development may frequently be delayed or put off indefinitely by the influence of the site value on rentals or on the purchase price of the new dwelling. Given prevailing high rates of interest on ordinary housing loans and relatively short amortization periods, the would-be house-owner in an underdeveloped country is at a considerable disadvantage. There seems to be a need for strict regulation of urban sites and of the holding of undeveloped urban property, if speculative values are to cease to restrict housing development. The rise in site values, for instance, in Latin America, has virtually eliminated millions of people from the housing market and reduced the scope of innumerable housing projects. It has also contributed to the spread of unregulated settlements. It appears fundamental that some sort of "urban reform" parallel in many ways to land reform should be worked out. A combination of a drastic capital gains tax on urban properties in excess of a minimum value and regulations to prevent accumulation of urban wealth in private hands, and especially concentration of private property in low-income urban zones, would appear to be inevitable in the coming years. To be effective, urban reform would also have to place some restriction on indiscriminate private sales by holders of subsidized housing.

A new approach to problems of urban development would also seem to call for a revision of taxation of urban property in general, especially in order to introduce the principle of progressive rates. Costly modern suburban development expenditures for the upper middle-class in Latin American cities should be offset by high local rates and special assessments, and, in general, large wealthy-quarter estates, often involving extensive sites, should be subject to effective assessment and progressive rates. Urban property taxes in large Latin American cities, where tax capacity is relatively higher among certain groups, are in effect low, and even nominally low.

The effective rate of the Mexican property tax on urban property is approximately one-half of 1 per cent of true or fair market value, compared with the nominal rate of 1.09 per cent of appraised value. . . . The nominal tax rate in Caracas is 6 per cent of potential rents; in Montevideo it is 0.65 per cent of appraised value (excluding surtax) . . . [but] effective rates must have been only a small fraction of nominal rates. The heavier effective rate in Mexico results mostly from better administration rather than higher nominal rates. [However], revenue from the property tax is approximately [only] 1 per cent of national income originating in the Federal District [of Mexico], about twice the share found in Caracas, but less than half the share found in American cities with populations of one million or more. . . . Mexican property tax rates . . . are modest by comparison with rates in most American cities, and, in fact, with prevailing rates in many jurisdictions where the level of economic development is no higher than in the Federal District of Mexico.[34]

Thus there is ample room for further increases in effective rates, and there is no really valid reason for not introducing progressive rates, although some expert fiscal opinion stands for maintaining proportionality.[35]

Taxation and regulation of urban site values, and the broader policy of urban reform, should be regarded in the more general context of the reality of the extensive marginal communities, for which new expenditure priorities now seem to be indicated. Urban reform may be socially desirable generally, as a measure towards a more egalitarian society, but it is particularly needed as part of a rational scheme for urban development, before the large underdeveloped cities are engulfed by squatter settlements and the ideal of a "green belt" around the large towns is substituted by a "brown belt" or a "filth belt," as is already beginning to be evident in many parts of the world. Authorizations to build expensive homes in middle-class suburbia should, in the interests of the owners themselves, be restricted or conditioned upon contributions to the financing of squatter developments or other schemes in the lower-income zones and to the improvement of substandard housing. The underdeveloped city cannot afford millionaire homes and millions of hovels side by side.

Technological innovation for the underdeveloped city is needed. Much technical progress in urban planning and in construction relates to what the wealthy communities of the industrially advanced nations are able to do in their own terms. Urban planning concepts, like industrial technology, would appear to require adaptation to the less-developed framework. Frequently, the proposals of urban planners, rich in imagination and humanistic ideals, are devoid of economic content; they are insufficiently related to the starting conditions or to the actual social possibilities of implementation, and they fail to quantify the many variables involved in bringing about results, nor do they take into account broader economic alternatives. Urban planning is part of a process; by itself it is necessarily incomplete. Closer association with economists and sociologists concerned with urban development is indispensable, for a totality of economic and social factors must come into the picture. In particular, the economics of the underdeveloped city, as distinct from the rich city of the Western industrial nations, must be made the object of careful study, and the whole interrelationship of urban development and overall economic and social development needs to be clarified.

Greater awareness of these problems in the less-developed countries is bound to lead to the adoption of national policies of urban development, in which suitable machinery may be set up to bring the growth and housing policies of the major cities under the scope of central or federal authorities, without restricting in any way the local functions or restraining local initiative. The industrial nations are moving in this direction, and much of the concern of planners now has to do with urban development as an integral part of national development. The less-developed countries, in view of their demographic prospects and their trends in urbanization, outlined earlier, are in equal need of national policies, if not more so. Urban growth, industrialization and regional planning can hardly be conceived today as separate processes. The expansion and modernization of transportation, both within cities and between them, has to be part and parcel of the same process and the same policies. New priorities in public expenditure, reflecting these objectives, are urgently needed in the poorer countries.

The underdeveloped cities are often projected into the future not on the basis of what they are and are likely to be, given their basic present conditions, or on the basis of a realistic process of change, but according to the models of the already outmoded cities of the industrially developed nations. This occurs equally in the latter nations, where policy-makers "have occasionally been trying to solve the problems of the city that was."[36] It must be conceded that any prognostication is risky, but most projections tend to be conservative in the extreme. Projections based on present conditions can be overly pessimistic. "Sociologists and economists who base their projects for future economic and urban expansion on the basis of forces now at work, projecting only such changes as may result from speeding up such forces, tend to arrive at a universal megalopolis, mechanized, standardized, effectively dehumanized, as the final goal of urban evolution."[37] This urban doomsday is not yet the outlook of sociologists, economists, or urban planners in the less-developed areas—if anything, they show insufficient awareness of the implications of urbanization—but there is certainly a built-in projection of present conditions. A recently published master plan for Monterrey, Mexico, where population is estimated to grow from the present one million to over five million by the year 2000, fails to consider any alternative to the private automobile and bus as a means of internal transportation, although the plan is well-conceived in most respects.[38] But, will automobiles as we now know them really be necessary by the year 2000? Even a city subway system may be obsolete by then. Urban development experts need not immerse themselves in science fiction, but alternative reasonable assumptions may easily be introduced in the projections.

There is clearly a need to increase knowledge of the present situation of cities in the underdeveloped nations. It is no less essential to reappraise the outlook, to work out revised approaches and policies, to try to achieve a new understanding, by all sectors, of the complex issues of tomorrow. Urban areas will benefit from overall economic and social development, but their own healthy development can be a positive contribution in turn to achievement of the broader objectives. The bleak prospect which, for lack of adequate policies, is now in sight is a proliferation of underdeveloped cities; it certainly calls for change. Ultimately, we are dealing not with land and concrete, or freeways, housing projects and community centers, or with water, parks or smog, but with people—human beings who must live and work together, who may aspire to be alone together, and who are unfortunately in the habit of multiplying (together) to an extent hitherto unforeseen.

NOTES

1. Among the particularly valuable sources, the following may be mentioned: Papers presented by the United Nations Population Division, other related bodies and individual experts to the UN Interregional Seminar on Urban Development Planning and Policy, Pittsburgh, October–November 1966; papers presented to the World Population Conference, Belgrade, September 1965; Luis Lander and Julio César Funes, "Urbanismo y desarrollo," in *Hacia una política de integración para el desarrollo de la América Latina*. Proceedings of the Sixth Inter-

American Planning Congress, Caracas, November 6–11, 1966 (San Juan, Puerto Rico, Inter-American Planning Society, 1967), pp. 60–110; and Rubén D. Utría, "The Housing Problem in Latin America in Relation to Structural Factors in Development" in *Economic Bulletin for Latin America*, XI (October 1966) (United Nations, ECLA), pp. 81–110.

2. UN Population Division, *Trends in World Urbanization, 1920–1960*, paper submitted to the Interregional Seminar mentioned in footnote 1; derived from Table 2.

3. An apparently stricter definition of "less-developed areas" estimates only 321 million in this group in 1960, that is, 42.4 per cent of the total. This grouping presumably excludes Japan, where the degree of industrialization and urbanization is much higher and the rate of demographic increase much lower than in most other Asian countries, although per capita income is below Western levels. However, the subdivision of the 321 million by region is not available, and for this reason the higher figure is used in the text. (Cf. *ibid.*, Table 11.)

4. *Ibid.*, Table 4.

5. For these four regions as a whole the increase was 116 per cent; under the stricter definition (see footnote 3), it was 138 per cent. (*Ibid.*, Tables 2 and 11.)

6. *Ibid.*, derived from Table 1.

7. *Ibid.*, Tables 7–9. The stricter definition of "less-developed areas" reduces the share of the latter in the aggregate population of cities 500,000 and over to 39.5 per cent, and the ratio of inhabitants in these cities to total urban population to 43 per cent (Table 11).

8. *Ibid.*, Table 9. About 25 per cent was in cities of 100,000 and over.

9. Medium projection. Cf. John D. Durand, *"The Modern Expansion of World Population,"* Proceedings of the American Philosophical Society, CXI (June 1967), Table 1.

10. *Ibid.*, Table 5.

11. Data for Brazil from John Durand and César Peláez, "Patterns of Urbanization in Latin America," *Milbank Memorial Fund Quarterly*, XLIII (Part 2, October 1965), Tables 4 and 5. Data for Mexico, Venezuela, Panama and Dominican Republic from Carmen Miró, "The Population of Latin America," *Demography*, 1 (No. 1, 1964), Table 8.

12. Lander and Funes, *loc. cit.*, Table 13.

13. R. Utría, *loc. cit.*

14. J. F. C. Turner, *Uncontrolled Urban Settlements*, paper submitted to the Interregional Seminar cited in footnote 1. This paper contains an excellent analysis of the problems in-

volved, with examples from many parts of the less-developed world. See also R. Utría, *loc. cit.*

15. R. Utría, *loc. cit. et passim,* and UN Population Division with the collaboration of Prof. Sidney Goldstein, *Urbanization and Economic and Social Change,* Interregional Seminar cited in footnote 1.

16. A survey conducted in seven Latin American capitals showed an average number of live-born children per woman of childbearing age ranging from 2.25 in Rio de Janeiro to 3.27 in Mexico City (leaving out Buenos Aires, where it was 1.49). Cf. Carmen Miró, "Some misconceptions disproved: a program of comparative fertility surveys in Latin America," in B. Berelson (ed.), *Family Planning and Population Programs* (Chicago, 1966), p. 639, Table 2.

17. Economic Commission for Latin America, *El proceso de industrialización en America Latina,* Anexo Estadístico, Santiago, Chile, 1966, pp. 11 and 13.

18. From B. Hopenhayn, *Ocupación y desarrollo económico en América Latina,* ILPES, Santiago, 1966, quoted by F. H. Cardoso and J. L. Reyna, *Industrialization, Occupational Structure and Social Stratification in Latin America,* in Cole Blasier (ed.), *Constructive Change in Latin America,* University of Pittsburgh Press, 1968, footnote 11, p. 54.

19. *Ibid.,* p. 44.

20. Felipe Herrera, President of the Inter-American Bank, in a speech at the University of Salvador, Bahia, Brazil, Sept. 23, 1967.

21. Centro Latinoamericano de Demografía, *Encuesta sobre immigración en el Gran Santiago,* quoted by Teresa Orrego Lyon, "Algunas consideraciones sobre marginalidad urbana," *Temas del BID,* Inter-American Development Bank, Washington, IV (September 1967), p. 30.

22. R. Utría, *loc. cit., passim,* quotes several; see also papers presented at Interregional Seminar, Pittsburgh, cited in footnote 1. A recent interesting comparative study of Latin American slums may be found in Lloyd H. Rogler, "Slum Neighborhoods in Latin America," *Journal of Inter-American Studies,* IX (October 1967), pp. 507–528.

23. R. Utría, *loc. cit.,* pp. 96–97.

24. Both estimates are quoted in a thoughtful review of the question recently published by the Banco Francés e Italiano para América del Sur, "El problema de la vivienda en América Latina," *Estudios Económicos,* I (1967), pp. 49–67. The ratio per thousand inhabitants in Western Europe was 7.4 in 1961.

25. R. Utría, *loc. cit.,* p. 97.

26. The source quoted in footnote 24 contains alternative calculations by various authors. The problem still remains insoluble.

27. R. Utría, *loc. cit.*

28. *Ibid.*, p. 86, Table 1. It should be emphasized that these are data used as averages in a "planned" solution to the housing shortage. Ordinarily, land values are a higher proportion of total cost, especially for middle-class one-family housing, where they may reach as much as 50 per cent or more.

29. Lander and Funes, *loc. cit.*

30. *Ibid.*, p. 98.

31. From an Inter-American Development Bank report.

32. From "Profile" on Charles Abrams, in *The New Yorker*, 1967.

33. Improvements in squatters' settlements could also take the form of certain "collective" services to offset the need for provisional or partial housing, or narrow minimum space standards. I have in mind such things as dormitories, communal kitchens, baths, laundries, children's areas, recreation clubs, and so on, which have been tried out in many places.

34. Oliver Oldman et al., *Financing Urban Development in Mexico City* (Cambridge, Mass.: Harvard University Press, 1967), pp. 79–80. The reference is to places in Africa, Brazil, and India.

35. The authors of the previously quoted book come out strongly *against* progressive rates. Cf. *ibid.*, p. 81.

36. Lowdon Wingo, Jr., "Urban Space in a Policy Perspective," in L. Wingo, Jr., ed., *Cities and Space—The Future Use of Urban Land* (Baltimore: The Johns Hopkins Press, 1962), p. 4.

37. Lewis Mumford, *The City in History* (New York: Harcourt, Brace and World, 1961), p. 527.

38. Departamento del Plan Regulador de Monterrey, N. L. y Municipios Vecinos, *El Plan Director de la Subregión Monterrey* (Monterrey: Dirección General de Planificación [Gobierno del Estado de Nuevo León], 1967).

IV

URBANIZATION IN SELECTED COUNTRIES AND CITIES

CHAPTER TEN

THE ARGENTINE SYSTEM OF CITIES: PRIMACY AND RANK-SIZE RULE*

CÉSAR A. VAPÑARSKY

Theoretical Approach

The problems posed by the idea that the relations between size and rank order of cities within an area constitute a meaningful phenomenon are particularly elusive. A considerable amount of work has been accomplished in this respect, but a real explanation of the regularities—as well as the deviations from a regular pattern—found in empirical research seems still to be lacking.

On this basis, it may seem that new empirical research can add very little to the existing body of knowledge unless a new attempt at a theoretical explanation is advanced first. We think this is not true. First, the study of

* This essay was prepared for the 1967 Summer Workshop in Engineering and Biological Analogues in the Social Sciences, directed by Richard Jung and organized by the Center for Environmental Quality Management at Cornell University, Ithaca, N.Y. It is based upon "Rank-Size Distribution of Cities in Argentina," an M.A. thesis completed in 1966 by the author under the chairmanship of Allan G. Feldt at Cornell University. A shorter version of this essay appeared under the title "On Rank-Size Distributions of Cities: An Ecological Approach," *Economic Development and Cultural Change* 17 (4) (July 1969):584–95. The author acknowledges the support he has received from the Consejo de Investigaciones Científicas y Técnicas of the Argentine Republic and from the Organization of American States while conducting the original research.

changes over time in the rank-size distribution of cities in a given area can lead to the finding of tendencies systematically related to some changing characteristic of the underlying ecological system as a whole. Second, it is also important to consider whether the same regularities found for the rank-size distribution of cities in an area as a whole will also be found for the distribution in each subarea, whatever the criterion adopted to draw the division. On the other hand, in an analysis over time as well as in an analysis for spatial divisions at one point in time, it is possible to state some hypotheses to guide the research, even in the absence of a complete theoretical framework, including an exhaustive explanation of the found regularities.

The present research concerns the analysis of the rank-size distribution of cities—over time as well as for subareas at one fixed point in time—in one specific country, Argentina, in which sufficiently reliable census data exist for five different dates along a period of nearly one hundred years (1869–1960).

MODELS OF CITY-SIZE DISTRIBUTION

Two quite different empirical regularities have been noted throughout the literature. Mark Jefferson[1] advanced the observation that the largest city in a country frequently is far greater than the second one, and proposed the "law of the primate city." On the other hand, apart from some earlier attempts, Zipf[2] was the first to call widespread attention to regularities linking the rank and size of the whole system of cities in an area. Zipf observed that, given an area sufficiently large, quite often the rank and size of cities follow a pattern such that the size of the kth city is $1/k$ the size of the largest city in the area. This is the empirical regularity known as the "rank-size rule."

According to the rank-size rule, we can predict the pop-

ulation P_k *of the kth city* knowing the population C of the
first one. The corresponding formula is:

$$P_k = C/k$$

Equivalently, the rank-size rule can be formulated by saying that the rank of any city multiplied by its population
yields a constant C. Solving the equation above for C, the
population C *of the largest city* can be predicted when the
rank k and the population P_k of any other city are known:

$$kP_k = C$$

Graphed in log-log paper, the rank-size rule yields a series
of points lying in a straight line with slope -1 and whose y-
intercept is log C.[3]

Zipf looked for an explanation of this empirical regularity on the basis of his "principle of least effort." His attempt is not generally accepted as successful, however.
More recent attempts, in particular those of Simon and
Ward,[4] have tried to derive the rank-size rule from stochastic processes. This kind of approach suggests a promising line of research because, under the assumptions of
each of these proposals, the exact fulfillment of the rank-
size rule is considered as the most probable steady state of
a stochastic process in a system.[5] Therefore, if those assumptions are accepted, the need for explanation is shifted
from the reasons why the model has to hold to the reasons
why deviations from it do in fact occur.

A remark is necessary at this point about the relations
between primacy and rank-size rule. A frequent emphasis
in empirical research directs attention to the relations between or among the top cities, either the two largest or at
most the five or six largest cities, without taking into account the distribution of the rest of the cities in the area.
In this kind of approach, the rank-size rule and the
primacy of a single city are compared as alternative, mutually exclusive models. However, primacy and rank-size

rule appear as alternative models only when attention is directed exclusively to the largest cities in an area. To analyze the whole range of the distribution is quite a different problem. In this case, if the largest city is far greater than the second largest, but the rank-size rule holds for the rest of the distribution, it is perfectly acceptable to claim that this model still applies except for one deviant case, however important, and to look for a specific explanation of the deviant case instead of rejecting the model. The same reasoning applies even if not only the largest but the two or three largest cities in an area are larger than predicted by the rule.

HYPOTHESES

The question of whether the rank-size rule can be expected to hold in any area, whatever the criterion established to delimit it, has been advanced by Hoover.[6] In the same vein, the question can be asked: What are the conditions associated with the existence of a "well-defined pattern" of rank-size distribution of cities in an area? As stated above, two "well-defined patterns" are available as models relating rank and size of cities, namely, primacy and rank-size rule. Since they are not mutually exclusive models when the entire distribution of cities is the subject matter of research, it can be expected that the conditions associated with the fulfillment of each one derive from different general characteristics of the area under study.

If a region is regarded as an ecological system, one defining characteristic of a region is its degree of *closure*. As defined by Feldt,[7] "closure is the proportion of all existing interactions beginning or terminating within a particular system which are also completed within the same system." That is, closure is a quotient that varies between 0 and 1. Closure is 1 if no interaction occurs between the system and the external world; closure is 0 if all interactions initiated or terminated within the system are completed outside it. The latter is a limiting case, and it is obvious that it is no longer possible to speak of a "system" here.

First, a very general hypothesis can be formulated in this respect, namely that, since closure is a property of well-defined systems, a necessary condition to find a "well-defined pattern" of rank-size distribution of cities is a relatively high degree of closure of the area under analysis.

Second, for regions that are sufficiently well defined— that is, having relatively high closure—the lower the degree of closure (the more the region is inherently dependent upon other regions to maintain a steady state), the higher can be expected to be the degree of primacy of the city that establishes the main link between the given area and the external world. This is a second and more specific hypothesis, relating closure to primacy.

With respect to the rest of the distribution, however, closure is hypothesized to be related to a well-defined pattern only as a necessary condition, as stated above. A *third* hypothesis links fulfillment of the rank-size rule not to closure but to another characteristic of an area, namely, its degree of internal *interdependence.* Considering as units of analysis all the agglomerations within the area, internal interdependence can be defined as the total amount of interaction that takes place between all possible pairs of units, divided by the total population living in these units. Low interdependence means relative isolation of the units from each other in the area. The corresponding hypothesis is that the higher the interdependence, the higher can the fulfillment of the rank-size rule for the whole distribution of cities be expected to be, since the existence of a high level of interaction among the different units in the system is required for the differentiation of the system into a complete hierarchy of city sizes.

Referring these concepts to the analysis of Argentina, it

is necessary to note that an entire country, the most important political unit in the modern world, is typically a well-defined ecological system. Such a unit exhibits relatively high closure, which is probably greater than that of any other area either smaller or greater than the country itself and is likely, therefore, to have a well-defined pattern of rank-size distribution of its cities. However, countries differ in their degree of closure as well as in their degree of interdependence. Consequently, four logical possibilities arise, namely:[8]

1. *High closure and low interdependence.* This combination would characterize a very underdeveloped area that is also practically isolated from the external world, a situation becoming increasingly difficult to find in the modern world. No well-defined pattern in the rank-size distribution of cities can be expected. Even more, no city of appreciable size is likely to occur.

2. *Low closure and low interdependence.* The primacy of the city (or cities) establishing the main link with the external world is expected in this case; at the same time, no well-defined pattern can be expected for the rest of the distribution. This was the case of Argentina until the end of the nineteenth century.

3. *Low closure and high interdependence.* While the first city (or cities) will tend to show primacy, the rest of the distribution can be expected to fulfill the rank-size rule. This is the case of Argentina at present.

4. *High closure and high interdependence.* The hypothesized conditions for the fulfillment of the rank-size rule by the whole distribution of cities, including the largest one, are accomplished. The classical example, given by Zipf, among others, is the United States.

Thus far the discussion has been centered on the analysis of alternative patterns of city distribution to be found in one specific type of area: *a country as a whole*. But the present study is also concerned with the analysis of city distributions in *subareas within the country*.

These subareas will hardly present the character of an ecological system as clearly defined as the country as a whole. Therefore, the patterns of rank-size distribution of cities for these subareas may not be as clearly shaped as the pattern for the country as a whole. But the division of the country into smaller regions can be made according to quite different criteria. Therefore, as a corollary of the *first* and very general hypothesis stated above, it was hypothesized in this case that the criterion that maximizes the degree of closure of the resulting subareas provides the type of regions where the most clear shape of city distribution is likely to be found. Since the closure of subareas thus obtained will be normally lower than that of the whole country, however, according to the *second* general hypothesis, primacy is always expected. Finally, according to the *third* general hypothesis, the degree of fulfillment of the rank-size rule by the rest of the distribution will depend on the degree of internal interdependence within each subarea thus obtained.

A remark must be made about the very small localities in a given area, constituting the lower part of the rank-size distribution. In fact, although the rural village is practically unknown in Argentina, very small agglomerations of a few hundreds of people perform only the function of serving the surrounding rural area, lacking specifically "urban" functions. It has been observed in the literature that very small places are fewer than predicted by the rank-size rule, and the previous observation is assumed to account for this fact.[9] Granted that a rank-size distribution of cities must stop at some minimum size of agglomeration, in this research, localities of less than 1,000 people were excluded from the universe to which the model was applied. This minimum size, based upon impressionistic images of the characteristics of Argentine agglomerations, is far lower than limits adopted in most available empirical research on this subject.

Finally, it should be observed that in this analysis no explanation is advanced on the reasons why the rank-size rule can be assumed as a model. Rather, the validity of this model for a system of high closure and high interdependence is accepted on the basis of the work of Zipf, Simon, Ward, and others. The hypotheses advanced are restricted solely to relations between fulfillment of primacy and/or rank-size rule in the city-size distribution, on the one hand, and levels of closure and interdependence of the area under analysis, on the other.

METHODOLOGICAL REMARKS

To test the hypotheses just exposed, a clear methodological criterion to measure deviations from the rank-size rule in empirical distributions of cities was required.

The deviations of an actual distribution of cities from the rank-size rule are often measured by plotting on log-log paper points representing the whole range of cities in an area and comparing them to the straight line of slope -1 that corresponds to the rank-size rule. Actually, different criteria can be adopted to make this comparison.

In most current empirical research the "best-fitting line" —that is, the regression line of rank on population—is drawn, and its slope is measured. The divergence shown by this slope from the theoretical slope -1 characterizing the rank-size rule is considered as a measure of deviation. However, positive deviations of large cities can seriously affect this slope, even if most of the distribution does fulfill the rank-size rule. On the other hand, a regression line may show a slope -1 in spite of considerable deviations along the distribution, provided that these deviations compensate themselves.

Since the model postulates a slope of -1 as the most probable steady state, a criterion for comparison was adopted in which not the best-fitting line of the whole distribution but deviations of individual cities (or groups of cities adjacent in rank order) were measured with respect to a line of slope -1. This line, in turn, was obtained by drawing a best-fitting line of fixed slope -1 of the whole distribution down to localities of just over 1,000 population, and excluding the one or more cities if they showed strong deviations in the direction of primacy. The quantitative measure of deviations was facilitated by an alternative analytic procedure that, for the sake of brevity, is not exposed here.

Findings

THE ARGENTINE RANK-SIZE DISTRIBUTION OF CITIES OVER TIME

In studying the rank-size distribution of Argentine cities over a period of approximately one hundred years (1869–1960), we would expect to find relatively high primacy but not a well-defined pattern for the rest of the cities at first, followed by increasing primacy and a good fit of the rest of the distribution to the rank-size rule in following years—that is, we would expect a change in the distribution accompanying a change from relatively high closure and low interdependence to lower closure but high interdependence, since this is the general trend characterizing the Argentine socioeconomic history at least up to the thirties. These expectations were fulfilled.

The rank-size distributions of cities corresponding to the five national censuses of population hitherto realized have been plotted in Figure 1. Only the population of places over 2,000 people is available in the third census (1914), and only that of places over 10,000 people in the fifth census (provisional data, 1960). The other three censuses, however, recorded the population of all places of 100 people or more, so that the distribution could be drawn in these cases down to the stated lower limit—that is, includ-

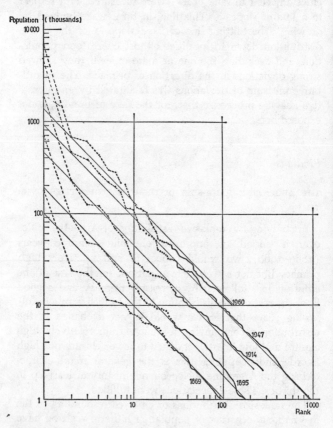

FIGURE 1. Argentina. City-size distribution at each census date. (Best-fitting line of slope -1 drawn excluding largest city in all except first census date.)

ing all places of more than 1,000 inhabitants. On the other hand, the original census data were rearranged according to a uniform definition of agglomerations as urbanized areas rather than as administrative units as defined in the censuses.

The primacy of Buenos Aires was remarkable long before the first census was undertaken in 1869. It has been continuously increasing since then to such a degree that Buenos Aires is at present one of the most extreme examples of primacy in the world—that is, in 1960 it had 6,700,000 inhabitants, more than ten times the population of Rosario, the second Argentine city. Both the rapid growth and the increasing primacy of Buenos Aires are the result of characteristics of Argentine economic growth. Buenos Aires grew as the main national link to Europe in the exportation of meat and grains and the importation of manufactured goods, thus becoming the central node of the whole network of communications in the country. The process of increasing internal interdependence coincided with a process of decreasing closure of the country, whose whole economy grew upon the rapid development of a national export base. During recent decades, both the creation of a national industry directed to the domestic market and the expansion of the tertiary sector took place on the basis of already existing locational advantages of Buenos Aires, so that the powerful pressures previously developed toward centralization in the primate city could not be overcome.

From the second census (1895) on, the increasing primacy of Buenos Aires is accompanied by a consistent fulfillment of the rank-size rule by the rest of the cities in the country. As stated above, rank-size rule and primacy are not considered here as mutually exclusive models of city distributions.

Figure 1 shows the actual distribution of cities at each census date compared to a line of slope -1 representing the corresponding theoretical distribution that follows the rank-size rule at each date. The largest city was excluded in drawing this line in all except the first census date.

Although the distribution for 1869 (first census) shows the already present primacy of Buenos Aires, the rest of the distribution does not respond to a well-defined pattern. By 1895 (second census) the increase in internal interdependence led to a considerably closer fit to the rank-size rule by all except the largest city. Except for some marginal areas, a high degree of internal interdependence in the whole country was practically achieved toward 1914 (third census). Two important factors in shaping the ecological characteristics of Argentina have been the development of new cultivated areas and of the railway system, and both came to an end approximately toward this date. Correspondingly, the distribution of all cities except the largest fit closely the rank-size rule in 1914 and at the dates of the following censuses, 1947 (fourth) and 1960 (fifth). Some intermediate deviations from the rank-size rule do exist, which were analyzed in the original research in terms of the specialized character of the cities involved.

REGIONAL RANK-SIZE DISTRIBUTIONS OF CITIES IN ARGENTINA IN 1947

The second part of this research concerns the analysis of subsystems of cities in Argentina at one point in time (1947). Three forms of regional delimitation were examined. Since "natural" regions and/or administrative regions are in principle totally unrelated to either closure or interdependence in an ecological sense, no perceptible fit to the rank-size rule and only scattered and meaningless evidences of primacy were expected under either of these first two criteria of regionalization.

First, a division into homogeneous regions[10] based on physiographic features favoring different ways of human occupation was studied. One region revealed almost complete absence of cities (only one place existed, of about 3,300 people). On the other hand, some of the largest cities in the country were located just at the intersection of two or even three regions, making arbitrary any decision as to the assignment of each of these cities to a single region. One of these arbitrary-decision criteria resulted in a large series of cities in one region that deviated in the direction of primacy toward the upper end of the distribution. In summary, this method of delimitation of regions resulted in poor and meaningless approximations to rank-size distributions.

The second criterion referred to the analysis of rank-size distributions of cities for fourteen provinces and nine national territories existing in 1947, and shown in Figure 2. In some of these administrative areas the distributions were shapeless, in another one the rank-size rule was not fitted by cities under 12,000 people, and some administrative units had too few cities to admit the validity of any model of rank-size distribution. This second method of regional delimitation proved to be also inappropriate for the application of any model of rank-size distributions of cities.

However, the analysis of rank-size distributions in regions delimited taking into account the notions of closure and interdependence showed a quite different picture. The country was partitioned into six clearly defined nodal regions by way of an analysis of differential population density at the level of counties. This procedure determines regions of relatively high closure. The resulting map was very similar to a map of economic regions that had been prepared by an Argentine federal office[11] on the basis of an analysis of intercity telephone calls, and which is shown in Figure 2. The latter was finally adopted, since the only important difference it showed was the separation of the southern part of the country, considered as a single nodal region in the former, into a nodal region with center in the city of Bahía Blanca and a sort of residual area scarcely populated in the extreme South. The resulting city-size distributions, briefly described below, exhibit primacy of one or a few cities, followed by a fairly well-fitted rank-

FIGURE 2. Argentina. Nodal regions. (Interprovincial limits indicated in dotted lines.)

size rule in the rest of the distribution. The only exception is the shapeless distribution of the mentioned residual area.

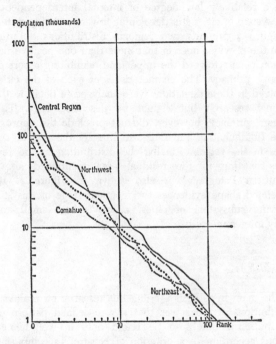

FIGURE 3. Argentina. Four regional city-size distributions exhibiting a primate city and the rank-size rule fulfilled by the remaining cities. 1947.

Figure 3 shows four regional distributions exhibiting a pattern similar to that of the whole country: a primate city and the rank-size rule approximately fulfilled by the rest of the cities. One of these cases, however, the region of Bahía Blanca, presents consistently negative deviations toward the upper end and positive ones toward the lower end of the distribution, not so pronounced but somewhat resembling the distribution of the whole country at an early date (1869). As in the latter case, this would indicate a relatively low degree of internal interdependence in a system of cities still developing toward a steady state.

Figure 4 presents two regional distributions differing from the previous ones in that more than one positive deviation occurs toward the upper end, exhibiting a sort of "group" primacy. The characteristics of each of the cities involved in these deviations were analyzed in detail in the original research but cannot be described here. This "group" primacy, however, did not preclude the approximate fulfillment of the rank-size rule by the rest of the cities in the region. Finally, the distribution of the few cities existing in the residual area mentioned above (southern Patagonia) is also drawn in Figure 4. Its undefined shape evidences the incipient stage of this still evolving subsystem of cities, which is both small and badly interconnected.

Conclusions

The main hypothesis guiding this research on rank-size distributions of cities was that a well-defined pattern of distribution is likely to be found only in well-defined regions according to a criterion of closure. In comparing different regions of relatively high closure (or the same region at different points in time), the shape of their rank-size distributions of cities was expected to be associated with the level of closure and the level of interdependence of each region. The corresponding hypotheses were tested for the Argentine system of cities at different points in time and for Argentine regions delimited according to different criteria of regionalization at one point in time.

The results obtained confirmed the hypotheses. Primacy was expected to be associated with relatively low closure

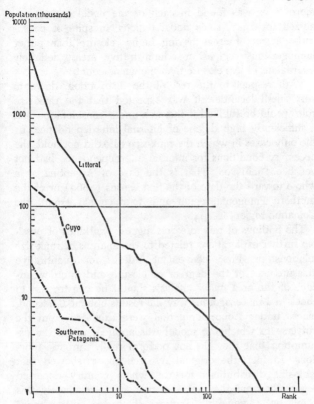

FIGURE 4. Argentina. Two regional city-size distributions (Littoral and Cuyo) exhibiting "group" primacy and the rank-size rule fulfilled by the remaining cities; and one distribution of undefined shape in a residual region (southern Patagonia). 1947.

and, indeed, the primacy of the largest city in Argentina, Buenos Aires, increased over time as the closure of the country diminished. On the other hand, primacy of one or

more cities was found in each of the nodal regions analyzed for 1947, since nodal regions, in spite of constituting a set of areas having higher closure than either
homogeneous regions or administrative areas, definitely
are regions of less closure than the whole country.

With respect to the rest of the distribution, down to
very small localities, it was expected that the rank-size
rule would be fulfilled if the area under consideration had
a sufficiently high degree of internal interdependence. In
the only cases in which the rank-size rule did not hold, the
necessary conditions for internal interdependence had not
yet been achieved. That is the case of Argentina as a
whole toward the date of the first census (1869) or of the
southern Patagonia region and, to a certain extent, the
Comahue region, in 1947.

The findings of this research suggest two kinds of possible further explorations related to the analysis of rank-size
relationships. First, convenient indexes for quantitative
measurement of the degrees of closure and interdependence of the area under analysis should be constructed to
check in a more rigorous way the results obtained. Second,
places under 1,000 population were excluded from the
universe to which the model was applied, under the assumption that they do not perform really "urban" functions. In fact, the original research report showed that
rank-size distributions for the whole country departed
negatively from the rank-size rule at approximately this
point, but regional distributions showed a cutting point
more or less defined between 500 and 2,000 people according to the case. An analysis of the functions performed by these smaller centers as contrasted to places in
the range of size immediately over them would reveal
whether the assumption was correct.[12]

Finally, it was far from the purposes of this research to
propose a complete theoretical explanation of the processes
leading to a specific pattern of rank-size distribution of
cities. However, the work done indicates the importance

of some theoretical considerations. First, primacy and rank-size rule are shown to be complementary rather than mutually exclusive models. Current theoretical formulations tend to forget that the primacy of one city, however large, is only one instance of deviation from a distribution of hundreds or even thousands of individual cases—provided that cities are considered the units of analysis rather than population living in different classes of cities in a hierarchy of sizes. Second, the definition of the region in which the rank-size rule is drawn is crucial for the testing of hypotheses and the explanation of empirical distributions. In principle, no well-defined pattern can be expected in a region arbitrarily delimited. This research emphasizes closure as the criterion for delimitation of meaningful regions in the analysis of systems of cities. Third, each of the two available models relating rank and size of cities appears to be fulfilled under different characteristics of the area under analysis: primacy depending on the level of closure, rank-size rule on the level of interdependence. Given the difficulties found in available research to establish valid correlations between either of these models and socioeconomic characteristics of the area, the exploration of these and other properties of ecological systems as variables of the utmost importance seems promising.[13] The results of this research point clearly in this direction.

NOTES

1. Mark Jefferson, "The Law of the Primate City," *Geographical Review* 29 (Apr. 1939):226–32.

2. George K. Zipf, *National Unity and Disunity* (Bloomington, Ind.: Principia Press, 1941) and *Human Behavior and the Principle of the Least Effort* (Cambridge, Mass.: Addison-Wesley, 1949). See references to earlier studies on this regularity in Otis D. Duncan, "The Measurement of Population Distribution," *Population Studies* II (July 1957):27–45.

3. The rank-size rule is a special case of a series of distributions highly skewed in the shape of a reversed J. Variously, it

has been treated as a Pareto, a lognormal, and a Yule distribution. See Otis D. Duncan, op. cit.; Herbert Simon, "On a Class of Skew Distribution Functions," *Biometrika* 42 (Dec. 1955):425–40, repr. as Chap. 9 in *Models of Man* (New York: John Wiley & Sons, 1957); Brian J. L. Berry and William L. Garrison, "Alternate Explanations of Urban Rank-Size Relationships," *Annals of the Association of American Geographers* 48 (Mar. 1958):83–91; Benjamin Ward, "City Structure and Interdependence," *Papers and Proceedings of the Regional Science Association* 10 (1963):207–21.

4. Herbert Simon, op. cit.; Benjamin Ward, op. cit.

5. Brian J. L. Berry briefly discusses rank-size distributions of cities in a framework of general systems theory in "Cities as Systems Within Systems of Cities," *Papers and Proceedings of the Regional Science Association* 13 (1964):147–63. Perhaps the best presentation of general systems theory, especially concerned with living systems, is a series of three articles by James G. Miller, "Living Systems: Basic Concepts," "Living Systems: Structure and Process," and "Living Systems: Cross-Level Hypotheses," *Behavioral Science* 10 (July 1965):193–237, and 10 (Oct. 1965):337–411. A system of cities is considered in the present essay as an ecological system; consequently, regularities in rank-size distributions of cities are regarded as depending on the states of ecological variables. From a general ecological viewpoint, John B. Calhoun, "Social Welfare as a Variable in Population Dynamics," *Cold Spring Harbor Symposia on Quantitative Biology* 22 (1957):339–56 regards the fulfillment of the rank-size rule as representing a "climax community."

6. Edgar M. Hoover, "The Concept of a System of Cities: A Comment on Rutledge Vining's Paper," *Economic Development and Cultural Change* 3 (Jan. 1955):196–98.

7. Allan G. Feldt, personal communication. The concept of closure had not yet been widely developed in the theoretical literature, although the fundamental attributes of more or less closed systems have been discussed in some detail in relation to many empirical studies. See, for example, Robert Redfield, *The Little Community* (Chicago: University of Chicago Press, 1955); Horace C. Miner, "The Folk-Urban Continuum," *American Sociological Review* 17 (Oct. 1952):529–37; Colin Clark, "The Economic Functions of a City in Relation to its Size," *Econometrica* 13 (Apr. 1945):97–113. A few empirical attempts to measure the level of closure of a system may be seen in P. Neff and R. M. Williams, "The Identification and Measurement of an Industrial Area's Export Employment in

Manufacturing," *Proceedings of the Western Committee on Regional Economic Analysis* (1952); and Allan G. Feldt, "The Metropolitan Area Concept: An Evaluation of the 1950 SMA's," *Journal of the American Statistical Association* 60 (June 1965):617–36. Finally, Alexander Szalai, "Cohesion Indices for Regional Determination," *Papers of the Peace Research Society* 4, Cracow Conference (1965):1–6, presents a careful analysis of criteria for determining the level of closure of a region. The technical vocabulary employed to refer to this concept varies widely from each of these works to the other.

8. Considering these four logical possibilities as a sequence ordered from the first to the fourth, they roughly correspond to North's typical stages in regional economic growth. See Douglass C. North, "Location Theory and Regional Economic Growth," *Journal of Political Economy* 63 (June 1955):243–58.

9. See, for example, Charles T. Stewart, Jr., "The Size and Spacing of Cities," *Geographical Review* 48 (Apr. 1958):222–45.

10. Professor Daus' division of Argentina into "natural regions" was adopted. See Federico A. Daus, *Geografía y unidad argentina* (Buenos Aires: Nova, 1957).

11. Consejo Federal de Inversiones, República Argentina, *Bases para el desarrollo regional argentino* (Buenos Aires: CFI, 1963).

12. In the framework of central place theory, many investigations on the functions performed by different classes of places in the lower levels of a hierarchy of sizes have been accomplished. See, for example, John E. Brush and Howard E. Bracey, "Rural Service Centers in Southwestern Wisconsin and Southern England," *Geographical Review* 45 (Oct. 1955):559–69.

13. Brian J. L. Berry, in "City Size Distributions and Economic Development," *Economic Development and Cultural Change* 9 (July 1961):573–87, has shown that there is no correlation between lognormalcy of the city-size distribution and either degree of economic development or degree of urbanization. On the other hand, Arnold S. Linsky, in "Some Generalizations Concerning Primate Cities," *Annals of the Association of American Geographers* 55 (Sept. 1965):506–13, formulated several hypotheses relating occurrence of primacy and socioeconomic and demographic-ecological variables. He found that high primacy is in any case precluded in large countries. Hence, an ecological variable, size, was critical in the mere definition of the area chosen to test his hypotheses.

CHAPTER ELEVEN

URBANISM AND URBANIZATION IN MEXICO: SITUATION AND PROSPECTS*

LUIS UNIKEL

Introduction

The geographic concentration of population constitutes at present one of the most important processes in the contemporary world. This phenomenon, diffused throughout the world, is characterized by important changes in the distribution and composition of population, by progressive incorporation of large sectors of the population into an urban life style, and, in general, by continuous, and at times accelerated, transformations in the rural-urban structure of the nations of the world, especially the developing countries.

In Mexico, these changes have been occurring rapidly, due to, among other factors, a process of urbanization, which intensified after 1940. It is apparent that this phenomenon will continue during the next ten years at a pace meriting greater attention than it has received to date. Attention must be paid not only to investigation of this process, but also to steps that public and private sectors should take to maximize economic and social benefits and

* Originally published in *Disyuntivas sociales*, ed. Miguel S. Wionczek (Mexico City: SEP/setentas, No. 5, 1971). The author gratefully acknowledges the collaboration of Omar Lazcano in the preparation of this essay. English translation by Felicity M. Trueblood.

minimize the innumerable problems arising from urbanization.

The present essay has three main objectives: (1) to inform the reader of the principal features of Mexican urbanization from 1900 to date; (2) to furnish an idea of the magnitude of urban development that may possibly occur in Mexico from 1970 to 1980; and (3) to provide a series of reflections regarding the urban phenomenon in general, with specific reference to the Mexican case.

Definition, Causes, and Effects of Urbanization

A rigorous, theoretical definition of the process of urbanization presents serious difficulties. Contributing to the problem is the unquestioned relationship of this phenomenon with factors as vast and complex as modernization and economic development. Nevertheless, there is consensus that urbanization is a multidimensional phenomenon at work in the basic elements of society: the economic, the social, the social-psychological, the political, and the demographic-ecological. At the same time, it is commonly accepted that one of urbanization's best-known dimensions, and most important notwithstanding its limited range, is the demographic-ecological.[1]

Thus, urbanization is "a process of concentrating population and human activities at central spatial points."[2] The phenomenon of concentration may take place in already existing cities or through the creation of new urban localities, causing an increase in the proportion of population described as urban.

According to the above definition, the main conditioning elements of urbanization are the growth of urban population, physical expansion of the cities, and migration of rural population to urban centers. In turn, each of these elements is generated or developed by other factors. For example, the natural increase of urban population is influenced by the level and distribution of income, the degree of sociocultural progress, the age and sex structure of the population, etc. Physical expansion of the cities is caused by the movement of the population and its activities from the center of the metropolis to the periphery, as well as from peripheral zones' own demographic growth. Finally, rural-urban migration is generated by a double play of forces, those that expel rural population (due to, among other factors, the ineffective land-tenure system, great demographic pressure on the latter resource, and accentuated rural marginality) and those that attract rural population to the cities. The latter include all those factors representing to migrants improved opportunities—real or illusory—for overcoming their problems, principally economic.

The effects of urbanization—much more evident and remarked than its causes—may be broadly classified into two categories: those occurring within cities (intraurban) and those taking place in a regional setting (interurban). The former have their origin in the concentration of industrial, financial, commercial, cultural, political, and administrative activities (which generate external economies and diseconomies of scale), and in extraordinary increases in urban services, public works, urban lots, housing, transportation, employment, etc. Interurban effects are the result of greater interdependence among cities and between these cities and their hinterland, due basically to the growing movement of persons, vehicles, goods, and information. The second section of this essay will treat certain of these aspects in greater detail.

Urbanization from 1900 to 1970[3]

LEVEL AND PACE OF URBANIZATION

Mexico has undergone two stages in its urbanization process. The first, 1900–40, may be described as slow; the second, 1940–60, and by extension to 1970, may be classified as rapid. The relative slowness and rapidity of the urbanization process express the different positions and movements recorded by the level of urbanization in Mexico.[4]

From 1900 to 1940, the process of urbanization in Mexico was determined by highly diverse demographic, socioeconomic, and political factors. The prerevolutionary period (1900–10) was characterized by isolation of the rural population due to nonexistent or limited communication between rural and urban centers. This was in large part responsible for the fact that Mexico City was the only urban center to grow to any considerable degree during this period.

The 1910–21 period was, on the contrary, a period of great social agitation. Among other events during this period, the semifeudal system binding the peasant population to the soil was destroyed. As a result, cities grew in population, with Mexico City recording the greatest demographic increase.

After 1921, and until the late 1930s, the Mexican population entered a period of relative stability. Rural-urban migration decreased considerably, in large part because of the cessation of military activities and because of the effects of the agrarian reform policy, which in those years began to be important. Nevertheless, in the late 1930s, migratory currents to Mexico City, Guadalajara, Monterrey, and certain northern border cities resumed and even intensified. The latter phenomenon was influenced by the expropriation of the Mexican petroleum industry, the creation of state financial organisms for development, construction of the national highway system and large hydroelectric and irrigation works, the effects of U.S. water and irrigation policies on Mexico's northern border, and the diverse effects of the Second World War.

The second stage, 1940–60, was characterized by three basic features: first, a rapid rate of urbanization (that of the 1940–50 decade was of such magnitude that it will never be achieved again); second, continuous and accelerated increase in the rate of natural population growth, from 2.7 per cent annually 1940–50 to 3.1 per cent in the 1950–60 decade. The latter has caused, notwithstanding the important volume of rural-urban migration, a change in the relative weight that rural migration to the city and natural population increase have traditionally had upon the growth of urban population. From 1940 to 1950, rural-urban migration was the most significant factor in urban growth, while in the succeeding ten years it was natural population increase. The third outstanding feature of these twenty years of urbanization was the decrease in the population predominance of the urban area of Mexico City with respect to the eight next largest cities, after 1950. Yet, the latter process almost halted from 1960 to 1970 (see Table 4), due primarily to the fact that during this decade the high annual rate of growth of the population of the Mexico City urban area surpassed that of 1950–60.

Decrease in primacy, a reflection of the formation of regional development centers (principally Guadalajara and Monterrey) and of the formation of subsystems of better-integrated cities, is cause and effect of a series of increasingly more complicated economic and sociopolitical processes occurring in Mexico. Outstanding among these are the growing industrialization of the nation and qualitative changes taking place in certain of its industrial branches, such as petrochemicals; deterioration in the standard of living of the peasant; formation of a middle class with increasingly demanding aspirations; and improvement in and expansion of the communication and transportation network throughout the nation, especially in rural areas.

URBAN GROWTH, 1900–70

During the present century, the urban population of Mexico—that living in localities of 15,000 or more inhabitants[5]—grew more rapidly than the total population of the nation. Nevertheless, this growth was not homogeneous during the entire period, as can be seen in the two previously mentioned stages: slow growth, 1900–40, and rapid growth, 1940–60 (Tables 1 and 2).

Table 1

MEXICO

Total Population, Urban Population, and Population of 17 Largest Cities, 1900-1970

Population and Percentages	1940	1950	1960	1970
Population (thousands of inhabitants)				
(1) Total	13,607	19,649[d]	34,923	49,100[e]
(2) Urban[a]	1,434	3,928	12,747	22,100[c]
(3) 17 largest cities[b]	97.3	3,005	8,969	15,100[g]
(4) Urban area of Mexico City[c]	345	1,560	4,910	8,567[g]
Percentages				
(2) / (1)	10.5	20.0	36.5	45.0
(4) / (1)	2.5	7.9	14.1	17.4
(4) / (2)	24.1	39.7	36.9	38.8
(3) / (2)	67.8	76.5	70.4	68.3

[a]Urban population is defined as that inhabiting localities of 15,000 or more persons. See footnote 5.
[b]This corresponds to the 15 urban areas having 100,000 or more inhabitants in 1960, with the addition of the cities of Aguascalientes and Ciudad Juárez.
[c]This includes the population residing in the physically-contiguous area having as its center Mexico City (12 districts) and extending without consideration for politico-administrative limits into the State of Mexico.
[d]Luis Unikel, "The Process of Urbanization in Mexico...," table 13.
[e]Population estimated as of 30 June 1970, based on preliminary data from the January, 1970, census. It does not include underenumerated population.
[f]Population estimated on the basis of the hypothesis that the average annual increase in the percentage of urban population from 1960 to 1970 was 2.1%, a rate 5% higher than that assumed for 1960-1980. For the latter analysis, see Luis Unikel, "El proceso de urbanización," in *El perfil de México en 1980* (Instituto de Investigaciones Sociales de la Universidad Autónoma de México) (Mexico City: Siglo XXI, 1970), Volume II, pp. 223-253.
[g]Estimate based on preliminary data from the 1970 census.

Sources: Calculations based on general population censuses. See also Luis Unikel, "The Process of Urbanization in Mexico...," *loc. cit.*, and preliminary data from the 1970 census.

Table 2

MEXICO

Average Annual Increases in Urban and Total Population and Their Relationship, 1900-1970

Population and Relationship of Increases	1900-1940	1940-1960	1900-1970	1960-1970[a]
Total (1)	0.91	2.80	1.46	3.37
Urban (2)	2.33	5.29	2.66	5.37
Relationship (2) / (1)	2.56	1.89	1.82	1.59

[a]Estimated data. See Table 1, notes e, f, and g.
Source: Table 1.

In each of these two stages, urban population as a percentage of total population almost doubled, in spite of the fact that the second stage was only half as large as the first. This fact is reflected incontrovertibly in the number of cities and their population. In 1900, there were 33 urban centers in Mexico, with a total population of 1.4 million inhabitants; in 1940, there were 55 cities, with a population of 3.9 million; and in 1960, urban localities had risen to 123, with a population of 12.7 million (see Table 3).

Table 3

MEXICO

Distribution of Population by Size of Locality, 1900, 1940, and 1960

Groups of Localities According to Population Size	1900			1940			1960		
	Localities	Inhabitants (thousands)	%	Localities	Inhabitants (thousands)	%	Localities	Inhabitants (thousands)	%
National total	52,749	13,607	100.0	105,508^h	19,649^i	100.0	89,005^h	34,923^h	100.0
Urban	33	1,435	10.5	55	3,928^j	20.0	123	12,747^j	36.6
1,000,000 and more^a	—	—	—	1	1,560	7.9	1	4,910	14.1
500,000–999,999^b	—	—	—	—	—	—	2	1,511	4.3
100,000–499,999^c	2	446	3.3	5	781	4.0	14	2,548	7.3
50,000– 99,999^d	4	280	2.0	8	589	3.0	20	1,533	4.4
20,000– 49,999^e	17	536	3.9	23	694	3.5	51	1,630	4.7
15,000– 19,999	10	173	1.3	18	304	1.6	35	615	1.8
Non-urban	52,716	12,172	89.5	105,453	15,721	80.0	88,882	22,176	63.4
Mixed	146	1,128	8.3	195	1,492	7.6	342	2,757	7.9
10,000–14,999^f	25	294	2.2	35	431	2.2	72	881	2.5
5,000– 9,999^g	121	834	5.4	160	1,061	5.4	270	1 876	5.4
Rural	52,570	11,044	81.2	105,258	14,229	72.4	88,540	19,419	55.5
2,500– 4,999	395	1,327	9.8	436	481	2.4	747	2,531	7.2
1,000– 2,499	1,609	2,411	17.7	1,934	3,968	20.2	3,203	4 761	13.6
Less than 1,000	50,566	7,306	53.7	102,868	9,780	49.8	84,590	12,127	34.7

^a Metropolis.
^b Regional centers.
^c Large cities.
^d Medium cities.
^e Small cities.
^f Mixed urban localities.
^g Mixed rural localities.
^h Does not include localities enumerated with others or uninhabited localities.
^i This datum differs from that provided by the VII Census of Population, by less than 4,390 inhabitants, due to three errata in the state volumes of this Census: 2,009 inhabitants in the city of Mérida, 2,345 inhabitants in the state of Durango, and 45 inhabitants in the state of Oaxaca.
^j This population differs from that obtained from census information for localities of 15,000 and more inhabitants because it includes the nation's principal urban areas: 6 in 1940, 21 in 1950, and 28 in 1960.

We shall now describe briefly the magnitude and certain characteristics of the growth of urban population in Mexico by discussing the three distinct ways in which this growth is achieved.

GROWTH OF URBAN POPULATION: EXISTING AND RECLASSIFIED CITIES

The notable change in the level of urbanization at work during the two previously mentioned stages may be analyzed as a function of the growth of cities existing at the beginning of each period and of localities which, due to their own internal growth, were reclassified from nonurban to urban. From 1900 to 1960, urban population grew by 11.3 million, 82.2 per cent of which corresponded to the growth of already existing cities, and the remainder, 17.8 per cent, to cities reclassified as urban. This phenomenon appeared with differing intensity in the two periods 1900–40 and 1940–60; thus, in the former period the percentage corresponding to already existing cities was 74.8, while in the latter it was 84.2.

There were, however, exceptional cases of cities that ceased to belong to the group of urban localities during the periods under consideration. The most outstanding case was recorded in the state of Mexico, where El Oro, once a prosperous mining city, suffered heavy emigration after the loss in importance of its principal economic activity.

GROWTH OF URBAN POPULATION THROUGH PHYSICAL
INTEGRATION

This is a relatively recent phenomenon in Mexico, the result of the city's territorial expansion toward its periphery and its absorption of peripheral localities. In 1940, Mexico had six urban areas, the most notable of which were the cities of Mexico, Orizaba, and Tampico. By 1960, the number had increased to twenty-eight, among which, apart from Mexico City, Guadalajara and Monterrey were outstanding. The northern border cities—which include cities undergoing the most rapid demographic growth—constitute special cases since their physical expansion, linked to that experienced by their neighboring cities on the U.S. side, has developed international urban areas of strategic importance to both countries. Such is the case of the urban area of Ciudad Juárez-El Paso, with nearly one million inhabitants.

It must be noted that of the urban increase recorded in

Mexico through physical integration in the 1940–60 period (876,000 inhabitants), approximately 70 per cent corresponded to the urban area of Mexico City.

In spite of the fact that this phenomenon has not had great weight on urban growth in the past, it is expected that it will assume greater importance in the future if present tendencies continue. Its implications may also be significant. By way of illustration, consider the political effects of urban expansion into *ejidal* (agricultural community) lands; the economic effects, as the already limited availability of agricultural lands, generally productive and often under irrigation, is further reduced; the ecological-urban, as cities are permitted to continue to grow and develop; and politico-administrative, when the physical expansion of a city takes place, as in the cases of Mexico City and Torreón, in two separate federal entities.

NATURAL AND SOCIAL GROWTH OF URBAN POPULATION

Average annual increases in urban population, 1900–60, have systematically surpassed increases in total population —that is, if it is assumed that urban as well as total population grow at the same rate, total growth of urban population has been greater than its natural growth. This implies a process of rural-urban migration which, with highs and lows, was continuous from 1900 to 1940. As might be expected, this phenomenon was particularly intense in the 1910–21 period, because of the revolutionary movement. From 1920 to 1930, migration from country to city retained a certain importance as the nation entered a period of relative calm and institutionalization.

On the opposite side of the ledger, urbanization underwent from 1930 to 1940 the greatest deceleration of the entire period, due to an important relative reduction in rural-urban migration. This decrease was possibly the result of the extensive agrarian reform program undertaken during this decade. It is probable that the distribution of lands and construction of the first important irrigation works rooted in the countryside at least temporarily the peasant population which, under other circumstances, would have migrated in greater numbers. On the other hand, the few existing cities, some of which were still affected economically by the revolutionary movement of 1910, did not offer sufficient attractions.

From 1950 to 1960, Mexico experienced a phenomenon similar to that of 1930–40: The relative weight of natural increase of urban population surpassed that of country-city migration. Nevertheless, what happened in the 1950–60 decade, as distinct from 1930–40, may be attributed in greater measure to the elevated rate of natural increase of urban population than to a reduction in migration. The latter was, in absolute terms, as numerous as that of 1940–60, the period in which Mexico recorded its highest rate of urbanization.

Finally, the 1960–70 decade has probably witnessed, according to estimates by S. Eckstein,[6] massive country-city migration on a scale superior to that of any of the preceding decades. If such be the case, the number of migrants may have surpassed 3 million persons. Yet, in view of the fact that total population—and certainly the urban —increased 10 per cent over the preceding decade, it may be asserted that, as was true in the 1950–60 decade, country-city migration has played a role of less relative importance than natural increase in the expansion of Mexico's urban population.

THE URBAN STRUCTURE

The distribution of urban population by size of locality indicates an extremely important evolution that in theory has been favorable to the nation's socioeconomic development. Accordingly, the elevated primacy of Mexico's system of principal cities began to fall after 1950, in spite of almost systematic increases since 1900 (see Table 4). Due to the acceleration in growth of the urban area of Mexico City, however, from 5.5 per cent annually 1950–60 to 5.7 per cent in the 1960–70 decade, the decrease in the index of primacy[7] during the past decade only occurred at the level of two cities. The remaining indices were constant, as noted in Table 4 below.

Table 4
MEXICO
Indices of Primacy, 2 to 10 Cities, 1900-1970

Indices of Primacy of:[a]	1900	1910	1921	1930	1940	1950	1960	1970[d]
2 cities	4.4	3.9	4.3	5.7	6.5	7.2	6.1	5.9
4 cities	1.7	1.6	1.9	2.4	2.7	2.9	2.7	2.7
6 cities	1.2	1.1	1.3	1.7	2.0	.2.2	2.1	2.1
8 cities	0.9	0.9	1.1	1.4	1.6	1.8[b]	1.8[b]	1.8
10 cities	0.8	0.8	0.9	1.2	1.4	1.6[c]	1.6[c]	1.6

[a]Expressed by Ip (n) = $\frac{P_1}{P_2 + P_3 + \ldots P_n}$ in which P_1, P_2, P_3 and P_n are the populations of the cities occupying ranks 1, 2, 3, and n.
[b]The exact values are 1.82 and 1.79, in 1950 and 1960, respectively.
[c]The exact values are 1.57 and 1.59, in 1950 and 1960, respectively.
[d]Calculations on the basis of estimated figures.
Source: Luis Unikel, "Urbanización," *loc. cit.*, p. 134, table V-11.

This means that from 1960–70, the demographic disproportion of the urban area of Mexico City vis-à-vis the principal cities next to it in size decreased only imperceptibly. On the other hand, from 1900 to date, the population of Mexico City has sustained constant increase in the percentage it represents of total national population, estimated in 1970 at 17.4 per cent (Table 1).

DISTRIBUTION OF NONURBAN POPULATION

The distribution of Mexico's population according to different sizes of localities is characterized as much by the relatively high proportion of population living in urban centers as by the hundreds of thousands of localities with scant population scattered throughout the nation. With a few exceptions, these localities of extremely limited population have a precarious standard of living, lack elementary public services, are frequently geographically isolated, have scarce sources of income, and are vulnerable to external factors. In sum, they are localities difficult to integrate into a pattern of modern development.

The distribution of nonurban population demonstrated relative slowness during the first forty years of the present century, and relative rapidity in the 1940–60 period. The rural population, which in 1900 had risen to 81.2 per cent, decreased slowly to 72.4 per cent in 1940, and thenceforward decreased even further from year to year. In spite of the latter, Mexico continued to be, in 1960, predominantly rural (55.5 per cent of the population lived in localities with less than 5,000 inhabitants). In 1970, the rural population was almost 50 per cent of total Mexican population. In absolute numbers (without adjustment), rural population reached 24.2 million in that year.

The relative decrease in population residing in localities of less than 2,500 inhabitants during the period of slow urbanization was minor. The percentage, which in 1900 was 71.4, was maintained almost immutably until 1940; after this year the percentage decrease was more rapid, reaching 48.3 per cent in 1960. A similar phenomenon occurred with the proportion of population residing in localities having less than 1,000 inhabitants. These highly significant percentage drops were nothing more than the product of massive and continuous migration from rural to urban zones, particularly from 1940 to date. The displacement of rural-urban population prior to 1940 was, in comparison with what occurred later, of little magnitude.

Finally, it must be emphasized that, in spite of the important "disruralization" occurring in Mexico, the population inhabiting very small localities continues to rise in absolute terms. The population living in localities of less than 1,000 inhabitants increased from 9.8 million in 1940 to 12.1 million in 1960. As of June 30, 1970, 13.7 million persons were living in these localities, representing 28.1 per cent of the total national population.

Urbanization in 1970 and 1980

In 1970, the urban population of Mexico was estimated at approximately 22.1 million,[8] or 45.0 per cent of the 49.1 million inhabitants of Mexico, according to preliminary figures from the last census adjusted to June 30, 1970. In accordance with the estimated amount of urban population, the latter recorded an annual increase of 5.4 per cent in the 1960–70 decade, almost equal to the 5.5 per cent of the preceding decade.

Risk is inherent in all population projections, and especially in one involving the number and size of cities. Nevertheless, we consider projections necessary if only to obtain an idea of the magnitude of the possible changes that demographic urbanization in Mexico will undergo from 1970 to 1980. Preliminary projections of probable urban population and structure in 1980 are based upon the following considerations:

a. The rate of urbanization will continue to decelerate, as has been true from 1950 to date.[9] Thus, the proportion of urban to total population will fluctuate between 50 and 54 per cent.

b. The structure of Mexican cities will continue to demonstrate a tendency toward a system of less pre-eminent cities, implying that the concentration of population in cities having more than 50,000 inhabitants, excluding the urban area of Mexico City, will be more rapid than the growth of total urban population.

Based upon the above assumptions and in accordance with a projected population of 71.9 million in 1980,[10] it has been estimated that urban population (in localities of 15,000 or more inhabitants) will fluctuate between 36 million and 39 million inhabitants.

The results of preliminary projections, obtained by means of the "proportional indices" method,[11] indicate that Mexico will have the following urban structure in 1980:

a. Three cities will have more than 1 million inhabitants: the urban area of Mexico City, with between 12.5 million and 13.8 million; the urban area of Guadalajara, with more than 2.5 million; and the urban area of Monterrey, with 2 million inhabitants.[12]

b. Six cities will have between 500,000 and 1 million inhabitants: Ciudad Juárez, Puebla, León, Tijuana, Mexicali, and Chihuahua.

c. Between 35 and 37 cities will have more than 100,000 and less than 500,000 inhabitants.

d. Between 31 and 36 cities will have more than 50,000 and less than 100,000 inhabitants.

e. Between 185 and 192 cities will have 15,000–50,000 inhabitants.

In spite of the reservations with which they should be considered, the above figures are not improbable and contain various implications for the reader: the unquestionable speed at which the population of Mexico will continue to concentrate in urban centers; the formation of an urban structure increasingly diffused throughout the nation; the possible rise of a greater number of cities of regional importance, primarily in the intervals between sizes of cities in *b.* above and, to a lesser degree, in *c.* above; a growing interconnection among a larger number of cities, independent of their nexuses with Mexico City; the consolidation of subsystems of cities (already under way), such as that running from Guadalajara to the cities of northern Baja California, that of Bajío cities and other areas, and the formation of new subsystems, such as that of the isthmian zone of Veracruz and Oaxaca and its branches reaching outward toward the southern part of Mexico.

In sum, in 1980, Mexico will not only be a predominantly urban country, true to its level of urbanization, but it will also have a network of cities of different sizes covering almost the entire nation. The city system will continue to demonstrate the well-known predominance of the urban area of Mexico City; however, the number of cities with growth rates superior to that of Mexico City will increase substantially.

Reflections on the Urbanization Process

URBANIZATION AND URBANISM

The process previously described demands serious thinking regarding causes and consequences—positive and negative—of such a complex phenomenon. Due to the rapidity and intensity with which this phenomenon is taking place in Mexico, it is necessary to remind those involved in the study, planning, and achievement of urban and regional projects of the unavoidable necessity of evaluating the errors and successes of what has been done in this area in Mexico. If such evaluation is not performed, urbanization as a factor in socioeconomic development will continue to be unexploited, leading almost certainly to worsening of Mexico's urban problem.

The ideas and reasoning propounded in this second section confirm the author's previously expressed uneasiness. Yet, given the relative universality of the urban phenomenon, the case of Mexico is not exceptional. It consequently offers features and characteristics found in other countries having different levels of development, though, obviously, Mexico also has its own peculiarly Mexican traits.

At present, everything appears to indicate that demographic-ecological urbanization is an irreversible process.

Forecasts of the situation, even long-range, share the feeling that concentrated (urban) population will maintain a rate of growth superior to that of total population. Thus, even though world population is not converted into an "ecumenopolis," as C. Doxiadis[13] has predicted will occur during the course of the twenty-first century, there still are today a number of megalopolises—the physical union of two or more metropolitan zones—as well as a tendency of these megalopolises to expand in size and multiply in the nations of the six continents. One of the most notable causes of this new urban phenomenon is occurring in the United States, in which it is estimated that in the year 2000, 60 per cent of the population will live in four megalopolises, one of which, that of the California coast, will occupy a land area of 130,000 square kilometers along a strip of almost 1,000 kilometers in length.[14] The urban area of Tijuana, Mexico, will form part of this megalopolis.

During the 1960s, several decades before the above phenomena will occur, the urban problem worsened in rich as well as in poor countries. The urban phenomenon became more complex and more directly related to social, economic, and politico-administrative development than twenty or thirty years before. This was due to rapid and drastic changes in urban life style caused, primarily, by technological innovations in communications and in the transportation of persons, goods, and information. This transformation has been far more radical in the great urban centers of the developing countries, for various reasons: greater rates of demographic growth; a greater proportion of population with rising expectations and improved resources to satisfy such aspirations; more drastic psychosocial repercussions on large population groups having a low cultural level and inadequate preparation for adapting rapidly to the effects of extremely advanced technology constantly emanating from the more industrialized countries, etc.

In Latin America, the repercussions of urbanization—the most rapid in the world—have given rise to opinions such as the following (which summarizes the present and future importance of the region's urban phenomenon): "It is not an exaggeration to say that the development of Latin America is the development of its urbanization."[15]

Yet, the developed countries also have serious limitations in their struggle to satisfy the basic needs of their growing urban populations. For example, a study of housing in the United States indicates that in 1968 only 1.5 million housing units were built, when 3 million new units were necessary.[16] In Latin America, the housing situation is many times more precarious. United Nations studies prove the financial inability of Latin American countries to meet the accumulated quantitative deficit in urban housing. It has been conservatively estimated that the amount of annual investment needed in Latin America to build ten housing units per 1,000 inhabitants would reach almost 40 per cent of present global gross investment (equivalent more or less to 17 per cent of gross product).[17] And even with this investment, all that could be achieved would be to keep the housing deficit from increasing. As is logical to suppose, Latin America's economic ability to satisfy other basic needs of the urban population such as employment, transportation, and education is even more limited than its ability in housing.

With respect to the problem of financing, Urquidi has expressed an idea that has generally been ignored: The housing problem, and with even greater reason the entire urban problem, will not be solved solely by obtaining adequate financial resources, but rather by recognizing that it is also a problem of basic concepts.[18] To this, Utría adds: "One observes a contemplative attitude in the face of progressive increase in the housing and community services deficit and an apparent ornamental-urbanistic intent in the treatment of urban planning."[19]

The gulf between planners' ideas and reality is increasingly more profound. This is the result in large measure of an unscientific and subjective approach to the urban problem, which has been ineffective in the face of reality: unrestricted and speculative trade in urban lots; unilateral application of zoning and subdivision laws; governmental systems deficient in dealing with real estate, waste, and misuse of urban land, etc.

Nevertheless, the commonly used concept of urban anarchy and chaos has a reason for being. Its explanation lies not only in a lack of planning, but also often in badly focused planning, or rather in urban "planning" idealized and important in the eyes of vested interests. As C. Wright Mills has written:

> The absence of a discernible order in our environment has been much discussed. To me, this seems stupid. Isn't it possible that capital gain and the accumulation of capital are the common denominator of all this order? Aren't private real-estate interests and unfettered publicity characteristics of our environment? For them, our cities are not the least bit disordered; on the contrary, they find our cities as orderly as the files containing their property deeds.[20]

D. Stea warns that theories and practices of urbanism that consider planning and urban design only as large-scale architecture will be of little use and will only defer the problem of cities in the second half of the twentieth century.[21] That the problems of urban growth still need to be clarified is attested to, in part, by the large number of problems that have not yet been solved. There are many indications that the problems that "solutions" have attempted to alleviate have increased in number and severity. "It has been said that the majority of so-called solutions to problems of urban development are nothing more than partial, short-term answers or badly stated questions."[22]

Notwithstanding the above criticisms, it would be improper and unjust to blame the urbanist and urbanism for the problems of large cities and the unfortunate attempts to remedy these problems. Many other factors—social, economic, political, administrative, ecological, and historical—intervene in the complex urban dynamic; certain problems, especially politico-administrative, have the greatest influence on possible solutions to urban problems. As an illustration, it has been declared that the paradox of the so-called U.S. urban crisis consists of the waste of technological advances (due to the extreme slowness with which institutional changes occur—as much in population attitudes as in social structures and politico-administrative machinery), which could make housing more innovative in exploiting these technological advances.[23] Various additional factors could be enumerated that have a decisive influence on the growth of the urban problem, as much in developed as in developing countries. These the planner can contemplate only as a spectator, either for lack of knowledge, or, primarily, because they lie beyond his grasp.

The foregoing has attempted to express that, in the face of the indissoluble union of urbanization, socioeconomic development, and the politico-administrative system, explanation for the urban dynamic and therefore the problems it generates must be sought, not merely in the city, but rather in a broader context of growth and social change on a regional, national, and international scale.

RELATIVE ADVANTAGES AND DISADVANTAGES OF THE CITY

In spite of the fact that governments and many urban technicians express their disagreement with the existence, and especially with the growth of large cities, such is the power of the urbanization process—particularly in the developing countries—that it can be considered impossible to halt. In the face of this fact, a new approach is appearing that adopts a different attitude, one might say a more realistic attitude, based upon the attempt to resolve or alleviate the urban problem without eliminating urban growth or large concentrations of human beings.

This point of view abandons the exclusively critical posture toward the city and urbanization in general, and recognizes, on the other hand, that this process not only brings problems, but also positive effects. One of the latter is—in addition to those well-known effects related to scientific, technological, and cultural advancement—reduction of demographic pressure on agricultural lands, through country-city migration. This process, generally considered as negative, has given rise, even when caused by factors of rejection of the countryside, to the physical incorporation of millions of rural inhabitants into urban areas. It is true that many of these migrants become part of the growing numbers of marginal population, which constitutes, on the one hand, a heavy burden for the large city, and, on the other, ". . . human resources potentially more adaptable to the modernization process than those who remained behind, more attached to traditional norms and probably with less desire to risk everything for a new form of future life."[24] In this respect—given the hardly propitious conditions of Latin America's rural zones—it might be worthwhile to ask whether urban life, precarious as it may be for marginal population, constitutes in comparative terms an improvement.

Another positive aspect of urbanization is that it creates expectations and raises the level of aspirations, as much of migrant as of native population. "Migration decided, the new urban family assumes, in spite of the limitations it finds, an expectant attitude, if not an altogether optimistic one, in the face of an environment comparatively richer in possibilities and interaction."[25] Unfortunately, it must also be admitted that these aspirations are exaggerated by the diffusion of behavior patterns (products of mass communication) deriving from the value systems and consumption patterns of rich nations. As a result, the "imitation effect" has two main consequences: the development of frustration and an increase in the degree of aggression; and the channeling of restlessness and energies in the form of phantasy. To this must be added that a certain social mobility is beginning to be observed among marginal population groups. Portes, Turner, and other researchers have found in their field work in *barriadas* (shantytowns) in Santiago and Lima that

> far from being the menacing belt of misery imagined by the upper and middle classes, the whole complex of peripheral population settlements may be defined with more certainty as a belt of social security. The marginal area undoubtedly shelters the new city of the poor. Those who inhabit these zones do not appear to be, however, the poor at the end of a descending career, the most miserable, apathetic and frustrated, but rather precisely those who have moved to the periphery in search of a minimum of security through a residence of their own.[26]

It might be added that urbanization encourages industrialization and permits provision of urban services in greater number and better quality (even if over the long term, a term that could be reduced if subdivision laws were to be enforced) to a larger proportion of the population. Were it not for industrialization, it would be materially impossible for the population to receive these services, except in subsidized form.

There remain many unanswered questions, however, important questions related to urban problems: Is the large city the best or only option available to marginal population in order to obtain a more or less regular income, an acceptable dwelling, and basic public services? What factors explain the fact that the marginal population of large cities endures miserable living conditions, without returning to place of origin or demonstrating open disconformity through organized protest? Is it necessary to sacrifice a

generation of marginal population—consciously or unconsciously—so that its members' children will have the opportunity to attain an improved standard of living? How is
it possible to accelerate and give material embodiment to
what is today only the expectation of economic and social
improvement?

To these questions must be added the serious problems
generated or aggravated by urbanization: scarcity of employment for migrant as well as native population; costs of
urbanization beyond the financial reach of developing
countries; and politico-administrative, ecological, and social
problems in general. Thus, in the face of urbanization's
advantages and disadvantages, an important question
arises: Do the benefits of urban development compensate
for the high economic and social cost of such development?
According to Petersen, it is not feasible for developing
countries to aspire to the benefits of modern urban and industrial society if at the same time they attempt to avoid
not only the cost of social change but also the city as the
resulting product.[27]

It is not necessary to undertake detailed investigations
to know that the distribution of advantages and the social
and economic price that city dwellers pay for such advantages—according to different social groupings—are extremely unbalanced and unjust. For example, while a certain few benefit from the increase in added value and
capital gains generated by the growth and concentration
of population (particularly with respect to speculative
buying and selling of real estate), the vast majority do not
have institutional access to a city lot, a house, or basic
public services. It must not be forgotten that the countryside also contributes directly or indirectly to the financing of urbanization. In countries such as Mexico, an important percentage of foreign exchange is obtained from
the export of agricultural raw materials. Thus, in addition
to the traditional disadvantages in the exchange relationship between country and city, the former contributes
an important part of the foreign exchange necessary to im-

port machinery and pay royalties for the use of foreign patents, which in large measure are used by urban industry. If one adds to this the fact that imported machinery and technology are, to a great extent, destined to establish capital-intensive industries that absorb little labor, one sees closing one of the many vicious circles of a developing society: urbanization-industrialization-socioeconomic development. In fact, many urban problems—such as the formation of large zones of marginal population—are due in great measure to the disparity between those who enjoy the use of the city's benefits and those who pay the costs implied.

As Turner writes,

> the existence of uncontrolled urban settlements is the product of the difference between the popular demand for housing and the offer made by society in institutional form. . . . Shantytowns and other uncontrolled forms of urban settlement are not social aberrations but rather a perfectly natural, and often a surprisingly adequate, response to the situation. The tragedy is not that such settlements exist—this is inevitable—but that so many of them are so much worse than they could be.[28]

Therefore, to consider the city a necessary evil is not the solution. New approaches avoiding unrealistic presentations of urban problems, physical as well as human, are required. For this purpose, it will be necessary among other things to formulate and undertake a kind of "urban reform" that distributes in a more equitable way the benefits and costs of the present-day city, and the city of the future, in Latin America.

THE RELATIONSHIP BETWEEN DEVELOPMENT AND PLANNING

It is unquestioned that the greatest laboratory of human behavior is the city. Nevertheless, this social context has been losing relative independence (by its very nature the

city cannot be autonomous or self-sufficient) to the extent
that the nations of the world have urbanized and inter-
communication has intensified. Thus, urbanization is cause
and effect of intraurban (urban environment) and interurban (nonurban environment) processes covering regional
and national space.

Until the present time, in the majority of countries and
especially in developing ones, development and national,
regional, and urban planning have taken place in almost
total isolation from each other. One of the reasons for this
disconnection is that urban and regional planning have
been formulated and put into effect for certain cities or
zones of the nation, while national planning has concentrated on sectoral development or certain large projects.
Plans at this level pay little attention to the spatial factor
and do not give proper importance to the location of economic and social activities or to territorial distribution of
urban and rural population. Sectoral plans contain the implicit belief that a suitable allocation of capital will also
result in an adequate distribution of labor, population, and
socioeconomic activities in general. The majority of sectoral development plans—as in the case of Mexico—do
not define zones or cities that should grow more rapidly
than others, or which economic sectors have priority in
investment allocated to each region. This circumstance,
aggravated by disconnected plans, can cause such serious
problems as the formulation and undertaking of investment programs and projects whose objectives are incompatible with development (in the short- or long-term) of
the nation, a region, or a city. This can occur because in
national plans covering sectors of economic activity the
implications for regional and urban development and
growth of investment on such a scale are not considered.
At the same time, at the urban level, public works
(planned or unplanned) are continuously under construction, financed by public and private sectors in the absence
of a hierarchy of planned public investment (receiving

regional or national directives) and without any notion of the effects such actions have on the regional and national environment. For example, the construction of a means of rapid transit, like the metropolitan train, "Metro," independently of its lesser or greater efficacy in alleviating the problems of urban transportation, must be considered as a factor affecting the nation's balance of payments, since it is partially financed by credits from abroad.

Regarding private investment, the problem is more serious; in many developing countries the principle of *laissez faire* still reigns. Zoning and urban subdivision laws are generally inoperative, because they are obsolete, because through lack of urban development plans they do not lead to a specific end, or because they are evaded, partially or completely, by speculators and subdividers of urban land. In general, actions on an urban scale are undertaken without consideration for their effects on the region or nation.

Limited national-regional-urban communication reflects differing interests, as much on the part of administrators as of technicians. The latter believe that the national is more important than the regional or urban, while the administrators believe the contrary. In reality, the three levels of study and planning are interdependent and should not be undertaken in an isolated manner, notwithstanding the great technical, financial, and politico-administrative difficulties it is necessary to overcome. To the foregoing must be added the greater or lesser dependence to which the developing countries are subjected by those nations in hegemony; thus, the direct or indirect investment of ruling countries affects the course of socioeconomic development and the urbanization process in the most backward countries.

Lack of national-regional-urban co-ordination exists among technicians and between them and executive administrators. Technicians manipulate (in their intent to solve interdependent problems) extremely different con-

cepts, working instruments, and approaches, causing incompatibility of objectives and goals. This necessarily
makes studying and planning cities, regions, and the nation from an interdisciplinary and interspatial perspective
difficult.

The need to plan the nation's development increases as
the number and intensity of forces affecting the economy,
social change, and urbanization become more complex. In
this context, the region—as much the natural (a hydrographic basin) as the nodal (city-periphery)—must constitute the territorial unit permitting development of an integrated planning system at different levels: local,
regional, and national. The international scale should also
be considered, for the reasons previously expressed.

The problem of formulating and undertaking plans of
this type, in spite of their implicit worth and logic, has not
been resolved. The repeated attempts of certain countries
(with scant success and at high cost), among which Great
Britain and France are outstanding, confirm this. In a
recent study of planning and political economy in Great
Britain and France, the authors make certain observations
that must be emphasized and considered by regional
studies and plans of developing countries. For example,
they affirm, somewhat doubtfully, that "integration of regional plans into a national development plan permits a
coherent vision of the strategy required for different regions at different moments in time."[29] The authors are
more categorical when they present problems that have
arisen and that lack solution:

> Therefore, the argument in favor of the type of regional
> policy at present under way in Great Britain and France
> still remains to be proved. A broad cost-benefit analysis
> is needed, which still has not been achieved, in order to
> arrive at firm conclusions . . . in France, the immense
> cost of regional development in terms of financial outlay
> and of its effects on the growth of the national economy

have given rise to an increasingly selective approach and a deliberate concentration on a small number of predetermined growth poles whose expansion will benefit the region as much as the nation. The approach to the problem of the expansion of the Paris region elaborated in the Fifth Plan provides indications of the difficulties implicit in harmonizing national and regional growth and the growing tendency in official circles in favor of more exacting determination of the real costs of regional development.[30]

The French experience in regional planning is of great utility to the Mexican case, because, among other reasons, the French Government, through integration of its regional and national planning, is attempting to reduce what has come to be called the macrocephaly of the Paris urban area. The same thing is being attempted in Mexico with its capital city, Mexico City.

In spite of the fact that what has been achieved in Great Britain in the field of regional development is less adaptable to the Mexican situation, it still constitutes the most important effort carried out over the longest space of time —since 1937—for the purpose of achieving more balanced regional economic development at the same time as achieving slower economic and demographic growth of Greater London. For this reason, it may be significant to mention that British technicians and officials, like the French, express doubts regarding the path followed by regional policy. To this effect, Denton and his colleagues, on referring to the time factor, write in their study that a regional policy destined primarily for achievement of medium-term objectives will not necessarily be appropriate for the national interest over the longer term. The authors emphasize that

Such arguments, although perfectly valid in terms of the particular objective in mind—for example, a medium-

term development program—leave hanging the most
transcendent question, namely, whether it is compatible
with the long-term national interest, let us say 20 or 30
years, to give special incentives to businesses to locate
in the least prosperous regions.[31]

Research into Mexico's regional dynamic has been
sparse, and, unfortunately, there is still a lack of will on
the part of governmental organisms and even research
centers (with a few exceptions) to introduce the spatial
variable into studies of Mexico's socioeconomic development. Notable regional disparities, caused among other
reasons by an intense and rapid process of urbanization,
make impossible postponement of studies and formulation
of national plans of urban-regional development that
would answer three questions: (1) Has the distribution of
population and socioeconomic activities been a factor
operating to the detriment of the regional and national
development of Mexico? And even if the answer to this
question is negative, it is indispensable to determine: (2)
Which pattern or patterns of distribution of population
and activities lead to improved or more rapid regional and
national development? Finally, assuming a sufficiently reasonable response for the Mexican case and one not solely
based on the schemes (unproved in theory or in practice)
of the general theory of development poles, the most
difficult of the three questions remains to be answered:
(3) How can an integrated city-region-nation plan be
carried out, and what financial, administrative, legal, and
political instruments and means must be put into practice
to achieve the objectives and goals which, in the short-
and long-term, are implicit in such a plan?

Fathoming the complexity of these questions lies beyond
the reach of this study. Yet their importance must be un-
derscored, as well as the urgent necessity of answering
them as quickly as possible, not only because it is considered feasible to modify substantially the present urban

structure of the nation, but also so that the nation's private and public sectors can enjoy elements of judgment permitting them to anticipate the events that will probably occur in the field of urbanization and to prevent, to the maximum extent possible, the lagging behind of studies, plans, and actions related to urban-regional development.

On achieving the suggested recommendations, substantial changes should be made in the approach that to date has been given to urban, regional, and national development. National planning should include the spatial factor (geographic distribution of investment) on an urban as well as a regional scale. Regional development strategy should be considered an instrument of national development to which all parts of the country contribute to the limit of their potentialities in order to achieve stated national objectives. One of the latter should be sustained development, at the same time that regional disparities diminish or at the very least do not increase. In other words, the strengths that each region contibutes to the nation's development should be of the same order of magnitude.

The nation-city-region programmatic connection demands that regional development not be exclusively based on hydrographic basins, as has been the case to date in Mexico. Rather, it will be necessary to include urban-region (nodal regions) plans to encompass the growing number of metropolitan zones, among which Mexico City's is outstanding in importance, with a population in January 1970 of 8.5 million inhabitants.

The effect of urban development on the multiplication of metropolitan zones covering two or more municipalities makes necessary taking more vigorous action with respect to the study, planning, and administration of such urban units. Under these circumstances, the municipality, considered independently, sees its limited economic and political capabilities to satisfy the needs of the city even more reduced. At the same time, conflicts of authority are created among contiguous municipalities injected into the development of the same urban unit. The situation becomes complicated when the metropolitan zone extends over two federal entities or two nations. Included among zones covering two or more municipalities, in 1960, were Mexico City, Guadalajara, Monterrey, Cuernavaca, Puebla, Orizaba, Tampico, Torreón, Veracruz, Colima, and others of smaller size. Today, the number of such cases is certainly larger. Mexico City, for example, includes part of the Federal District and the state of Mexico; Torreón includes municipalities from the states of Coahuila and Durango; and Tampico contains two municipalities from Tamaulipas and one from Veracruz.

Finally, the case of the metropolitan zones of the northern border cities of Mexico is a phenomenon of capital importance. This is true because of the number of cities involved, the growing numbers of population, and the geopolitical and economic strategic situation. Until the present time, the cities on the Mexican side of the border have only been treated in "regulating plans," meaning no plans at all, formulated between 1958 and 1964, under the sponsorship of the Ministry of National Patrimony. These plans were not linked to those that no doubt existed on the U.S. side.

Thus, plans and actions for these metropolitan zones, among which that of Ciudad Juárez-El Paso is outstanding, with one million inhabitants, must be achieved through a certain degree of co-ordination. Something similar will be needed for Tijuana and San Diego, which will probably unite in the remaining years of this century. The same will also be true for Matamoros-Brownsville, Reynosa-McAllen, Nuevo Laredo-Laredo, and other Mexican cities with adjacent cities on the U.S. side.

In sum, one of the alternatives Mexico could follow in its attempt to co-ordinate national and regional and urban planning, for the purpose of achieving greater, more accelerated, and better-distributed socioeconomic development,

is that of formulating regional development plans constituting bridges among national, urban, and metropolitan
plans. This implies the explicit formulation of objectives
and goals determined by the geographic location of investment as well as its sectoral distribution. Similarly, minimum incompatibility of objectives and goals, as much in
time as in space, should be sought.

Political and administrative obstacles and technical and
budgetary limitations made difficult translating ideas such
as the above into reality. Unfortunately, Mexico's experience in planning, whether urban, regional, or national, is
relatively scarce, with urban planning, technically speaking, the least developed.

In spite of the advantages that co-ordination of planning
according to different geographic levels could contribute,
it will also cause quite serious political and administrative
difficulties. One of the problems will be, once the nation is
zoned, that of allocating investment resources in accordance with certain aims and goals, such as, for example,
reducing underemployment, increasing internal product,
etc. The experience of other countries in this area indicates that there are always regions and cities that will
complain of discrimination and demand greater rights
than those allocated by a particular plan.

In turn, periodic modification of the limits of regions
and cities selected as objects of special action by higher
authorities, which can reduce the political problem,
presents serious technical and administrative complica-
tions. In synthesis, co-ordination of planning at different
geographic levels, difficult to explain in detail from a theoretical point of view, is highly complicated to put into
practice, especially in nations like Mexico, in which the
allocation of resources occurs in a predominantly centralized way. At any given moment, this same circumstance
could facilitate resource allocation sectorally as well as ter-
ritorially, but not co-ordination of national with regional
and urban planning. The latter demands political strength

and economic power from the other two levels, factors that at the present time are concentrated in the federal public sector.

In spite of the long road ahead before planning in Mexico, and particularly regional and urban planning, constitutes a basic instrument of governmental policy, it is only just to emphasize certain serious attempts that make one hopeful: the directing plan of the Monterrey subregion, studies and actions undertaken in the Guadalajara metropolitan zone, population research and actions being carried out by the present government of the state of Mexico, and, finally, the work of the Ministry of the Presidency relating to the metropolitan zone of Mexico City.

RESEARCH AND POLICY

On investigating the urban situation, as with all social problems, divergencies in points of view surface among those studying the phenomenon and those in a position to modify it. Such divergencies, principally of approach, in turn are reflected in the limited financial support provided to research and to the lack of attention given its results. This dilemma between research and action in the field of urban development is not necessary; indeed, there are no hard-and-fast reasons for it to exist. Both study and application of urbanization policies constitute parts of the same whole and cannot exist in isolation from each other. If the latter is the case, action will continue to be a mere palliative, a spectator watching as urban problems worsen, and research, merely an interesting intellectual exercise of little use to the decision-making official.

This situation is generated by a series of misunderstandings, especially in the matter of interests pursued by the social researcher and the decision-making official, or of those who decide the type of research to be undertaken and the resources available for so doing. To this problem must be added limited and inadequate communication between technicians studying the dynamic of the urban phenomenon and those formulating urban and regional development plans.

All parties involved say, and believe, that they are right, and accuse the others of lack of comprehension. In reality, both sets of reasoning are only partially complete. The social scientist is principally preoccupied with the dynamic of the urban process; the planner, with foreseeing and formulating plans leading to a solution to problems; and the politician, with his own solutions. Yet, the clear and logical interrelationship between the previously mentioned stages and objectives, conflict, and apparent incongruity continues to exist. Ways of reducing such disharmony consist of establishing greater and improved communication among those studying and attempting to resolve urban problems, and the decision-makers; greater utilization on the part of decision-makers of the nation's scarce human resources who have specialized in the field; developing new urban scientists of high academic level, not merely those with architectural or engineering training, but those with backgrounds in sociology, economics, psychology, and ecology, in order to generate interdisciplinary urban research in a systematic and increasing way through creation of urban and regional research institutes. These institutes could complement academic knowledge and become, in turn, centers in which urban, national, or regional problems are studied continuously and systematically, in accordance with the purposes of such institutions (long-term) and those of the public and private sectors (short- and medium-term). In brief, only the combined action of the urban scientist, the planner, and financial and executive authorities will accomplish the purpose at hand, which all supposedly share: improving the standard of living of the population of the nation and its different regions.

The foregoing is not easy to translate into action— even though it would be easy to intensify and improve the quality of regional and urban studies—due particularly to the need of the Executive to make continuous decisions without being able, in many cases, to await the answers provided by research. This is caused in large measure by the fact that limited financial and technical resources do not permit increasing the number of studies required by the public sector. This fact, in part, is responsible for the dilemma; its elimination can only be achieved in any case through successive stages. Such stages must provide, in the short run, diagnoses of the urban and regional situation, explanations of its dynamic, evaluations of existing instruments and means relating to the process, and support for formulation and achievement of urban and regional development policies.

The persistence of the *apparent* dichotomy between study of the urban and regional dynamic, and action at these levels in a nation like Mexico (with a rapid urbanization process) probably aggravates the whole regional and urban problem. Solutions will continue to be sought through regulating plans, instruments catalogued as useless and obsolete in nations in which urbanism is seeking new directions, such as England and the United States. Allocation of investment in many cases will not be handled on a priority basis, due to, among other factors, the lack of knowledge necessary to establish objectives and goals in harmony with reality and the social and economic needs of the nation. In sum, Mexico will continue to ignore the advances of the new urban science—in rapid formation in other countries, developed as well as developing —and will remain backward in urban matters, as has been true for the past three decades.

NEW PERSPECTIVES IN THE APPROACH TO THE URBAN PROBLEM

The ideas expressed herein are not an attempt to give a fatalistic image to urban problems or to dramatize in turn a situation that does not appear promising. My purpose is to present the phenomenon in the most realistic possible way, without ignoring the difficulty posed by treating a phenomenon of such increasing complexity.

Under the present circumstances, the world urban crisis is patent. This crisis is particularly true of the Latin American nations, and is a crisis forming an integral part of the general problems they face in their desire to achieve national development and simultaneously satisfy the needs of a constantly increasing population.

This first great dilemma of the development process presents, in turn, a series of more specific contradictions and dilemmas. These conflicts occur over, for example, technological progress and its high social cost; increase in agricultural productivity and the contamination of rivers, lakes, and seas by chemical products; subsidies to industries to install devices to stop toxic substances from contaminating the environment and higher consumer prices to defray the cost of such devices; the increasingly extended use of the automobile (irrational in size in relation to the number of persons it transports) and collective transportation; measures applied to resolve certain of the problems of large cities and the effects these measures have on increasing the cities' ability to absorb population; the interests of national vs. foreign business; and, in general, over social well-being and the private interest.

In other words, in what concerns the city, the city is not the main or only cause of the problems of our rural and urban society. Therefore, the urban crisis will not be resolved solely by reducing the size of large cities or halting their growth. The question is far more complicated. The urban problem is at once cause and effect of the regional, national, and international socioeconomic situation.

Many of the phenomena affecting the city cannot be eliminated by good wishes or by means of planning of an indicative type. It is necessary to recognize that factors external to the nations of Latin America—those resulting from economic, technological, and sociocultural dependence and that it has not been possible to control—influence not only demographic urbanization in a basic way, but also every aspect of social life. It must also be accepted that the existence of urban problems does not eliminate the advantages of the city; the latter will continue to generate external economies of scale, in spite of the diseconomies appearing in certain of its activities and zones. In fact, both the advantages and the problems are the result of the large size attained by certain cities. The critical question resides in determining when a city, such as for example the urban area of Mexico City, has reached the point of diminishing returns, or, in other words, decreasing cost-benefit quotients.

In spite of the technical difficulty implied by realization of studies giving an idea of the costs and benefits of a nation's urbanization, or of a city's growth, they must be attempted. On a more general level, the task of critical analysis of the successes and failures of attempts to alleviate urban problems cannot be delayed. In Mexico, this important evaluation has still not been undertaken.

The probable explanations for failures reside in: (1) erroneous presentation of urban problems; (2) inadequate application of existing instruments and means to solve such problems; (3) lack of suitable instruments and means; and (4) a combination of the three preceding factors.

In order to overcome this situation, according to a growing number of experiences in the field, the city should not be considered as a necessary evil or as an isolated and independent entity, but rather as an element with the potential of being a basic factor in the social, economic, and political progress of the Latin American nations. A type of urban reform, integrated with an agrarian reform, could be a way of exploiting this potential.

Fortunately, as much in urbanism as in regional and national planning, a renovating tendency is beginning that considers, in the former, social and political aspects, and in the latter, territorial.[32] In sum, the necessity of national plans for development is beginning to be recognized.

Similarly, studies emphasizing the inescapable need to undertake some form of urban reform are growing in number. Urban reform, reflecting the variations of each nation's political and socioeconomic system, must include among other things adopting a series of regulations relating to urban land use to make feasible the realization of urban development plans at a minimum cost to society; reducing inflation and land speculation to a minimum; avoiding the unrestricted accumulation of real estate in private hands in the face of growing concentration of economic power in a few social groups and deterioration of income distribution among the population; transferring to the public sector a greater proportion of the capital gains originating in urban growth and public works produced by the public sector, which are at present enjoyed by a small minority; halting premature subdivision of suburban land; guaranteeing the strict fulfillment of subdivision laws; and reducing the vast amount of investment frozen in real estate, which generates, over the short- and medium-term, great rewards with little risk and which could be employed more productively for social and economic ends. What is thus involved is that the public sector control the urban land market, considering it an article of prime necessity, as it does with other goods, respecting private property but reducing to the maximum speculation in and uncontrolled profit from urban land.

To achieve the above, institutional means and instruments to put such strategies into practice are needed. These tasks can be achieved through certain existing organisms by merely modifying some of their functions, or through new public entities in charge of study, planning, and action related to national and regional urbanization.

It will be necessary to introduce into the tax system

progressive taxes on vacant land, in such a way as to halt speculation and permit the use of such land by needy population, in accordance with established urban development plans. If this does not occur, the city will be forced to occupy land increasingly distant from its center in order to accommodate the growing numbers of people who cannot pay the high price of land. The latter aggravates the problems of transit and transportation of persons.

Urban reform, in addition to including the above measures of intraurban scale, must also have national and regional scope. Thus, a policy of national and regional urbanization must be formulated in which the functions of cities making up the nation's urban system are explicitly defined. In this respect, Hardoy has suggested the promotion of new spatial systems of cities that break with colonial and neocolonial models and exploit the advantages of gradual national and Latin American integration.[33]

In sum, Hardoy proposes breaking with the historic model, the result of internal and external colonialism, and modifying urbanization's present tendencies by creating a new series of centers to which can be channeled an important part of economic investment and new urban population. We must be prepared, in this case, for the possible expansion of existing cities, and assure that the latter is achieved at the least social and economic cost and with the maximum possible benefit.[34]

The above ideas may appear to be only idle "pipe dreams"; this is precisely the criticism I have made of conventional urbanism at the beginning of these reflections. Without believing necessarily that urban reform with certain of the characteristics outlined above will be achieved in Mexico, or, indeed, can be carried out at all, it is worthwhile to note the possible influence that events in other countries may have on Mexican urbanization.

For example, the United States is undergoing the greatest urban crisis in its history. This has caused confusion in the field of urbanism and quite generalized dissatisfaction on the part of students of urbanism. Similarly, there is a rapidly growing number of professors and professionals of urbanism who are unhappy with the present situation. Thus, demands for a change of approach in the study and practice of urbanism are increasingly intense. Among the modifications believed necessary in the United States are: more planners springing from the lower socioeconomic classes and not solely from middle- and upper-class groups; more black planners; and more women in the profession. The need for the urbanist to have a role in society different from that existing at the moment is discussed and propounded. Similarly, these specialists believe that restatement of the purposes and nature of urban planning education cannot be delayed. They also mention the need to augment substantially the discipline's level, to make it more scientific and more able to balance with the pragmatism that has dominated the field until the present time. To generalize, everything appears to revolve around the following basic question: How can education in urbanism be improved so that it responds to the needs of those wishing to follow this discipline, those using its services, and, especially, society as a whole? Without forgetting the differences existing between the U.S. situation and that of the Latin American countries, the above question has general validity and demands an answer, as much from the urbanist as from the planner.

In Mexico, as in the other Latin American countries, similar eagerness to answer such questions must be developed. For this purpose, it is necessary to know more of the background of Latin America's urban-national reality. This will permit the urban and regional planner to formulate plans that are not Utopian, and whose means and instruments can feasibly be put into practice and accepted by political decision-makers. Only in this way can the city cease being the center of great and growing social and economic disparities and become a setting better adapted to benefit the majority and not simply a privileged few.

NOTES

1. Aníbal Quijano has achieved the greatest advances in theoretical research into urbanization as a global and historical phenomenon of present-day society. See A. Quijano, "La urbanización de la sociedad en Latinoamérica," *Revista Mexicana de Sociología* XXIX (4) (1969):669–703. English translation included in this volume.

2. H. T. Eldridge, "The Process of Urbanization," *Demographic Analysis*, ed. J. Spengler and O. Duncan (New York: The Free Press of Glencoe, 1963), pp. 338–43.

3. The figures and main ideas presented in this section may be found in Luis Unikel, "Urbanización," *Dinámica de la población de México* (Mexico City: Centro de Estudios Económicos y Demográficos, El Colegio de México, 1970), pp. 117–43, and Luis Unikel, "The Process of Urbanization in Mexico: Distribution and Growth of Urban Population," *Latin American Urban Research*, ed. Francine F. Rabinovitz and Felicity M. Trueblood (Los Angeles: Sage Publications, 1971), pp. 247–302.

4. The level of urbanization of a territorial unit is the magnitude the phenomenon has achieved in this geographic area. The "level" may be measured through various types of indicators, one of which is the proportion of urban population. The rapidity of the process has been calculated by means of the mean annual increase in the level of urbanization, to which has been given the label "rate of urbanization." For further detail, see Unikel, "The Process of Urbanization," passim.

5. This limit derives from the study of Luis Unikel, "Ensayo sobre una nueva clasificación de población rural y urbana en México," *Demografía y Economía* (El Colegio de México): II (1) (1968):1–18. According to this study, localities are divided into four classes: rural (less than 5,000 inhabitants); mixed rural (from 5,000 to 9,999 inhabitants); mixed urban (from 10,000 to 14,999 inhabitants); and urban (15,000 or more inhabitants). This limit, calculated for the 1940–60 period, was used for the entire period under consideration only for purposes of comparative analysis.

6. S. Eckstein, "El marco macroeconómico del problema agrario mexicano," documento preliminar (Mexico City: Centro de Investigaciones Agrarias, 1968), pp. 146–70.

7. See Note *a*, Table 4.

8. This figure is not definitive and is subject to the changes implied in the calculations corresponding to the population of the nation's urban areas, which take into account the physical

integration of localities having less than 15,000 inhabitants into principal cities. Nevertheless, the population in 1970 (as of June 30) of the 181 localities having more than 15,000 inhabitants, including 1960 urban areas, was very close to 22 million inhabitants.

9. See the rates of urbanization in Luis Unikel, "Urbanización," Table V-3, p. 121. In addition, for an explanation of the decrease in urbanization, see p. 160 of this same study.

10. In spite of the declines in fertility that may occur from 1975 onward, it is estimated that the total population of Mexico in 1980 will fluctuate between 71.9 million and 73.6 million (medium hypothesis with decreasing fertility and high hypothesis with invariable fertility, respectively). See R. Benítez and G. Cabrera, *Proyecciones de la población de México 1960–1980* (Mexico City: Banco de México, S.A., 1966), pp. 47–50. The lower figure has been used for reasons of underenumeration, corrected in the cited projections but not in the censuses of 1960, which form the basis of the present estimate.

11. See Luis Unikel, "The Process of Urbanization," pp. 239–47. These figures are being verified by the Centro de Estudios Económicos y Demográficos of the Colegio de México by means of the more rigorous application of the "proportional indices" method and through use of preliminary data from the census of 1970.

12. The urban area of a city is understood to mean the city itself under discussion, plus its contiguous built-up area which, without following politico-administrative limits, obeys certain determined criteria of accessibility, density, and other analogues. The urban area, in the case of Mexico City, includes part of various municipalities of the state of Mexico adjacent to the Federal District.

13. The work and ideas of this Greek urbanist have stimulated a great deal of polemics, in spite of the fact that both his work and his ideas have had undeniable influence on present-day urbanism. His writings have principally been published in the magazine *Ekistics*, which he created. This magazine has been the outlet for what Doxiadis has named the science of human settlement. Regarding the ecumenopolis, see C. A. Doxiadis, "Ecumenopolis: Toward a Universal City," *Ekistics* 13 (75) (January 1962):3–18.

14. K. Lynch, "The Possible City," *Technology Review* (MIT) (January 1968):37.

15. Felipe Herrera, document No. 45-1 of the Reunión sobre

Financiamiento Municipal en Latinoamérica (Washington, D.C.: Inter-American Development Bank, January 1966), p. 1.

16. W. L. Hooper, "Innovation in Housing: Pipe Dreams of Practical Reality," *Technology Review* (January 1968):25.

17. Rubén Utría, "Los factores estructurales del desarrollo y el problema de la vivienda en América Latina," *Boletín Económico de América Latina* XI (2) (October 1966):246–75, cited in Víctor Urquidi, "La ciudad subdesarrollada," *Demografía y Economía* III (2) (1969):146–47. English translation included in this volume. Regarding the housing situation in Mexico, see J. Puente Leyva, "El problema habitacional," *El perfil de México en 1980*, pp. 253–303.

18. Víctor Urquidi, p. 147.

19. Rubén Utria, p. 272.

20. Cited by F. Ramón, *Miseria de la ideología urbanística* (Madrid: Editorial Ciencia Nueva, 1967), pp. 142–43.

21. D. Stea, "La conducta humana y el diseño urbano," *Revista de la Sociedad Interamericana de Planificación* II (7) (September 1968):12–13.

22. Víctor Urquidi, p. 150.

23. W. L. Hooper, p. 25.

24. W. Petersen, "Urban Policies in Africa and Asia," *Population Review* X (1) (January 1966):35.

25. J. Hardoy, "Urbanization Policies and Urban Reform in Latin America," *Latin American Urban Research*, Vol. II, ed. G. Geisse and J. Hardoy (volume) F. F. Rabinovitz and F. M. Trueblood (series). (Los Angeles: Sage Publications, 1972), p. 23.

26. A Portes, "El proceso de urbanización y su impacto en la modernización de las instituciones políticas locales," *Revista de la Sociedad Interamericana de Planificación* IV (13–14) (March–June 1970):16–17.

27. W. Petersen, p. 35.

28. J. Turner, "Uncontrolled Urban Settlement: Problems and Policies," *Urbanization: Development Policies and Planning* (New York: United Nations, 1968), pp. 108, 120.

29. G. Denton, M. Forsyth, M. MacIlenan, and PEP, *Planeación y política económica en la Gran Bretaña, Francia y Alemania* (Mexico City: Siglo XXI, 1970), pp. 335–36.

30. Ibid., p. 337.

31. Ibid. Other researchers such as Berry, Alonso, and Lasuen have thrown into doubt, partially or completely, the theory of development poles. See J. R. Lasuen, "Desarrollo y asentamiento," *Cuadernos de la Sociedad Venezolana de Planificación* 45–46 (1967); W. Alonson, "Urban and Regional

Inbalances in Economic Development," *Ekistics* 27 (162) (1969):351–55; and B. Berry, "City Size Distribution and Economic Development," *Regional Development and Planning*, ed. J. Friedmann and W. Alonso (Cambridge, Mass: MIT Press, 1965), pp. 138–58.

32. Entire issue, *Journal of the American Institute of Planners* XXXVI (4) (July 1970); Trevor MacMurray, "British Town Planning in Transition," *Technology Review* 72 (8) (June 1970):47–55. For the Latin American case, see Roberto Pineda and Jaime Valenzuela, "El proceso de urbanización y la enseñanza del planeamiento en América Latina," *Migración y desarrollo urbano,* ed. Ramiro Cardona (Bogotá: Asociación Colombiana de Facultades de Medicina, 1969), pp. 113–30; Facultad de Arquitectura de la Universidad de Colombia en Medellín, "La universidad y las entidades oficiales frente a los problemas de la planeación," ibid., pp. 131–40; Universidad Pontificia Boliviana, Facultad de Arquitectura, "La universidad y el proceso de urbanización," ibid., pp. 141–46.

33. J. Hardoy, p. 37.

34. Let us suppose that it was decided to decentralize 1 million inhabitants from the urban area of Mexico City from 1970–80, and remove them to the cities of Pachuca, Cuernavaca, Puebla, Querétaro, and Toluca. Generally, attention would be concentrated on the procedures necessary to displace this population, forgetting the effects this action would have on the receiving cities.

CHAPTER TWELVE

URBANIZATION AND DEVELOPMENT:
THE CASE OF SÃO PAULO*

PAUL SINGER

INTRODUCTION

This essay attempts to analyze the part urbanization plays in the capitalist development process in countries that were late in beginning to industrialize. The analysis will examine the function of large cities in the process of the formation of an industrial reserve force, in the light of the recent experience of São Paulo (Brazil). There is, of course, no attempt to generalize the characteristics of São Paulo's evolution to all cities in countries that are currently undergoing development. On the contrary, the part São Paulo plays in Brazil (like that of some large urban centers in other countries: Buenos Aires, Santiago, Mexico City, Caracas, etc.) is rather "opposed" to that of the other cities in the country, in the sense that capital accumulation tends to be concentrated in one or a few urban areas (São Paulo is one of these), draining the other regions economically, together with the cities they contain. Despite its "exceptional" nature, however, São Paulo is an adequate subject for analysis, to the extent that it presents a clearer picture of the process of accumulation on the national level.

The accelerated growth of large cities in undeveloped

* English translation by Ruth Huseman.

countries emphasized and brought into sharper focus a series of imbalances, primarily between supply and demand in the area of housing and urban services, that constitute specific urban problems. The perception of these problems and of the rapid growth of marginal population in the large cities provoked numerous critical appraisals of urbanization in undeveloped countries, many of which attack the process itself, showing themselves to be, at heart, anti-urban. The analysis that follows is directed against this kind of criticism, although it does not deny the gravity of urban problems and their consequences for the population that must cope with them, owing to the inability to fit urbanization into the context of a development that is occurring in a contradictory way. The reactionary nature of this kind of analysis, which stems from the concept of "urban explosion," becomes more evident when it is realized that it has close ties to the groups that came out against the "demographic explosion" and against industrialization which, since it uses advanced techniques, employs "few" workers. This kind of criticism of capitalist development, instead of pointing out its contradictions, attacks the consequences of structural change, condemning it for its "excessive" rate. The options that such criticism explicitly or implicitly proposes—control of urbanization, control of population, industrialization with less advanced (intermediate) techniques—are Utopian and tend to divert attention from the real problems of development.

1. ANTI-URBAN CRITICISM

The newly appointed mayor of São Paulo gained renown by declaring, shortly after taking office, that the city needed to stop growing, or otherwise it would be crushed under the weight of problems caused by too-rapid expansion. The mayor's statement contrasts with the slogan previously in vogue—"São Paulo cannot stop"—

which showed how much the citizen of São Paulo prided himself on the dynamism of his city.

The position of the mayor coincides, in a general way, with the fear shown by many analysts of urban problems in the face of the spectacular growth of modern cities, particularly in undeveloped countries.[1] The thesis of the superurbanization of recently industrialized countries finds an eloquent illustration in the case of São Paulo. In 1940, the entire continuous Brazilian urbanized area did not even occupy all the capital's territory, and contained 1,326,261 inhabitants. Hardly thirty years later, the urban area extended over 37 Brazilian *municípios,* containing 8,106,250 inhabitants. During this time the population grew at an annual mean rate of 5.5–6 per cent, doubling every twelve years.

What was, then, the result of this almost frightening urban growth? Obviously, the continued increase of urban problems: a housing shortage giving rise to the spread of slums and shantytowns (*favelas*); streets choked by traffic; a shortage of such basic urban services as running water and sewers, which reach a constantly smaller percentage of the total population; lack of telephones; overcrowded schools and hospitals, etc. There has also been a continuous increase in unemployment, delinquency, mental illness, and environmental pollution.

From the economic point of view, critics of urbanization view migration to the cities as a process through which productive agricultural workers become doers of odd jobs, bootblacks, and vagrants. From the social point of view, these same critics cite the uprooting of members of rural communities, who become "marginal" in metropolitan society.

This critical view of urbanization, which often delights in the fears aroused by large numbers (São Paulo will have a population of 20 million before the end of the country!) has spawned some amusing misinterpretations. The political Right, defender of the status quo, attributes all evils to demographic phenomena—excessive growth of the population and its massive migration to the cities—and by this means arrives at the well-known Malthusian moral according to which the poor are the ones principally responsible, owing to their reproductive and migratory behavior, for the worsening of their plight. The Left, which accepts as obvious the findings of anti-urban criticism, attempts to attribute to the anarchy of production, characteristic of capitalism, the excessive growth of large cites.[2] Thus, no one appears to be aware of the essence of the problem: Is the spectacular growth of large cities in underdeveloped countries the principal cause of their increased problems? After all, it is *not* self-evident that if the population of São Paulo, for example, were less numerous and therefore the demand for jobs and services of all kinds were also less numerous, the actual availability of jobs and services would be the *same*. In other words, criticism of urbanization is based on the assumption that there is no necessary relationship between the growth of urban population and expansion of the urban economy.[3]

2. URBANIZATION AS A PROCESS OF MOBILIZATION OF THE INDUSTRIAL RESERVE FORCE

One of the basic characteristics of the colonial economy that prevailed in Brazil (as in other Latin American countries) was a colossal waste of the work force together with a permanent shortage of laborers in the part of the economy integrated into the world market—that is, in the external market sector. When the export of Brazilian coffee began to increase, in the mid-nineteenth century, the greater part of the population was scattered in small subsistence economy units, or confined to the decaying sugar plantations of the Northeast or cattle ranches of the South. The coffee plantations were worked by slaves imported from Africa and, when the slave trade ended in 1850, by slaves brought from other parts of the country.

When slave labor began to grow scarce, recourse was had to the European immigrant, which, given the incompatibility of slave labor and free labor in the same sector of activity, finally brought about the abolition of slavery. What it is important to emphasize, in this context, is the reduced capacity for mobilization of the work force in the colonial economy, whose external market sector generally brought in laborers from abroad. The colonial economy did not possess a system of incentives capable of attracting those workers integrated into the subsistence sector, except when the land they worked was the property of planters (*fazendeiros*) who also produced for the external market. In this case, the workers' surplus production generally took the form of export commodities.

Between the abolition of slavery (1888) and the Revolution of 1930 there were important economic, social, and political changes in Brazil. The development process was begun through import substitution, with the establishment of important industrial parks to produce nondurable consumer goods (textiles, clothing, food), principally in Rio de Janeiro and São Paulo, and of an extensive commercial agricultural sector directed toward the internal market, in the states where large numbers of Germans and Italians had settled (Rio Grande do Sul and Santa Catarina). European immigration greatly increased, reaching its peak shortly before the First World War, with immigrants being absorbed into the coffee production sector and the new activities of the internal market sector. A limited process of urbanization began, with the relatively more rapid growth of the capitals that were centers of regional markets: Rio, São Paulo, Pôrto Alegre, Recife, and Belo Horizonte. São Paulo, in particular, possessed a regional market greater than the rest, since coffee production had shifted to its hinterland.

The most profound change occurred, however, after 1930: Constantly increasing interregional hostility, together with frequent revolts by young officers, led to the fall of the coffee oligarchy from power, which was then assumed by an alliance of politicians and *tenentes* from the peripheral regions of Brazil (the Northeast and Rio Grande do Sul). The governments that followed the Revolution of 1930 (headed, until 1945, by Getúlio Vargas), in addition to implementing a stronger industrialization policy, tried to break up the "armies of the *sertão*," restraining the power of the *fazendeiros*.[4] At the same time, they formulated labor legislation that applied only to urban areas (actually only to the largest cities), which gave urban wage-earners a standard of living substantially higher than that of rural masses. As a result, a system of incentives was created that attracted a growing number of rural workers to the cities. The greater part of the rural masses, confined to the subsistence economy, came to form a true reservoir of workers for the capitalist industrial economy, or, in the classic phrase of Marx, an industrial reserve force.

Mobilization of this force took place slowly, beginning with abolition of the states' autonomy between 1930 and 1945, which did as much to unify the internal market as to overthrow the local oligarchies, whose power over the rural population was thus considerably weakened. Construction of a network of highways, which came to interconnect the principal regions of the country, facilitated communications and gave an enormous stimulus to internal migration. Finally, it must be added that, beginning at this time, the steady fall in the death-rate, which began in the larger cities but soon spread to the interior, greatly accelerated the growth of population and therefore of the industrial reserve force. Increase in rural population in areas already densely populated (in the northeastern *zona da mata* and *agreste* and in the southern zones of colonization, for example) put pressure on the land, exacerbating the *latifúndio-minifúndio* dichotomy and bringing about strong migratory movements to pioneer agricultural regions and the cities.

Beginning in 1930, foreign immigration, for reasons as much external as internal, ceased to count a great deal. The number of immigrants arriving in Brazil was 622,397 between 1900 and 1909, reaching its highest level between 1910 and 1919: 815,463. During the following decade (1920–29) the number remained near this level: 788,170. But from then on the number of immigrants fell drastically: 332,768 between 1930 and 1939, and 114,405 between 1940 and 1949. During the 1950s, there was something of a recovery (586,670), but in the past decade the number of immigrants fell again, to approximately 200,000. It should be noted that even the greater immigration from 1950–59 counted for little, since during this time Brazil's total population increased by almost 20 million. But despite this decrease in foreign immigration there was continually greater assimilation of labor by the capitalist economy, thanks to a constantly larger increase in internal migration, primarily from rural to urban areas.

Of course, mobilization of the industrial reserve force, made up of rural masses tied to a precapitalist subsistence economy, did not take place only through urbanization, although this was the principal means. As a rule, industrial capitalism originates in the cities, and from there spreads to the country. Brazil is no exception to this rule. Import substitution brought about, in the first place, enlargement and diversification of the branches of the manufacturing industry, which caused great expansion of the urban economy. As a result, a large urban market for agricultural products, primarily food, came into being, and conditions were ripe for the penetration, on a limited scale even today, of capitalism into agriculture.[5]

The capitalist development of the Brazilian economy was strongly affected by this large-scale mobilization of the industrial reserve force, which led to an abundant supply of ill-qualified but docile workers, with limited aspirations. And so there arose a significant difference between the cost of skilled and unskilled labor, limited only by labor legislation, primarily the minimum wage. This explains the low level of mechanization in agriculture and construction, and the relative technological obsolescence in the older branches of industry, such as the textile and clothing industries. The persistence of numerous small artisans and craftsmen and the large segment of the labor force in domestic service are also explained by the low cost of labor.

3. METROPOLITANIZATION AND CONCENTRATION OF CAPITAL

Unification of the national market, physical as well as political, created the conditions, beginning in 1930, for growing concentration of capital, previously hindered by the market's regional fragmentation. Capital concentration appears under two different aspects, which mutually reinforce each other:

a. the concentration of activities in constantly larger establishments and firms, the result of the advantages—financial, commercial, productive, etc.—gained by a larger scale of operations;

b. the concentration of activities in certain areas, the result of external economies in the cost of transport and communication among complementary companies and of the use of industrial services (energy, water, sewers) and of financial and commercial services, etc., on a larger scale, reducing their cost.

To the extent that businesses are concentrated geographically, the market for each one is enlarged, thus facilitating greater capital concentration by entrepreneurs; to the extent that this occurs, the advantages of geographic concentration increase.

In Brazil, geographic concentration of capital occurred first of all in São Paulo for a variety of reasons, the most important of which was the fact that the city already had the largest industrial complex in the country, for the reason already shown: the large regional market formed by coffee production. When coffee production shifted to northern Paraná, beginning in the 1940s, it continued to be closely tied to São Paulo, whose hegemony over the national market could no longer be disputed.

Beginning in 1950, the process of import substitution reached industries producing durable consumer goods (automobiles, appliances); capital goods (machinery, equipment); and intermediate goods (steel, chemical and rubber products, paper). The establishment of these industries was largely the result of foreign capital investment, which brought mass-production techniques to Brazil. And so the new industries emerged already closely clustered, and most of them were located in the metropolitan area of São Paulo or its immediate surroundings: Baixada Santista, Campinas, and Vale do Paraíba. This formidable concentration of industrial activities gave rise, in turn, to an extraordinary growth of tertiary activities in the region: Commercial activity began to specialize as well as expand, as did financial activity; formal education expanded in scope, alongside a growing number of professional courses. Personal services also grew more important as de luxe establishments multiplied: hotels, beauty salons, country clubs, saunas, judo and yoga schools, etc., not to speak of the complete range of services required by the automobile and the driver, and semidomestic service in exurban and suburban residental areas. It is interesting to note that in greater São Paulo (the metropolitan area), the percentage of the work force employed in services rose from around 50 per cent in 1940 and 1950 to 60 per cent in 1960.

It is also interesting to discuss, in this context, to what extent the great concentration of activities in greater São Paulo coincided with the general economic advantages (those that permitted the development of the productive forces) and to what extent the concentration was the result of the capitalist characteristics of the Brazilian economy. It seems clear that there were disadvantages as well as advantages to agglomeration, greatly aggravated by the lack of adequate long-range planning. Since decisions involving the location of activities are made in a decentralized way, such planning is extremely difficult, if not impossible. Thus the main sources of the city's water, the Tiete River and its tributaries, were used in the sewer system, causing a severe shortage of drinking water, which is requiring costly hydraulic projects to bring water from more distant areas. In addition, the unrestricted use of automobiles on all city streets led to an excessive volume of traffic, making collective transportation difficult and necessitating a considerable amount of roadwork: widening streets, constructing elevated passageways, etc. The heavy concentration of tertiary activities in the historic center of the city contributed to an increase in certain transit flows, which aggravated traffic problems. A related problem that should be mentioned is the difficulty of constructing an underground transit system, because of the high cost of expropriating property.[6]

One of the characteristics of a capitalist economy is that the disadvantages of agglomeration, even though fundamentally caused by private enterprises, end by being paid for through socialization, since the solution to the problems thus raised is the task of the public sector, which finances the works with tax funds collected from the entire population. The automobile industry, for example, which is primarily responsible for the traffic problems its products cause, doesn't contribute proportionately more than any other "citizen" to their solution.

It must be realized, however, that the activities concentrated in São Paulo provide, thanks to their greater productivity, the surplus necessary for solution[7] of the problems they generate. In this sense, it would be wrong to think that the economy of greater São Paulo is no longer viable.

Its host of problems, which cause countless hardships for the population (long hours of waiting in the public transport system; bad sanitary conditions in poor neighborhoods, where housing is scarce and far from essential services, since real estate speculators handle the allocation of scarce resources according to the purchasing power of individuals), are the consequences of the delay in taking steps rather than the result of the absence of means to finance them.

4. SPEED OF GROWTH AND URBAN PROBLEMS

One might think (as did the mayor of São Paulo) that the problem lies basically in the excessive rate of growth of the metropolitan population, which causes the demand for urban services to increase at the same speed, at a rate that surpasses the capacity to acquire means to meet the demand. But actually the demand for services, in a capitalist economy, is just the solvent demand, and so it increases in relation to income rather than to population. A family that arrives in São Paulo and cannot find employment, having no other source of income, is not even able to request housing, and becomes a burden on welfare services, when it is not taken in by relatives or friends, as usually happens. When a family, however, begins to enjoy an income that it spends on housing, an automobile, etc., then indeed it does add to increased demand for urban public services. But in this case the income was generated at some point in the economy (thanks to the activity of members of this or some other family), so that the volume of resources of the urban economy was also increased.

In this context the problems of a city like São Paulo must not be confused with those of other cities where the machinery of transfer exists to guarantee the minimum vital needs of any new resident. Such machinery does not exist, except in almost symbolic terms, and those who are unable to integrate themselves into the economy in a legal and morally sanctioned way are, at worst, a charge on the services responsible for maintaining order. And so there exists an "explosive" demand for urban services of all kinds, which in large part remains unsatisfied. This occurs not because the population is growing too fast, but because urban income rises in an "explosive" way and the market mechanisms, which should generally balance supply and demand, simply fail to perform their task. And they fail because supply becomes inelastic in the short run when productive capacity is exhausted. It is impossible to meet a rapidly increasing demand for telephones, for connections to the water and sewer systems, for houses, for streets, etc., when the respective telephone systems, etc., are already being used to capacity. And so the only ways to reduce the gaps between supply and demand for urban public services would be either to check expansion of the urban economy or to engage in long-range economic planning. Everything leads one to believe that neither alternative is compatible with the method of capitalist production as it appears in Brazil at this time.[8]

Another part of the anti-urban argument is that excessive growth of urban population (in undeveloped countries) shows up under the form of a supply of labor that increases more rapidly than demand, causing a growing amount of unemployment (open, hidden, disguised) and of underemployment. First of all, it must be stated that the amount of open and hidden unemployment in São Paulo does not appear to be rising, according to the (meager) data available. Such unemployment also must not be very great. In 1953, in the district of São Paulo (which then constituted most of Greater São Paulo), 10 per cent of the men and 5 per cent of the women fifteen years of age and over were unemployed. More recently, in 1969, in the state of São Paulo (of which about 50 per cent of the population lives in Greater São Paulo), the percentages remained almost the same: 10 per cent of the men and 3.6 per cent of the women. Although recent data for the region are not available, it is probable that unemployment (open and hidden) is not excessive for a capitalist economy (in the United States, the equivalent rate would be 9–13 per cent in recent years, or double the rate of open unemployment).

As for disguised unemployment, not even indirect figures are available, since the very notion does not easily lend itself to measurement. An example of disguised unemployment would be someone whose marginal productivity is null or even negative. The classic example is that of the sixth salesman in a store in which five can easily take care of the customers. In the absence of clear estimates, it is usual to try to estimate disguised unemployment by the number of those who receive very low incomes. The assumption underlying this procedure is that a person's pay is commensurate with his marginal productivity. This neoclassical theorem calls for such market characteristics that its practical applicability is extremely limited. Many unqualified workers are ill-paid (in construction, for example), but this does not prove that they have low marginal productivity. One might ask: If there is a considerable difference between marginal productivity and salary, why does not employment expand, in construction, for example? There are several reasons: the limited demand for products of this type,[9] the shortage of other factors of production such as capital, a qualified work force, etc. Generally speaking, neither the labor market nor other markets of the metropolitan economy display the characteristics of free competition. Thus, the fields that use semiskilled labor—construction, bars, gardening, retail trade—are able to pay very low salaries without feeling motivated to expand employment to the point of exhausting the supply of this type of labor.

Whatever the amount of disguised and total unemployment in São Paulo, it is easy to see that it must be much *less* than in the majority of Brazilian cities, where the population grows more slowly or even decreases.† When one visits such cities, the unemployment of many people, in its various forms, is immediately evident. Obviously a large number of immigrants come to São Paulo from such cities. If there were some way to prevent them from coming to São Paulo to try their luck in the labor market, unemployment in São Paulo would perhaps decrease somewhat, but urban unemployment throughout the country would be still greater. At bottom, the great migratory movement to Greater São Paulo is nothing more than the relocation of the labor supply to a site of greater demand.

This does not mean, of course, that there are no Brazilian cities in which immigration causes expansion of the labor supply much stronger than actual demand. This is so above all in the regional capitals (Belém, Fortaleza, Recife), in which a number of unemployed are concentrated who were formerly dispersed in small communities. There do not appear to be valid arguments for preservation of the dispersion.

Here it might be well to distinguish between two types of unemployment that occur in capitalist economies that are still not completely developed: one arises from mobilization of social groups not previously integrated into the capitalist labor force (primarily women and people coming from the subsistence sector, together with young people entering the labor market); the other arises from the discharge of already employed workers, as a result of changes in production techniques or in the structure of real demand. This latter kind of unemployment occurs more frequently in the developed capitalist countries, is limited in scope, and assumes the aspect of frictional unemployment, since it is the consequence of the redeployment of labor among various businesses and sectors of production, except during periods of depressed economic

† Unfortunately, there are no figures available on the amount of unemployment in Brazilian cities. These kinds of data are only collected on a regional scale.

opportunity, when its volume grows considerably. But it is the first kind that predominates in countries like Brazil, resulting in the incorporation into the industrial reserve force of considerable masses of people who hope to participate in the heavily publicized consumer society. This kind of unemployment, which could be termed structural, is the result, in the final analysis, of insufficient prior accumulation of capital that would permit immediate use of the labor force made available through fundamental social changes in rural areas and small towns.

If one looks at the vast migratory streams crossing the territory of Brazil—streams made up of 30 million people out of a population of little more than 93 million, according to the 1970 census—it is easy to see that the industrial reserve force attains formidable dimensions in Brazil, since the great majority of migrants move in search of work. It is an immense effort devoted to locating the areas where capital accumulation is occurring and where, as a result, the demand for labor is growing. Often enough, the mere announcement that construction of a factory is under way attracts many workers to the area.

Greater São Paulo's rapid demographic growth is the result of the extent of structural unemployment in the country and of the fact that actually the increase is taking place on a large scale within its metropolitan limits. In comparison with other cities, it is probable that a large proportion of migrants who flock to the metropolitan area in fact succeed in integrating themselves into the productive process. This is the result of the fact that migratory currents generally cover short distances. Of the 8,403,444 migrants who lived in São Paulo in 1970, a total of 5,373,965 (or 64 per cent) came from within the state itself, and 888,615 (10.5 per cent) came from the neighboring state of Minas Gerais. Of the migrants who arrive in Greater São Paulo, almost 60 per cent come from within the state or from Minas Gerais. The inability (economic and social) of Brazilian migrants to encompass the whole of the nation in their search for work actually limits the growth of the population of Greater São Paulo, permitting differences in the employment level to arise among the various regions of Brazil. From this point of view, the growth of São Paulo's population would be even greater than it is if the geographic mobility of the labor force were perfect.

5. ANTICRITICISM

We can resume our initial discussion. It seems clear that the problems of metropolitan areas like Greater São Paulo are the result of geographic concentration of activities (and not of population) that is justified, in economic terms, within certain limits. There are no data that permit us to define, on the macroeconomic and social levels, an "optimal" degree of agglomeration (or dispersion) of activities. It cannot be concluded from this, however, that the agglomeration resulting from the separate decisions made by entrepreneurs, based on market indicators and personal inclinations, is the best. There are at least two reasons that invalidate this hypothesis. In the first place, market indicators are ineffective to the extent that each entrepreneur is unaware of the decisions of the rest and of the economic and social consequences of the sum of all decisions. Given the high cost of investment in land and buildings, correcting wrong decisions, even from a business's internal point of view, tends to be impractical in the short run. And so there are the transit bottlenecks, overloaded telephone lines, electrical blackouts, and other diseconomies of agglomeration. In the second place, the personal preferences of entrepreneurs and of chief managers of companies carry weight in decisions concerning their location, since this obviously affects the place of residence of their directors. Despite all the criticism of the quality of life in large cities, it is there that one finds the best schools, specialized medical services, a more active cultural life, and so on. Thus, when the location is not predetermined by fixed factors, such as proximity to the source of primary materials, the alternative that is ultimately preferred is that which allows the directors to live in a "nice city," which almost always means a large city. It can therefore be concluded that decentralized decision making, characteristic of capitalism, tends to be biased in favor of the superagglomeration of activities in metropolitan areas, a bias that is reinforced by the socializations of the diseconomies of agglomeration.

The conclusion that in capitalism there is a tendency to excessive geographic concentration of activities, which leads to hypertrophy of metropolitan areas, seems at first glance to coincide with the criticism of urbanization mentioned at the beginning of this essay. This resemblance, however, is only superficial. Actually, the causal relationship presented by anti-urban criticism, which sees in urban growth in undeveloped countries a "bulge" represented by an increase in population without corresponding expansion of the metropolitan economy, is the opposite of that brought out by analysis of the case of Greater São Paulo. What in fact happens is that capital accumulation occurs in a geographically concentrated form, which attracts great streams of migrants. The industrial reserve force, made up of a large segment of the population that becomes mobile to the extent that the chains tying it to rural areas are broken, heads for the large cities, which offer better prospects for employment.

It is not true, then, that urban "marginality" is a product of capitalist development, at least in the sense that it allegedly did not exist in the colonial economy. Such a proposition, even though it is articulated as a criticism of capitalism, is reactionary. Capitalism, when it destroys in rural areas relationships of production that predate and are opposed to it, sets in motion human masses that in a first phase join the industrial reserve force. Since capital accumulation is determined in a decentralized way, the function of the reserve force is to increase the capitalists' freedom of decision, who expand economic activity in areas best serving their interests. But this only means that elimination of the waste of the labor force, formerly submerged in the subsistence sector, is done in a contradictory way: It is necessary to mobilize millions of workers so that capital can utilize a part of them, keeping the rest in less invisible forms of unemployment.

In the same way, one cannot attribute to capitalism the fall in the deathrate and the resulting acceleration of demographic growth (at least as long as the birthrate remains high), since this is the result of scientific discoveries applied to the preservation of human life. The system, confronted with the resulting increase in the labor force, tries to capitalize on it, keeping salaries low and employing labor extensively as long as there are techniques of production that do not require a great deal of capital per worker. In the manufacturing industry these techinques grow constantly scarcer, but in the service sector they are still abundant. In São Paulo, excessive expansion of employment in the tertiary sector is the result, as has been seen in the increase in certain personal services, including domestic service, that utilize unskilled labor.

The real problem is not mobilization of the rural masses, which means their urbanization, but the insufficient mobility of the reserve force. Given the low purchasing power and the limited cultural horizons of the majority of migrants, they move only relatively short distances, often furthering their own urbanization in cities not chosen as centers of capital accumulation. In Brazil, certain cities of the North and Northeast, like Belém and Fortaleza, have grown faster in recent years than São Paulo. Capitalism does not possess mechanisms, except for state intervention, to oblige capital to focus on areas where labor force is available. Since the mobility of the labor force is not perfect, the system ended by adopting regional development plans having as their primary aim stimulation of streams of capital toward the most backward areas. In this way, new centers of geographic concentration of capital are created, as is the case with Salvador and Recife in the Brazilian Northeast. These new streams of capital are largely made up of public funds returned to the private sector—funds that are given back to taxpayers in proportion to taxes paid. Thus, incipient industrialization is taking place in the Northeast (and perhaps, in the future, in the North), being the creature of new companies formerly held back by capitalists from São Paulo and other areas of older industrialization. When the new industries become profitable, the surplus they produce tends to flow back to São Paulo, reinforcing capital accumulation in this area. In this way the system created mechanisms permitting São Paulo capital to exploit the Northeastern labor force without having to move away from São Paulo.

As for its future prospects, São Paulo is tending to become within Brazil a metropolis in the additional sense of appropriating and accumulating a growing portion of the most valuable goods produced in areas now being industrialized. This will only reinforce its economic hypertrophy, making its problems constantly more complex and difficult to solve. The foundations for the establishment of a large capital market are already being laid in São Paulo, where the Stock Exchange, the largest in the country, shows a daily activity equivalent to nearly U.S. $10 million. This capital market will have national functions, which means that São Paulo will be exporting financial services to the rest of Brazil. The revenue increase thus gained by the city benefits above all those classes with considerable purchasing power (brokers, bankers, speculators, *rentiers*), whose demand for urban services of the best kind is increasing rapidly. Already one notes the beginnings of suburbanization, whose foreseeable growth will absorb a considerable portion of public funds, while the poverty of areas inhabited by the poorer population becomes greater still. And so the city is adapting to the forms of conspicuous consumption imported from the developed capitalist countries, of which the unrestricted use of the automobile is the most important, while the needs of the great majority of the population are given constantly lower priority.

It is very clear that São Paulo is not going to stop growing, since it is the symbol and the epicenter of Brazilian capitalist development. The contrasts it exhibits only reveal the contradictions of a system which, in order to develop productive forces, is always raising new problems. Criticism of urbanization, by not taking into account this basic characteristic of capitalism, makes the mistake of trying to avoid these problems by limiting the system's dynamism, which is, after all, its only historical justification. A capitalism without contradiction and change is no more than a reactionary Utopia inspired by examination of isolated problems by those who refuse to analyze the essence of the system that gave them birth.

NOTES

1. A useful bibliography concerning the subject was assembled by Richard Morse, "Trends and Issues in Latin American Urban Research, 1965–1970," *Latin American Research Review* VI (1–2) (Spring and Summer 1971), who divides authors looking for a cure for "the real or imagined tertiarization malady" into "those absorbed in policy concerns (subdivided into hand-wringers and positive thinkers) and those more interested in identifying the enduring configurations of society than in devising panaceas for realigning the Latin American case with Western experience." Anti-urban criticism is represented above all by the "hand-wringers."

2. A good example of the more conservative point of view is expressed by Víctor Urquidi, "The Underdeveloped City," *Man in the City of the Future,* ed. R. Eells and C. Walton (London: Macmillan, 1968), who develops the thesis that "urbanization in the less-developed countries is necessary for modern development, but it is assuming some of the worst features of the growth of cities in the industrial nations and is being compounded by unprecedented social change stemming from high rates of population growth and massive movements of people

from rural to urban areas" (p. 75). See also essay included in this volume. An example of leftist anti-urban criticism is offered by Manuel Castells, "L'urbanization dépendante en Amérique Latine," *Espaces et Societés* 3 (July 1971). Castells describes urbanization in Latin America as accelerating rapidly, constituting large concentrations of population without corresponding development of productive capacity, beginning with the rural exodus and without assimilating migrants into the urban economic system, with the formation of a truncated and disarticulated urban network. According to Castells, all the urban ills of the continent are the result of dependence on international capitalism: "To the extent that there is national disintegration of the productive system, it is logical that the urban network should be disarticulated and truncated. But its disarticulation is only the result of an articulation of the social structure, created as much by the dominant society as by the dependent society" (p. 21). On this level of abstraction, dependence can be blamed on whomever one pleases.

3. The reasoning is, at bottom, similar to that of neo-Malthusianism: Unemployment (real or supposed) results from an excess of population in relation to accumulated capital, from which the conclusion can be drawn that if population were less there would be no unemployment. Population and economy are seen as evolving separately, which in fact almost never happens. For an analysis on the national level see my *Dinâmica Populacional e Desenvolvimento* (São Paulo: Edições CEBRAP, 1970).

4. In the Brazil of the pre-1930 period, the mobility of rural labor was restricted by a number of economic and psychosocial ties that bound the tenant farmers, *parceiros,* colonists, etc., to the landowner. These ties were backed by bands of armed thugs, led by *fazendeiros,* who in some areas came to make up real "armies of the *sertão,*" dissolved after 1930. The elimination of armed force to assure the landowners' domination over the workers is occurring slowly and is far from being completed. The same is true of the replacement of servile relationships of production by monetary capitalistic relationships (rent or wages).

5. Migration to the cities has a double effect on growth of the industrial reserve force: Migrants become part of it upon settling in urban areas, and at the same time they expand the solvent urban demand for agricultural products, which turns a growing portion of the production of the subsistence sector into commodities, or marketable surplus. It is through expansion of the urban market for agricultural products that capitalism pene-

trates agriculture, since it facilitates and makes profitable for
the owner the substitution of income paid in products or labor
by income paid in money or by profits deriving from exploitation of salaried labor.

6. It is evident that the difficulty in planning arises not only
from decentralized decision-making, but also from the antago-
nism of the interests of different classes. Any regulation concerning use of urban land, whether for construction or for
transit or parking, interferes with the rights of the owners of
the land and/or the vehicles.

7. Solution is meant in the sense of overcoming current
problems in the insufficient supply of services, which affect further development of these activities. Inadequate services affect
economic activity by making it less productive (due, for example, to worker fatigue caused by the shortcomings of mass
transit) or by raising costs (the higher cost of worker housing,
for example, makes higher wages necessary).

8. Morse (op. cit.) supplies extremely interesting data on
urban planning in Cuba, where geographic concentration of activities (above all in Havana) is giving way to creation of an
urban network of small and medium-sized cities. Although it is
too soon to evaluate the results of the experiment, it is certain
that the radical reorganization of the use of space in Cuba only
became possible thanks to socialization of the means of production, especially of urban land.

9. In a competitive market it is assumed that each company's
share of total supply is so limited that an increase in its share
does not affect the price. From this it follows that, as a result of
competition among companies, each expands employment until
the point at which marginal productivity (presumed to be constantly decreasing) is equal to salary paid. When, however, the
market is not competitive, expansion of supply by large companies tends to depress prices. Thus, if large construction companies expand production until the point at which marginal productivity and wages are equal, given a determined price level
of their products, they can expect that a greater volume of
buildings can be sold only at a lower price, so that when supply and demand are once again in equilibrium, marginal productivity would be *less* than salary (already paid). Under these
conditions, the oligopolistic company takes into consideration
the price elasticity of demand in determining its volume of
production and therefore of employment.